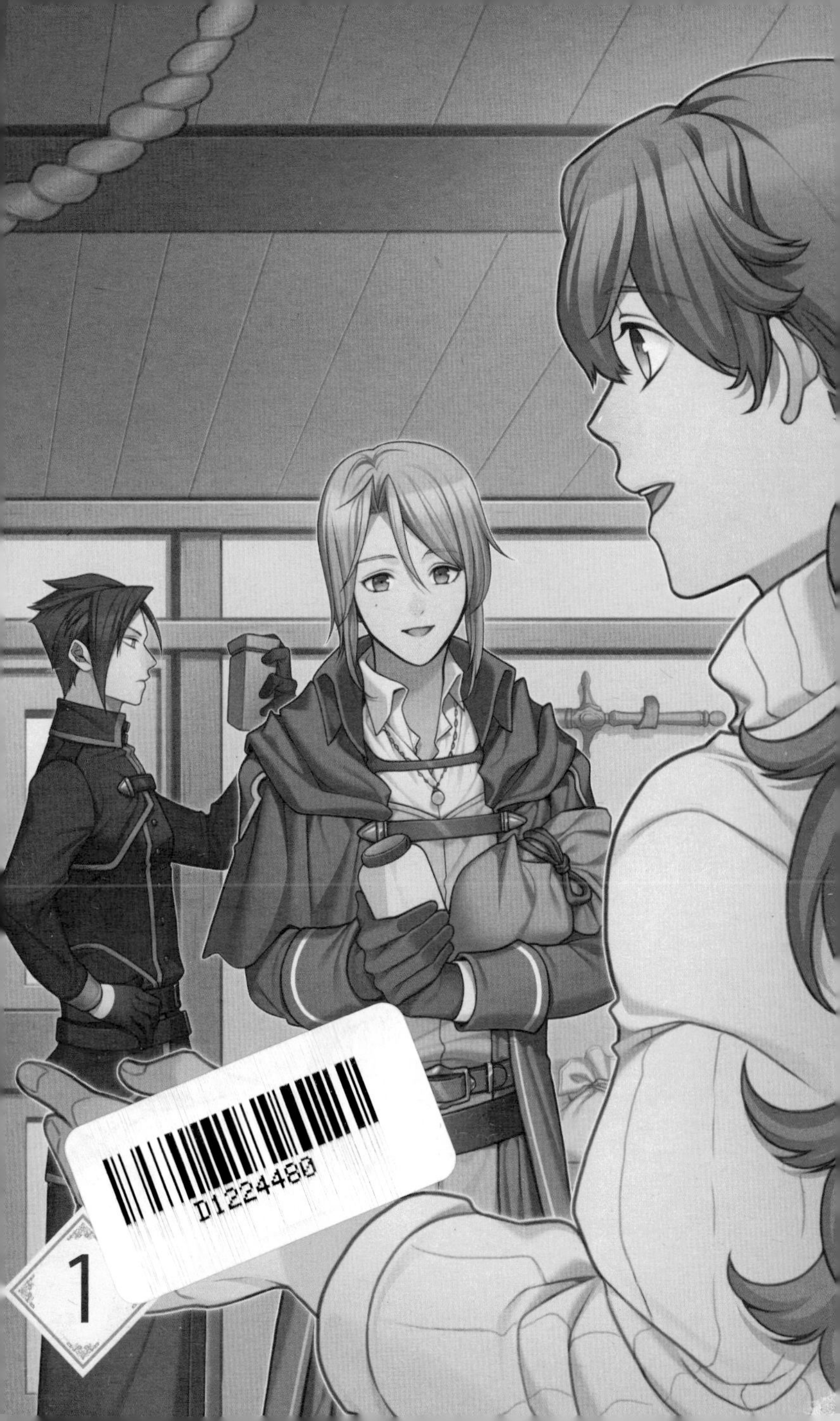
1

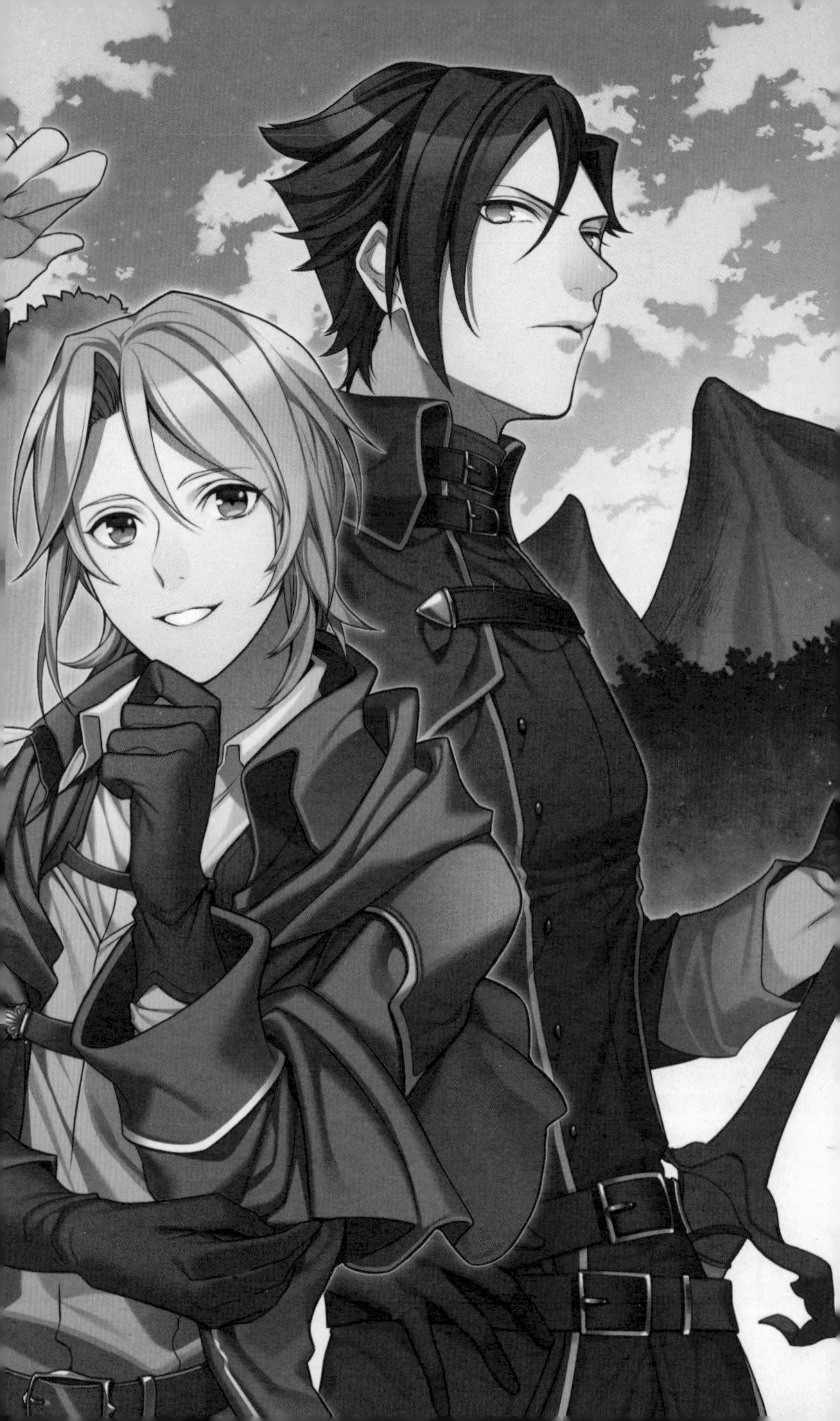

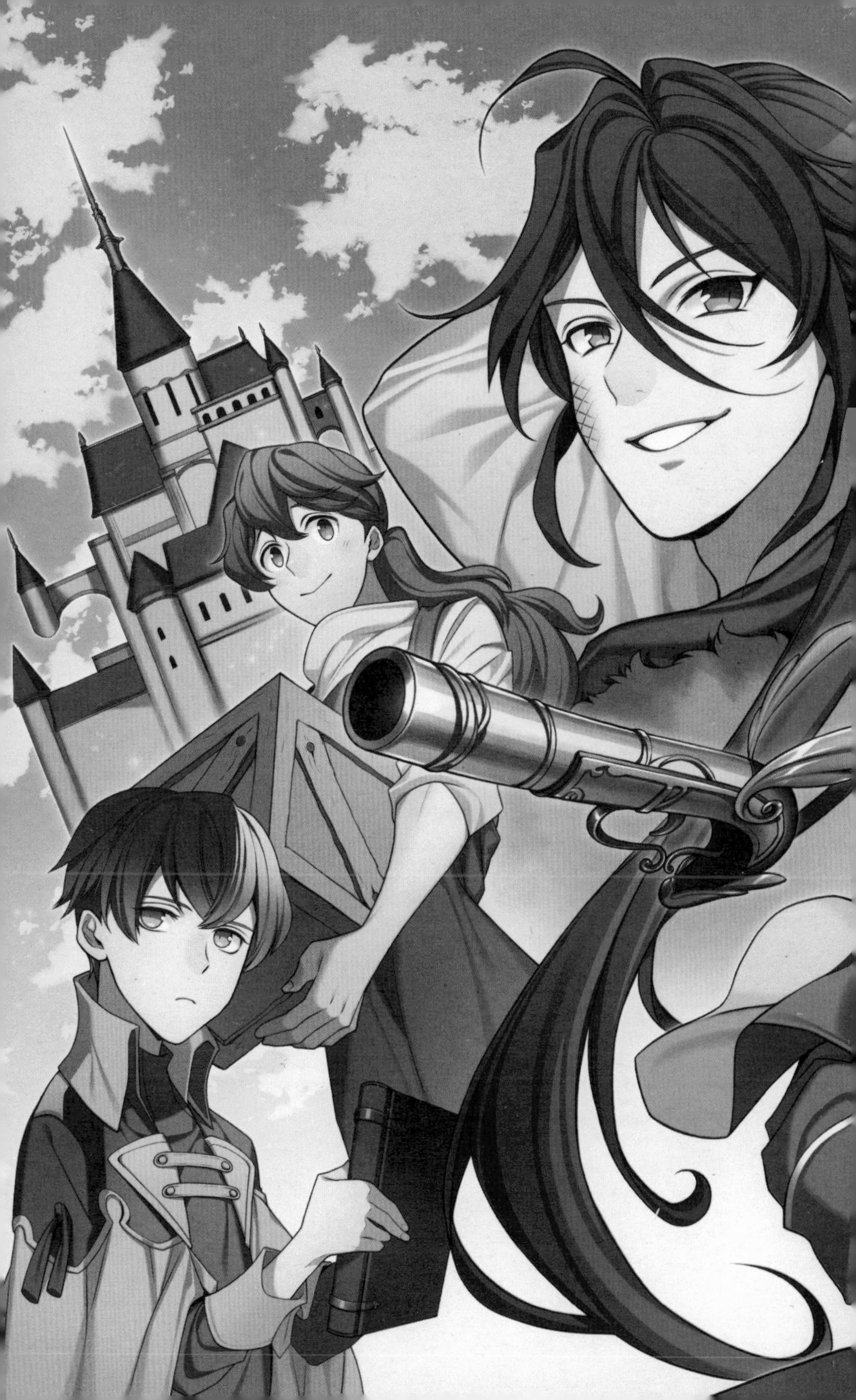

A Gentle Noble's
VACATION
RECOMMENDATION

Chapter 1

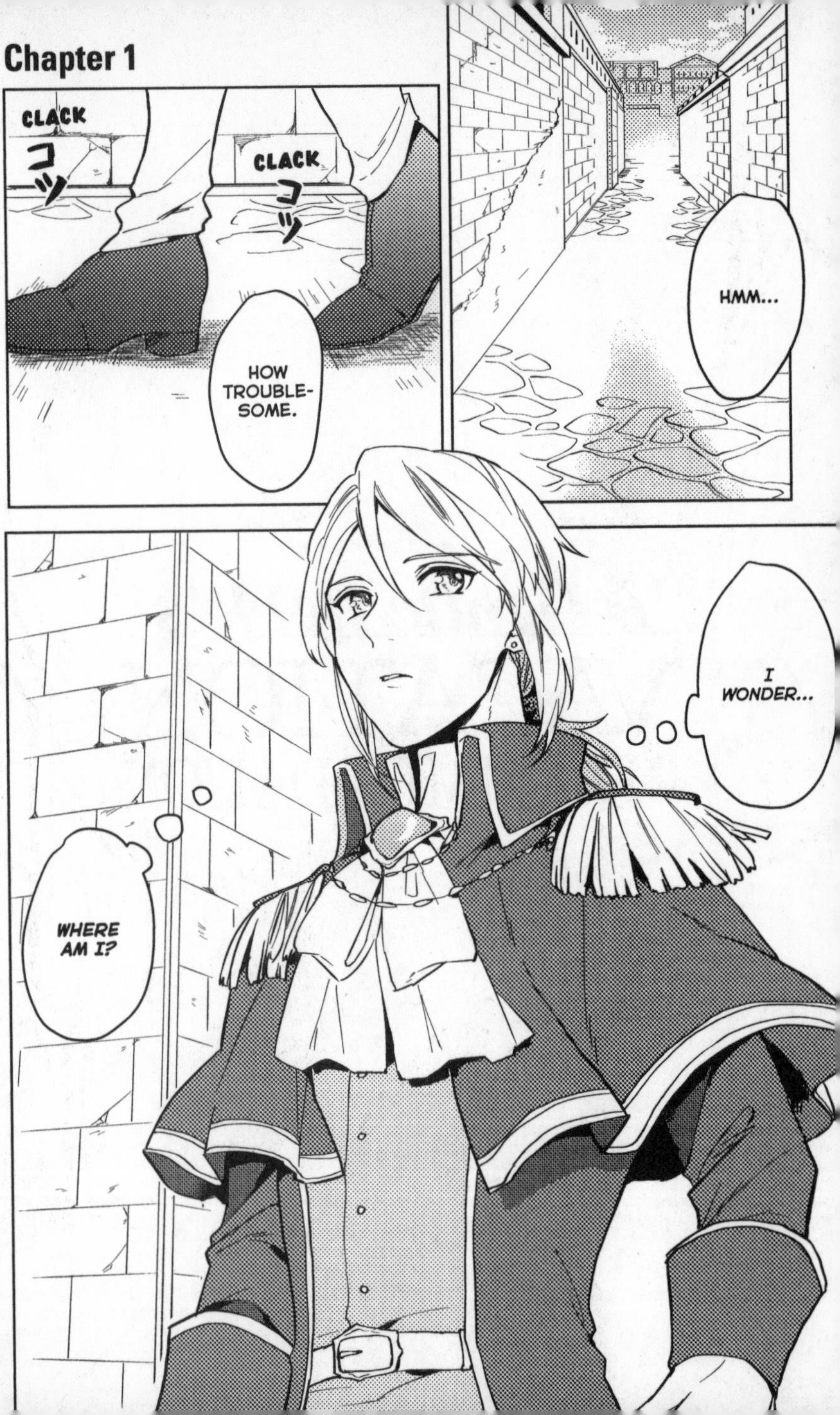
HMM...
CLACK
コツ
CLACK
コツ
HOW TROUBLE-SOME.
I WONDER...
WHERE AM I?

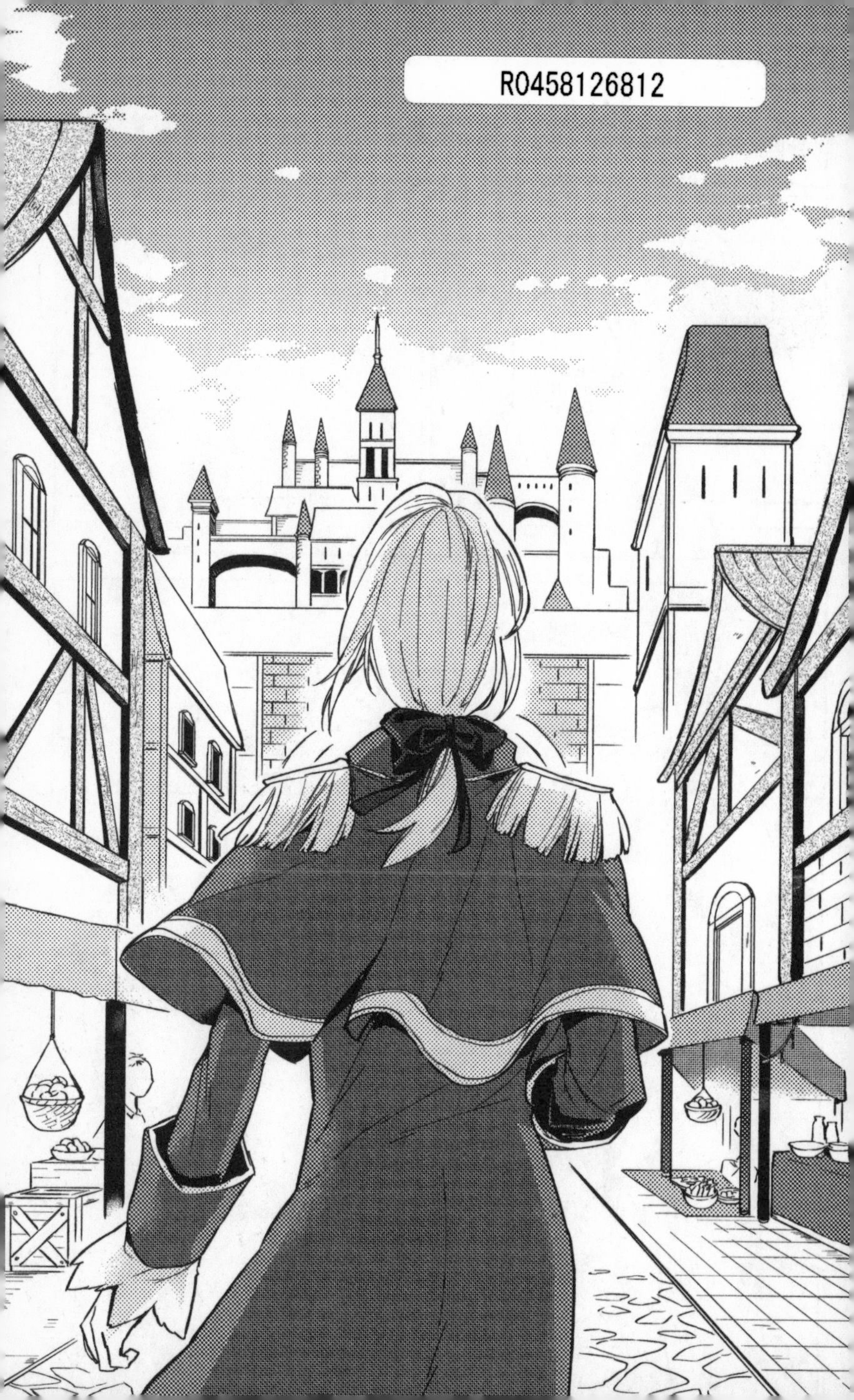

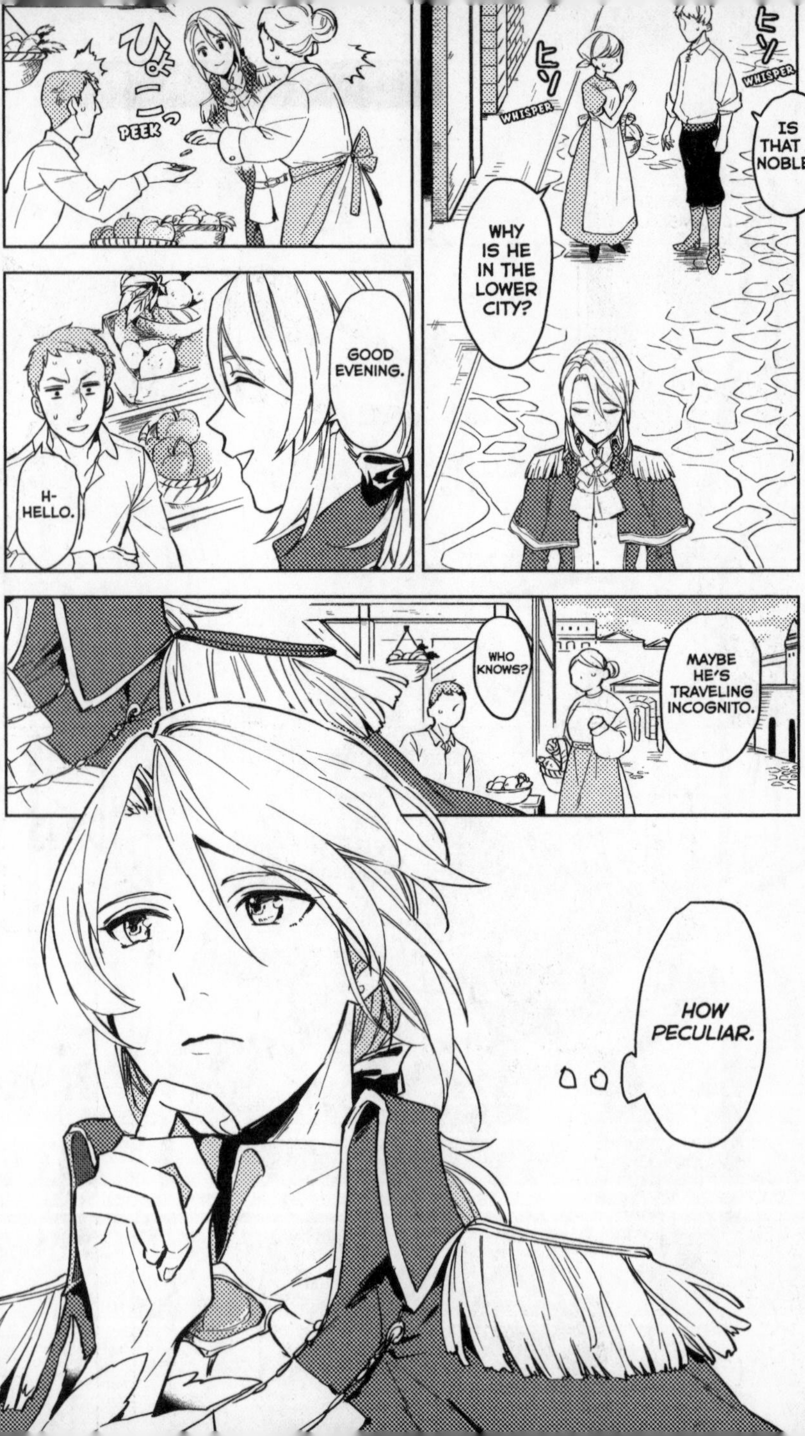
ヒソ
WHISPER
IS THAT A NOBLE?
ヒソ
WHISPER
WHY IS HE IN THE LOWER CITY?
ぴょーーっ
PEEK
GOOD EVENING.
H- HELLO.
MAYBE HE'S TRAVELING INCOGNITO.
WHO KNOWS?
HOW PECULIAR.

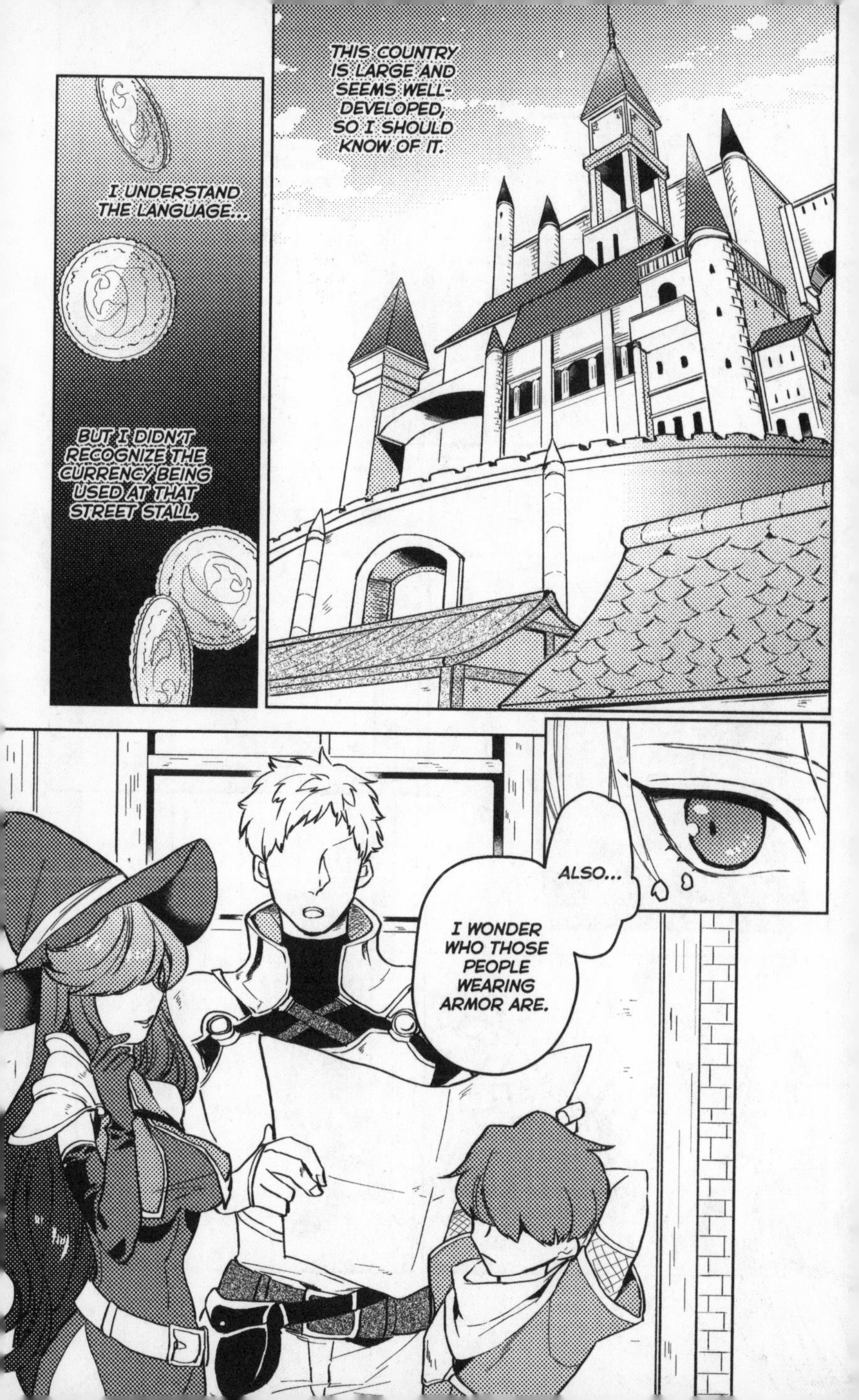
THIS COUNTRY IS LARGE AND SEEMS WELL-DEVELOPED, SO I SHOULD KNOW OF IT.
I UNDERSTAND THE LANGUAGE...
BUT I DIDN'T RECOGNIZE THE CURRENCY BEING USED AT THAT STREET STALL.
ALSO...
I WONDER WHO THOSE PEOPLE WEARING ARMOR ARE.

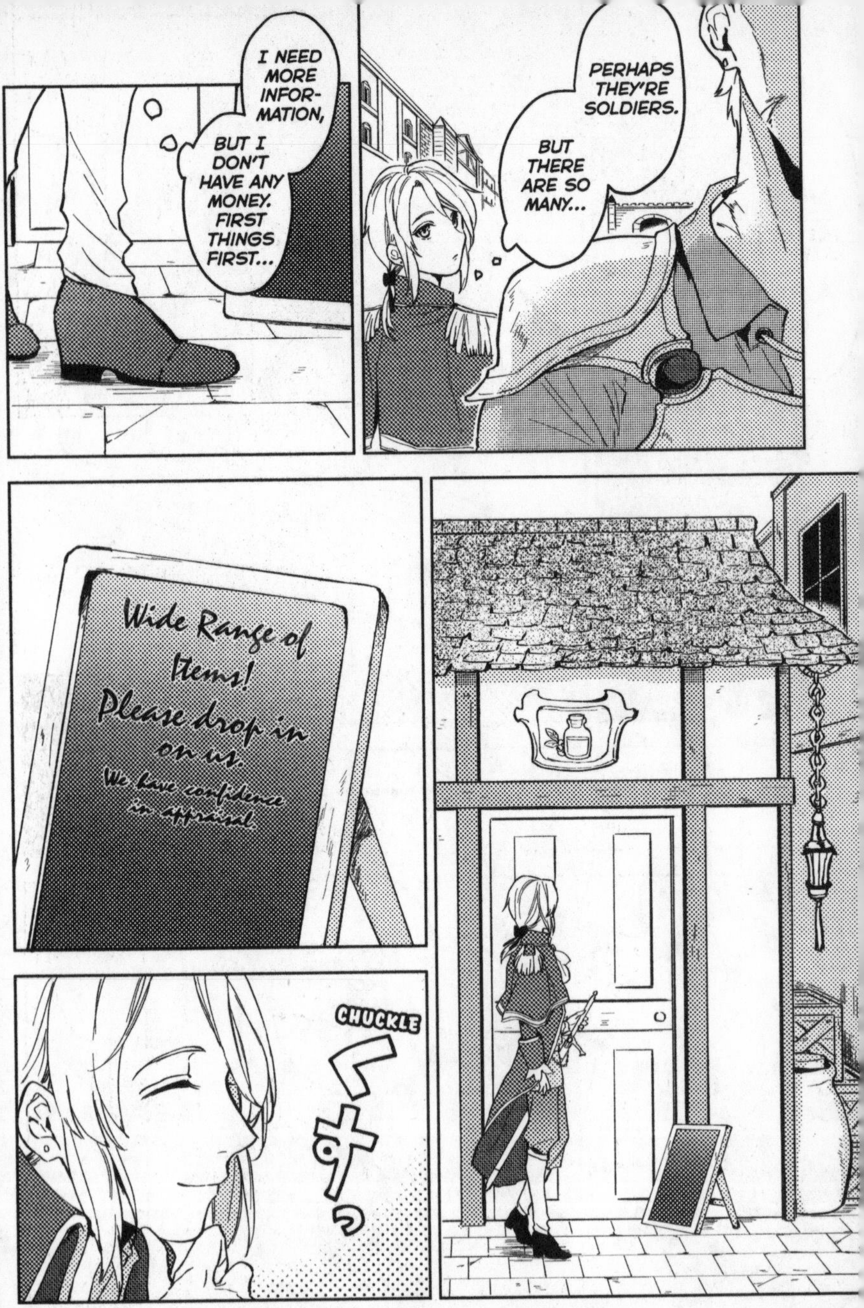
PERHAPS THEY'RE SOLDIERS.
BUT THERE ARE SO MANY...
I NEED MORE INFORMATION,
BUT I DON'T HAVE ANY MONEY. FIRST THINGS FIRST...
Wide Range of Items! Please drop in on us.
We have confidence in appraisal.
CHUCKLE
くすっ

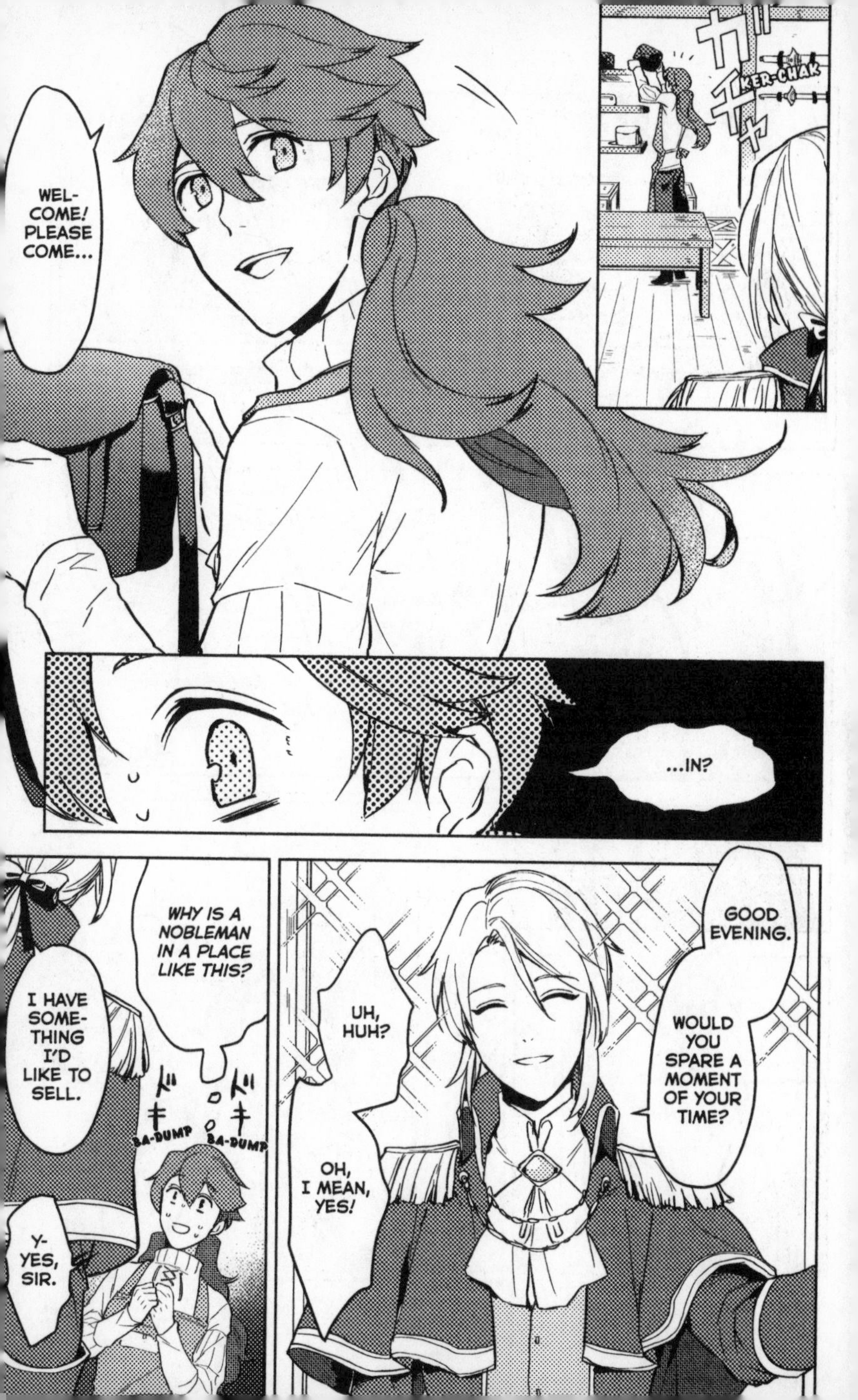
KER-CHAK
WEL-COME! PLEASE COME...
...IN?
GOOD EVENING.
WOULD YOU SPARE A MOMENT OF YOUR TIME?
UH, HUH?
OH, I MEAN, YES!
WHY IS A NOBLEMAN IN A PLACE LIKE THIS?
I HAVE SOME-THING I'D LIKE TO SELL.
ドキ
BA-DUMP
ドキ
BA-DUMP
Y-YES, SIR.

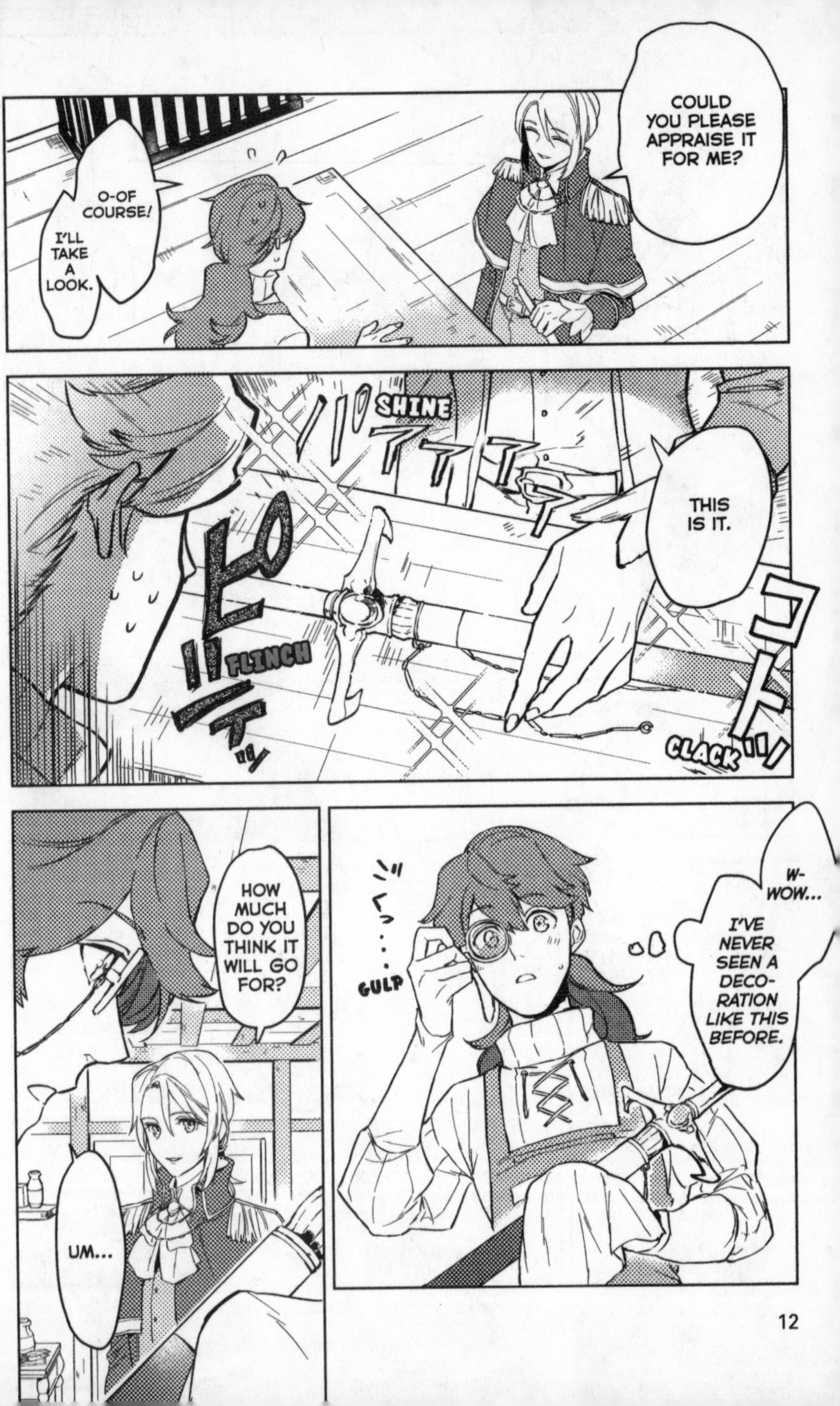
COULD YOU PLEASE APPRAISE IT FOR ME?
O-OF COURSE! I'LL TAKE A LOOK.
THIS IS IT.
CLACK
SHINE
FLINCH
W-WOW... I'VE NEVER SEEN A DECORATION LIKE THIS BEFORE.
GULP
HOW MUCH DO YOU THINK IT WILL GO FOR?
UM...

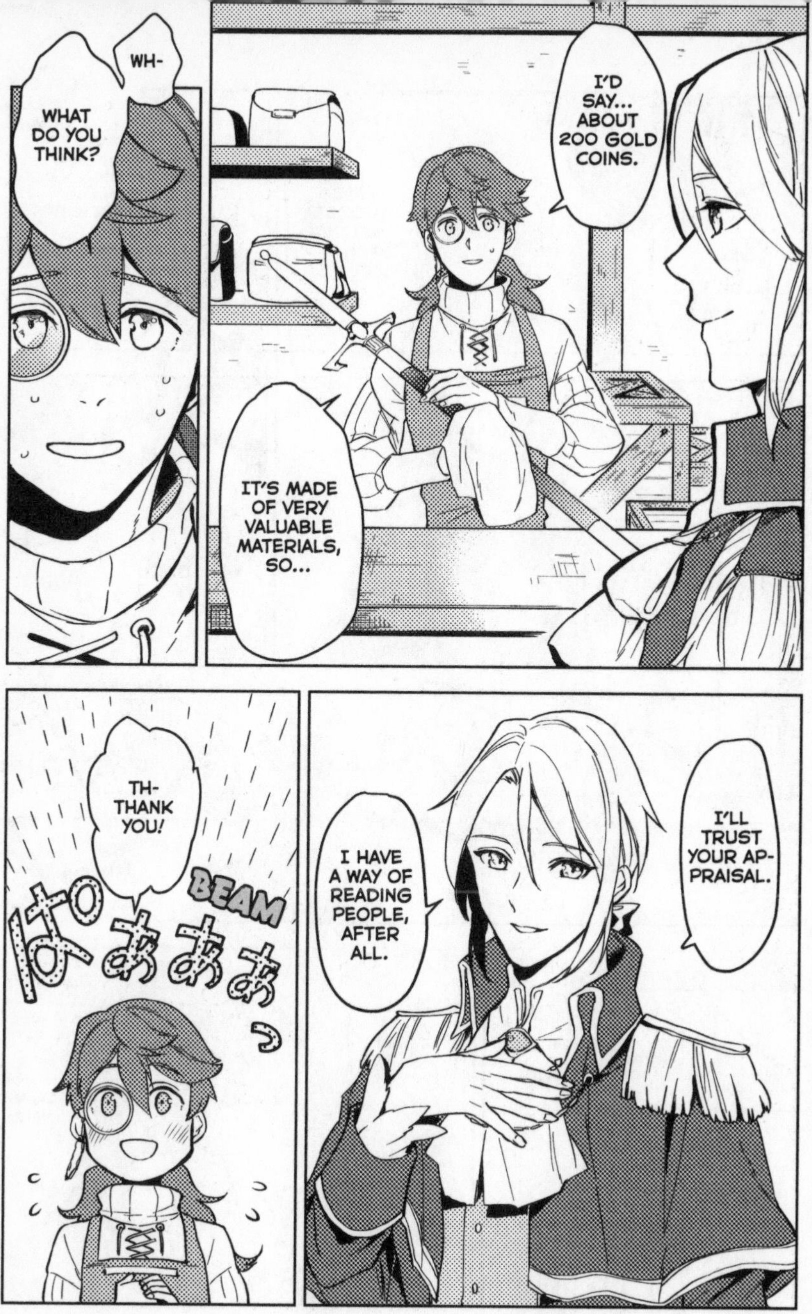
I'D SAY... ABOUT 200 GOLD COINS.
IT'S MADE OF VERY VALUABLE MATERIALS, SO...
WH-
WHAT DO YOU THINK?
I'LL TRUST YOUR AP-PRAISAL.
I HAVE A WAY OF READING PEOPLE, AFTER ALL.
TH- THANK YOU!
BEAM
ぱぁぁぁぁっ

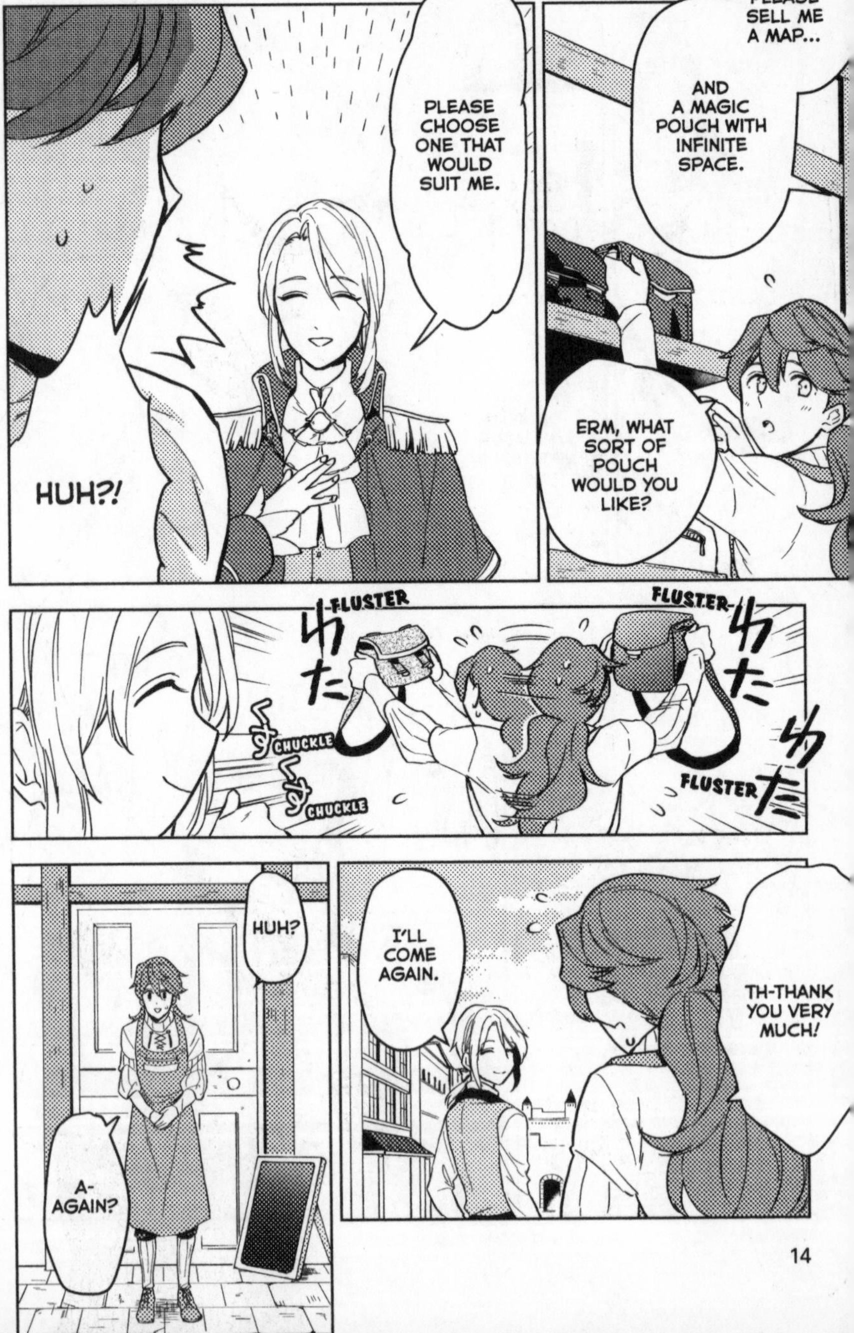
ALSO, PLEASE SELL ME A MAP...
AND A MAGIC POUCH WITH INFINITE SPACE.
ERM, WHAT SORT OF POUCH WOULD YOU LIKE?
PLEASE CHOOSE ONE THAT WOULD SUIT ME.
HUH?!
FLUSTER-
FLUSTER
CHUCKLE
CHUCKLE
FLUSTER
TH-THANK YOU VERY MUCH!
I'LL COME AGAIN.
HUH?
A- AGAIN?

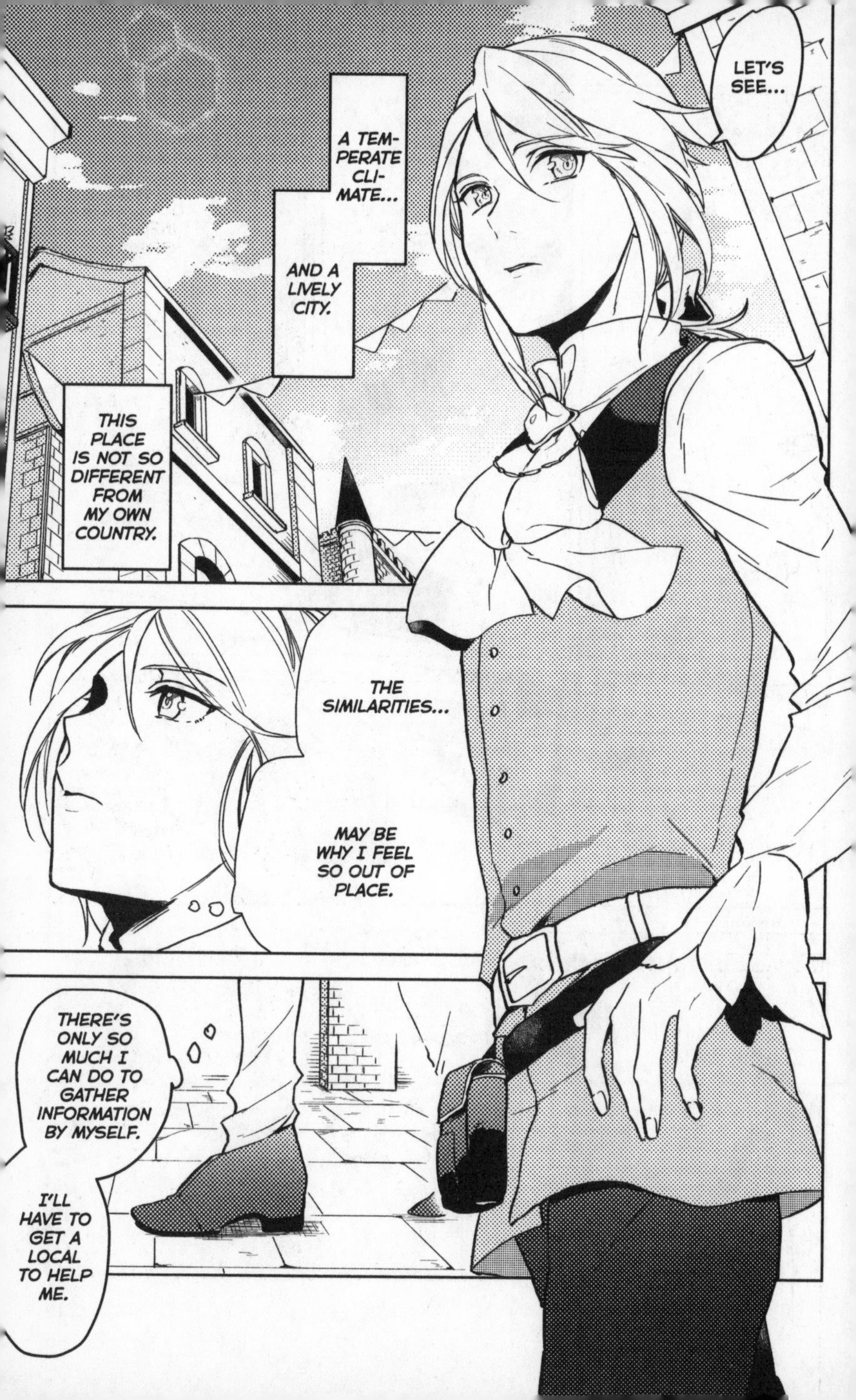
LET'S SEE...
A TEM-PERATE CLI-MATE...
AND A LIVELY CITY.
THIS PLACE IS NOT SO DIFFERENT FROM MY OWN COUNTRY.
THE SIMILARITIES...
MAY BE WHY I FEEL SO OUT OF PLACE.
THERE'S ONLY SO MUCH I CAN DO TO GATHER INFORMATION BY MYSELF.
I'LL HAVE TO GET A LOCAL TO HELP ME.

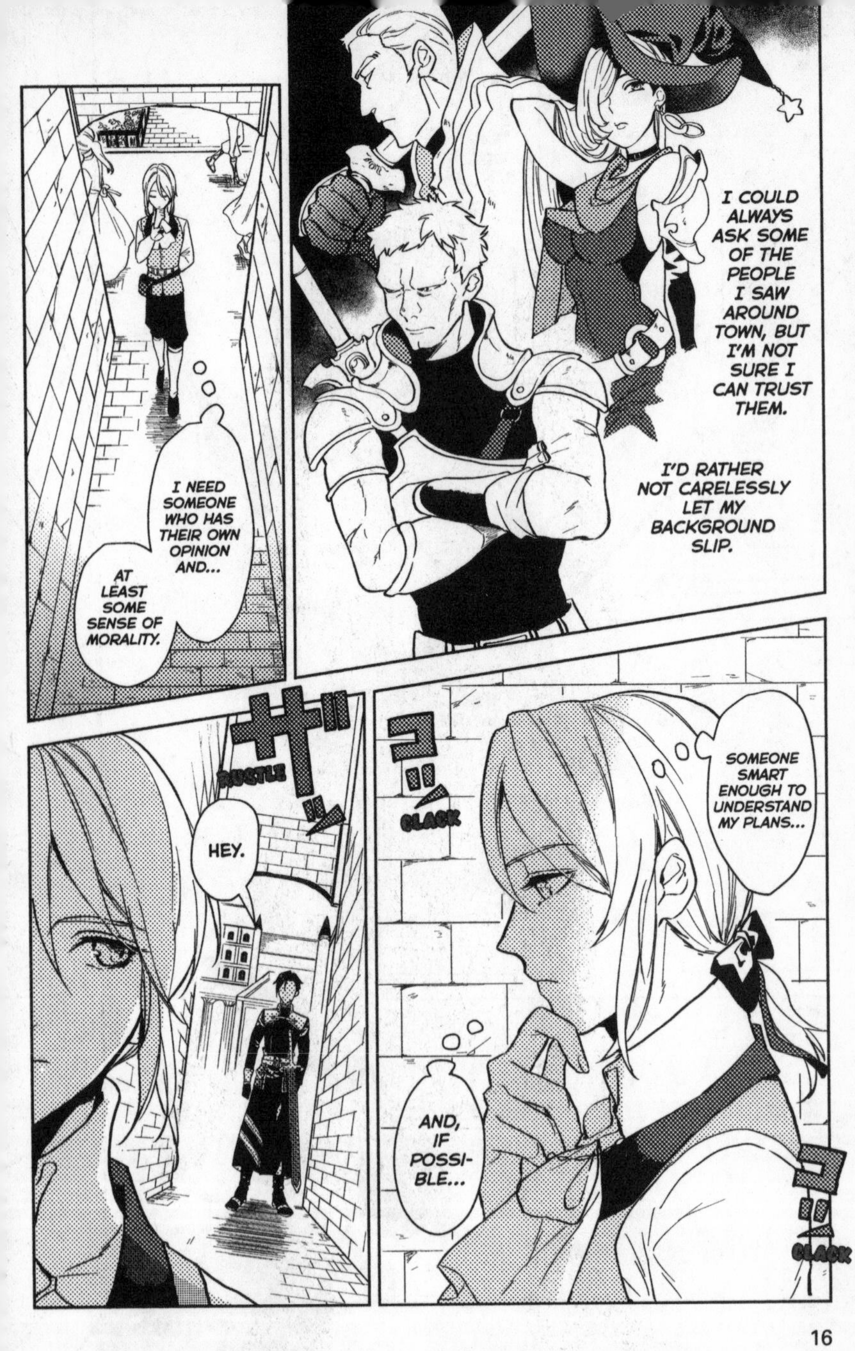
I COULD ALWAYS ASK SOME OF THE PEOPLE I SAW AROUND TOWN, BUT I'M NOT SURE I CAN TRUST THEM.
I'D RATHER NOT CARELESSLY LET MY BACKGROUND SLIP.
I NEED SOMEONE WHO HAS THEIR OWN OPINION AND...
AT LEAST SOME SENSE OF MORALITY.
SOMEONE SMART ENOUGH TO UNDERSTAND MY PLANS...
CLACK
AND, IF POSSIBLE...
CLACK
RUSTLE
HEY.

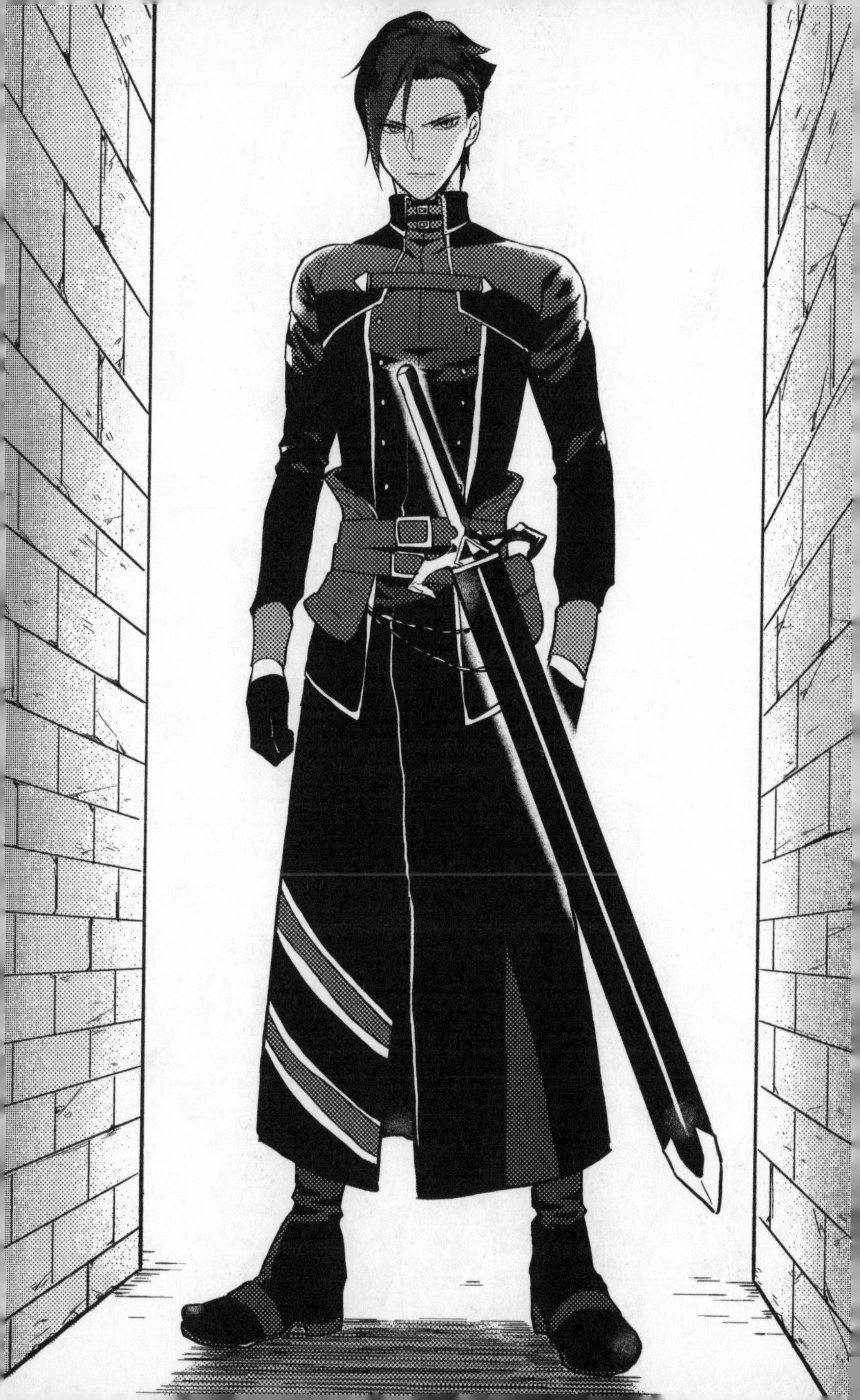

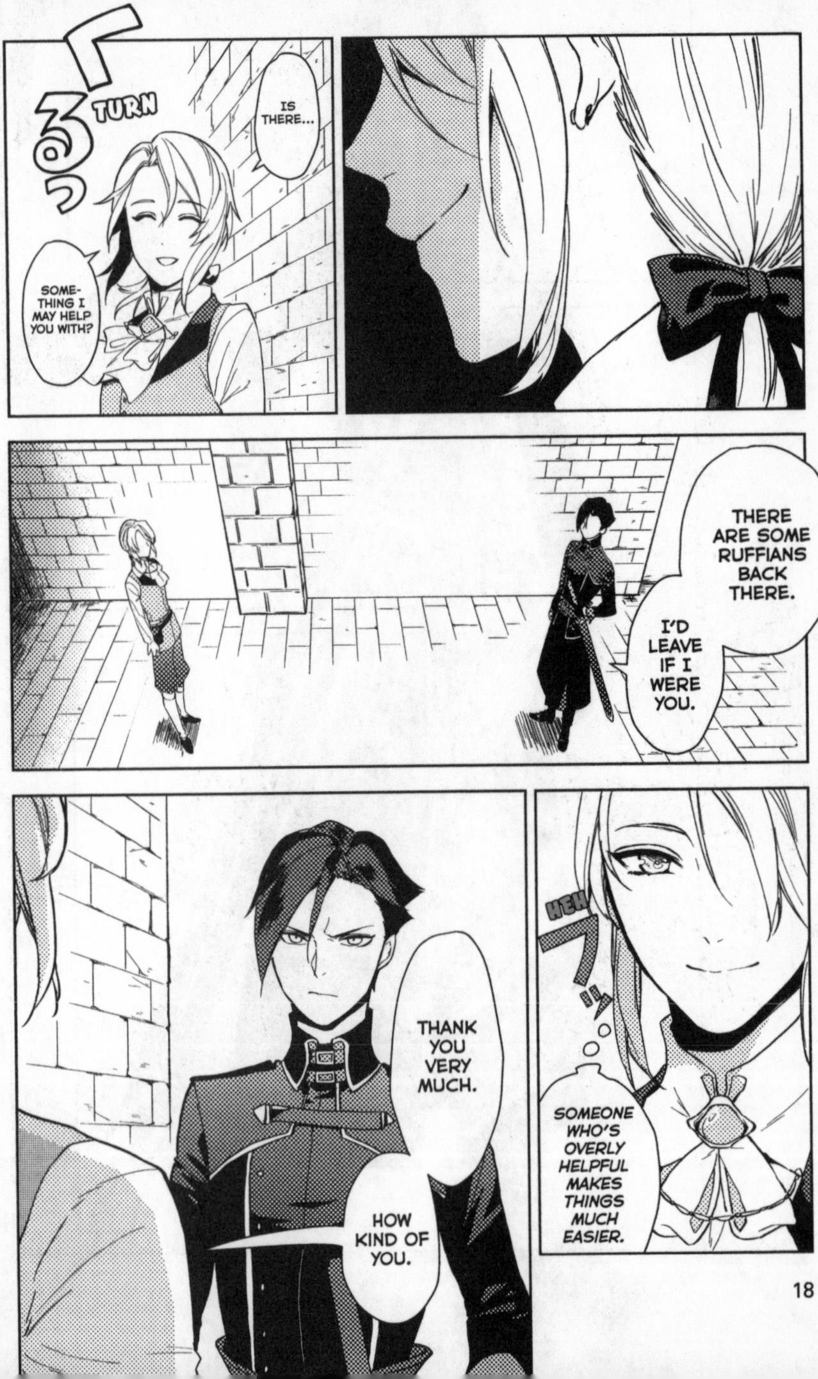
IS THERE...
TURN
SOME-THING I MAY HELP YOU WITH?
THERE ARE SOME RUFFIANS BACK THERE.
I'D LEAVE IF I WERE YOU.
HEH
SOMEONE WHO'S OVERLY HELPFUL MAKES THINGS MUCH EASIER.
THANK YOU VERY MUCH.
HOW KIND OF YOU.

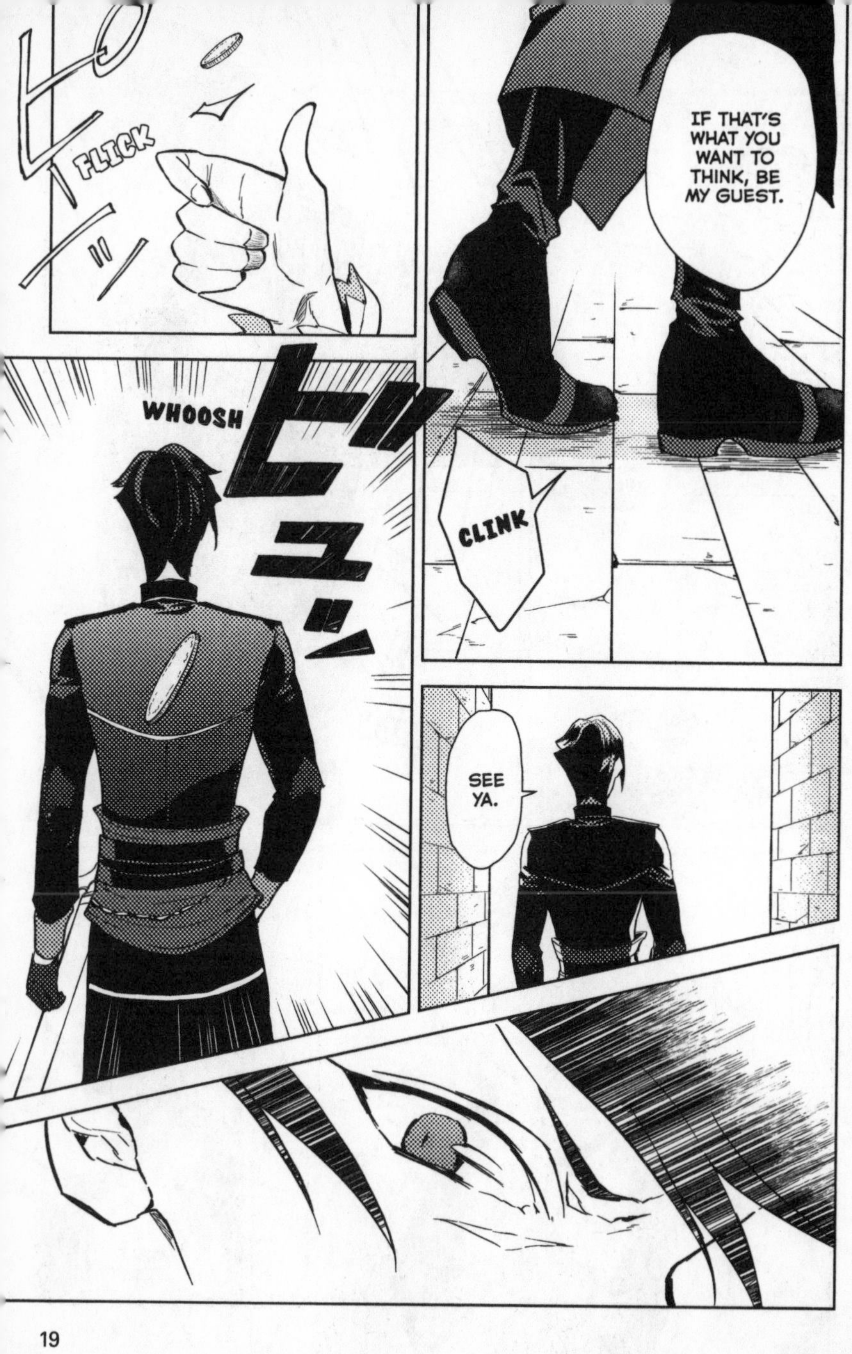
IF THAT'S WHAT YOU WANT TO THINK, BE MY GUEST.
CLINK
FLICK
WHOOSH
SEE YA.

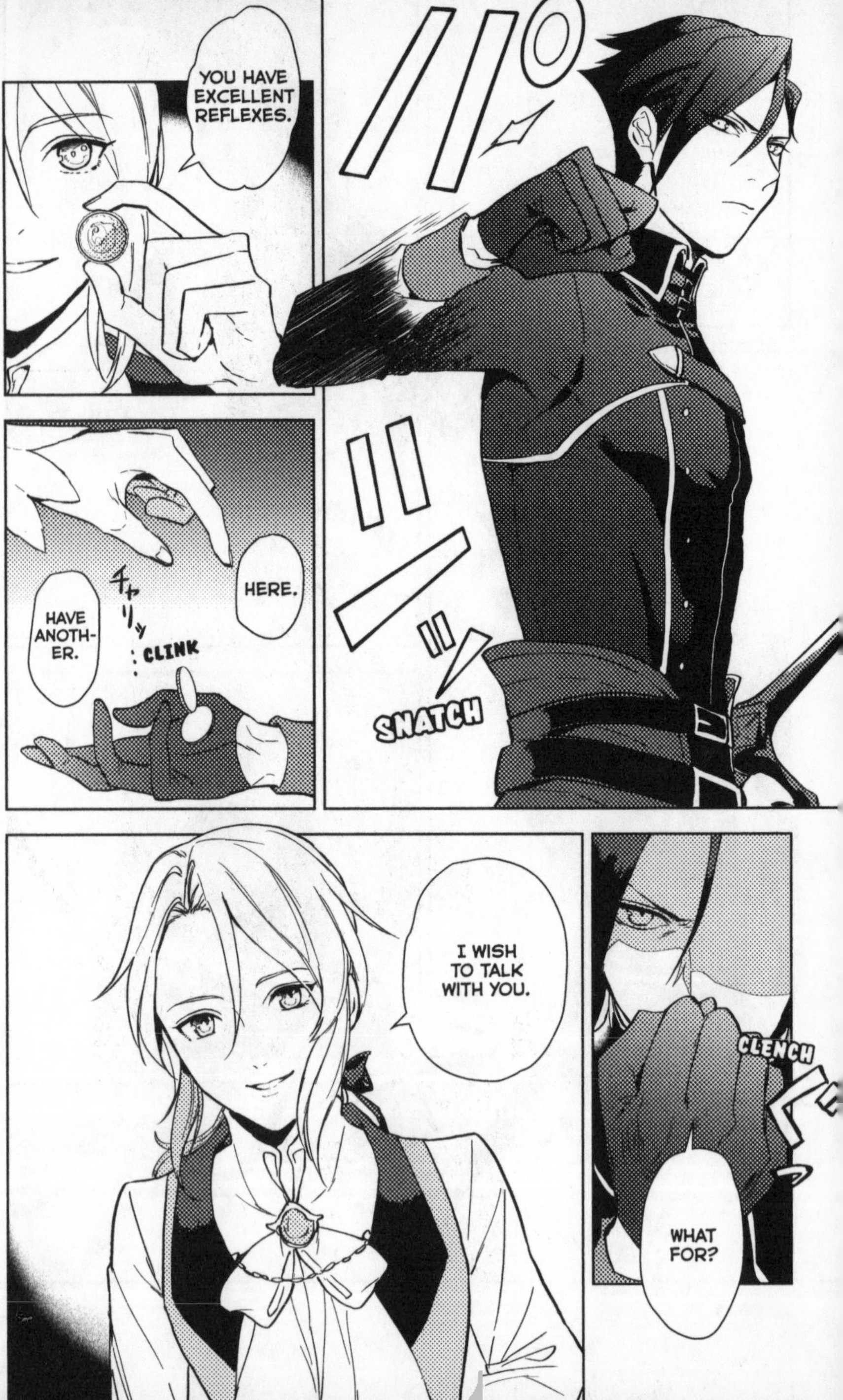
SNATCH
YOU HAVE EXCELLENT REFLEXES.
HERE.
HAVE ANOTHER-ER.
チャリッ
CLINK
CLENCH
WHAT FOR?
I WISH TO TALK WITH YOU.

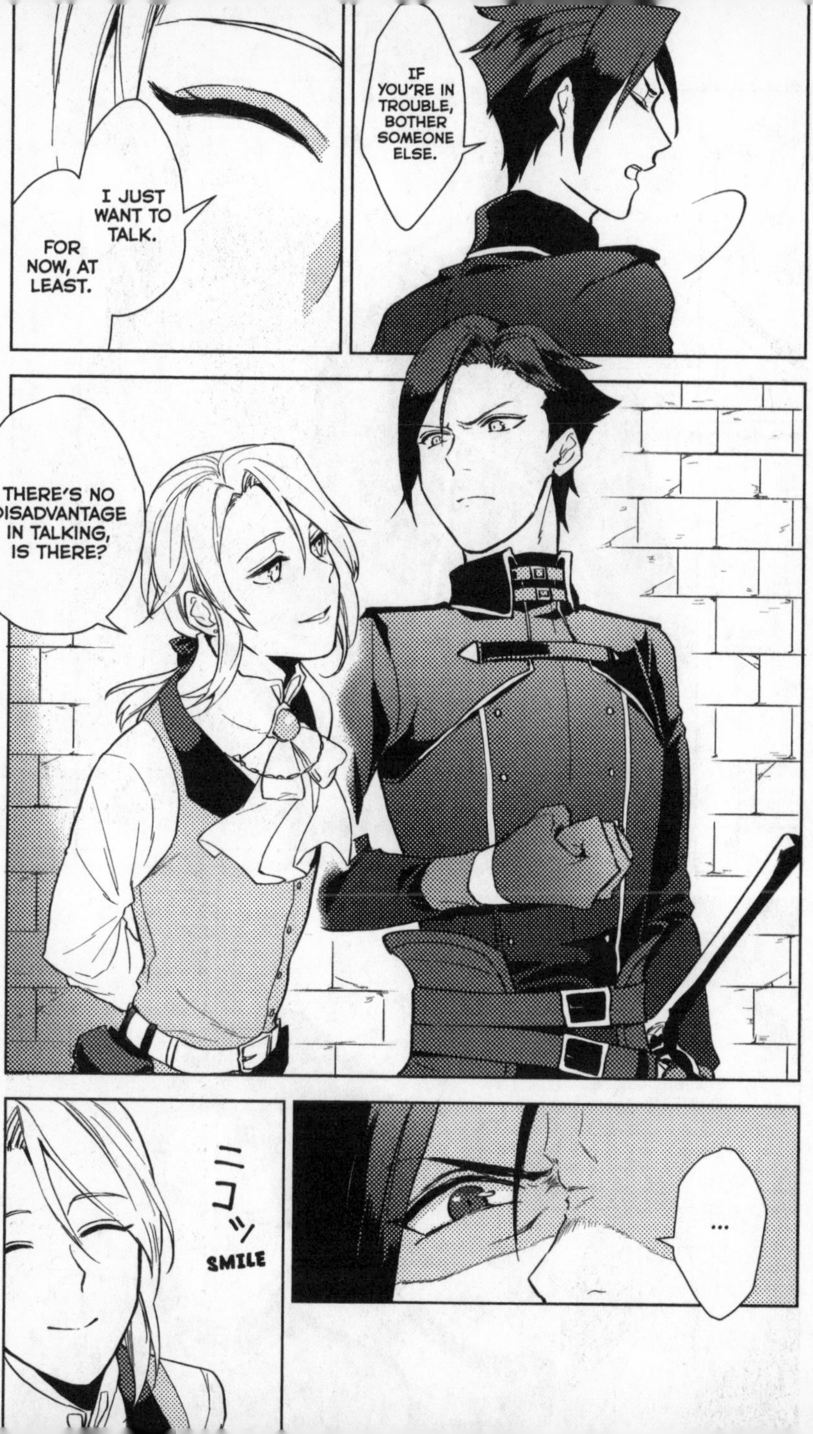
IF YOU'RE IN TROUBLE, BOTHER SOMEONE ELSE.
I JUST WANT TO TALK.
FOR NOW, AT LEAST.
THERE'S NO DISADVANTAGE IN TALKING, IS THERE?
...
ニコッ
SMILE

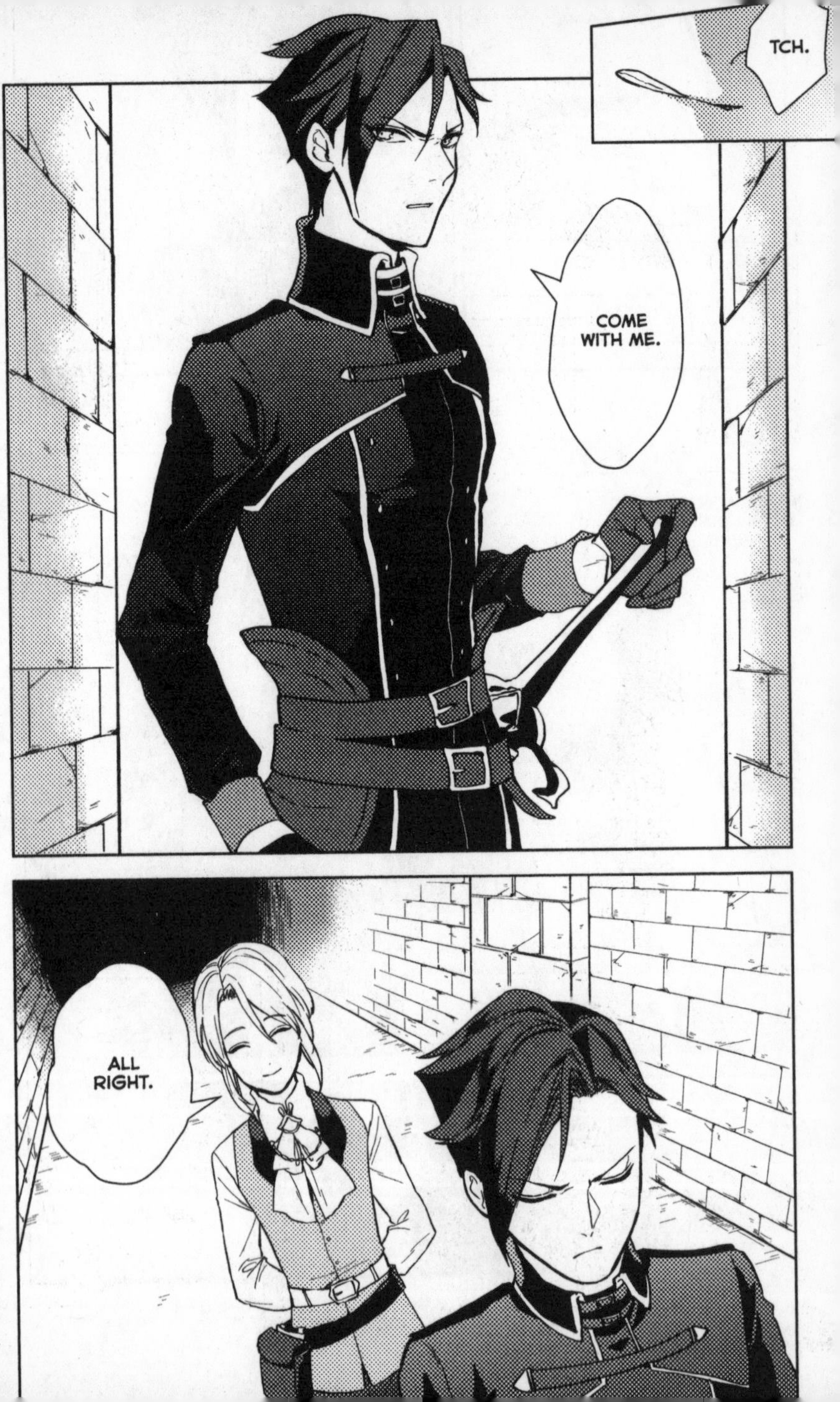
TCH.
COME WITH ME.
ALL RIGHT.

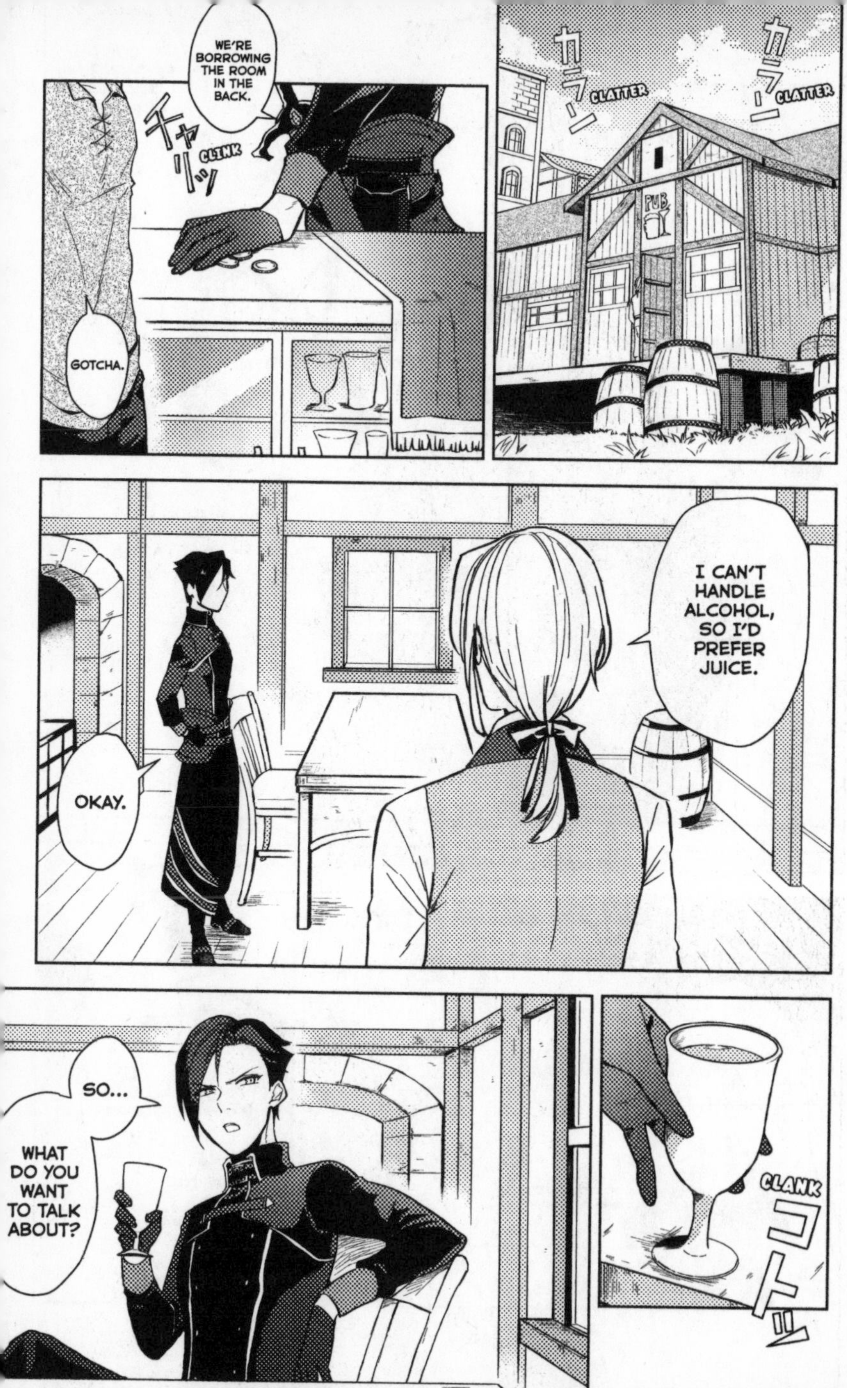
カラン
CLATTER
カラーン
CLATTER
PUB
WE'RE BORROWING THE ROOM IN THE BACK.
チャリッ
CLINK
GOTCHA.
I CAN'T HANDLE ALCOHOL, SO I'D PREFER JUICE.
OKAY.
CLANK
コトッ
SO...
WHAT DO YOU WANT TO TALK ABOUT?

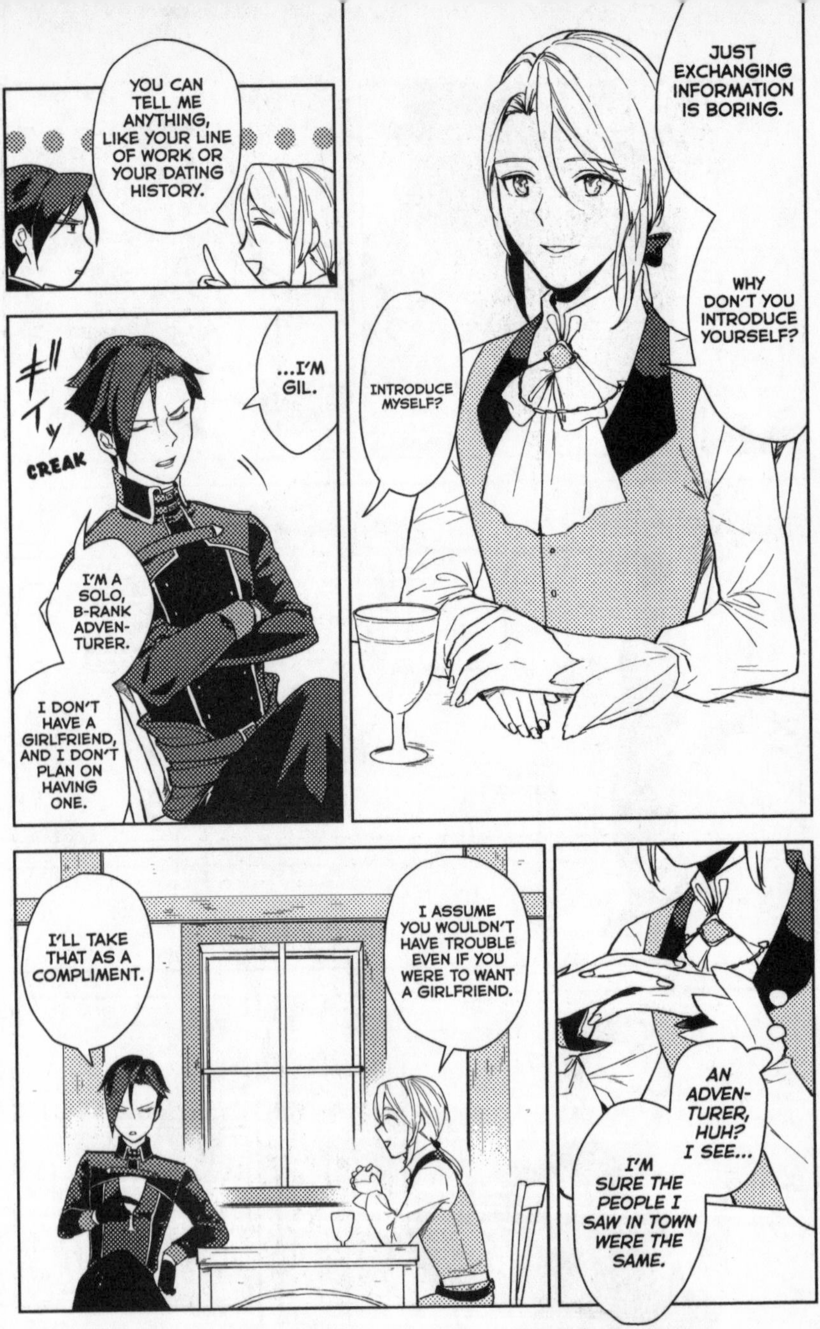
JUST EXCHANGING INFORMATION IS BORING.
WHY DON'T YOU INTRODUCE YOURSELF?
INTRODUCE MYSELF?
YOU CAN TELL ME ANYTHING, LIKE YOUR LINE OF WORK OR YOUR DATING HISTORY.
...I'M GIL.
ギイッ
CREAK
I'M A SOLO, B-RANK ADVEN-TURER.
I DON'T HAVE A GIRLFRIEND, AND I DON'T PLAN ON HAVING ONE.
AN ADVEN-TURER, HUH? I SEE...
I'M SURE THE PEOPLE I SAW IN TOWN WERE THE SAME.
I ASSUME YOU WOULDN'T HAVE TROUBLE EVEN IF YOU WERE TO WANT A GIRLFRIEND.
I'LL TAKE THAT AS A COMPLIMENT.

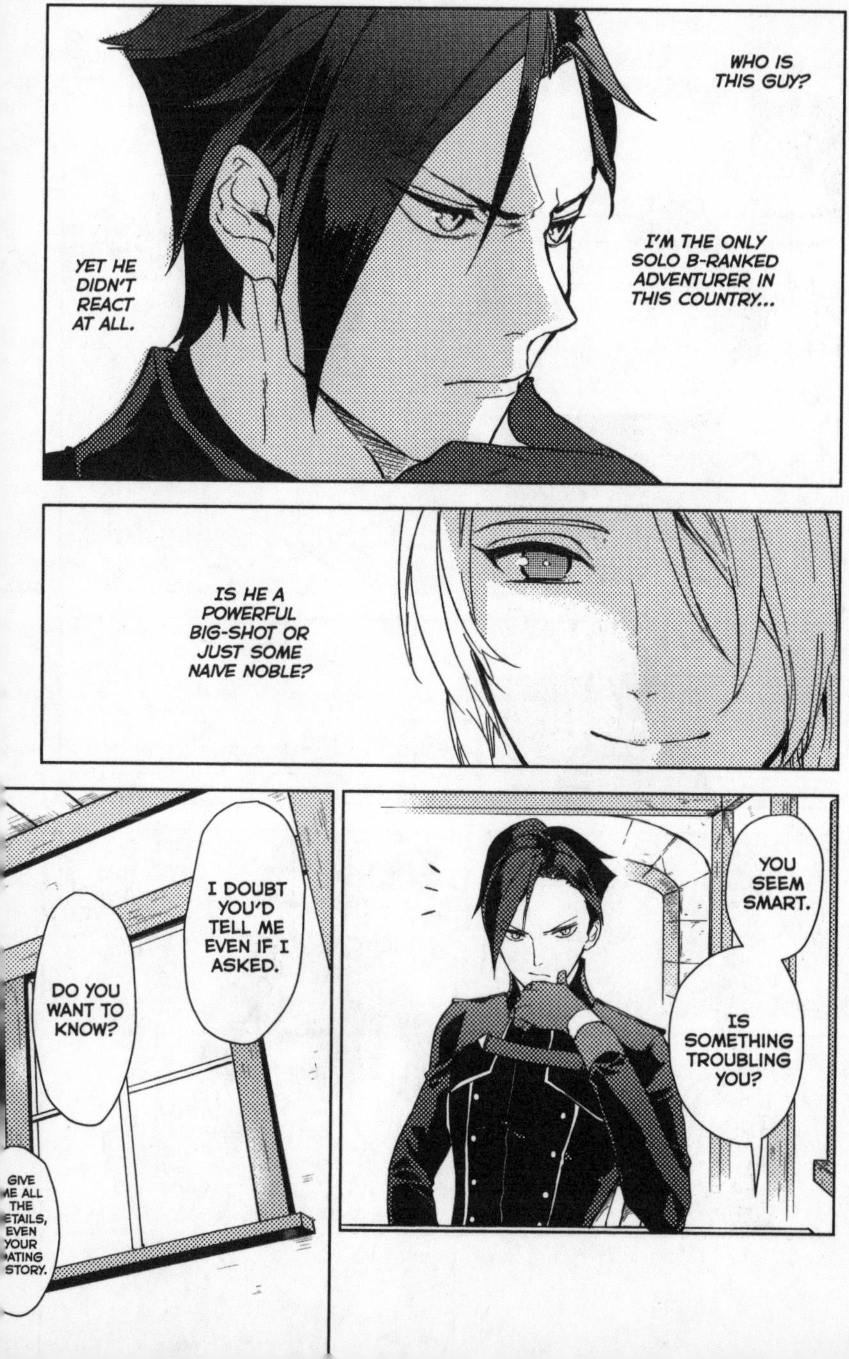
WHO IS THIS GUY?
I'M THE ONLY SOLO B-RANKED ADVENTURER IN THIS COUNTRY...
YET HE DIDN'T REACT AT ALL.
IS HE A POWERFUL BIG-SHOT OR JUST SOME NAIVE NOBLE?
YOU SEEM SMART.
IS SOMETHING TROUBLING YOU?
I DOUBT YOU'D TELL ME EVEN IF I ASKED.
DO YOU WANT TO KNOW?
GIVE ME ALL THE ETAILS, EVEN YOUR ATING STORY.

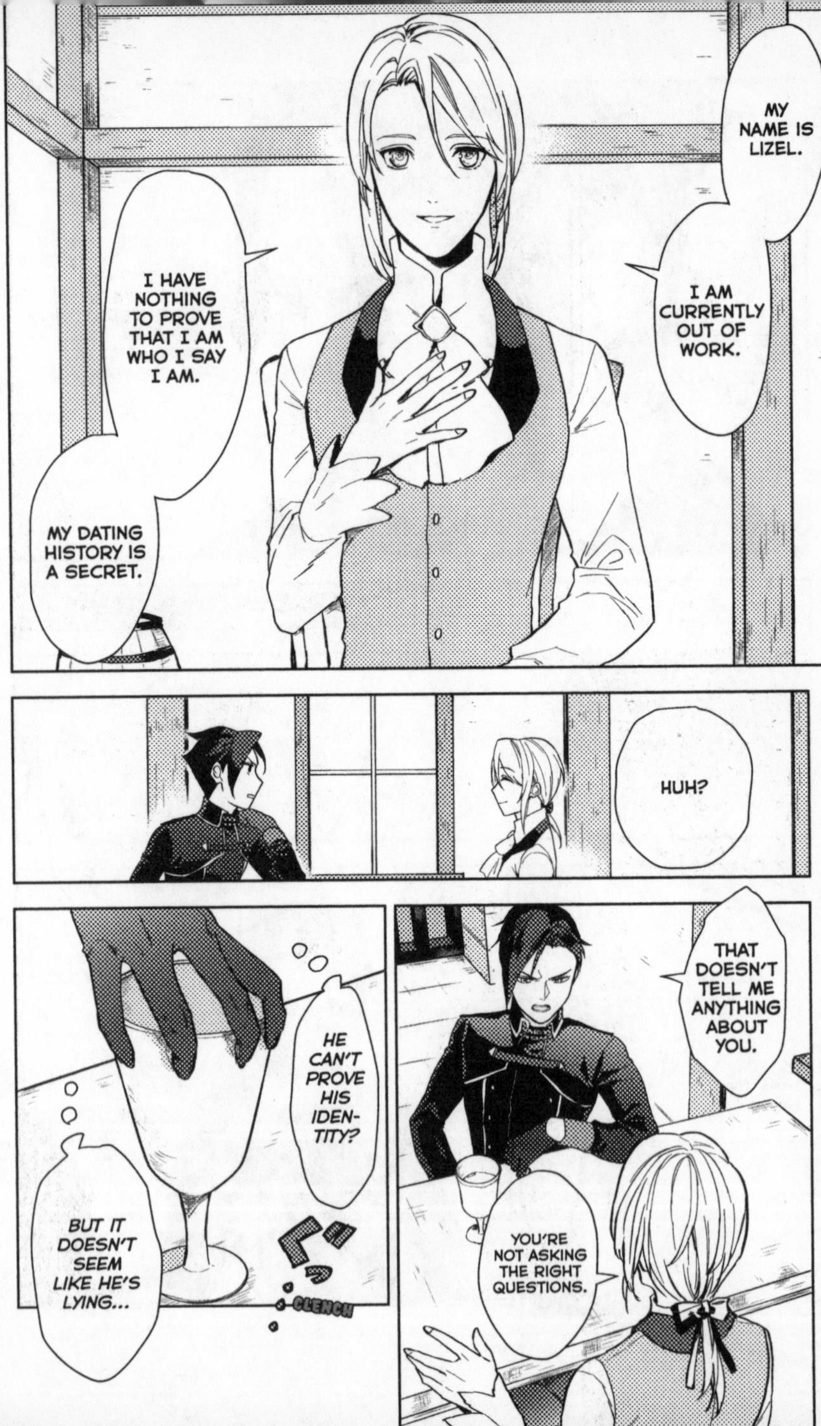
MY NAME IS LIZEL.
I AM CURRENTLY OUT OF WORK.
I HAVE NOTHING TO PROVE THAT I AM WHO I SAY I AM.
MY DATING HISTORY IS A SECRET.
HUH?
THAT DOESN'T TELL ME ANYTHING ABOUT YOU.
YOU'RE NOT ASKING THE RIGHT QUESTIONS.
HE CAN'T PROVE HIS IDEN-TITY?
BUT IT DOESN'T SEEM LIKE HE'S LYING...
CLENCH

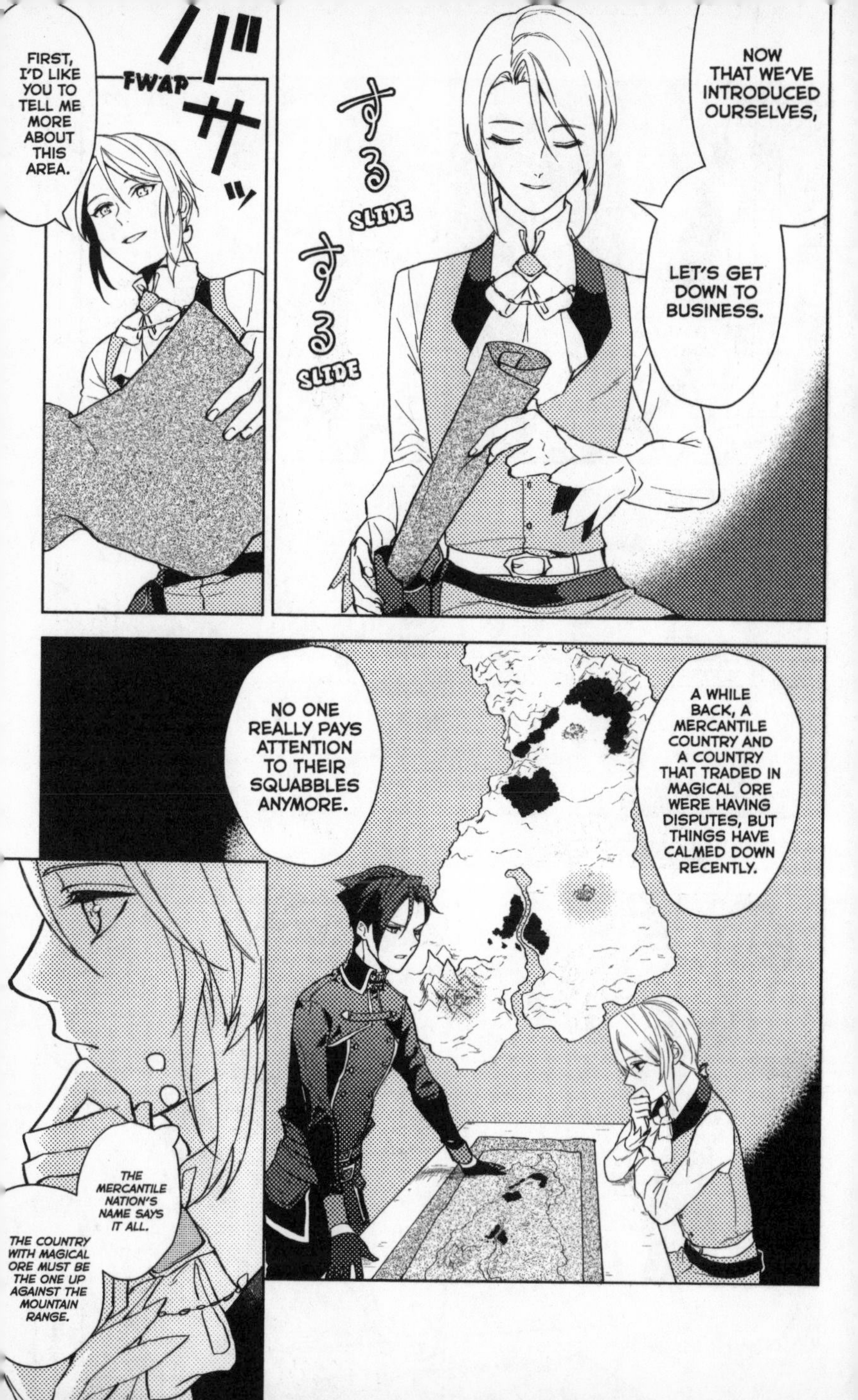
NOW THAT WE'VE INTRODUCED OURSELVES,
LET'S GET DOWN TO BUSINESS.
する
SLIDE
する
SLIDE
バサッ
FWAP
FIRST, I'D LIKE YOU TO TELL ME MORE ABOUT THIS AREA.
A WHILE BACK, A MERCANTILE COUNTRY AND A COUNTRY THAT TRADED IN MAGICAL ORE WERE HAVING DISPUTES, BUT THINGS HAVE CALMED DOWN RECENTLY.
NO ONE REALLY PAYS ATTENTION TO THEIR SQUABBLES ANYMORE.
THE MERCANTILE NATION'S NAME SAYS IT ALL.
THE COUNTRY WITH MAGICAL ORE MUST BE THE ONE UP AGAINST THE MOUNTAIN RANGE.

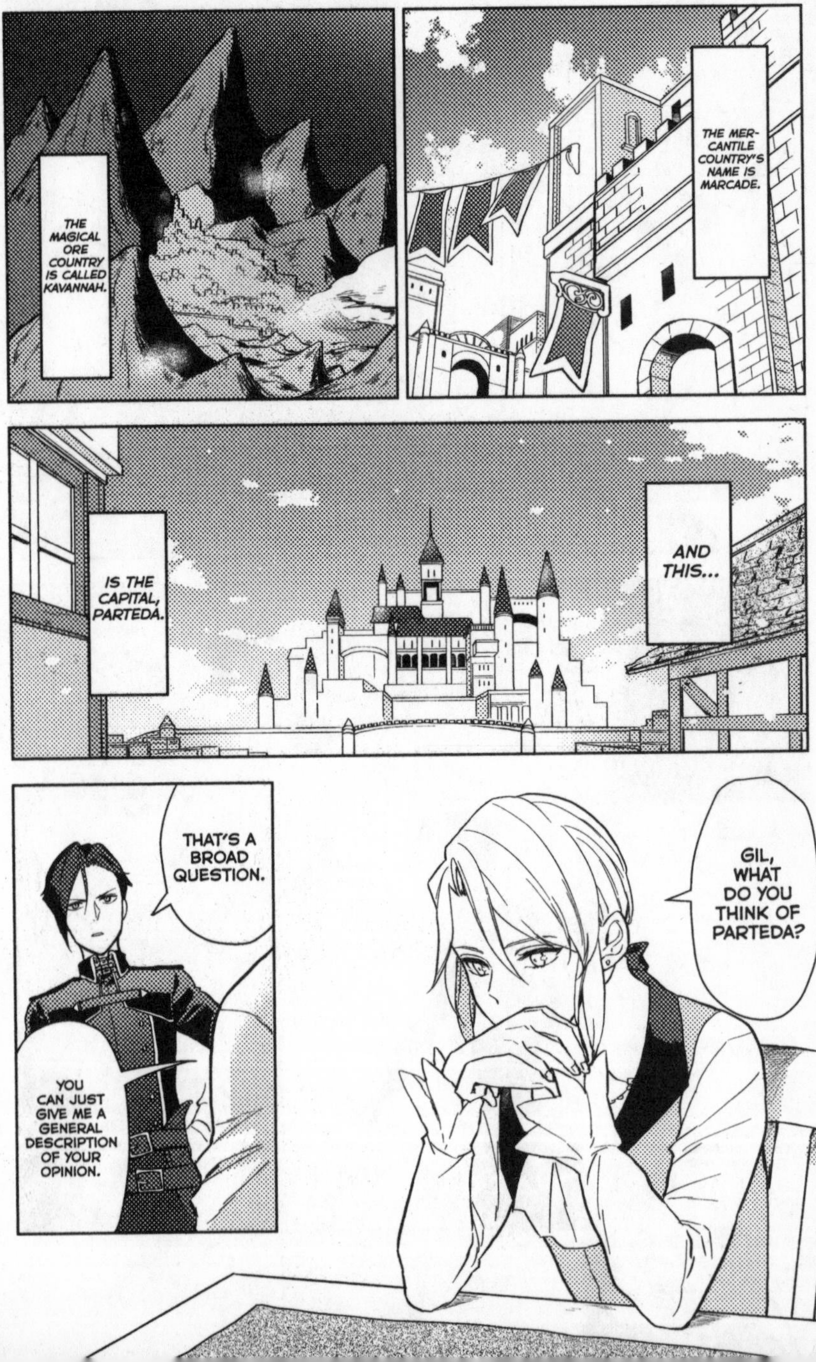
THE MER-CANTILE COUNTRY'S NAME IS MARCADE.
THE MAGICAL ORE COUNTRY IS CALLED KAVANNAH.
AND THIS...
IS THE CAPITAL, PARTEDA.
GIL, WHAT DO YOU THINK OF PARTEDA?
THAT'S A BROAD QUESTION.
YOU CAN JUST GIVE ME A GENERAL DESCRIPTION OF YOUR OPINION.

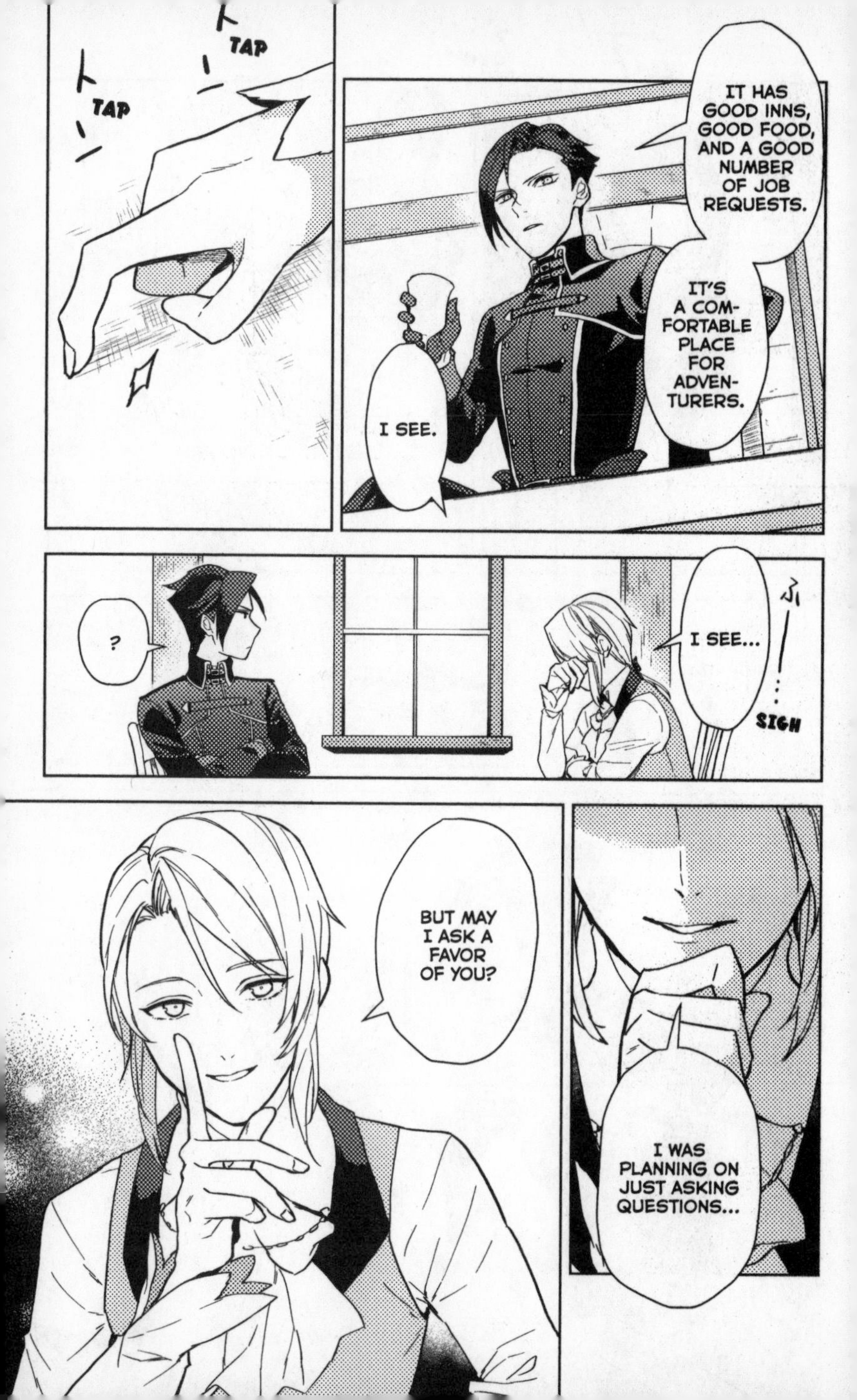
IT HAS GOOD INNS, GOOD FOOD, AND A GOOD NUMBER OF JOB REQUESTS.
IT'S A COM- FORTABLE PLACE FOR ADVEN- TURERS.
I SEE.
ト TAP
ト TAP
ふー… SIGH
I SEE...
?
I WAS PLANNING ON JUST ASKING QUESTIONS...
BUT MAY I ASK A FAVOR OF YOU?

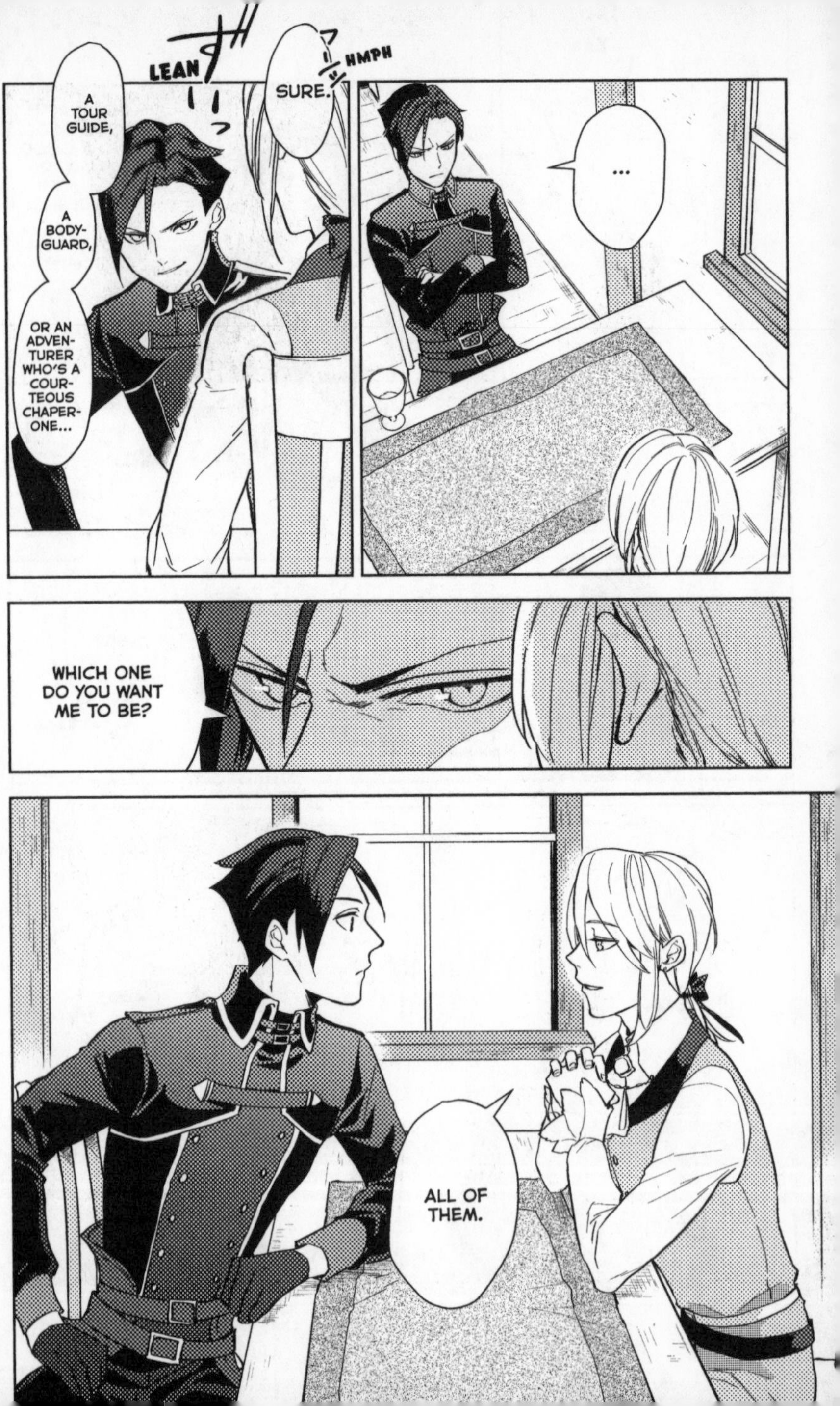
...
SURE.
HMPH
LEAN
A TOUR GUIDE,
A BODY-GUARD,
OR AN ADVENTURER WHO'S A COURTEOUS CHAPER-ONE...
WHICH ONE DO YOU WANT ME TO BE?
ALL OF THEM.

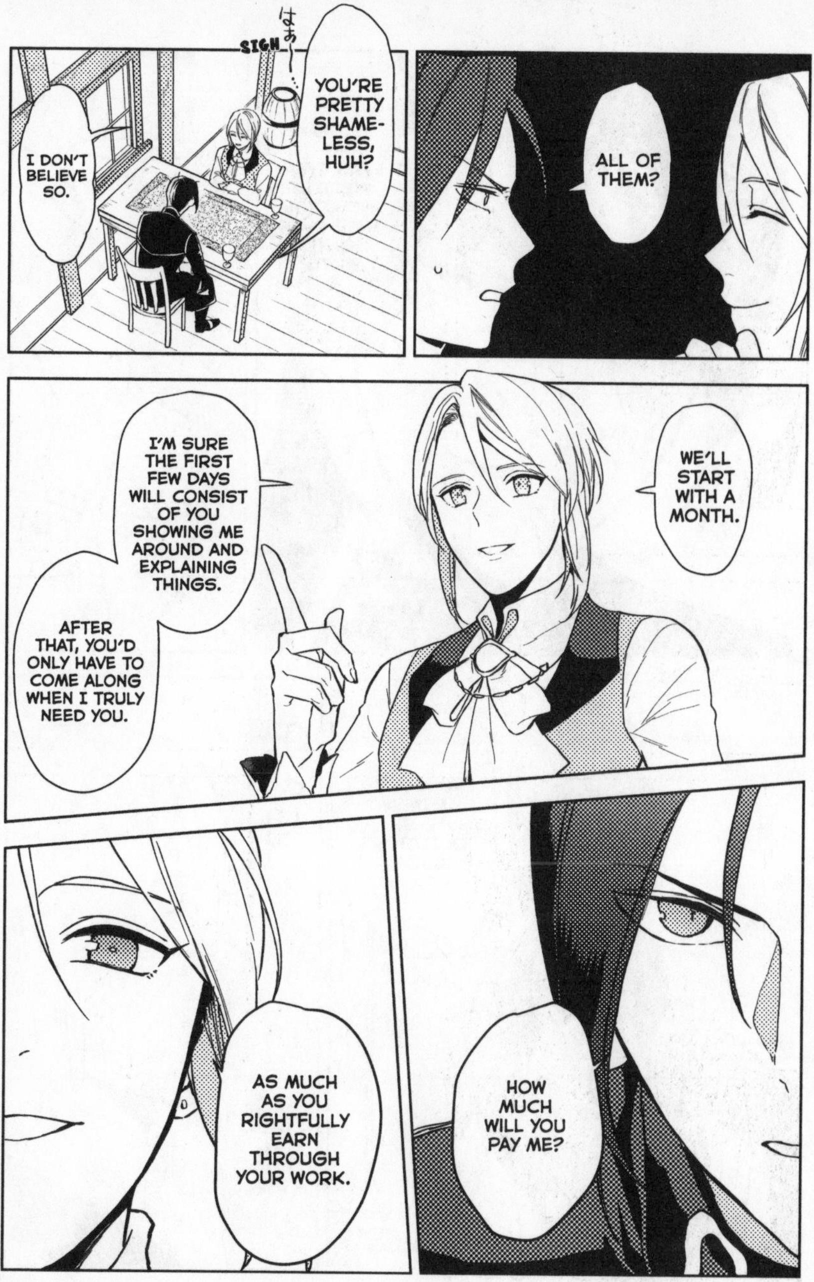
ALL OF THEM?
SIGH
はぁ~…
YOU'RE PRETTY SHAME-LESS, HUH?
I DON'T BELIEVE SO.
WE'LL START WITH A MONTH.
I'M SURE THE FIRST FEW DAYS WILL CONSIST OF YOU SHOWING ME AROUND AND EXPLAINING THINGS.
AFTER THAT, YOU'D ONLY HAVE TO COME ALONG WHEN I TRULY NEED YOU.
HOW MUCH WILL YOU PAY ME?
AS MUCH AS YOU RIGHTFULLY EARN THROUGH YOUR WORK.

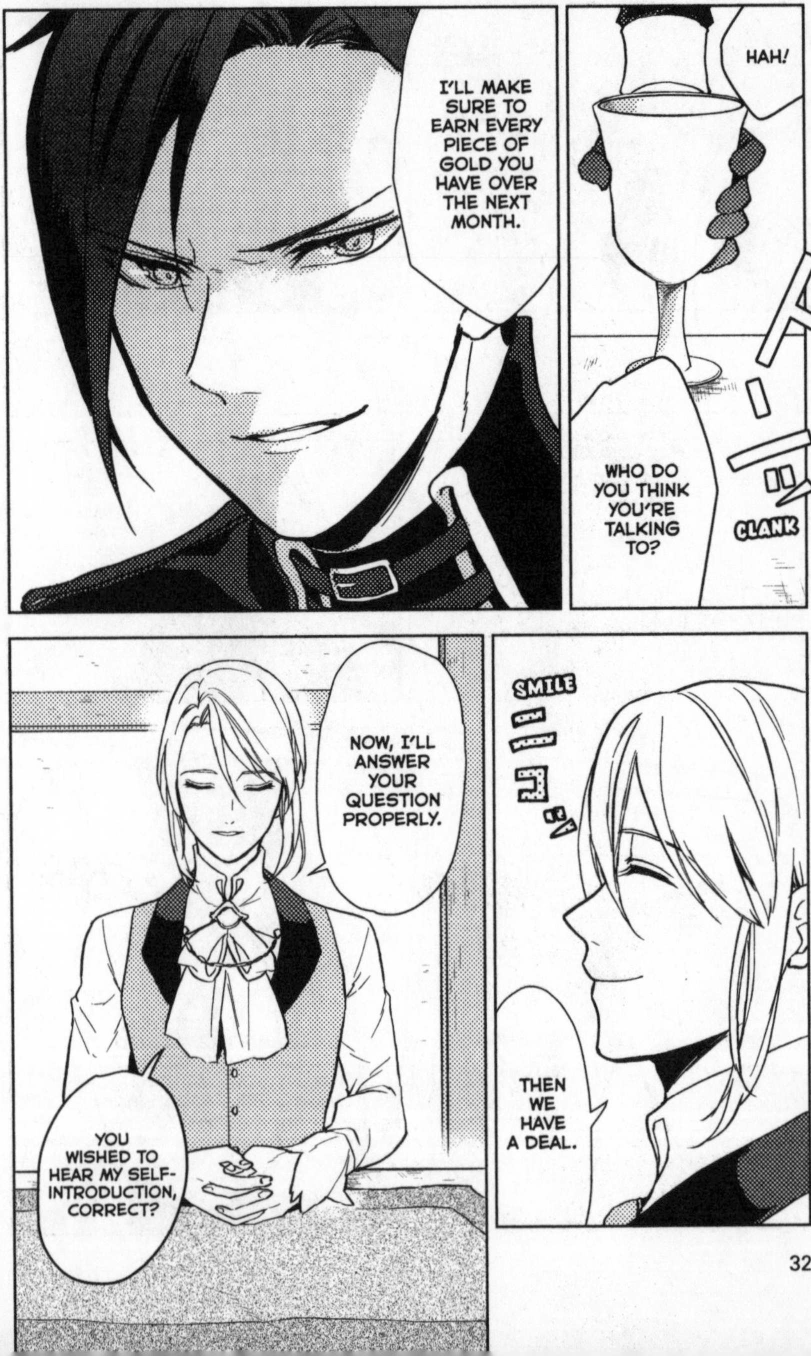
HAH!
WHO DO YOU THINK YOU'RE TALKING TO?
CLANK
I'LL MAKE SURE TO EARN EVERY PIECE OF GOLD YOU HAVE OVER THE NEXT MONTH.
SMILE
THEN WE HAVE A DEAL.
NOW, I'LL ANSWER YOUR QUESTION PROPERLY.
YOU WISHED TO HEAR MY SELF-INTRODUCTION, CORRECT?

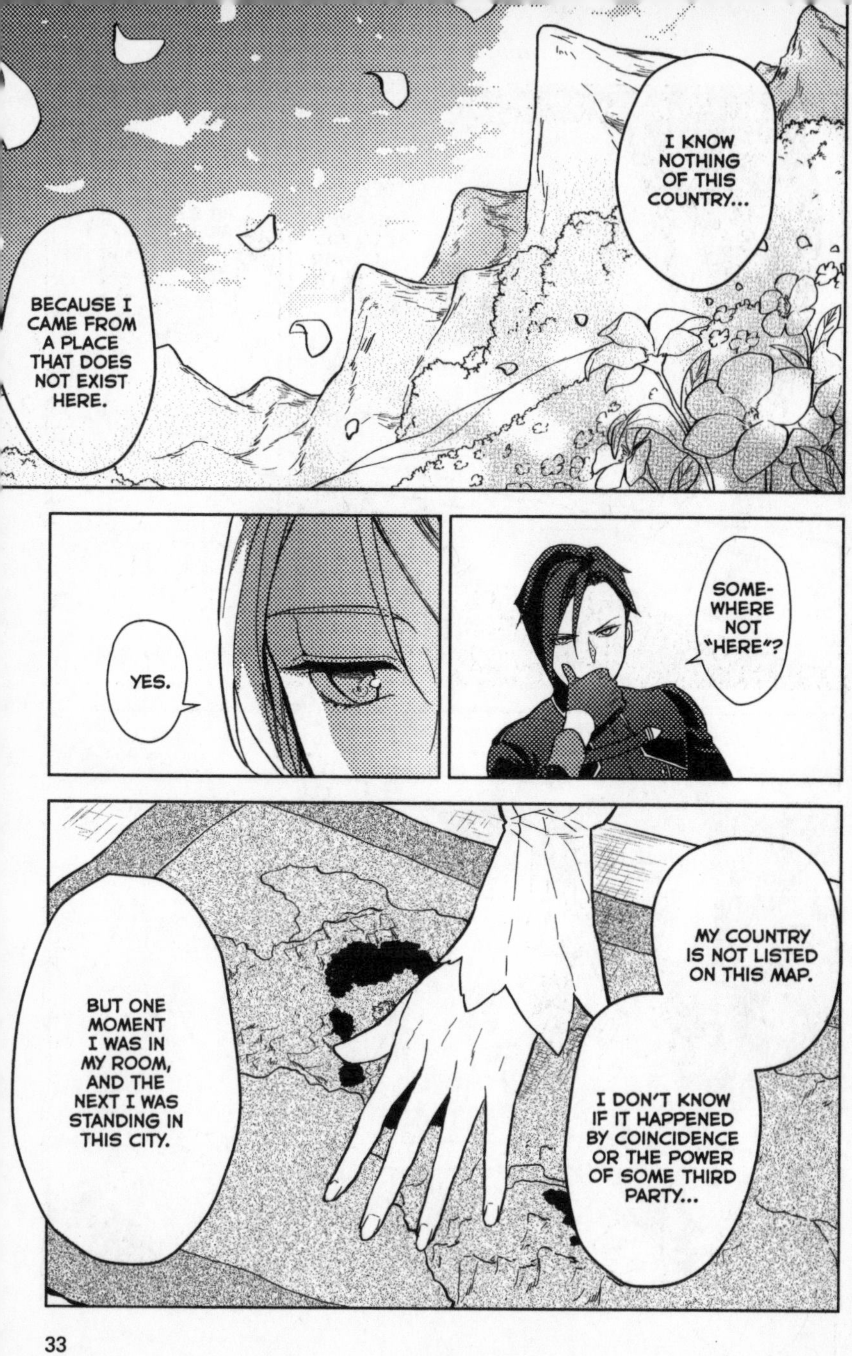
I KNOW NOTHING OF THIS COUNTRY...
BECAUSE I CAME FROM A PLACE THAT DOES NOT EXIST HERE.
SOME-WHERE NOT "HERE"?
YES.
MY COUNTRY IS NOT LISTED ON THIS MAP.
I DON'T KNOW IF IT HAPPENED BY COINCIDENCE OR THE POWER OF SOME THIRD PARTY...
BUT ONE MOMENT I WAS IN MY ROOM, AND THE NEXT I WAS STANDING IN THIS CITY.

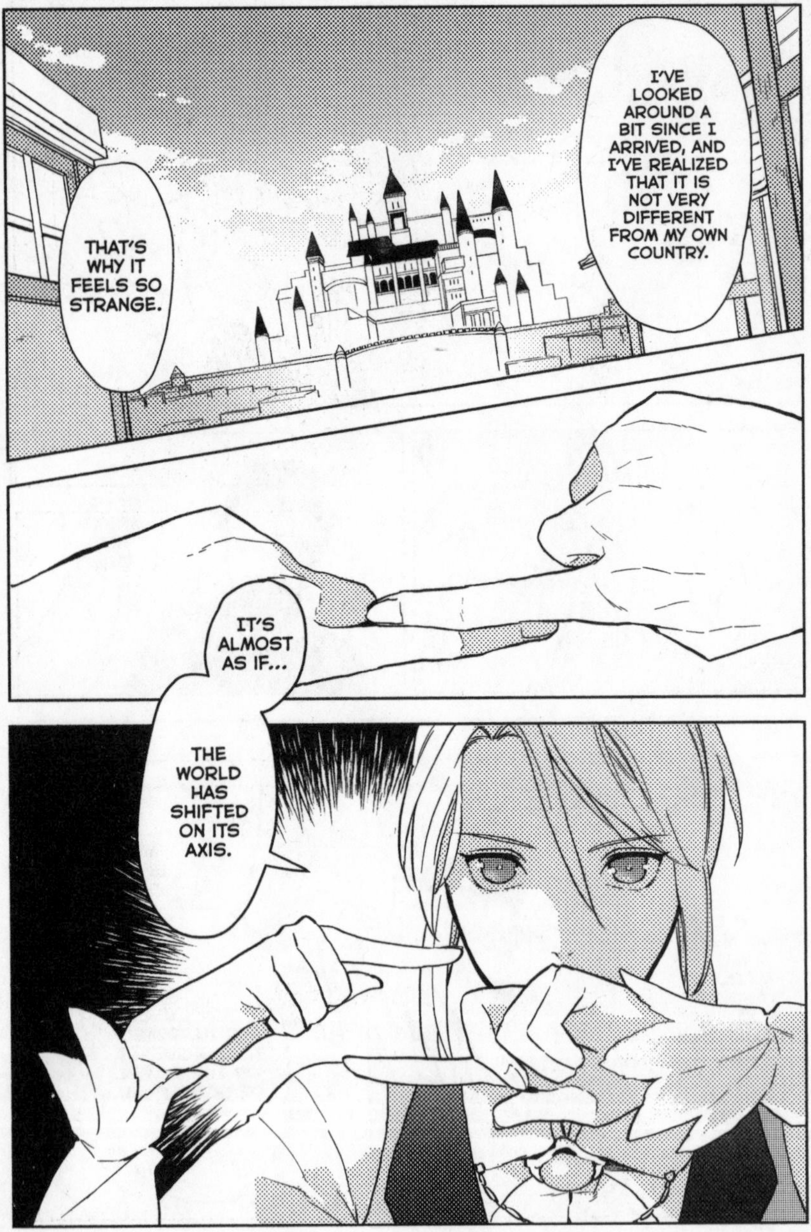
I'VE LOOKED AROUND A BIT SINCE I ARRIVED, AND I'VE REALIZED THAT IT IS NOT VERY DIFFERENT FROM MY OWN COUNTRY.
THAT'S WHY IT FEELS SO STRANGE.
IT'S ALMOST AS IF...
THE WORLD HAS SHIFTED ON ITS AXIS.

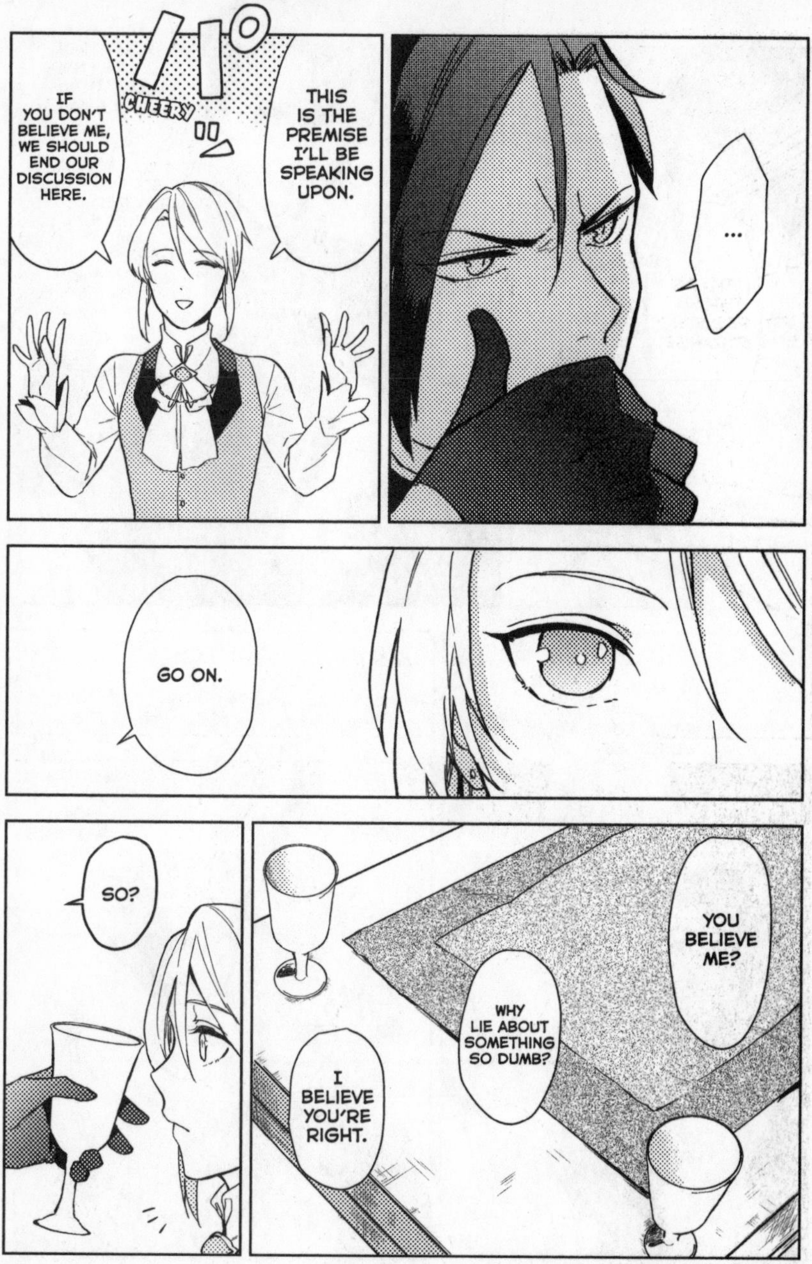
...
THIS IS THE PREMISE I'LL BE SPEAKING UPON.
CHEERY
IF YOU DON'T BELIEVE ME, WE SHOULD END OUR DISCUSSION HERE.
GO ON.
YOU BELIEVE ME?
WHY LIE ABOUT SOMETHING SO DUMB?
I BELIEVE YOU'RE RIGHT.
SO?

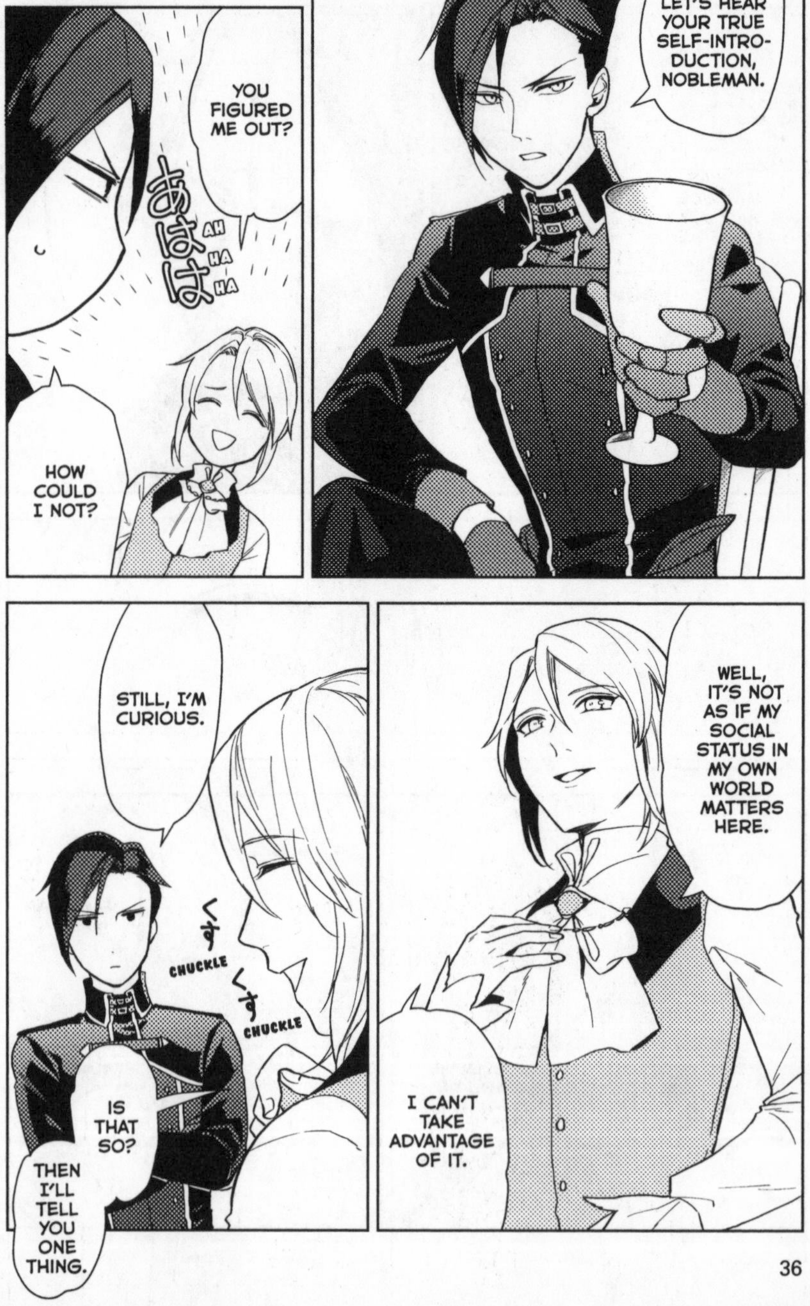
LET'S HEAR YOUR TRUE SELF-INTRO-DUCTION, NOBLEMAN.
YOU FIGURED ME OUT?
あはは
AH HA HA
HOW COULD I NOT?
WELL, IT'S NOT AS IF MY SOCIAL STATUS IN MY OWN WORLD MATTERS HERE.
I CAN'T TAKE ADVANTAGE OF IT.
STILL, I'M CURIOUS.
くす
CHUCKLE
くす
CHUCKLE
IS THAT SO?
THEN I'LL TELL YOU ONE THING.

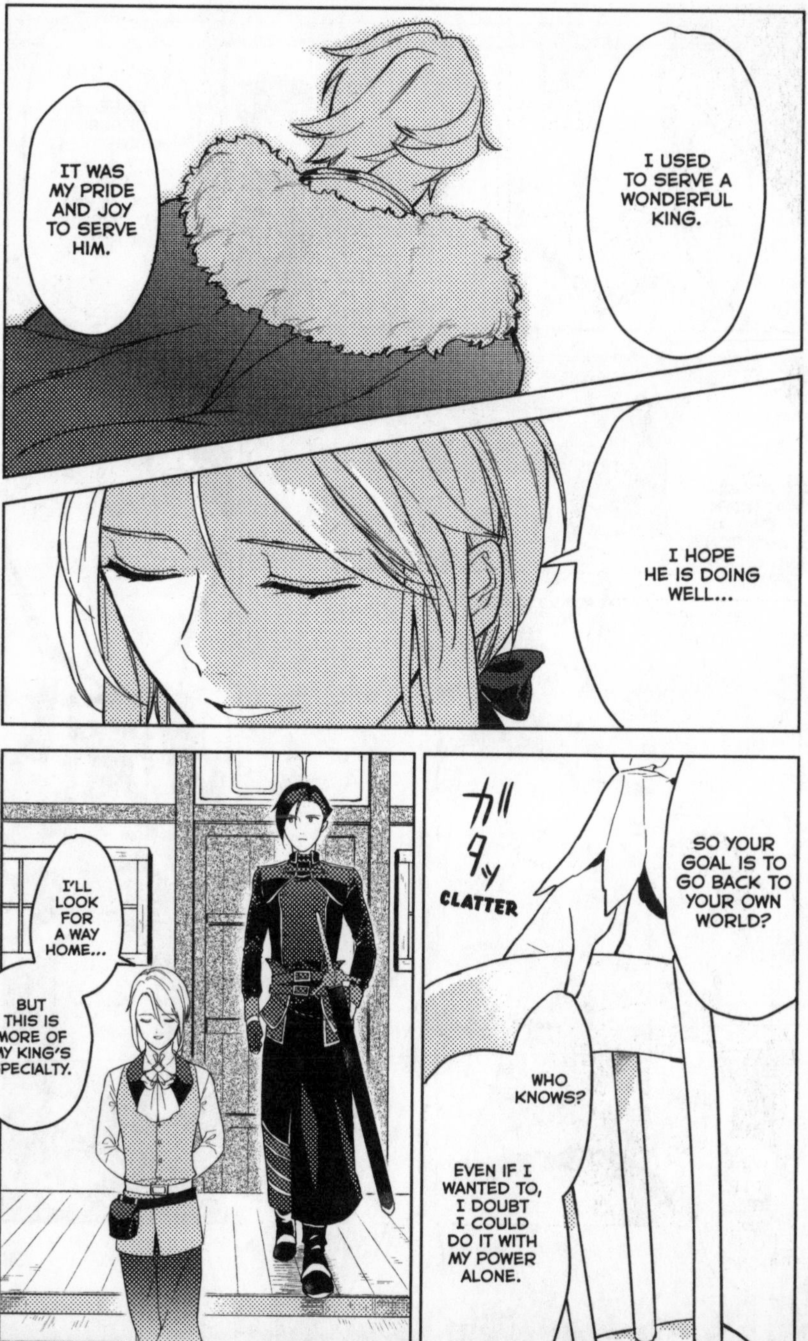
I USED TO SERVE A WONDERFUL KING.
IT WAS MY PRIDE AND JOY TO SERVE HIM.
I HOPE HE IS DOING WELL...
SO YOUR GOAL IS TO GO BACK TO YOUR OWN WORLD?
ガタッ
CLATTER
WHO KNOWS?
EVEN IF I WANTED TO, I DOUBT I COULD DO IT WITH MY POWER ALONE.
I'LL LOOK FOR A WAY HOME...
BUT THIS IS MORE OF MY KING'S SPECIALTY.

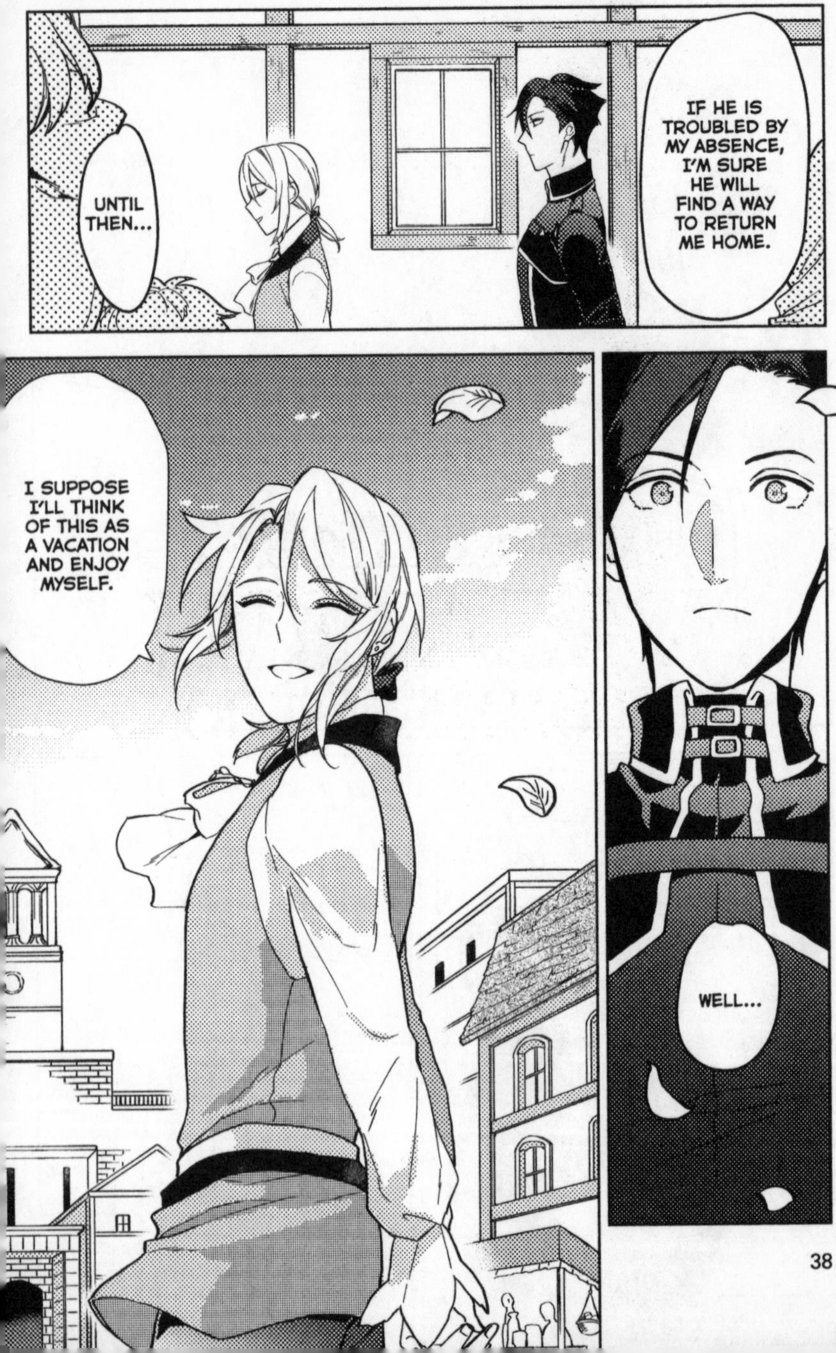
IF HE IS TROUBLED BY MY ABSENCE, I'M SURE HE WILL FIND A WAY TO RETURN ME HOME.
UNTIL THEN...
WELL...
I SUPPOSE I'LL THINK OF THIS AS A VACATION AND ENJOY MYSELF.

A Gentle Noble's
VACATION
RECOMMENDATION

Chapter 2

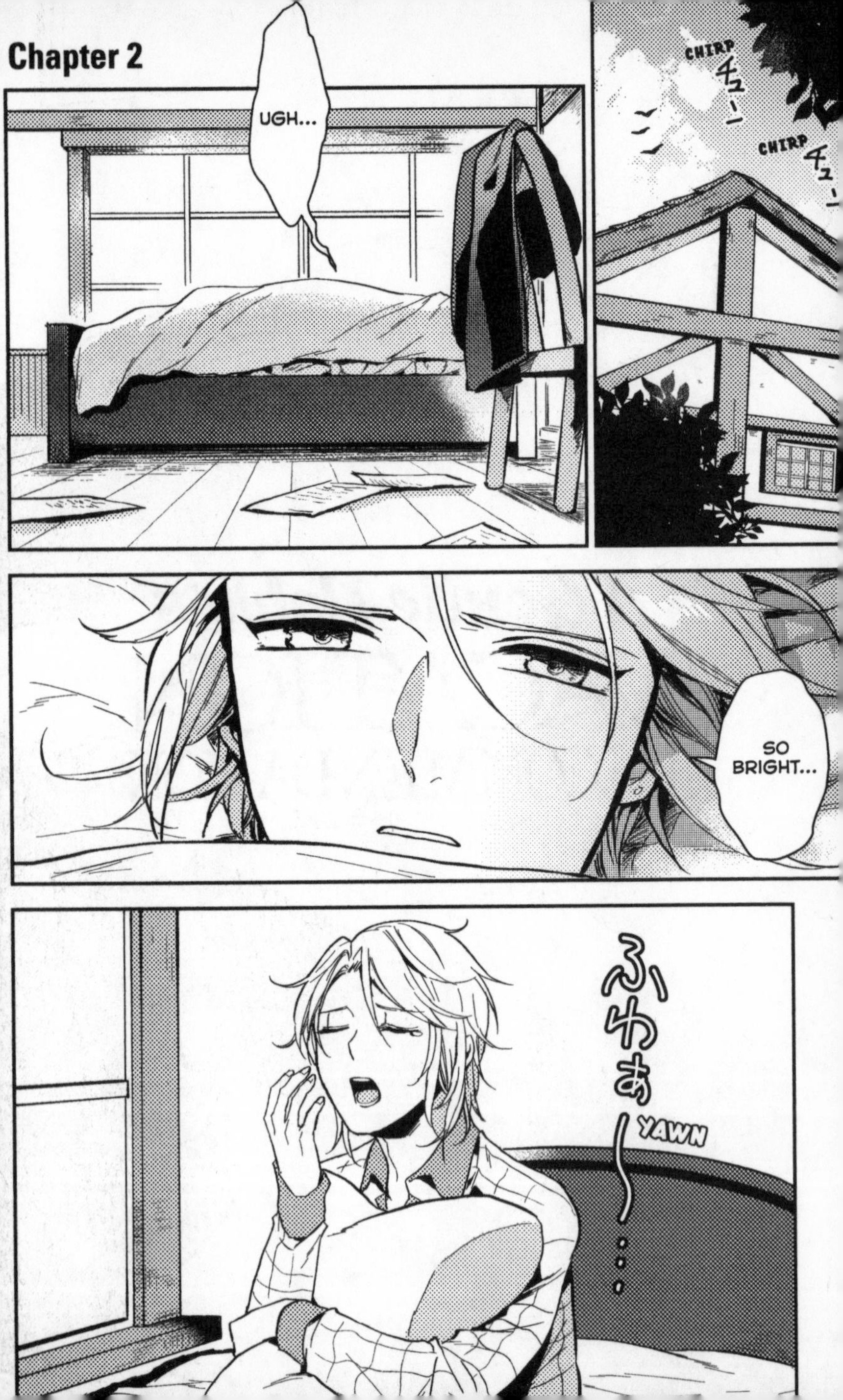
CHIRP
チュー
CHIRP
チュー
UGH...
SO BRIGHT...
ふわぁ~...
YAWN

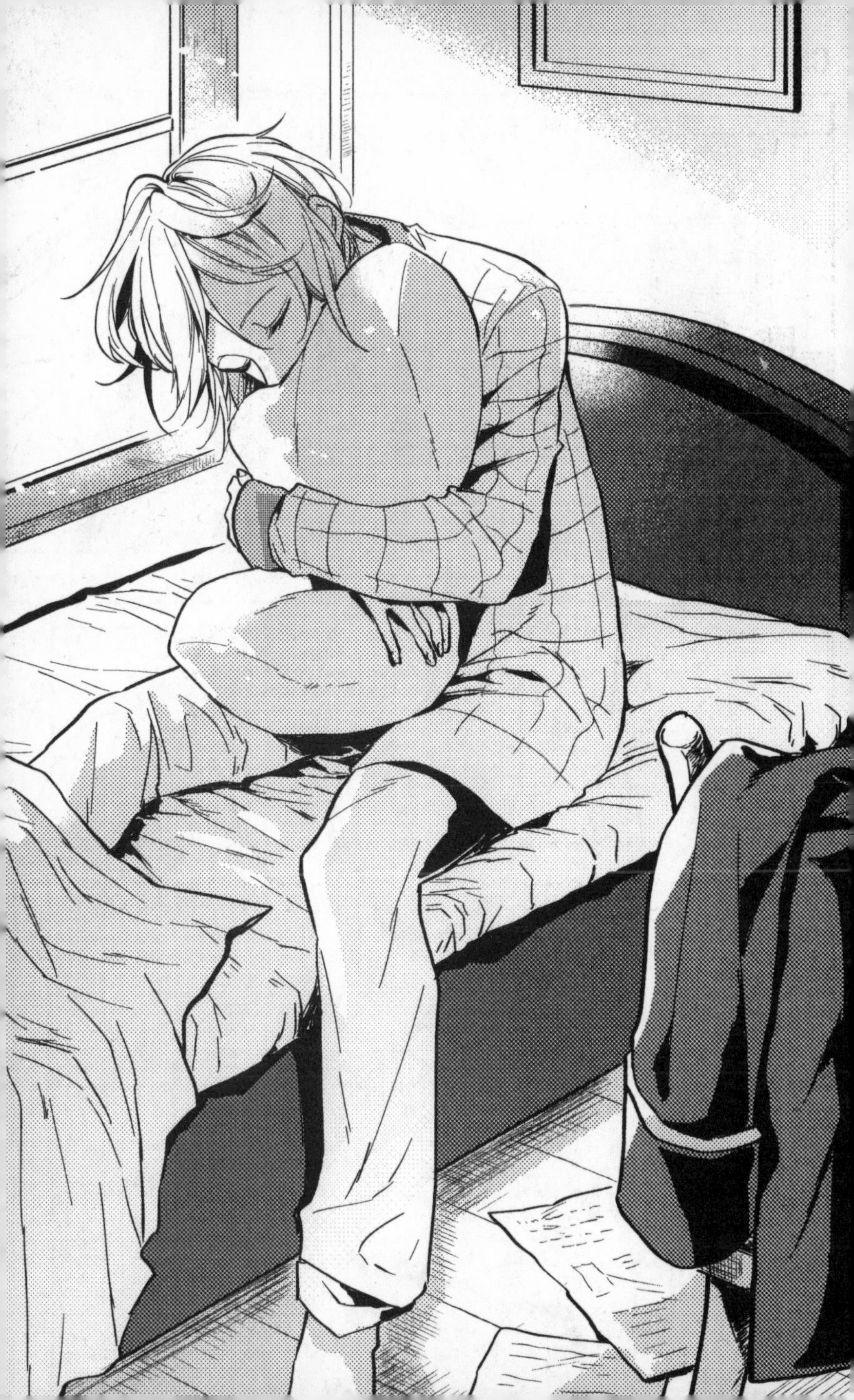

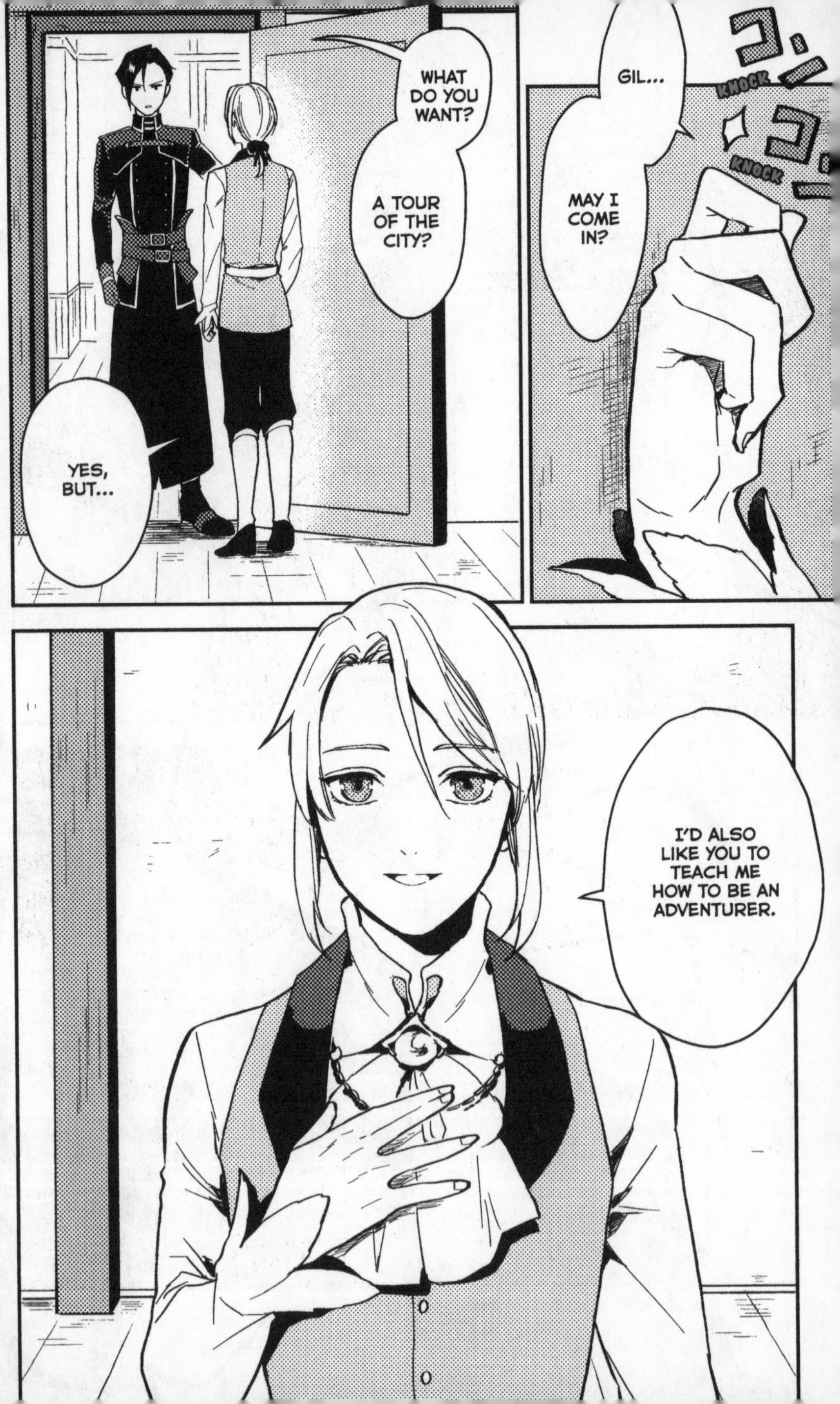
KNOCK
KNOCK
GIL...
MAY I COME IN?
WHAT DO YOU WANT?
A TOUR OF THE CITY?
YES, BUT...
I'D ALSO LIKE YOU TO TEACH ME HOW TO BE AN ADVENTURER.

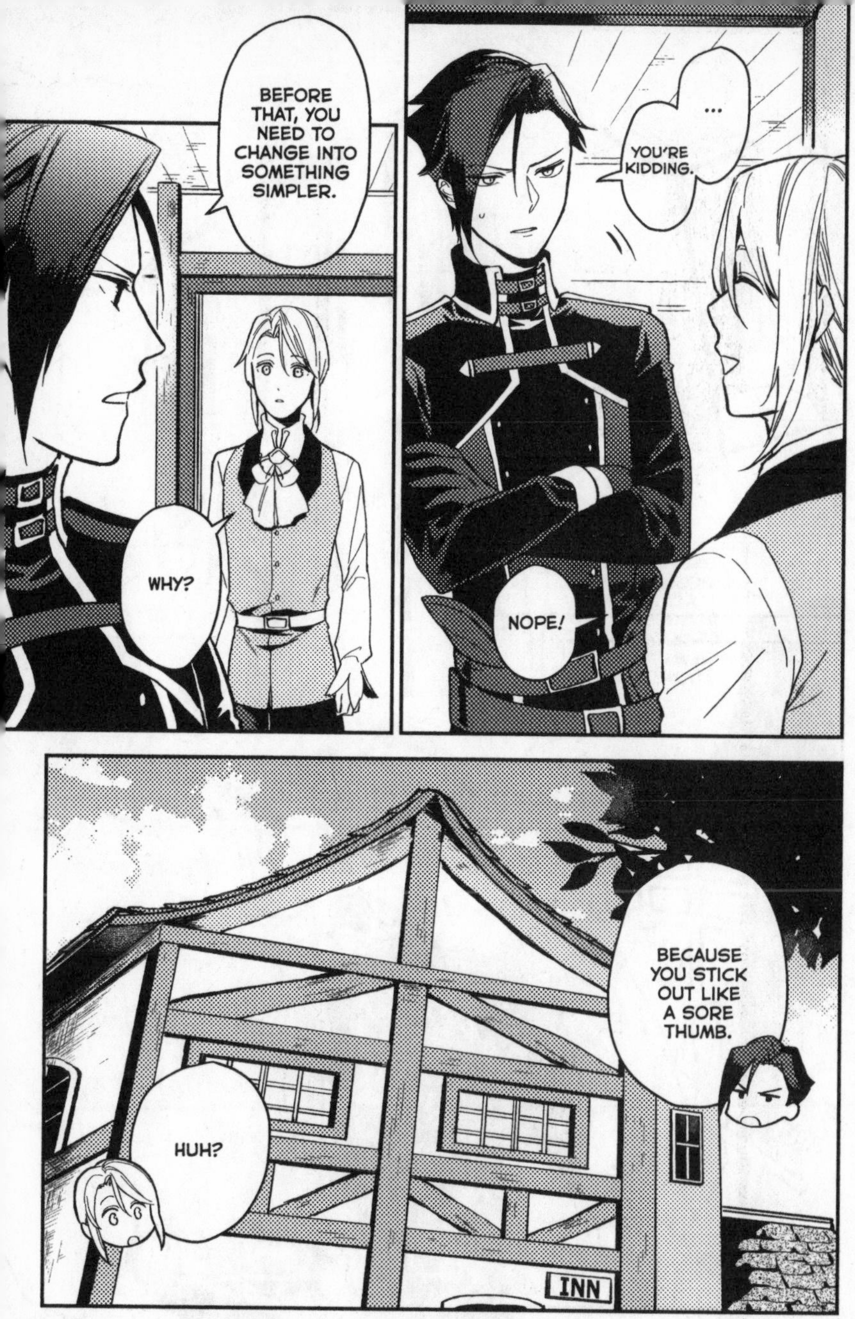
...
YOU'RE KIDDING.
NOPE!
BEFORE THAT, YOU NEED TO CHANGE INTO SOMETHING SIMPLER.
WHY?
BECAUSE YOU STICK OUT LIKE A SORE THUMB.
HUH?
INN

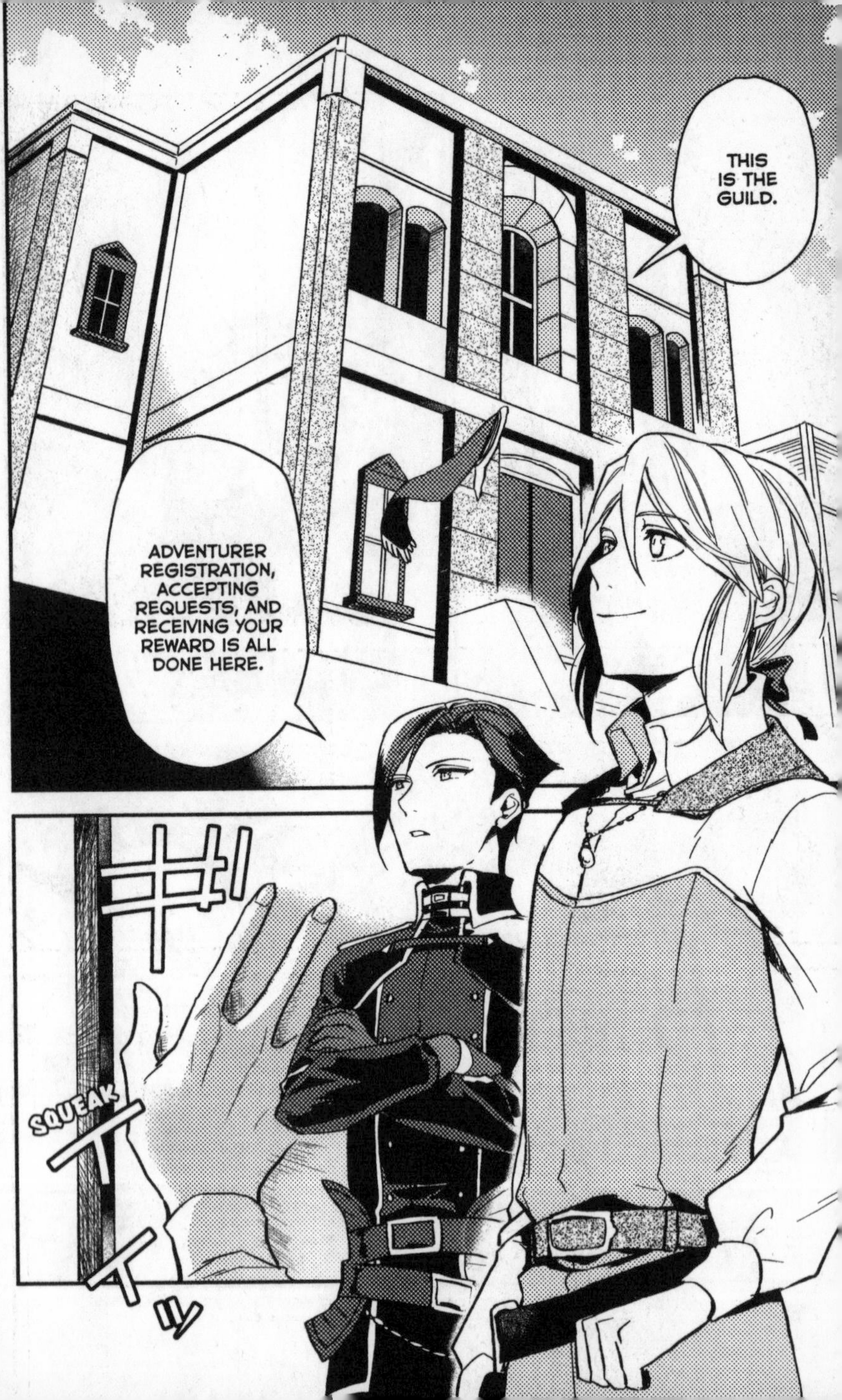
THIS IS THE GUILD.
ADVENTURER REGISTRATION, ACCEPTING REQUESTS, AND RECEIVING YOUR REWARD IS ALL DONE HERE.
SQUEAK

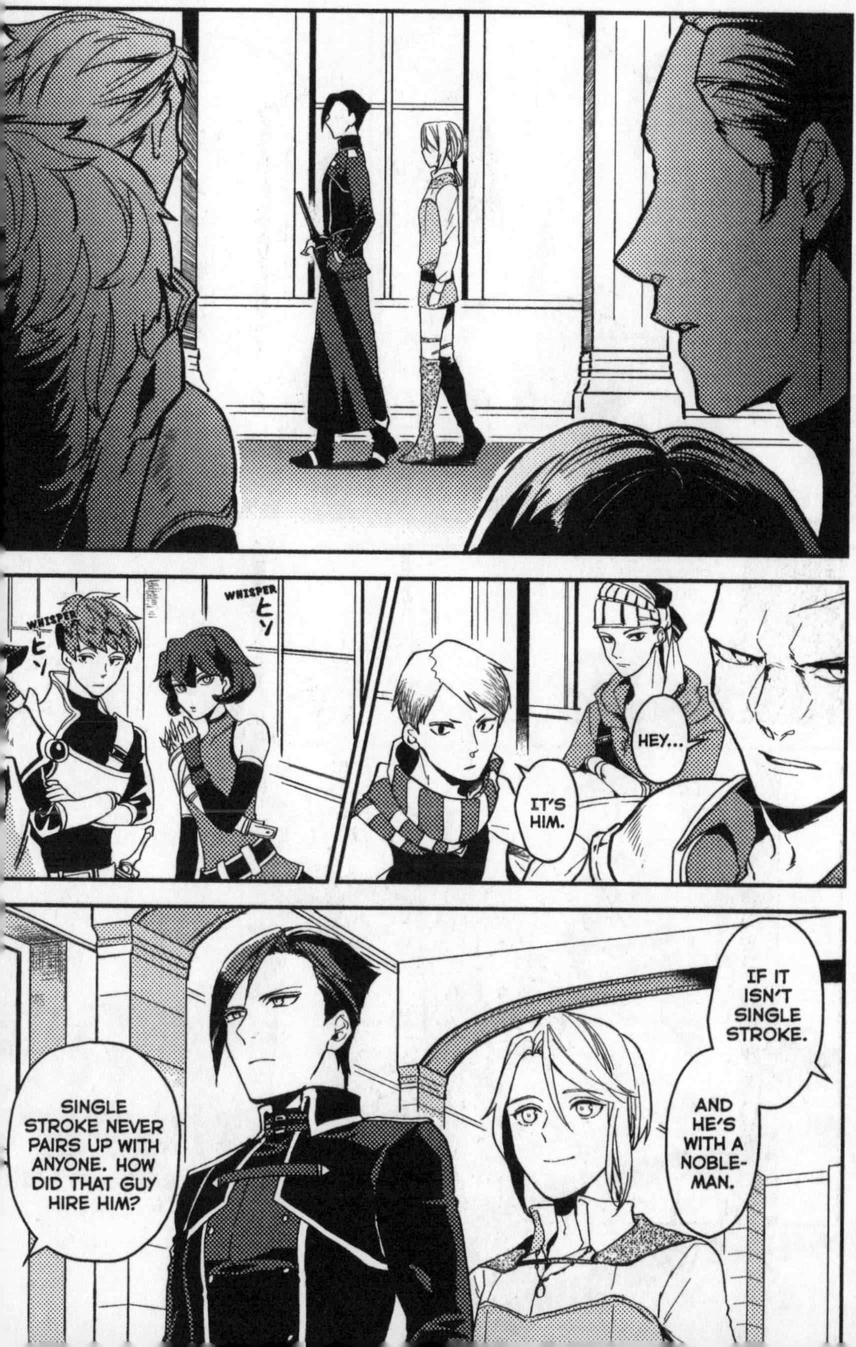
HEY...
IT'S HIM.
WHISPER ヒソ
WHISPER ヒソ
IF IT ISN'T SINGLE STROKE.
AND HE'S WITH A NOBLE-MAN.
SINGLE STROKE NEVER PAIRS UP WITH ANYONE. HOW DID THAT GUY HIRE HIM?

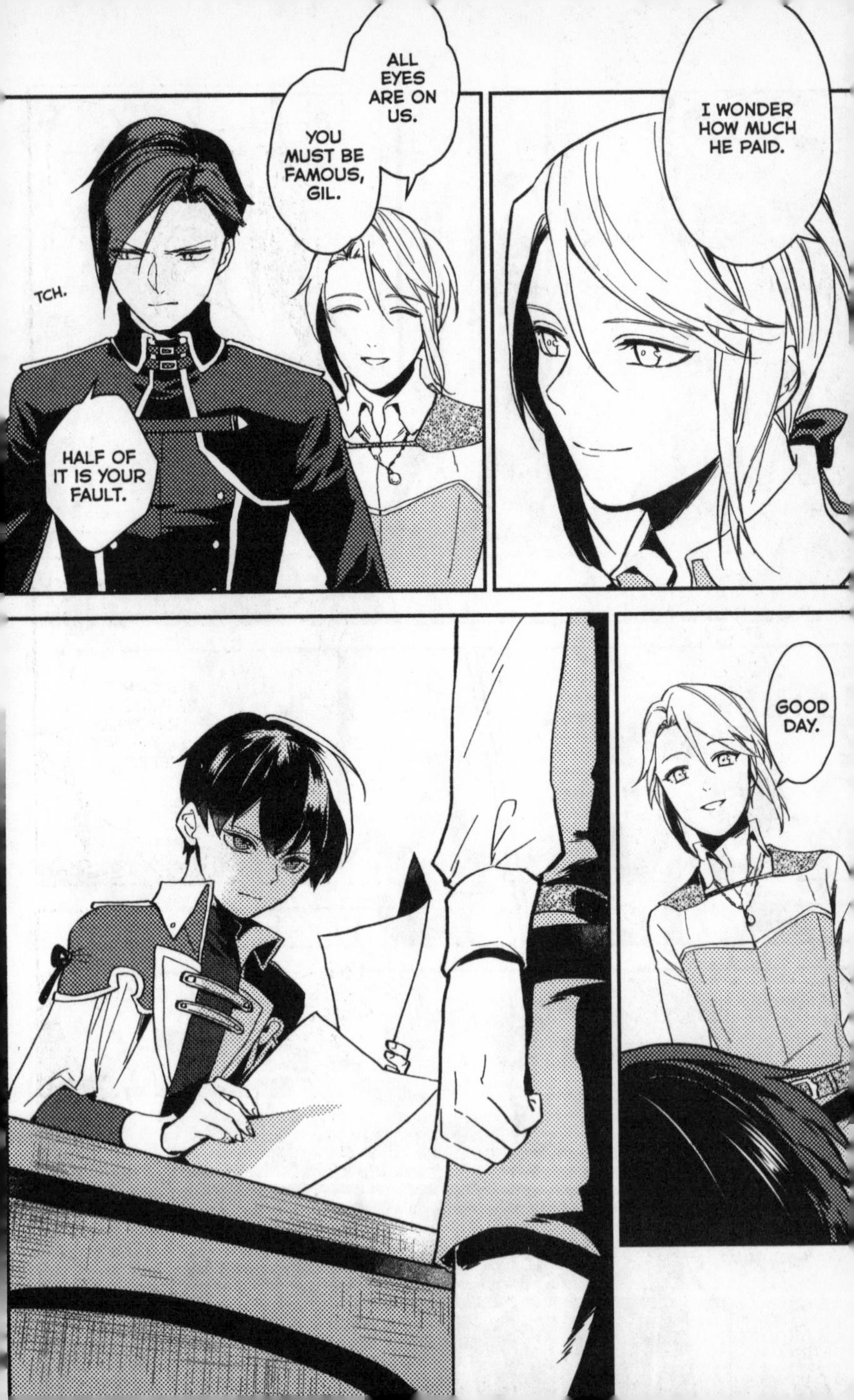
I WONDER HOW MUCH HE PAID.
ALL EYES ARE ON US.
YOU MUST BE FAMOUS, GIL.
TCH.
HALF OF IT IS YOUR FAULT.
GOOD DAY.

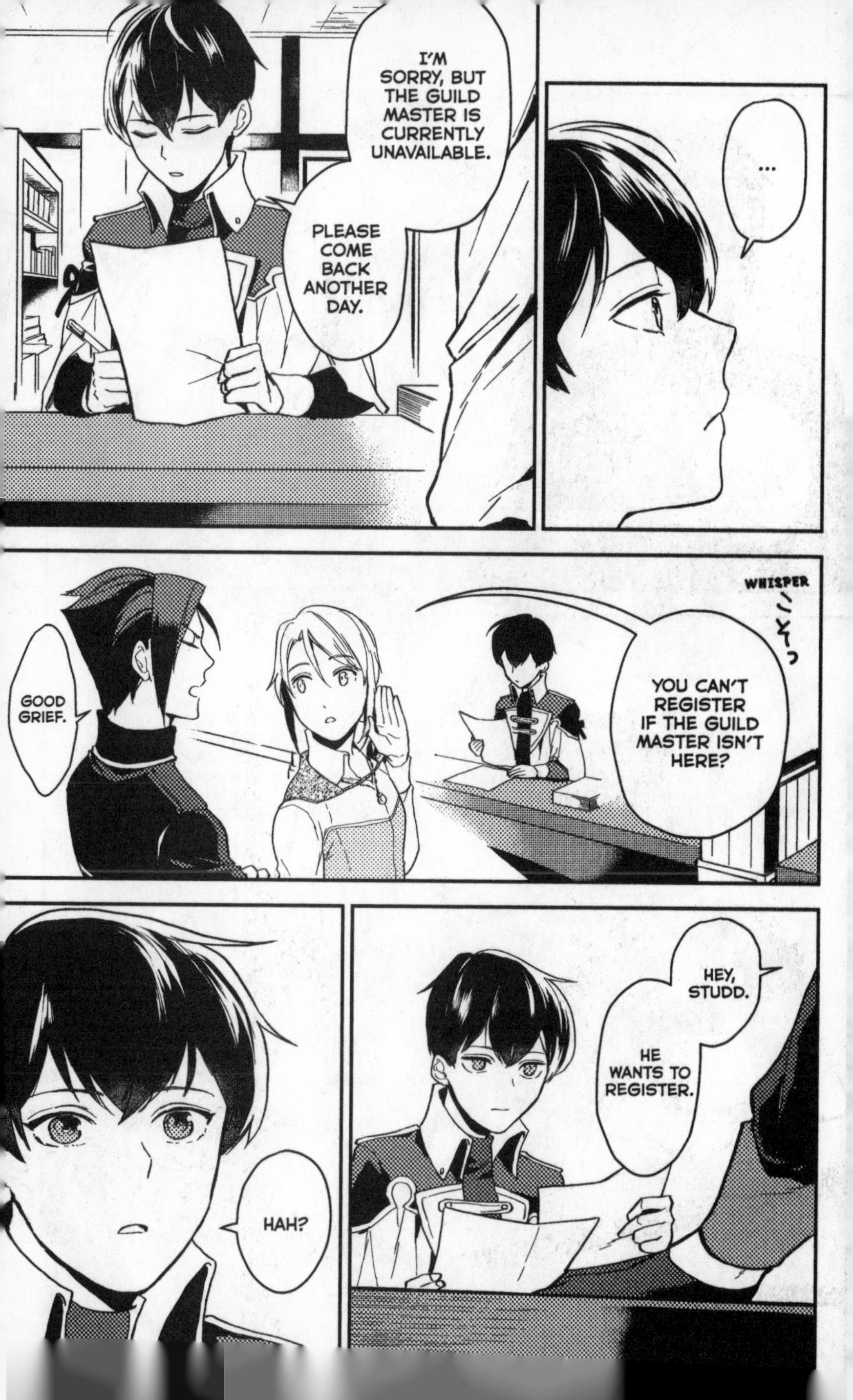
...
I'M SORRY, BUT THE GUILD MASTER IS CURRENTLY UNAVAILABLE.
PLEASE COME BACK ANOTHER DAY.
WHISPER
こそっ
YOU CAN'T REGISTER IF THE GUILD MASTER ISN'T HERE?
GOOD GRIEF.
HEY, STUDD.
HE WANTS TO REGISTER.
HAH?

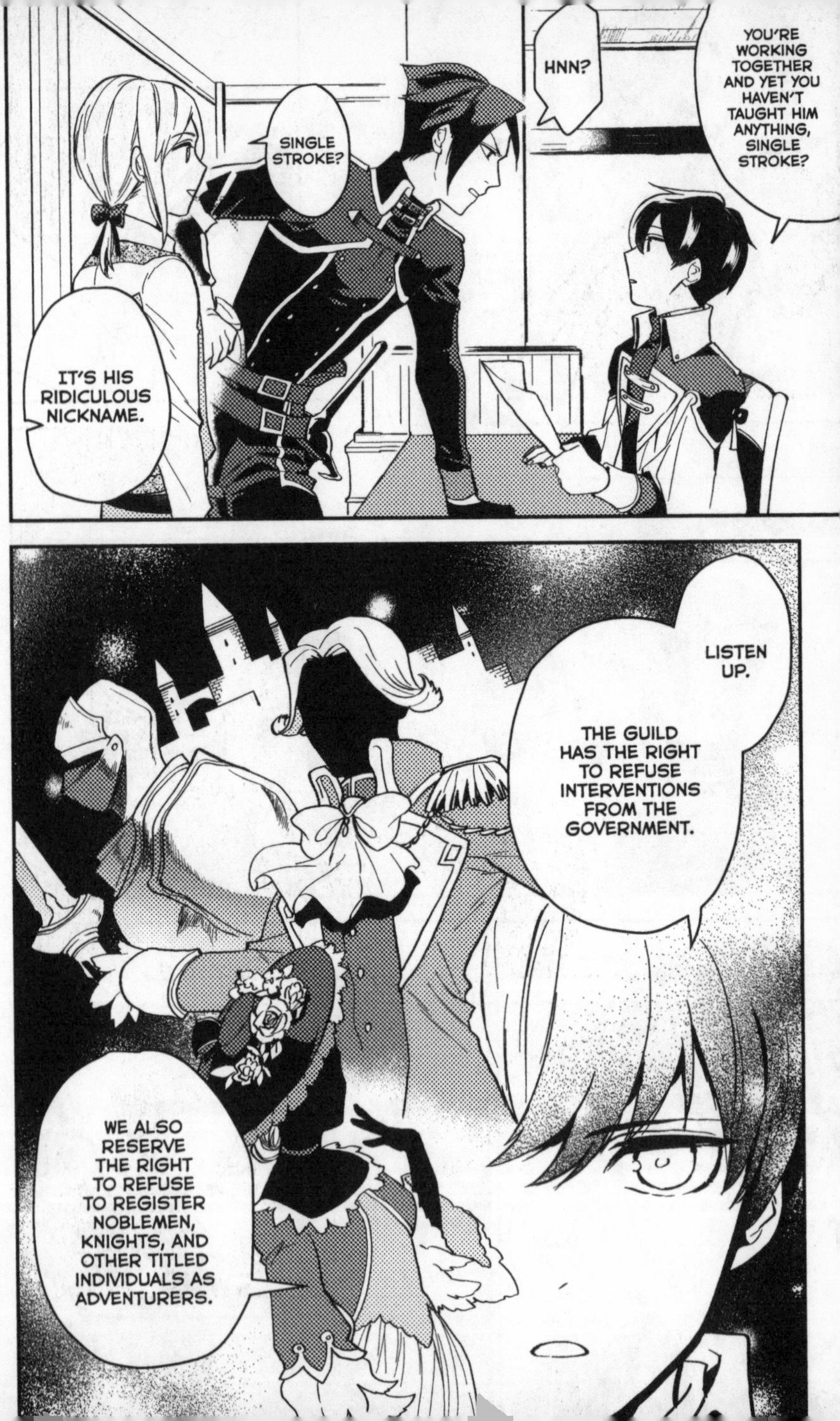
YOU'RE WORKING TOGETHER AND YET YOU HAVEN'T TAUGHT HIM ANYTHING, SINGLE STROKE?
HNN?
SINGLE STROKE?
IT'S HIS RIDICULOUS NICKNAME.
LISTEN UP.
THE GUILD HAS THE RIGHT TO REFUSE INTERVENTIONS FROM THE GOVERNMENT.
WE ALSO RESERVE THE RIGHT TO REFUSE TO REGISTER NOBLEMEN, KNIGHTS, AND OTHER TITLED INDIVIDUALS AS ADVENTURERS.

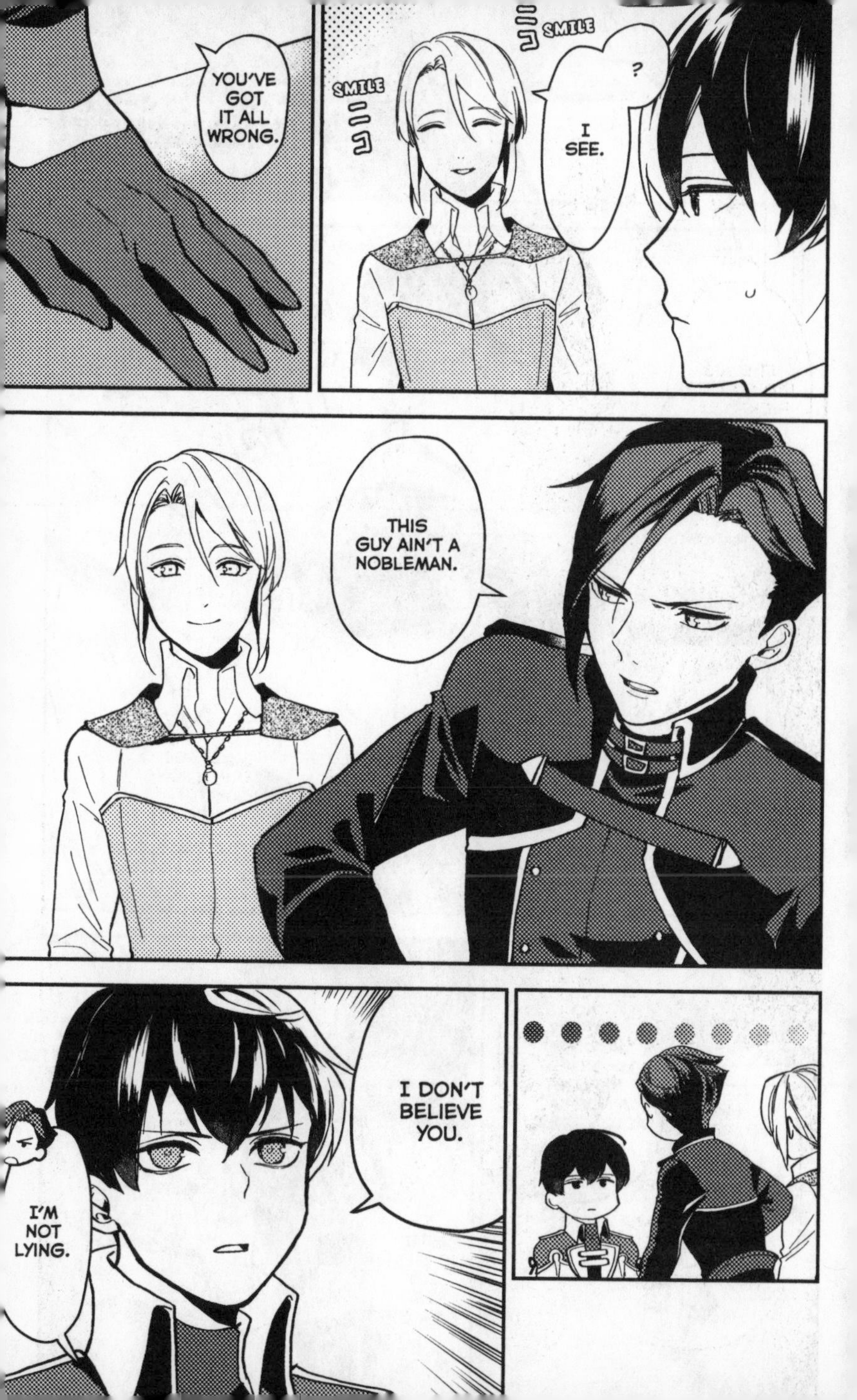
ニコ
SMILE
?
I SEE.
ニコ
SMILE
YOU'VE GOT IT ALL WRONG.
THIS GUY AIN'T A NOBLEMAN.
I DON'T BELIEVE YOU.
I'M NOT LYING.

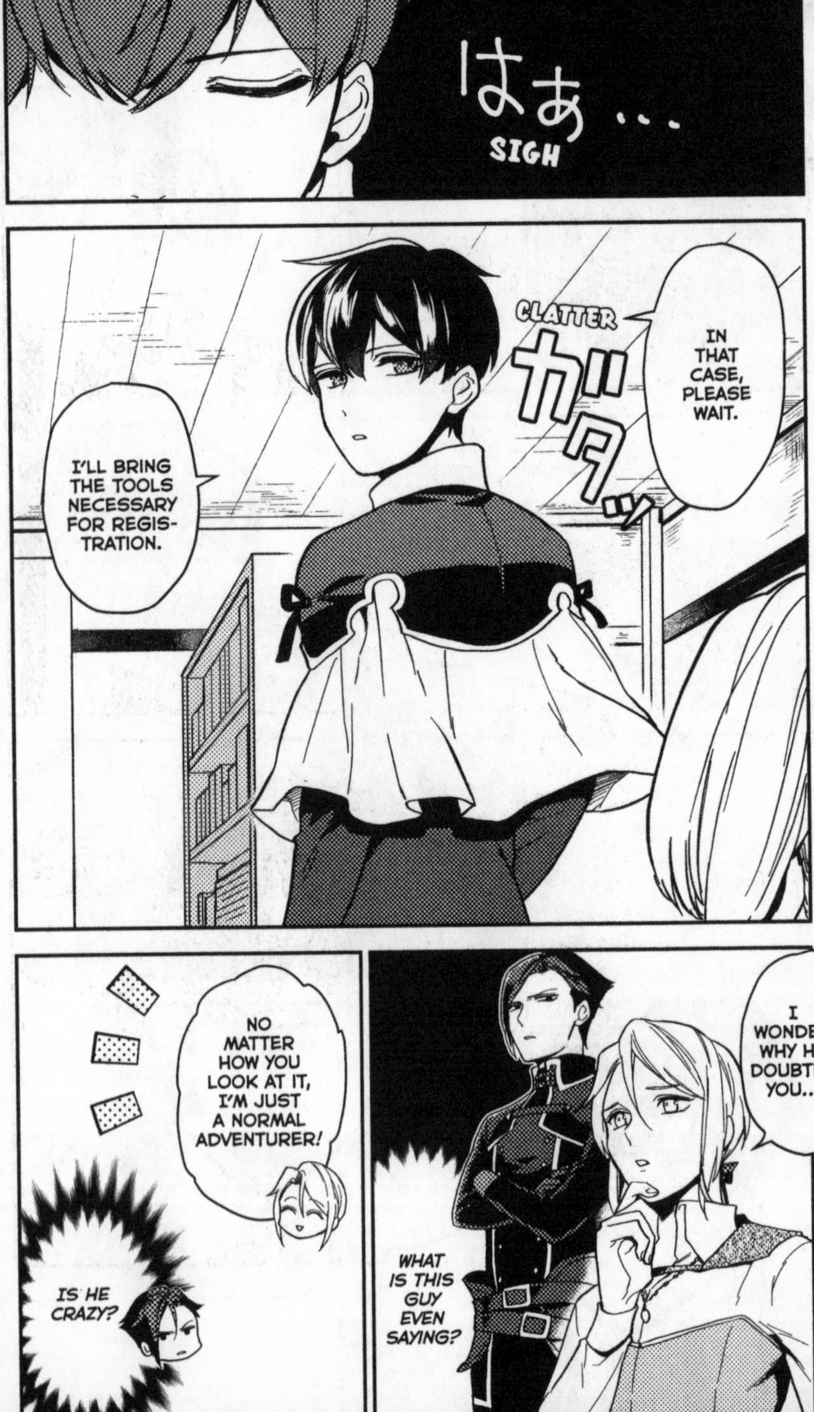
はぁ…
SIGH
IN THAT CASE, PLEASE WAIT.
CLATTER
ガタッ
I'LL BRING THE TOOLS NECESSARY FOR REGIS-TRATION.
I WONDER WHY HE DOUBTED YOU...
WHAT IS THIS GUY EVEN SAYING?
NO MATTER HOW YOU LOOK AT IT, I'M JUST A NORMAL ADVENTURER!
IS HE CRAZY?

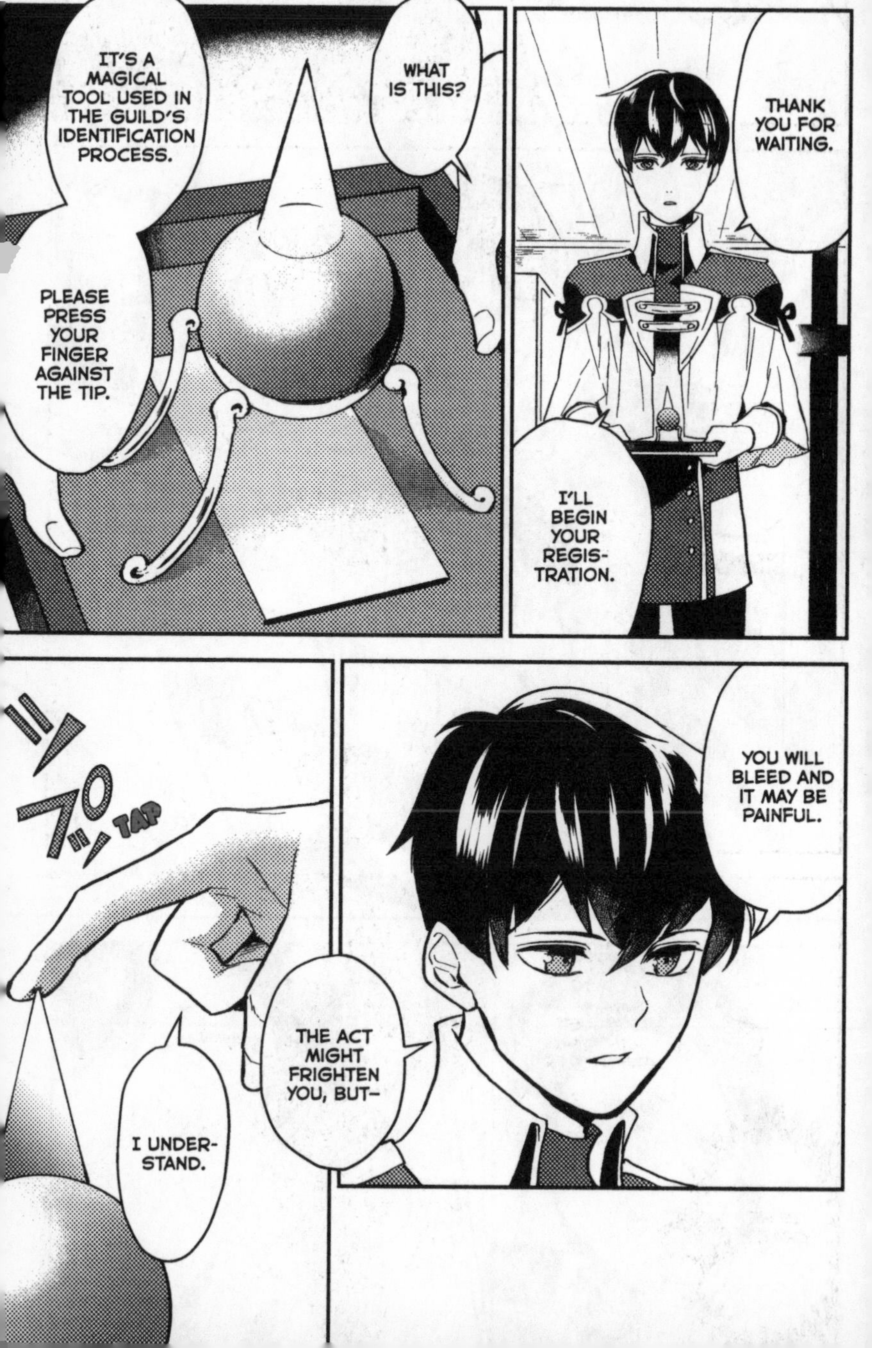
THANK YOU FOR WAITING.
I'LL BEGIN YOUR REGISTRATION.
WHAT IS THIS?
IT'S A MAGICAL TOOL USED IN THE GUILD'S IDENTIFICATION PROCESS.
PLEASE PRESS YOUR FINGER AGAINST THE TIP.
YOU WILL BLEED AND IT MAY BE PAINFUL.
THE ACT MIGHT FRIGHTEN YOU, BUT–
TAP
I UNDERSTAND.

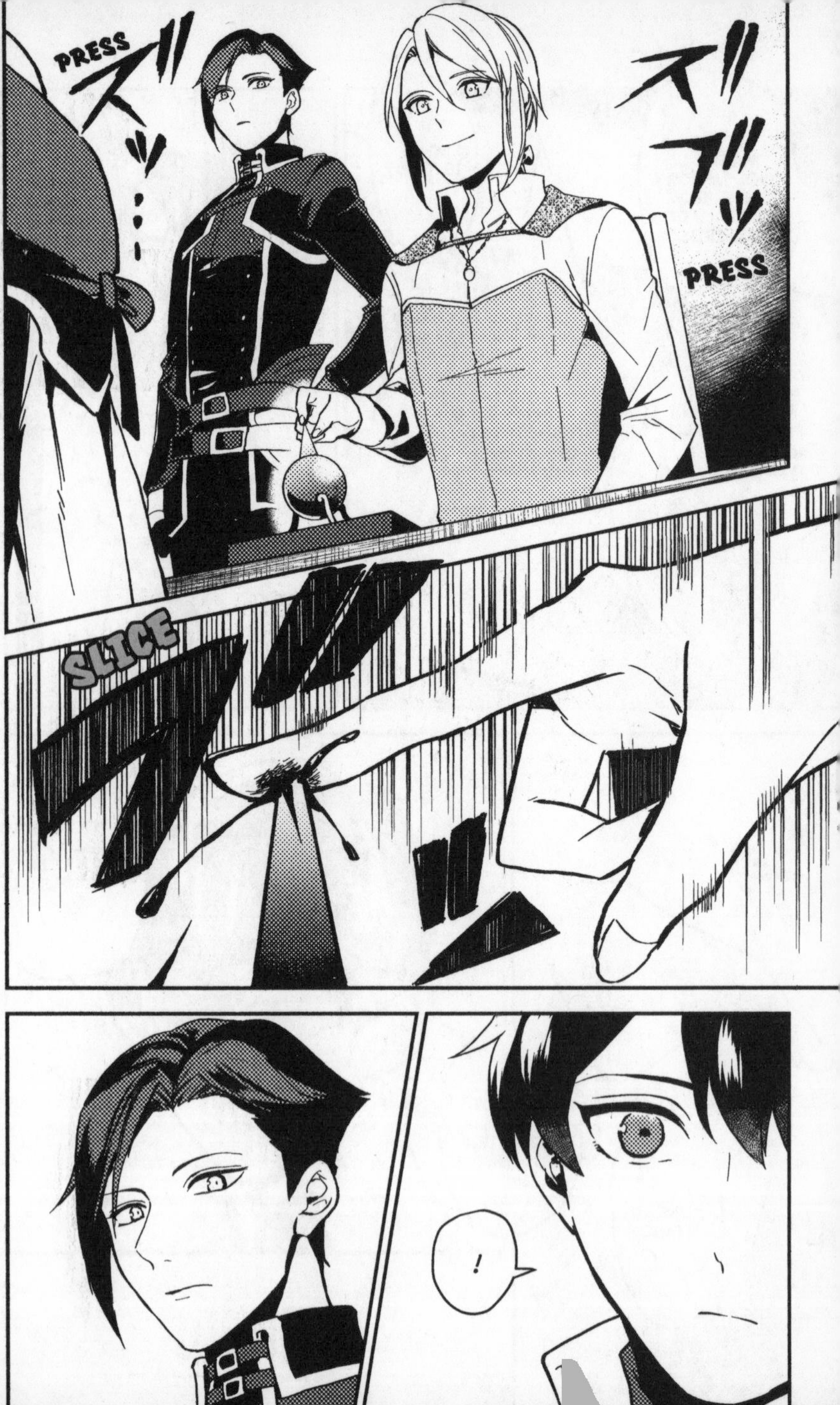
ズブッ
PRESS
ズッ…
PRESS
SLICE
!

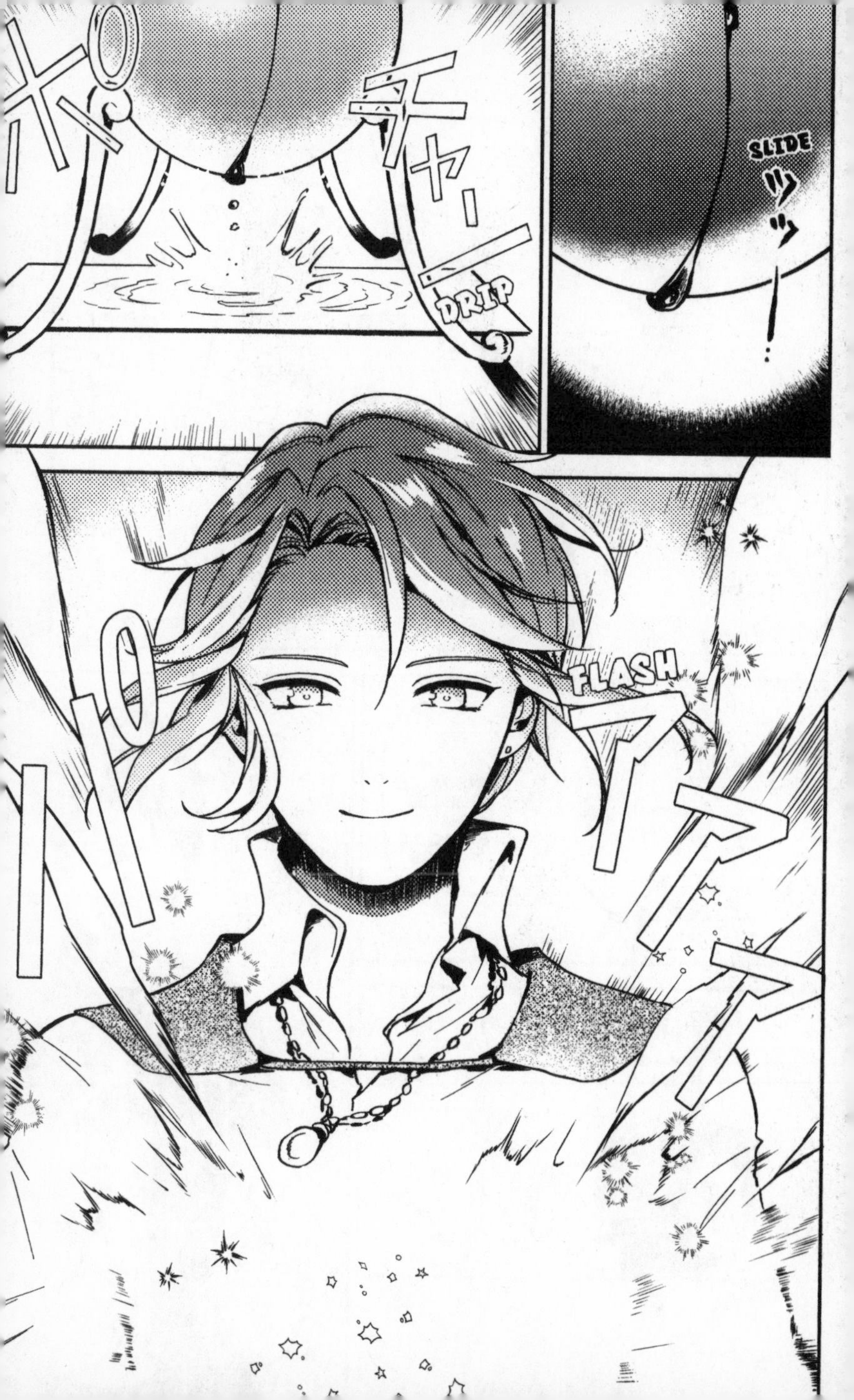
SLIDE
ツッ
ポチャー
DRIP
パアアア
FLASH

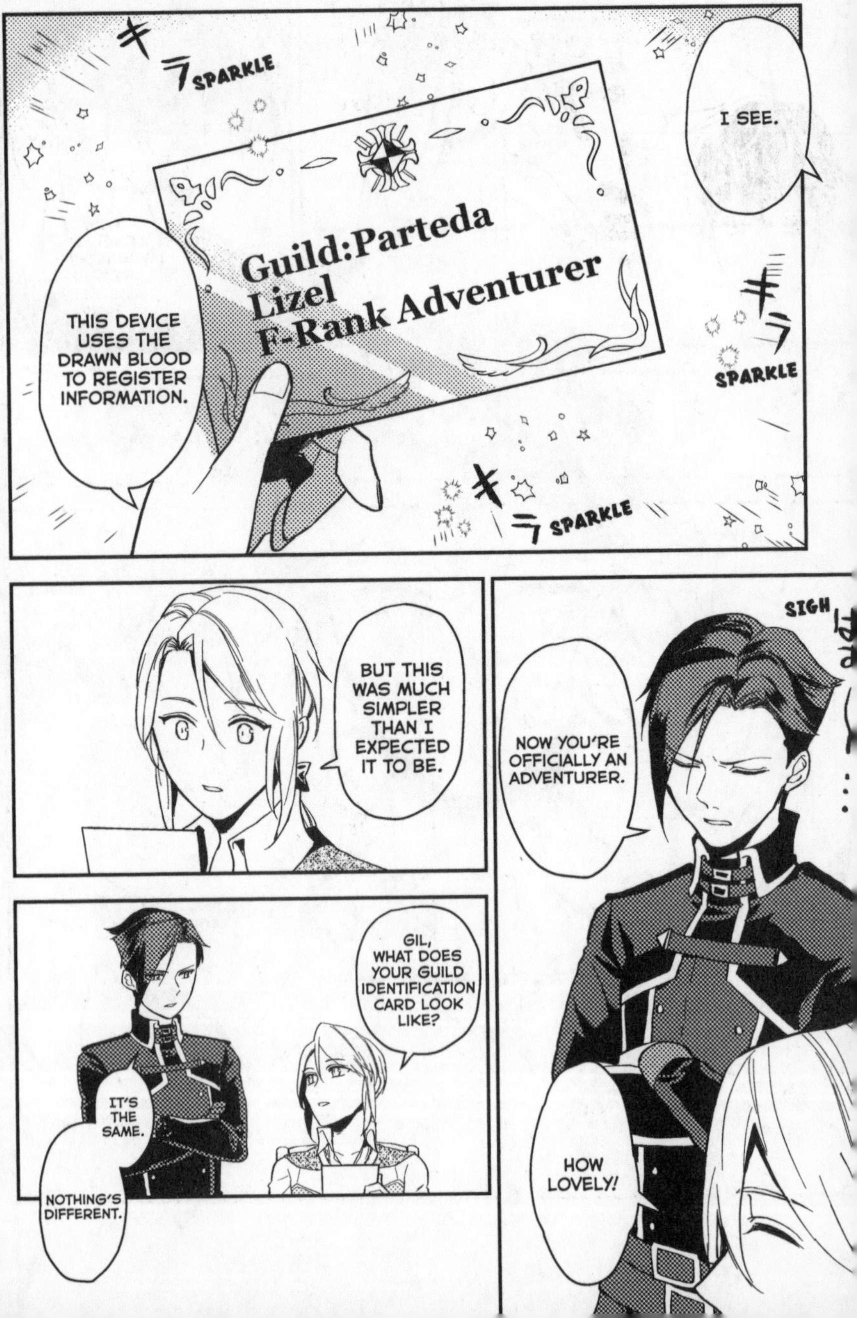
I SEE.
キラ SPARKLE
Guild:Parteda
Lizel
F-Rank Adventurer
キラ SPARKLE
THIS DEVICE USES THE DRAWN BLOOD TO REGISTER INFORMATION.
キラ SPARKLE
SIGH
...
NOW YOU'RE OFFICIALLY AN ADVENTURER.
HOW LOVELY!
BUT THIS WAS MUCH SIMPLER THAN I EXPECTED IT TO BE.
GIL, WHAT DOES YOUR GUILD IDENTIFICATION CARD LOOK LIKE?
IT'S THE SAME.
NOTHING'S DIFFERENT.

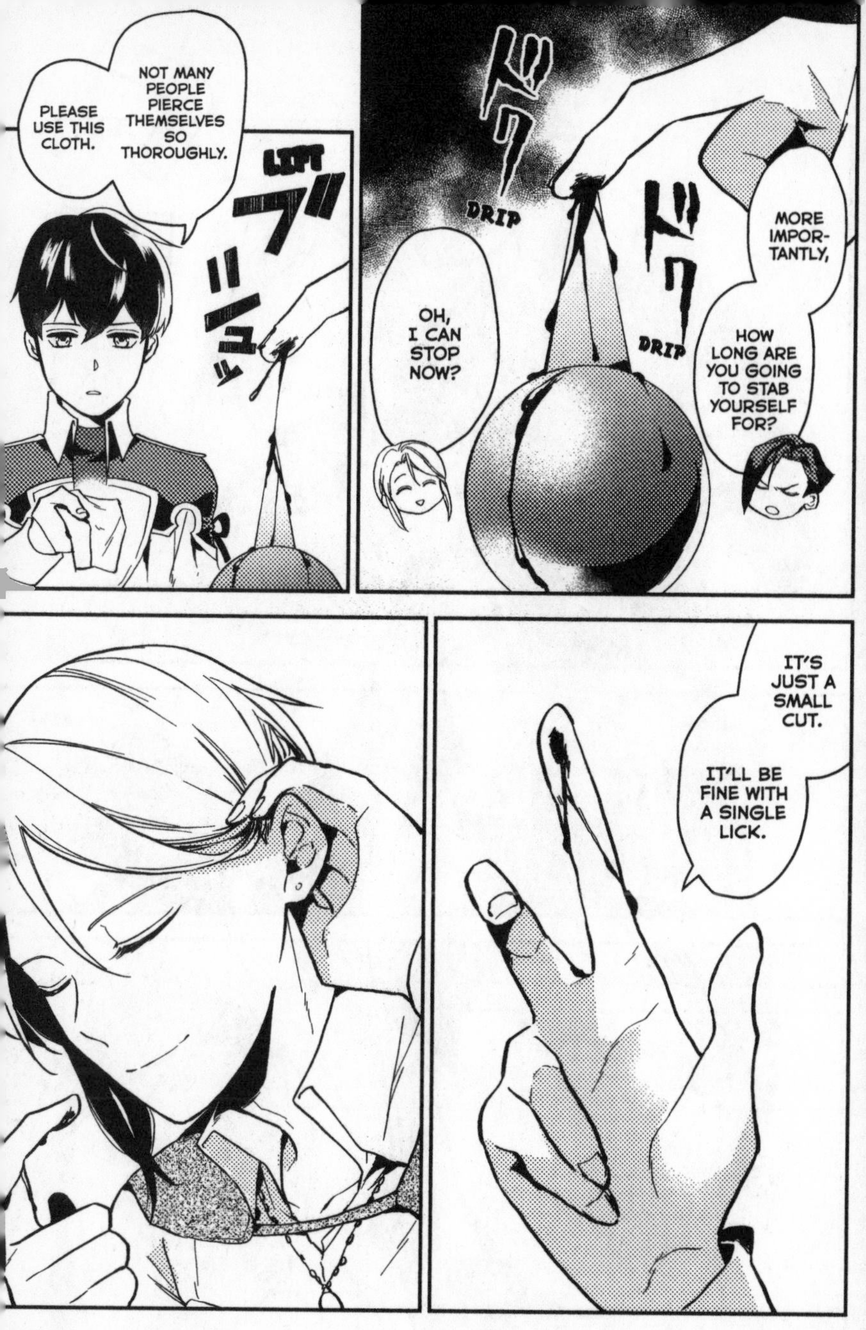
ドク
DRIP
MORE IMPORTANTLY,
HOW LONG ARE YOU GOING TO STAB YOURSELF FOR?
ドク
DRIP
OH, I CAN STOP NOW?
NOT MANY PEOPLE PIERCE THEMSELVES SO THOROUGHLY.
PLEASE USE THIS CLOTH.
LIFT
IT'S JUST A SMALL CUT.
IT'LL BE FINE WITH A SINGLE LICK.

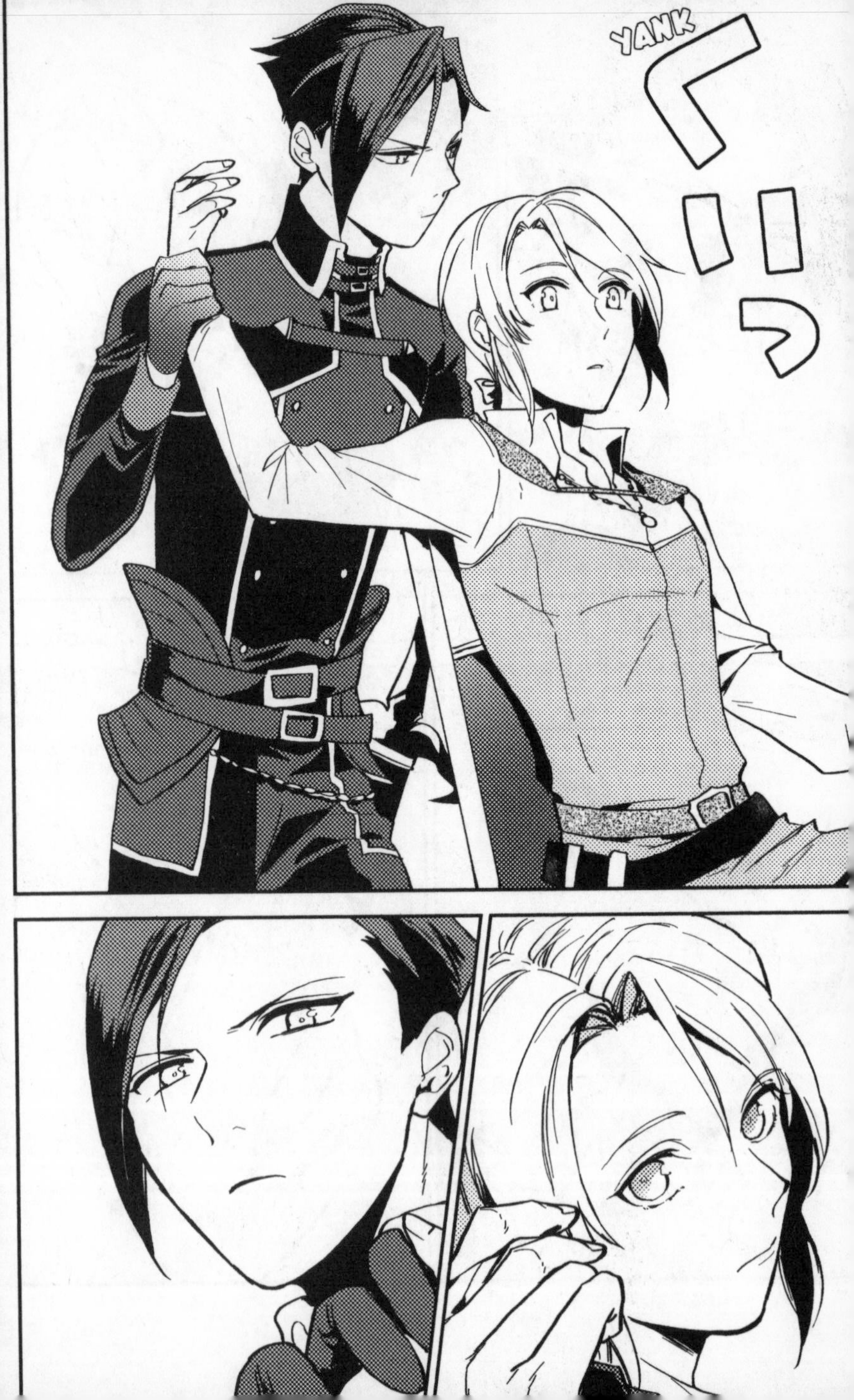
YANK

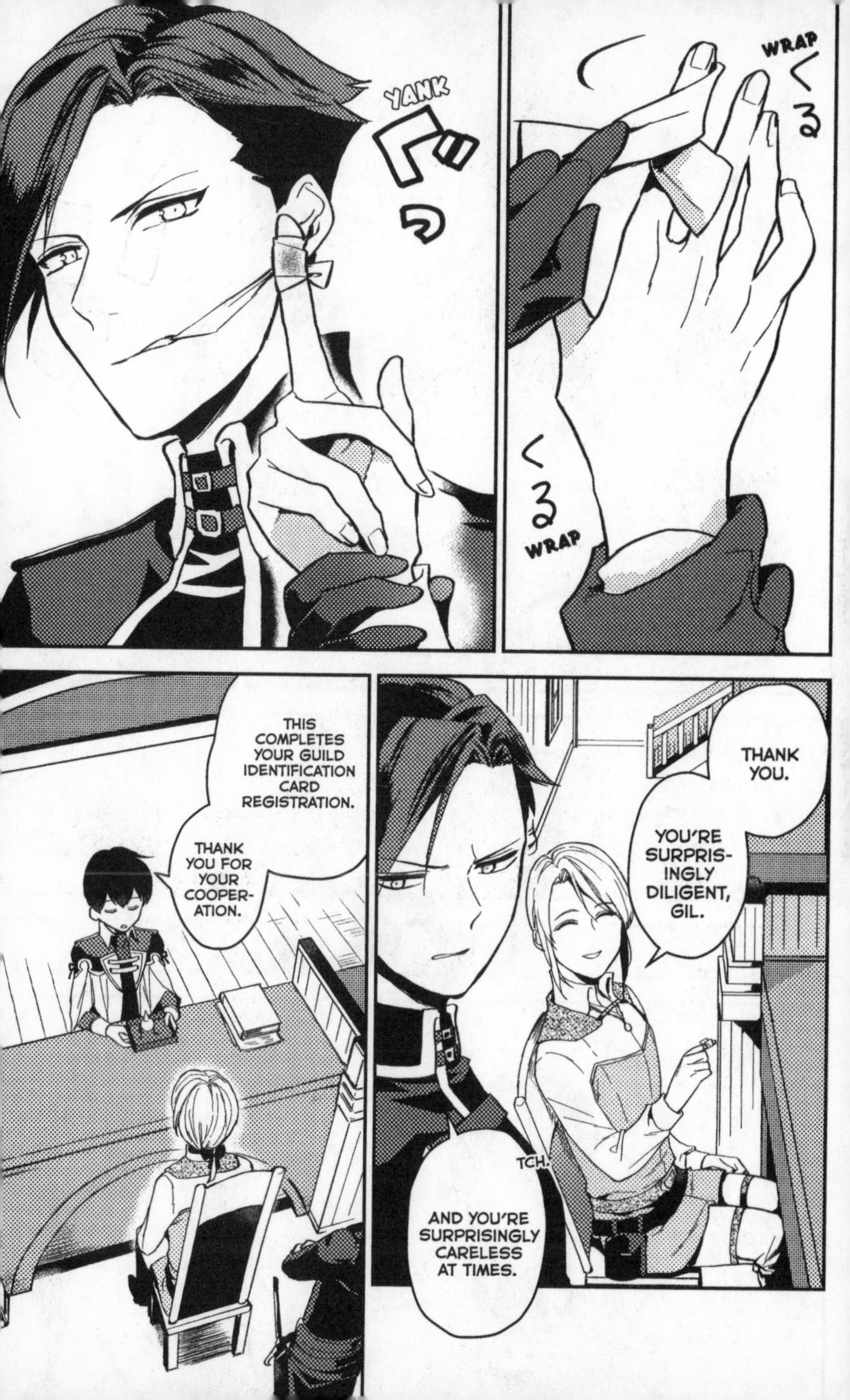
WRAP
くる
くる
WRAP
YANK
ぐっ
THANK YOU.
YOU'RE SURPRISINGLY DILIGENT, GIL.
TCH.
AND YOU'RE SURPRISINGLY CARELESS AT TIMES.
THIS COMPLETES YOUR GUILD IDENTIFICATION CARD REGISTRATION.
THANK YOU FOR YOUR COOPERATION.

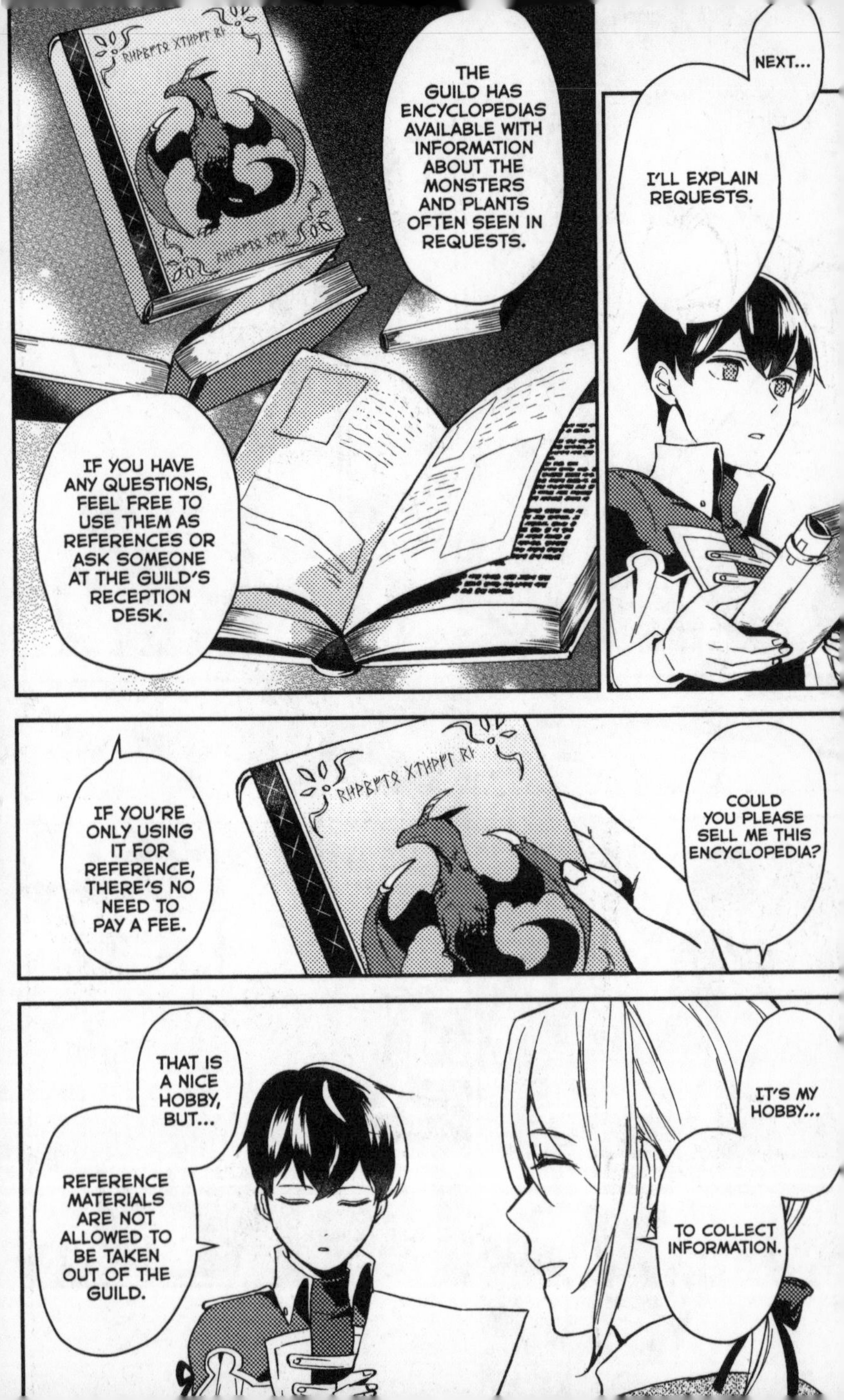
NEXT...
I'LL EXPLAIN REQUESTS.
THE GUILD HAS ENCYCLOPEDIAS AVAILABLE WITH INFORMATION ABOUT THE MONSTERS AND PLANTS OFTEN SEEN IN REQUESTS.
IF YOU HAVE ANY QUESTIONS, FEEL FREE TO USE THEM AS REFERENCES OR ASK SOMEONE AT THE GUILD'S RECEPTION DESK.
COULD YOU PLEASE SELL ME THIS ENCYCLOPEDIA?
IF YOU'RE ONLY USING IT FOR REFERENCE, THERE'S NO NEED TO PAY A FEE.
IT'S MY HOBBY...
TO COLLECT INFORMATION.
THAT IS A NICE HOBBY, BUT...
REFERENCE MATERIALS ARE NOT ALLOWED TO BE TAKEN OUT OF THE GUILD.

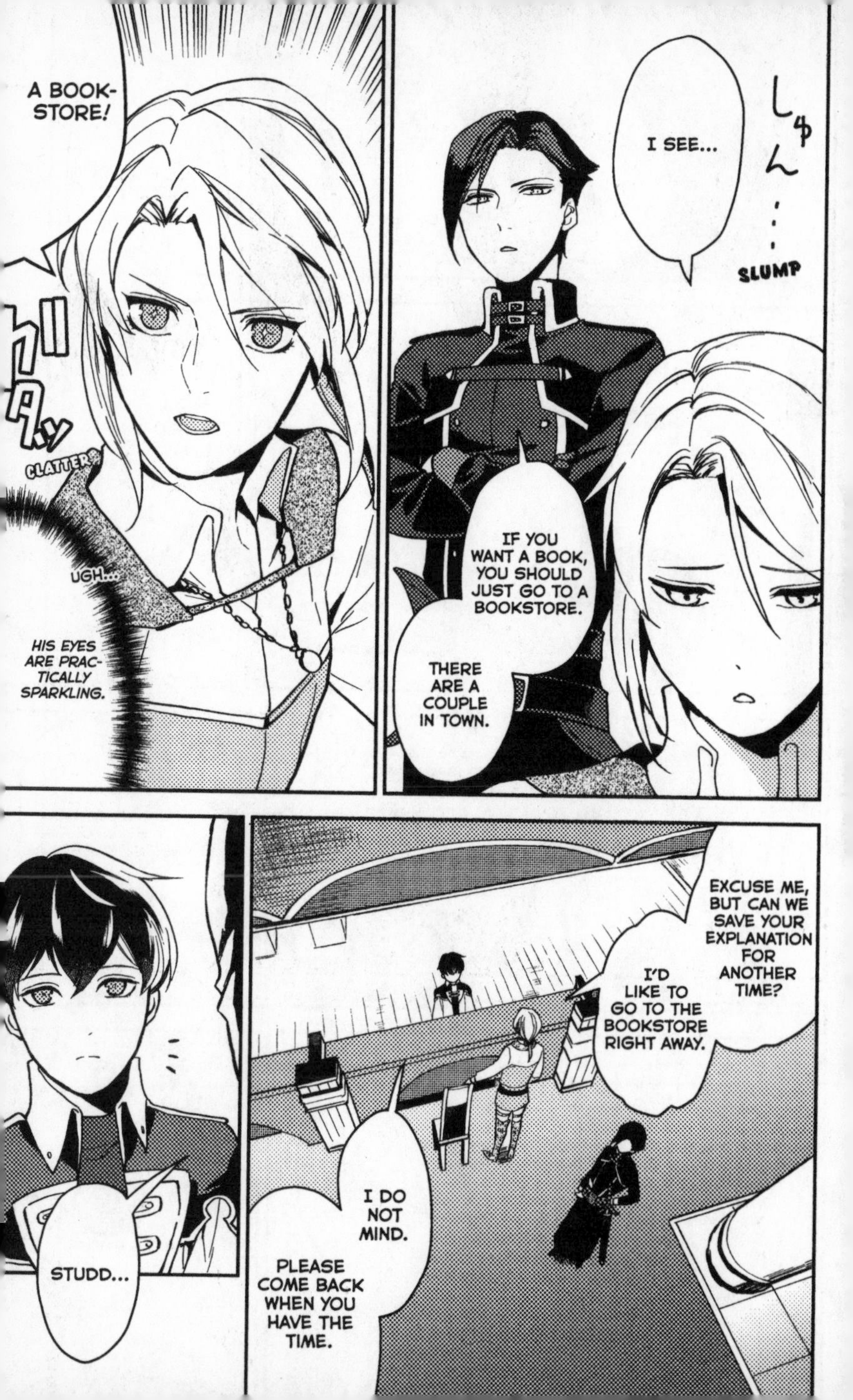

しゅん…
SLUMP
I SEE...
IF YOU WANT A BOOK, YOU SHOULD JUST GO TO A BOOKSTORE.
THERE ARE A COUPLE IN TOWN.
A BOOK-STORE!
ガタッ
CLATTER
UGH...
HIS EYES ARE PRACTICALLY SPARKLING.
EXCUSE ME, BUT CAN WE SAVE YOUR EXPLANATION FOR ANOTHER TIME?
I'D LIKE TO GO TO THE BOOKSTORE RIGHT AWAY.
I DO NOT MIND.
PLEASE COME BACK WHEN YOU HAVE THE TIME.
STUDD...

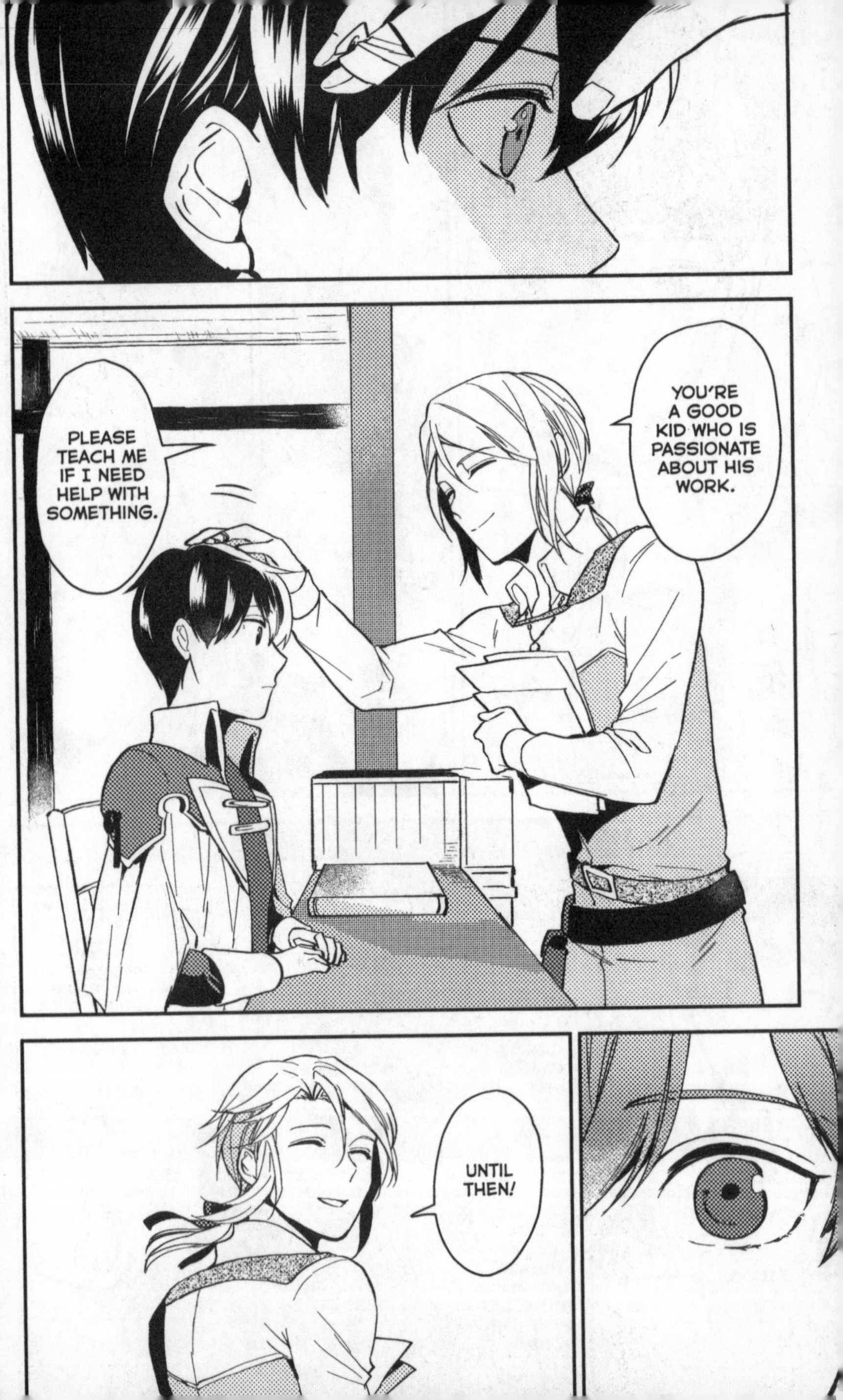
YOU'RE A GOOD KID WHO IS PASSIONATE ABOUT HIS WORK.
PLEASE TEACH ME IF I NEED HELP WITH SOMETHING.
UNTIL THEN!

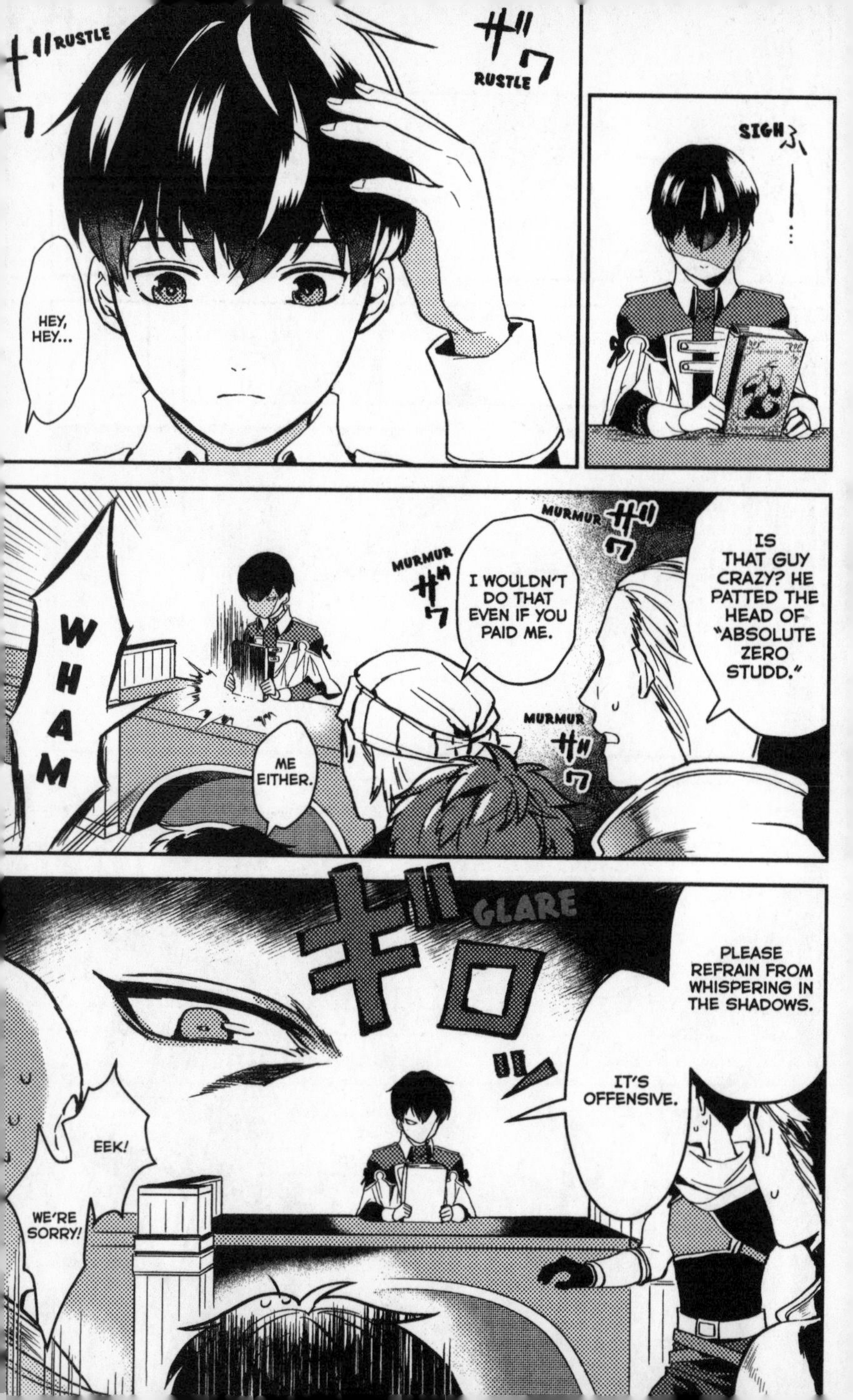
SIGH
—...
RUSTLE
RUSTLE
HEY, HEY...
MURMUR
IS THAT GUY CRAZY? HE PATTED THE HEAD OF "ABSOLUTE ZERO STUDD."
MURMUR
I WOULDN'T DO THAT EVEN IF YOU PAID ME.
MURMUR
ME EITHER.
WHAM
PLEASE REFRAIN FROM WHISPERING IN THE SHADOWS.
IT'S OFFENSIVE.
GLARE
EEK!
WE'RE SORRY!

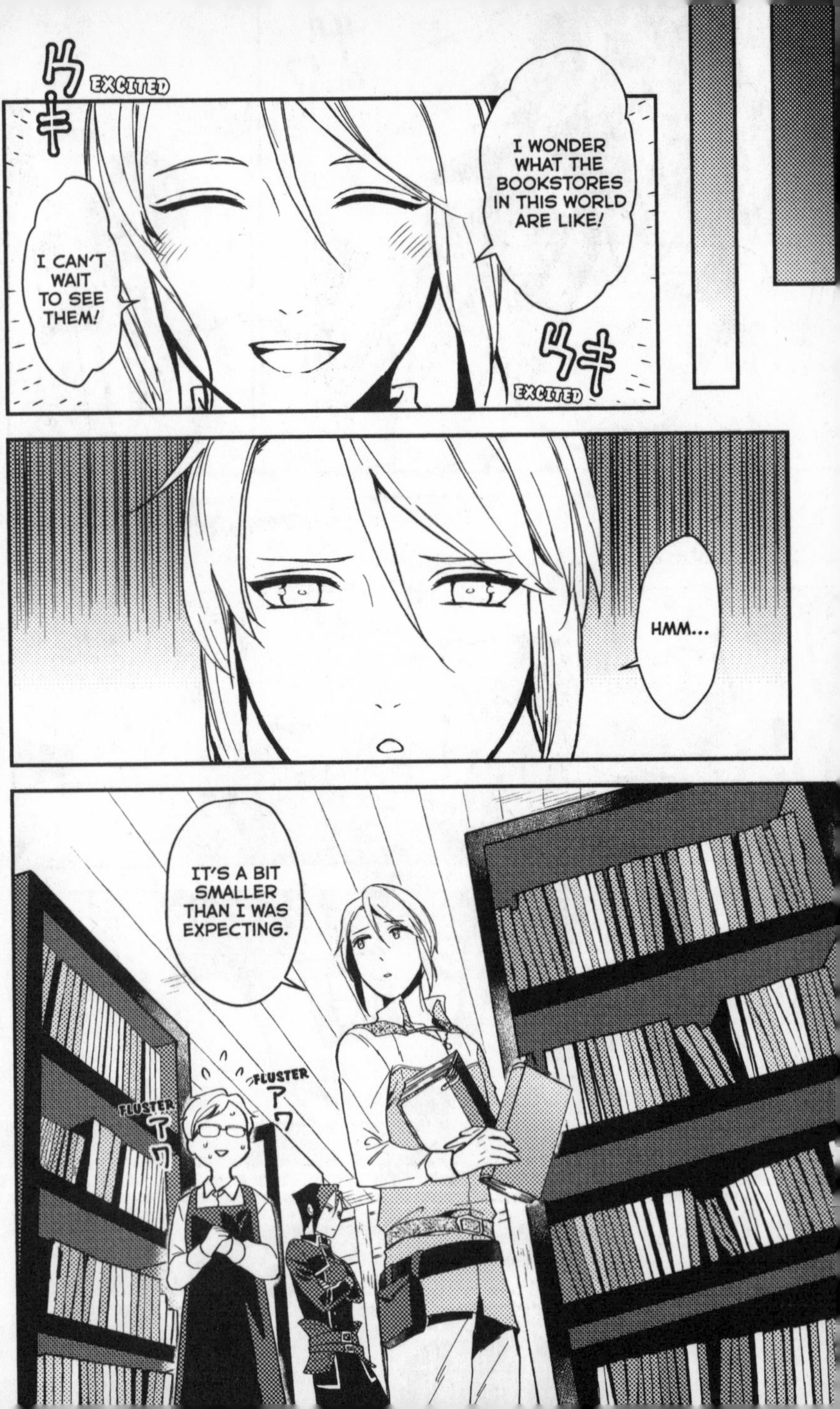
I WONDER WHAT THE BOOKSTORES IN THIS WORLD ARE LIKE!
ウキ
EXCITED
I CAN'T WAIT TO SEE THEM!
ウキ
EXCITED
HMM...
IT'S A BIT SMALLER THAN I WAS EXPECTING.
FLUSTER
アワ
FLUSTER
アワ

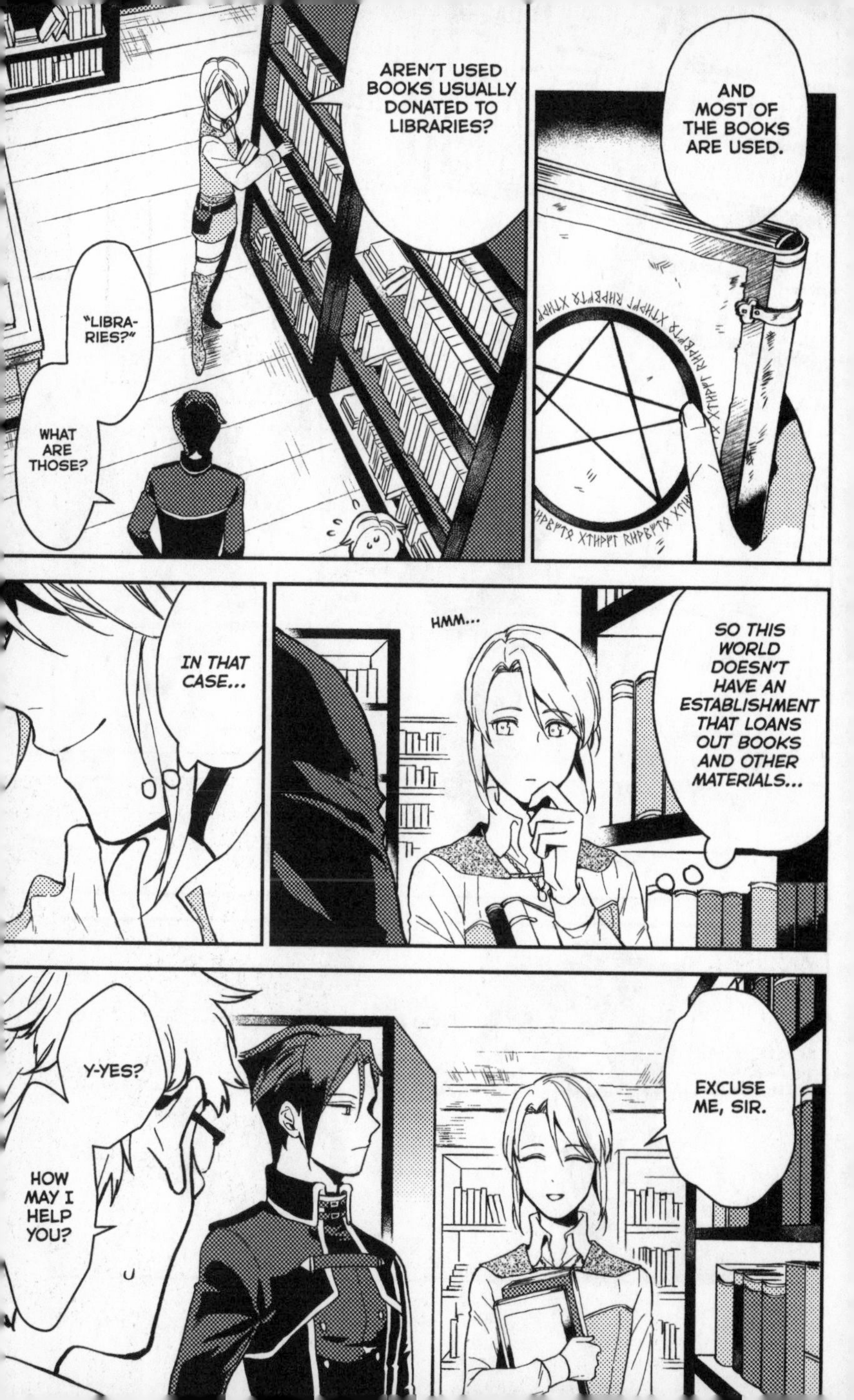
AND MOST OF THE BOOKS ARE USED.
AREN'T USED BOOKS USUALLY DONATED TO LIBRARIES?
"LIBRARIES?"
WHAT ARE THOSE?
SO THIS WORLD DOESN'T HAVE AN ESTABLISHMENT THAT LOANS OUT BOOKS AND OTHER MATERIALS...
HMM...
IN THAT CASE...
EXCUSE ME, SIR.
Y-YES?
HOW MAY I HELP YOU?

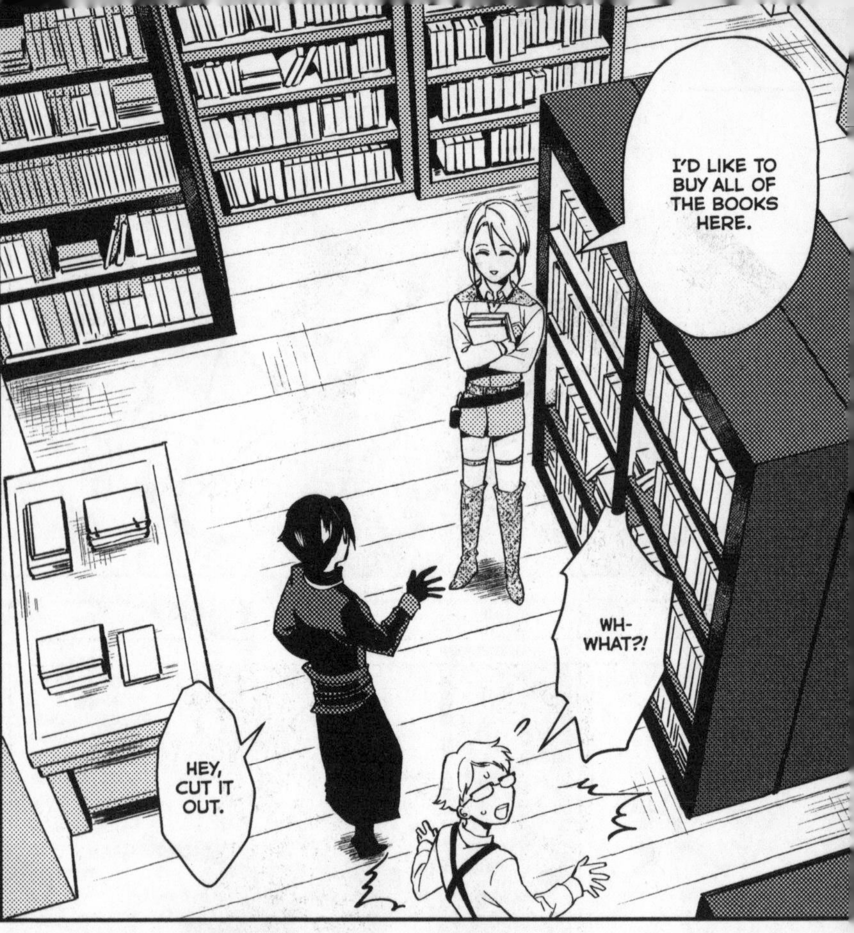
I'D LIKE TO BUY ALL OF THE BOOKS HERE.
WH- WHAT?!
HEY, CUT IT OUT.

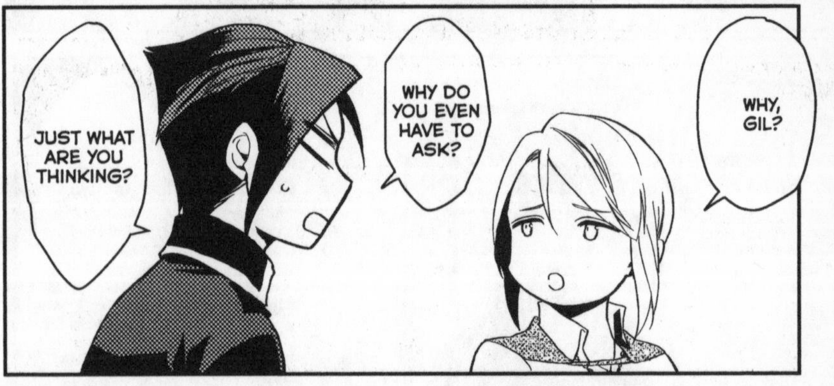
WHY, GIL?
WHY DO YOU EVEN HAVE TO ASK?
JUST WHAT ARE YOU THINKING?

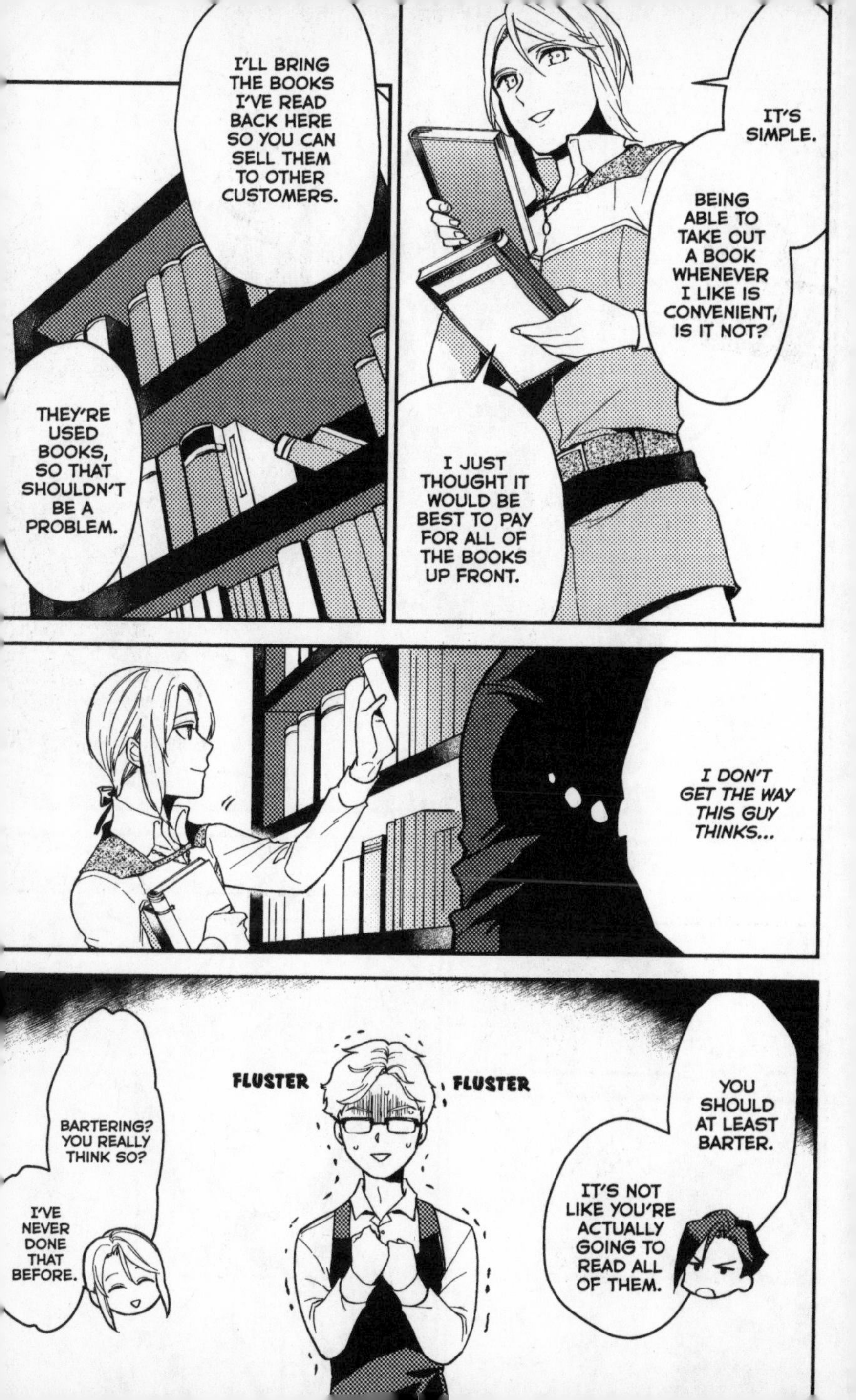
IT'S SIMPLE.
BEING ABLE TO TAKE OUT A BOOK WHENEVER I LIKE IS CONVENIENT, IS IT NOT?
I JUST THOUGHT IT WOULD BE BEST TO PAY FOR ALL OF THE BOOKS UP FRONT.
I'LL BRING THE BOOKS I'VE READ BACK HERE SO YOU CAN SELL THEM TO OTHER CUSTOMERS.
THEY'RE USED BOOKS, SO THAT SHOULDN'T BE A PROBLEM.
I DON'T GET THE WAY THIS GUY THINKS...
YOU SHOULD AT LEAST BARTER.
IT'S NOT LIKE YOU'RE ACTUALLY GOING TO READ ALL OF THEM.
FLUSTER FLUSTER
BARTERING? YOU REALLY THINK SO?
I'VE NEVER DONE THAT BEFORE.

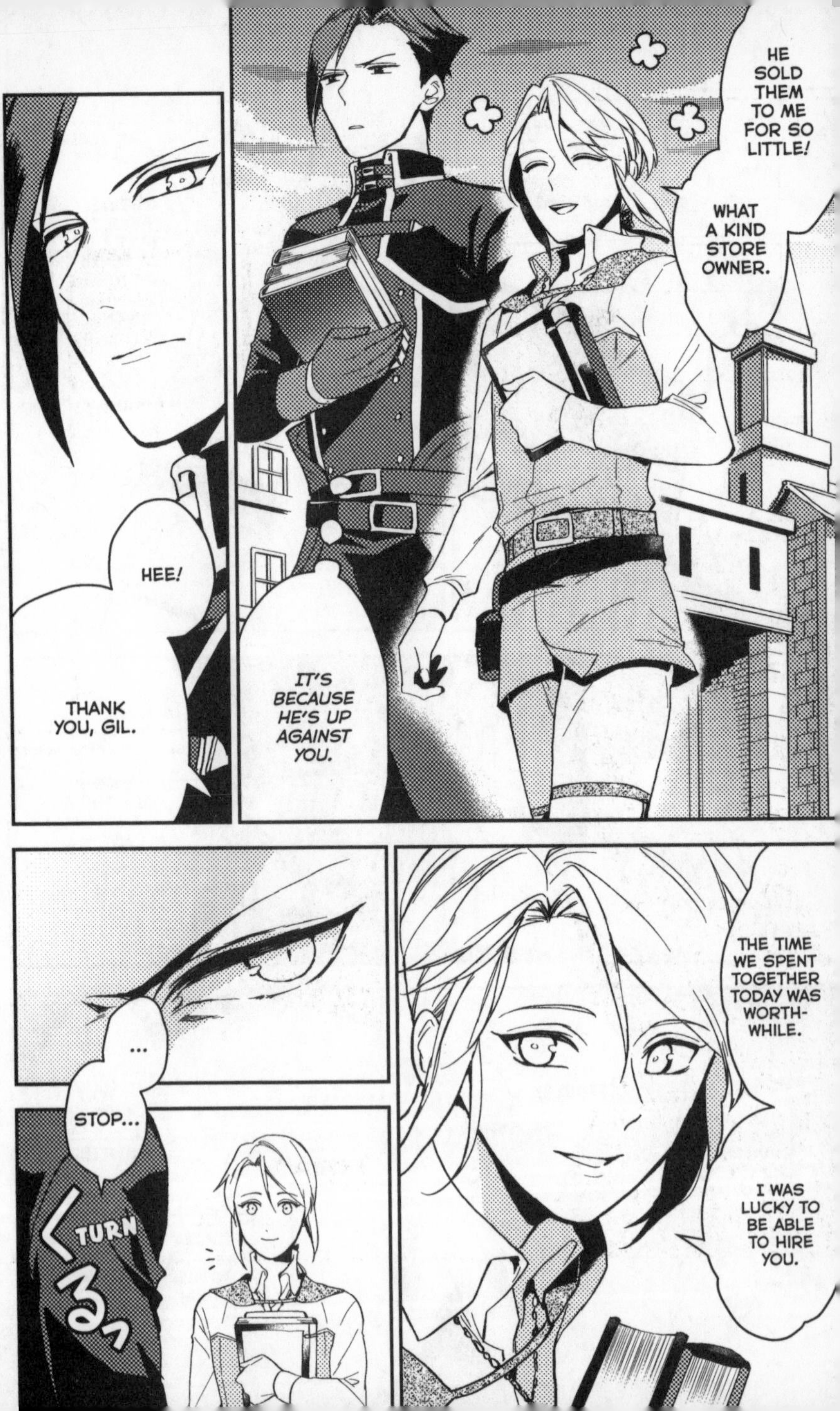
HE SOLD THEM TO ME FOR SO LITTLE!
WHAT A KIND STORE OWNER.
IT'S BECAUSE HE'S UP AGAINST YOU.
HEE!
THANK YOU, GIL.
THE TIME WE SPENT TOGETHER TODAY WAS WORTH-WHILE.
I WAS LUCKY TO BE ABLE TO HIRE YOU.
...
STOP...
TURN

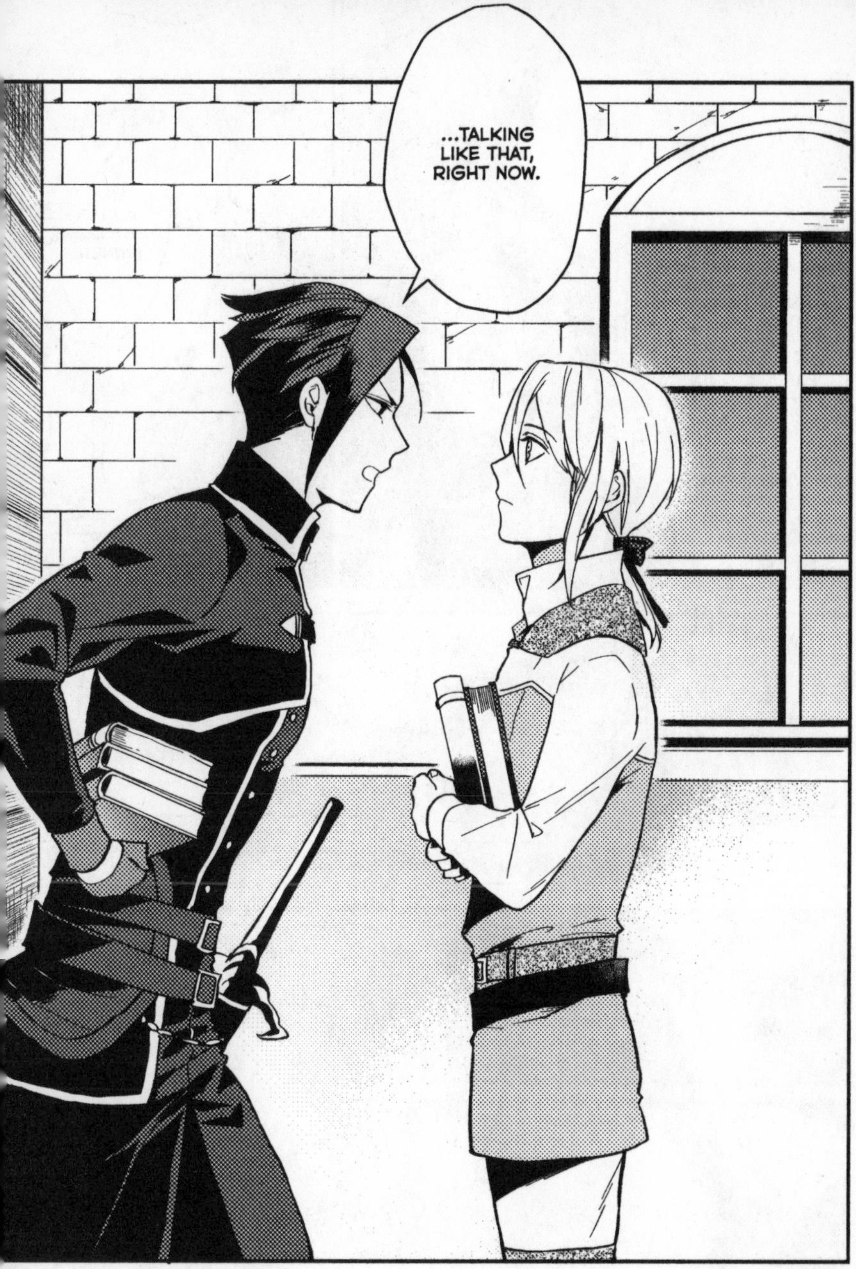
...TALKING LIKE THAT, RIGHT NOW.

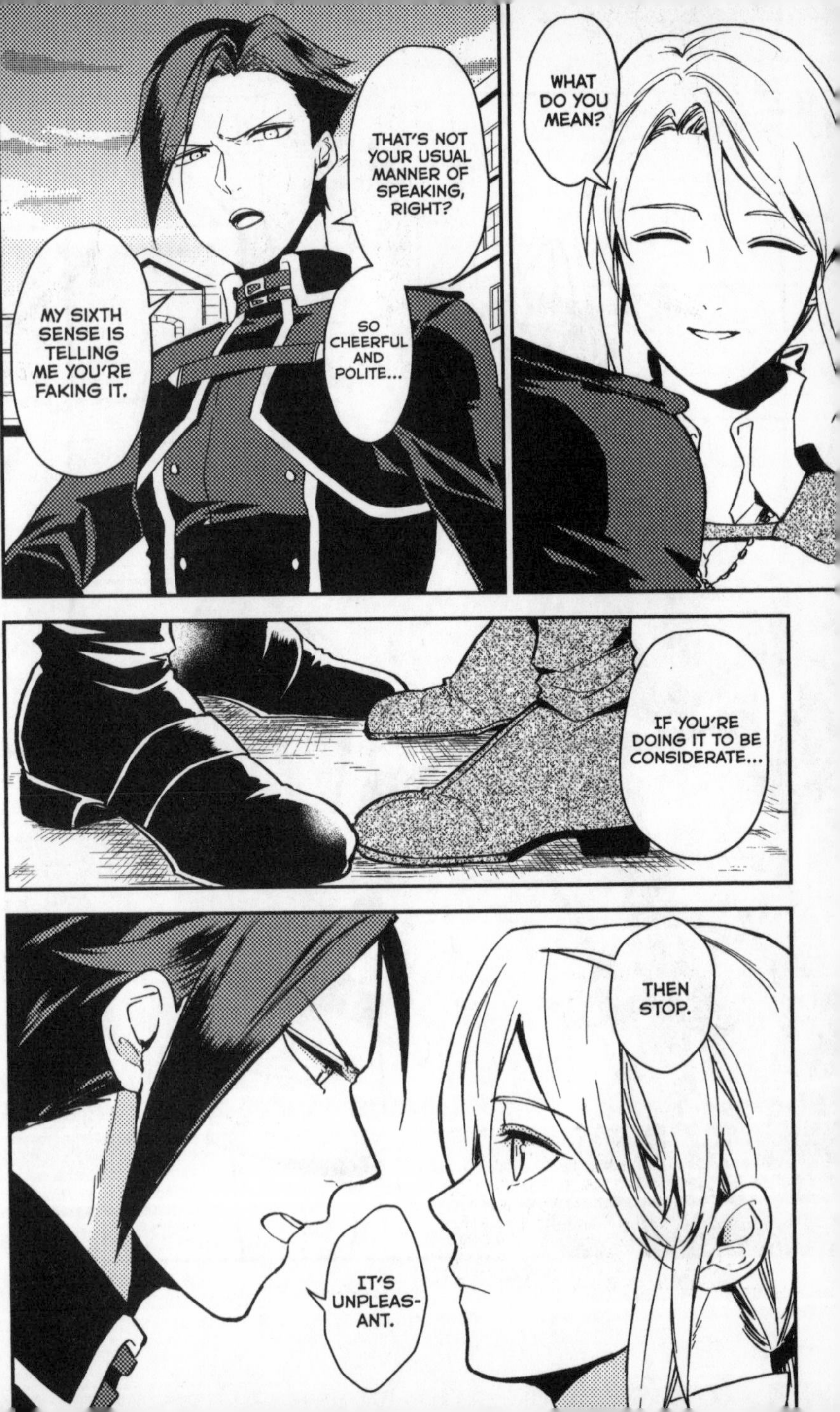
WHAT DO YOU MEAN?
THAT'S NOT YOUR USUAL MANNER OF SPEAKING, RIGHT?
SO CHEERFUL AND POLITE...
MY SIXTH SENSE IS TELLING ME YOU'RE FAKING IT.
IF YOU'RE DOING IT TO BE CONSIDERATE...
THEN STOP.
IT'S UNPLEASANT.

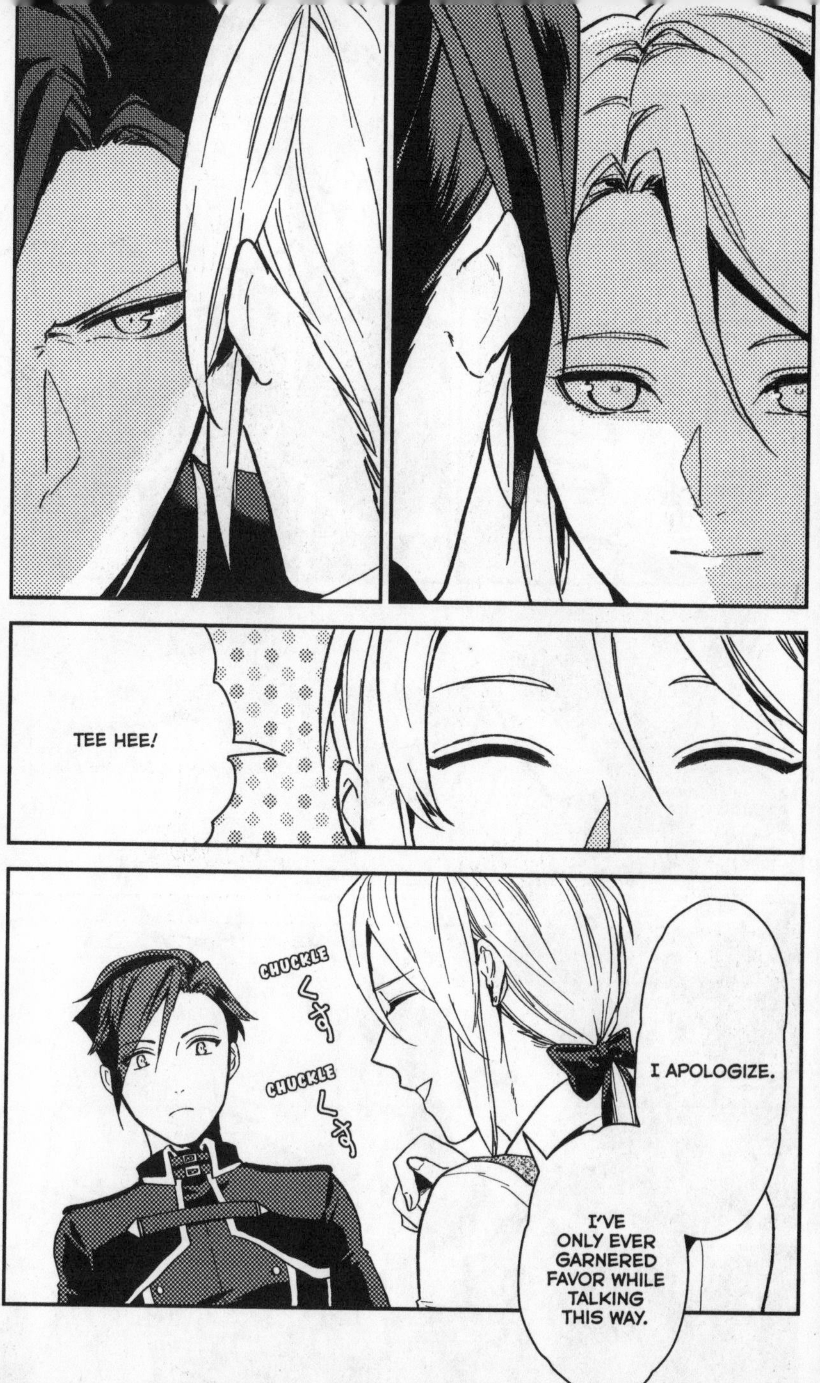
TEE HEE!
I APOLOGIZE.
I'VE ONLY EVER GARNERED FAVOR WHILE TALKING THIS WAY.
CHUCKLE くす
CHUCKLE くす

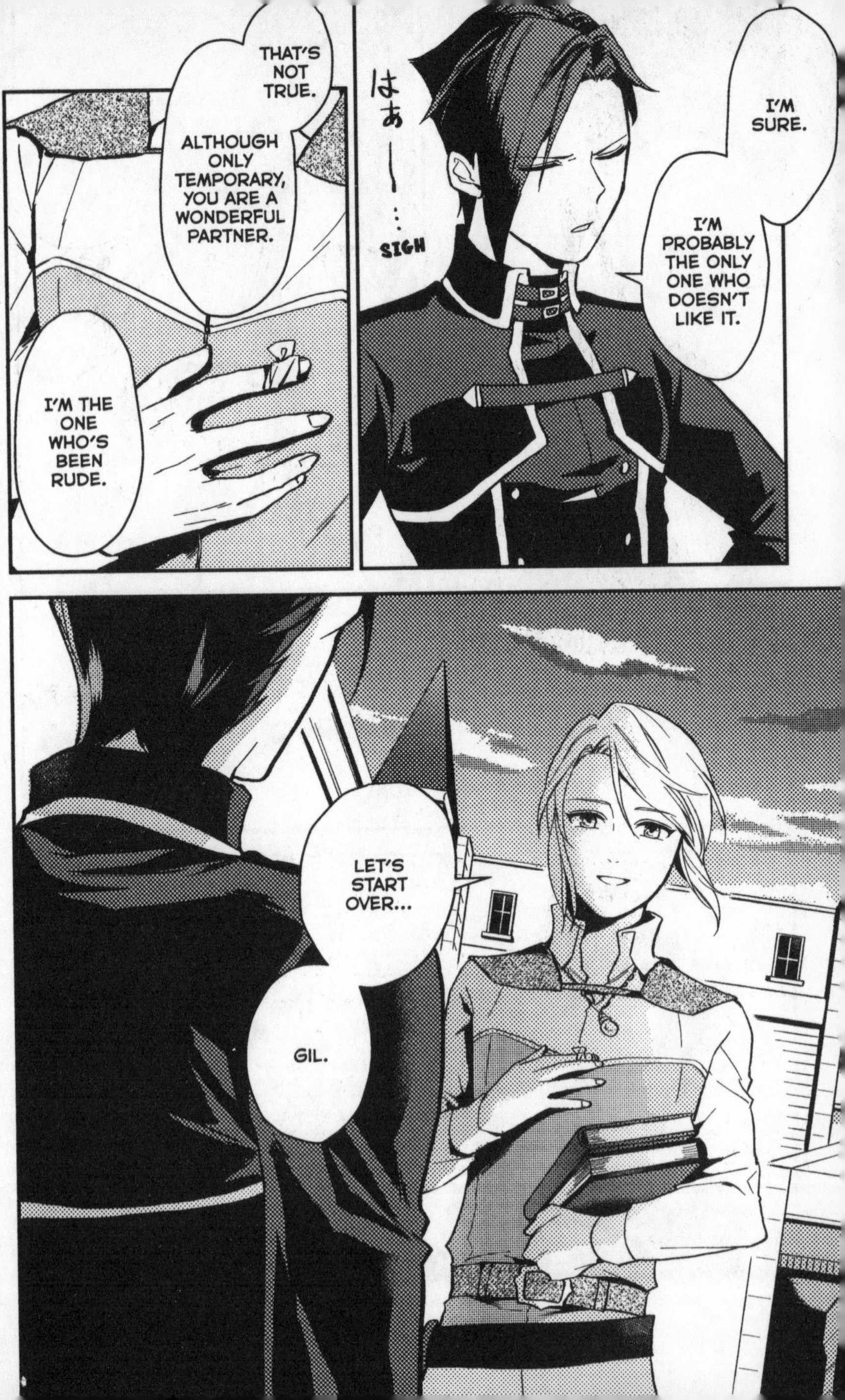
I'M SURE.
I'M PROBABLY THE ONLY ONE WHO DOESN'T LIKE IT.
はぁー…
SIGH
THAT'S NOT TRUE.
ALTHOUGH ONLY TEMPORARY, YOU ARE A WONDERFUL PARTNER.
I'M THE ONE WHO'S BEEN RUDE.
LET'S START OVER...
GIL.

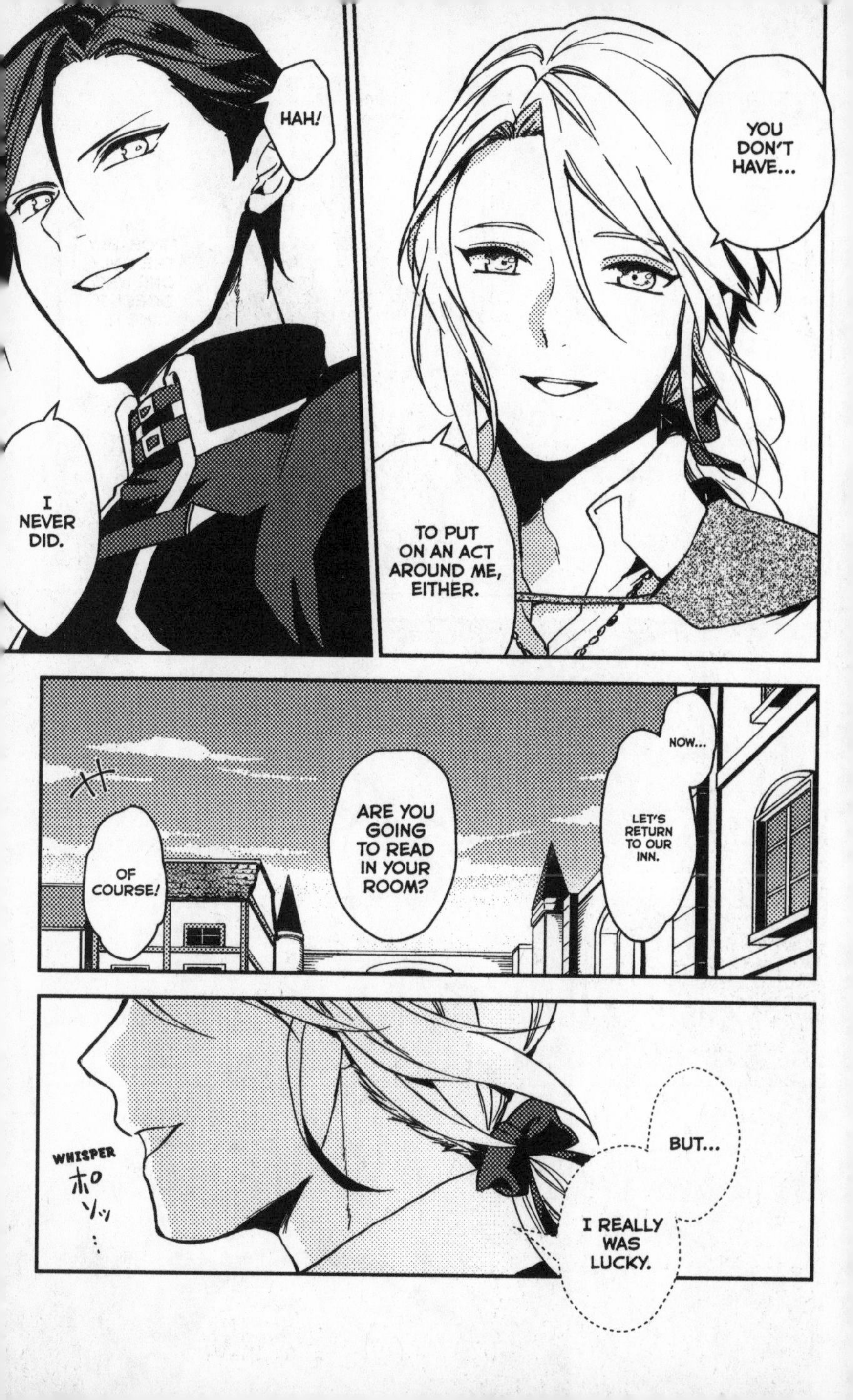
YOU DON'T HAVE...
TO PUT ON AN ACT AROUND ME, EITHER.
HAH!
I NEVER DID.
NOW...
LET'S RETURN TO OUR INN.
ARE YOU GOING TO READ IN YOUR ROOM?
OF COURSE!
BUT...
I REALLY WAS LUCKY.
WHISPER
ポソッ…

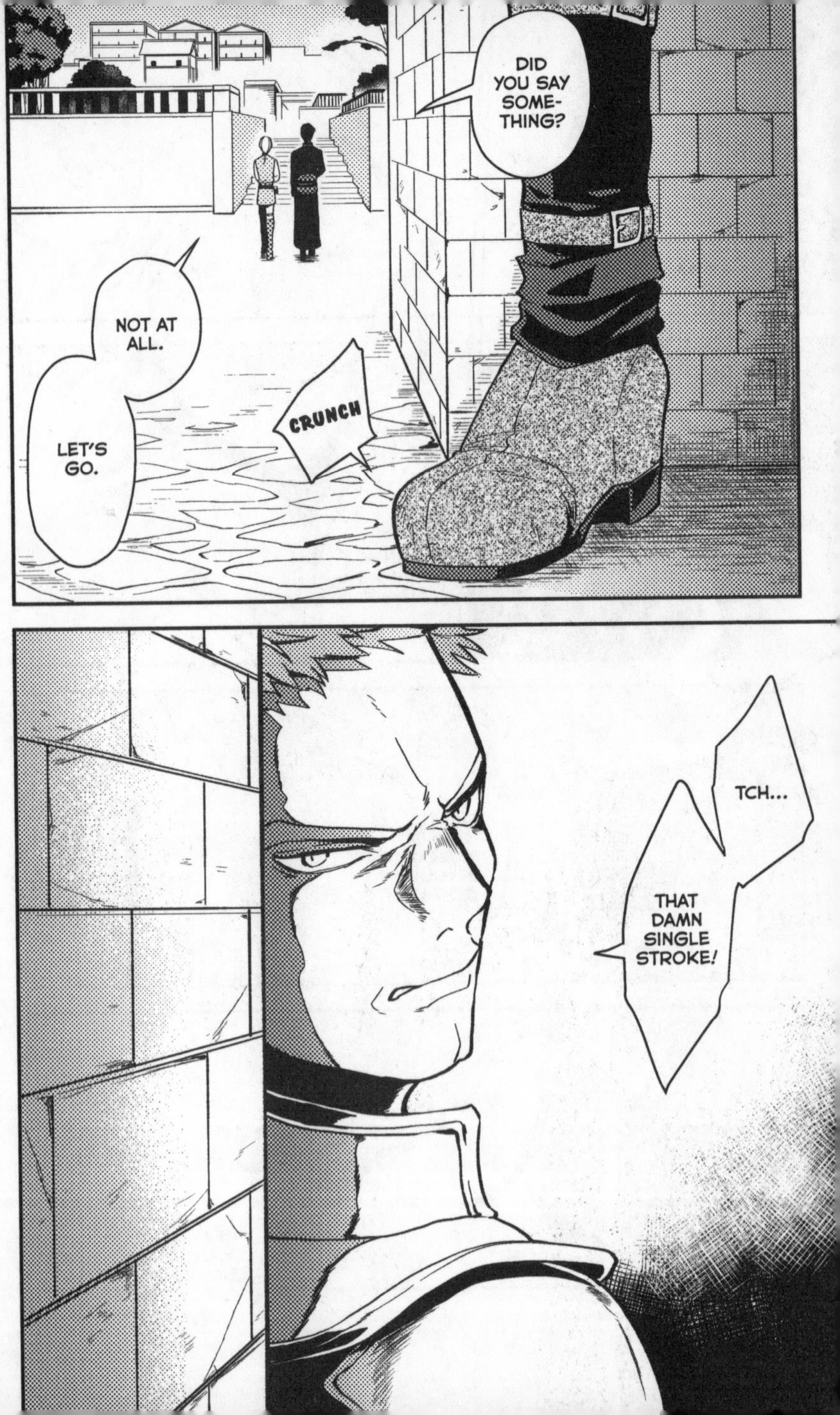
DID YOU SAY SOME-THING?
NOT AT ALL.
LET'S GO.
CRUNCH
TCH...
THAT DAMN SINGLE STROKE!

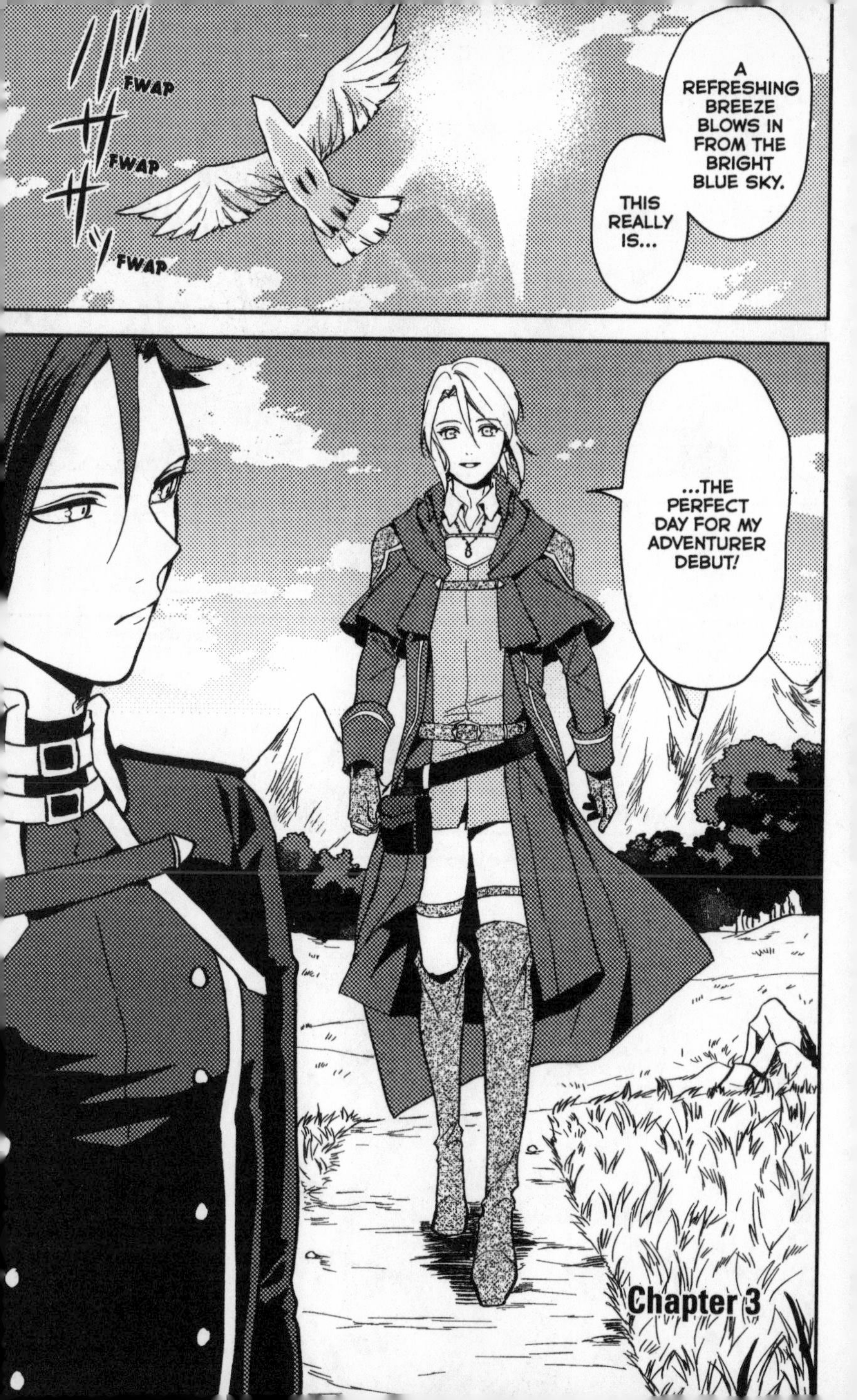
A REFRESHING BREEZE BLOWS IN FROM THE BRIGHT BLUE SKY.
THIS REALLY IS...
FWAP
FWAP
FWAP
...THE PERFECT DAY FOR MY ADVENTURER DEBUT!
Chapter 3

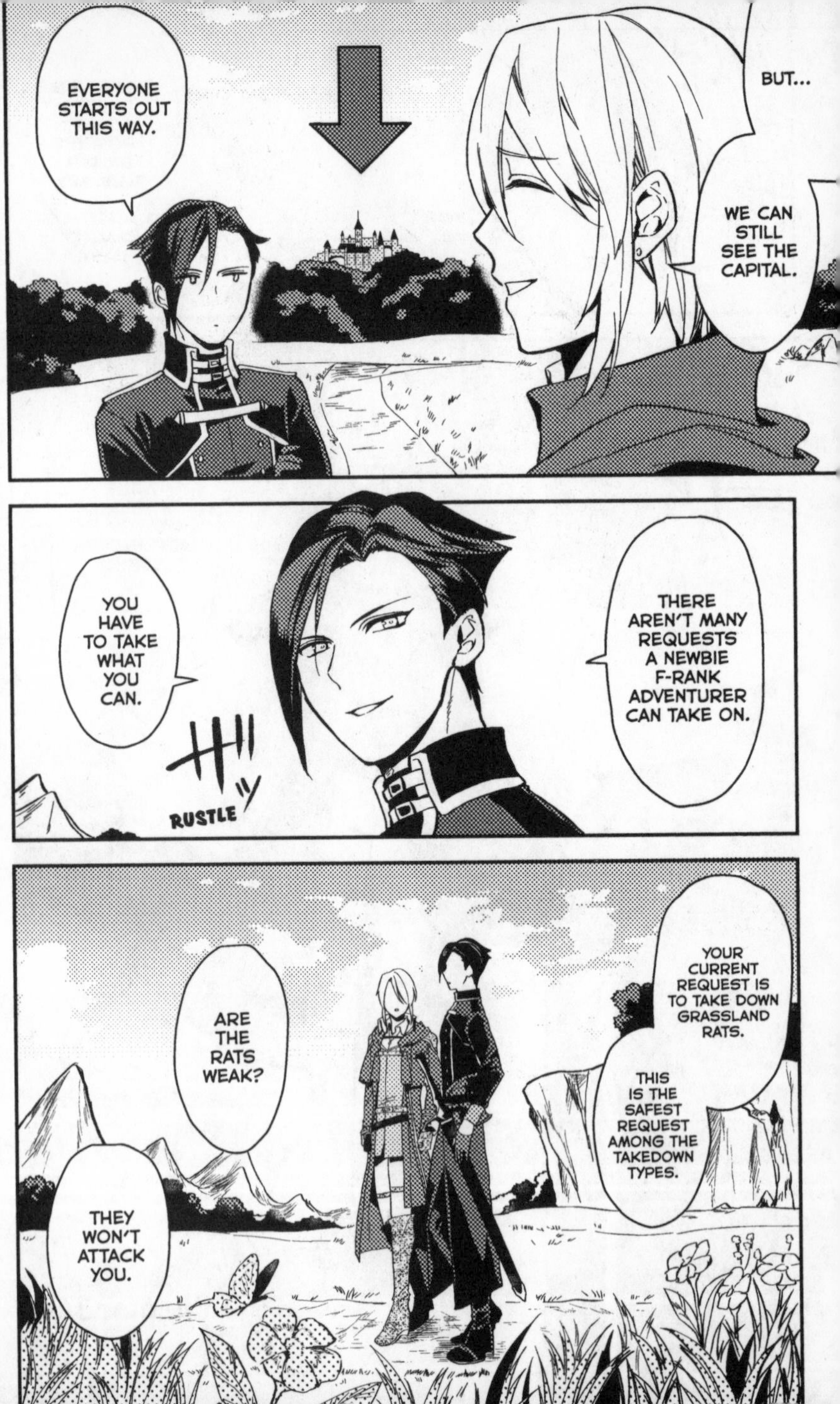
BUT...
WE CAN STILL SEE THE CAPITAL.
EVERYONE STARTS OUT THIS WAY.
THERE AREN'T MANY REQUESTS A NEWBIE F-RANK ADVENTURER CAN TAKE ON.
YOU HAVE TO TAKE WHAT YOU CAN.
RUSTLE
YOUR CURRENT REQUEST IS TO TAKE DOWN GRASSLAND RATS.
THIS IS THE SAFEST REQUEST AMONG THE TAKEDOWN TYPES.
ARE THE RATS WEAK?
THEY WON'T ATTACK YOU.

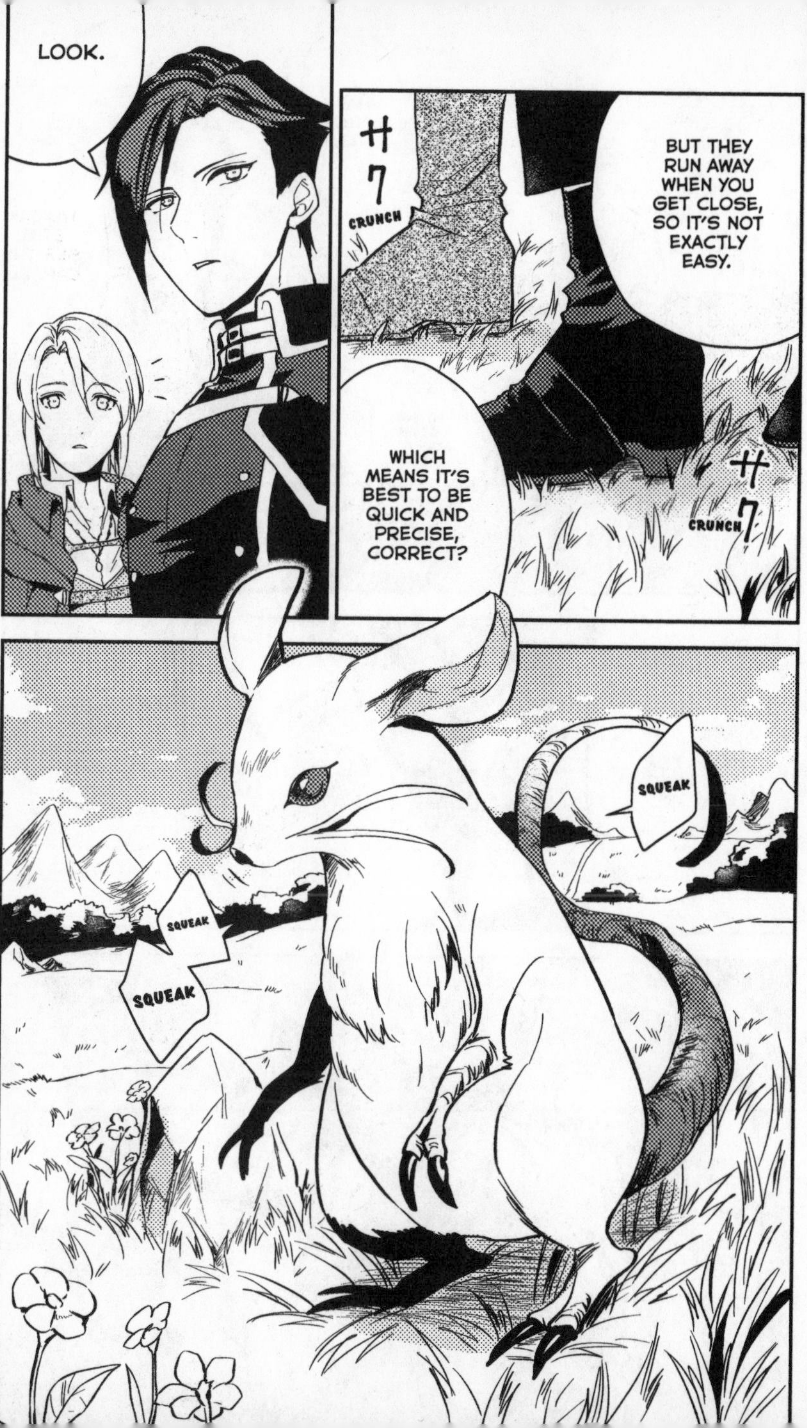
BUT THEY RUN AWAY WHEN YOU GET CLOSE, SO IT'S NOT EXACTLY EASY.
サク
CRUNCH
WHICH MEANS IT'S BEST TO BE QUICK AND PRECISE, CORRECT?
サク
CRUNCH
LOOK.
SQUEAK
SQUEAK
SQUEAK

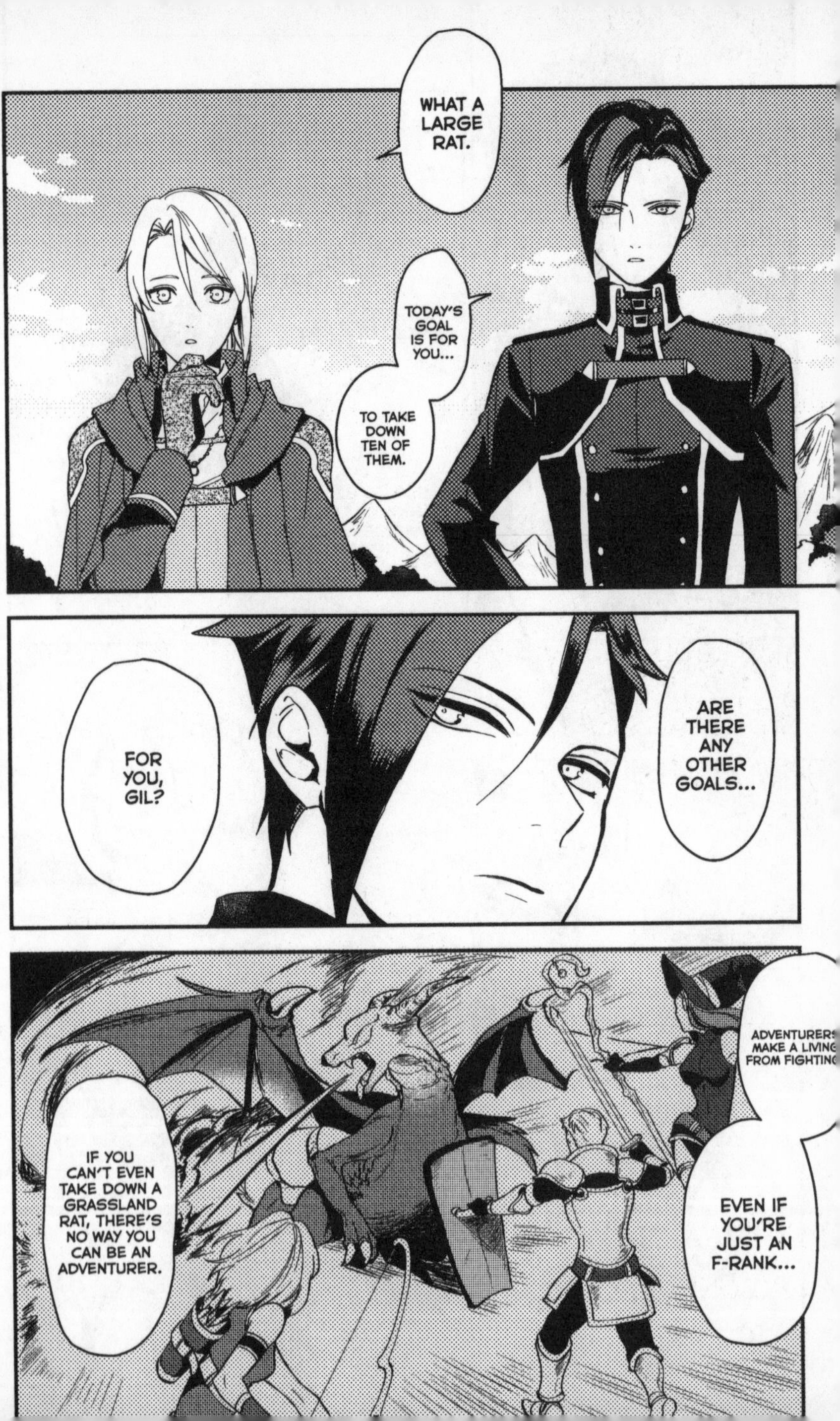
WHAT A LARGE RAT.
TODAY'S GOAL IS FOR YOU...
TO TAKE DOWN TEN OF THEM.
ARE THERE ANY OTHER GOALS...
FOR YOU, GIL?
ADVENTURERS MAKE A LIVING FROM FIGHTING
EVEN IF YOU'RE JUST AN F-RANK...
IF YOU CAN'T EVEN TAKE DOWN A GRASSLAND RAT, THERE'S NO WAY YOU CAN BE AN ADVENTURER.

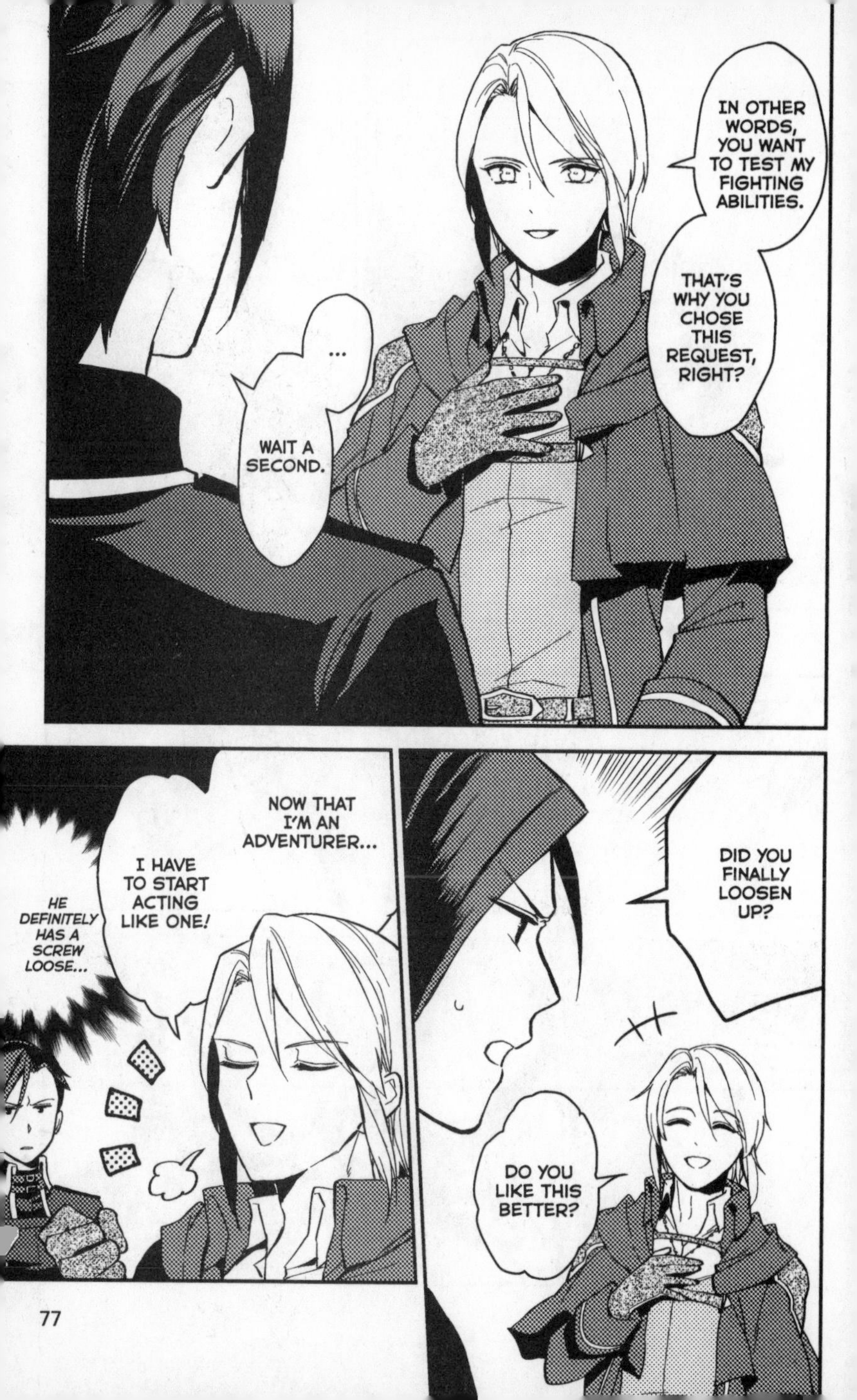
IN OTHER WORDS, YOU WANT TO TEST MY FIGHTING ABILITIES.
THAT'S WHY YOU CHOSE THIS REQUEST, RIGHT?
...
WAIT A SECOND.
DID YOU FINALLY LOOSEN UP?
DO YOU LIKE THIS BETTER?
NOW THAT I'M AN ADVENTURER...
I HAVE TO START ACTING LIKE ONE!
HE DEFINITELY HAS A SCREW LOOSE...

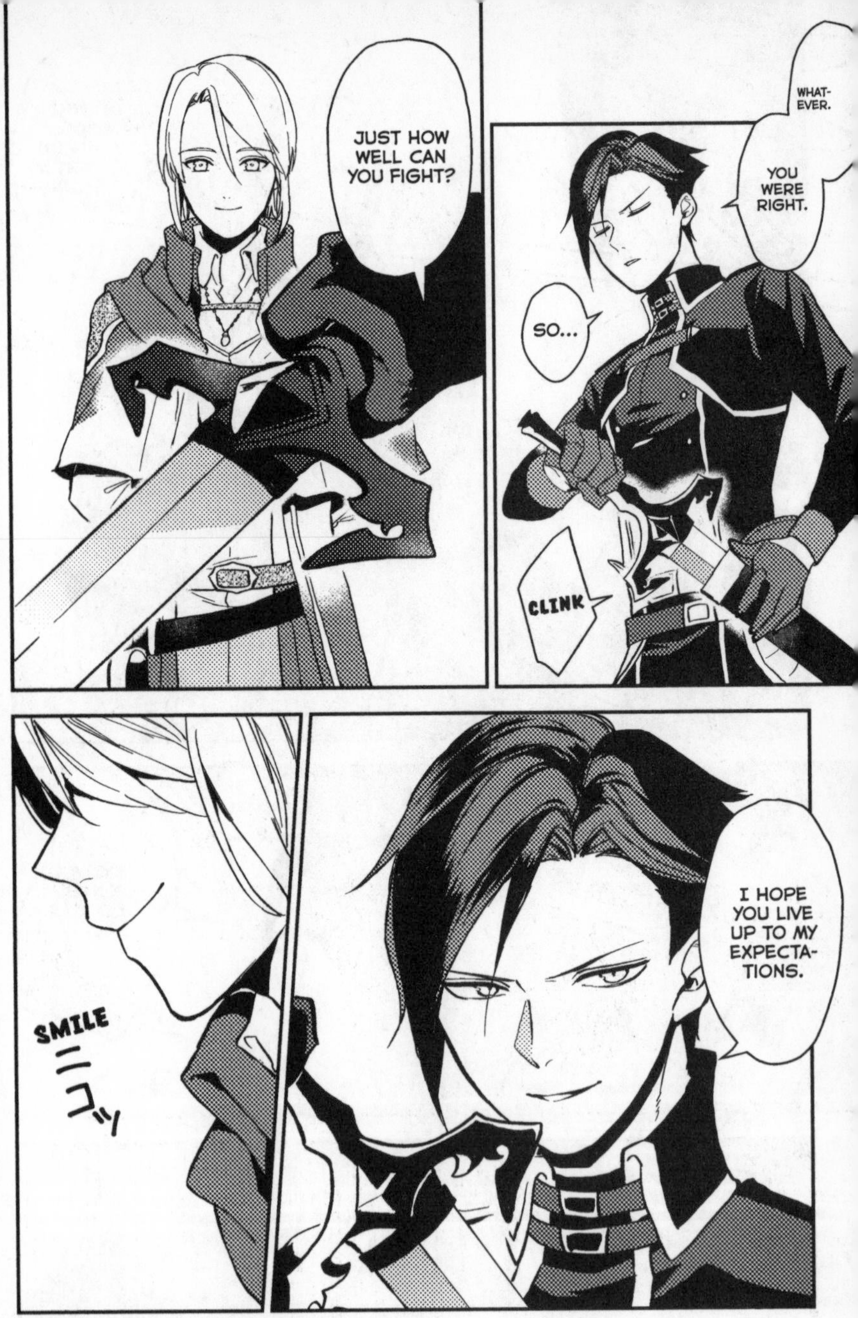
WHAT-EVER.
YOU WERE RIGHT.
SO...
CLINK
JUST HOW WELL CAN YOU FIGHT?
I HOPE YOU LIVE UP TO MY EXPECTATIONS.
SMILE
ニコッ

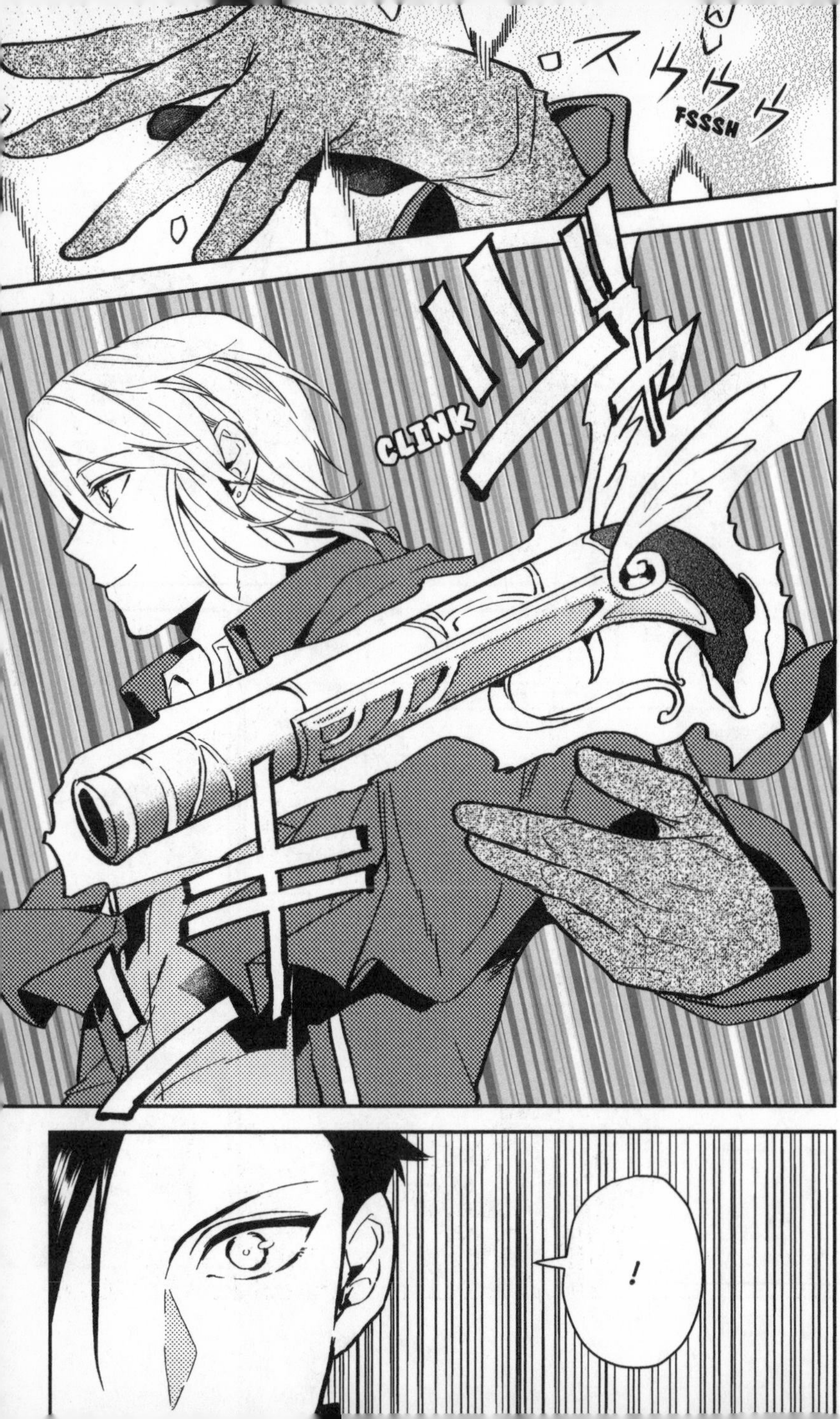
FSSSH
CLINK
!

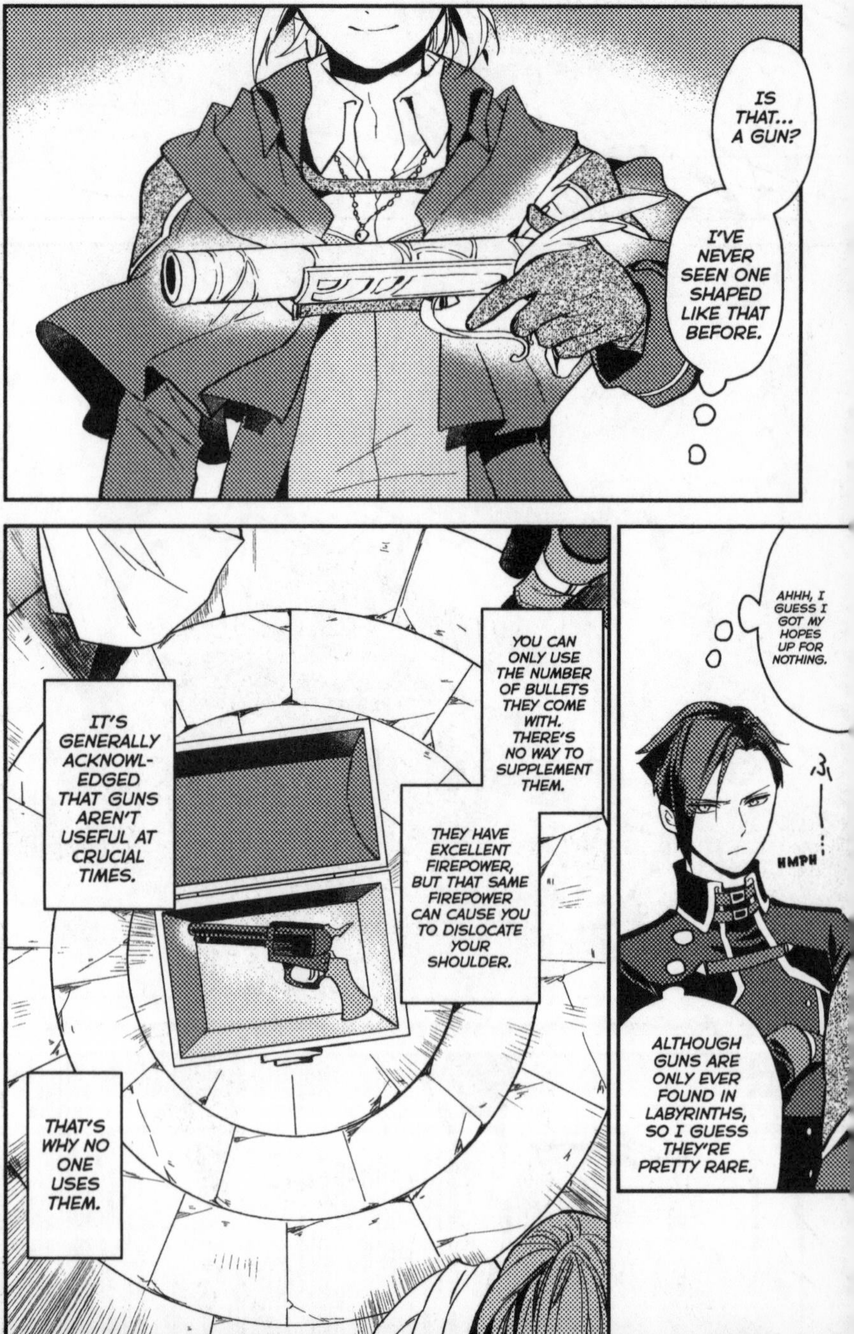

IS THAT... A GUN?
I'VE NEVER SEEN ONE SHAPED LIKE THAT BEFORE.
AHHH, I GUESS I GOT MY HOPES UP FOR NOTHING.
ふー…
HMPH
ALTHOUGH GUNS ARE ONLY EVER FOUND IN LABYRINTHS, SO I GUESS THEY'RE PRETTY RARE.
YOU CAN ONLY USE THE NUMBER OF BULLETS THEY COME WITH. THERE'S NO WAY TO SUPPLEMENT THEM.
THEY HAVE EXCELLENT FIREPOWER, BUT THAT SAME FIREPOWER CAN CAUSE YOU TO DISLOCATE YOUR SHOULDER.
IT'S GENERALLY ACKNOWL-EDGED THAT GUNS AREN'T USEFUL AT CRUCIAL TIMES.
THAT'S WHY NO ONE USES THEM.

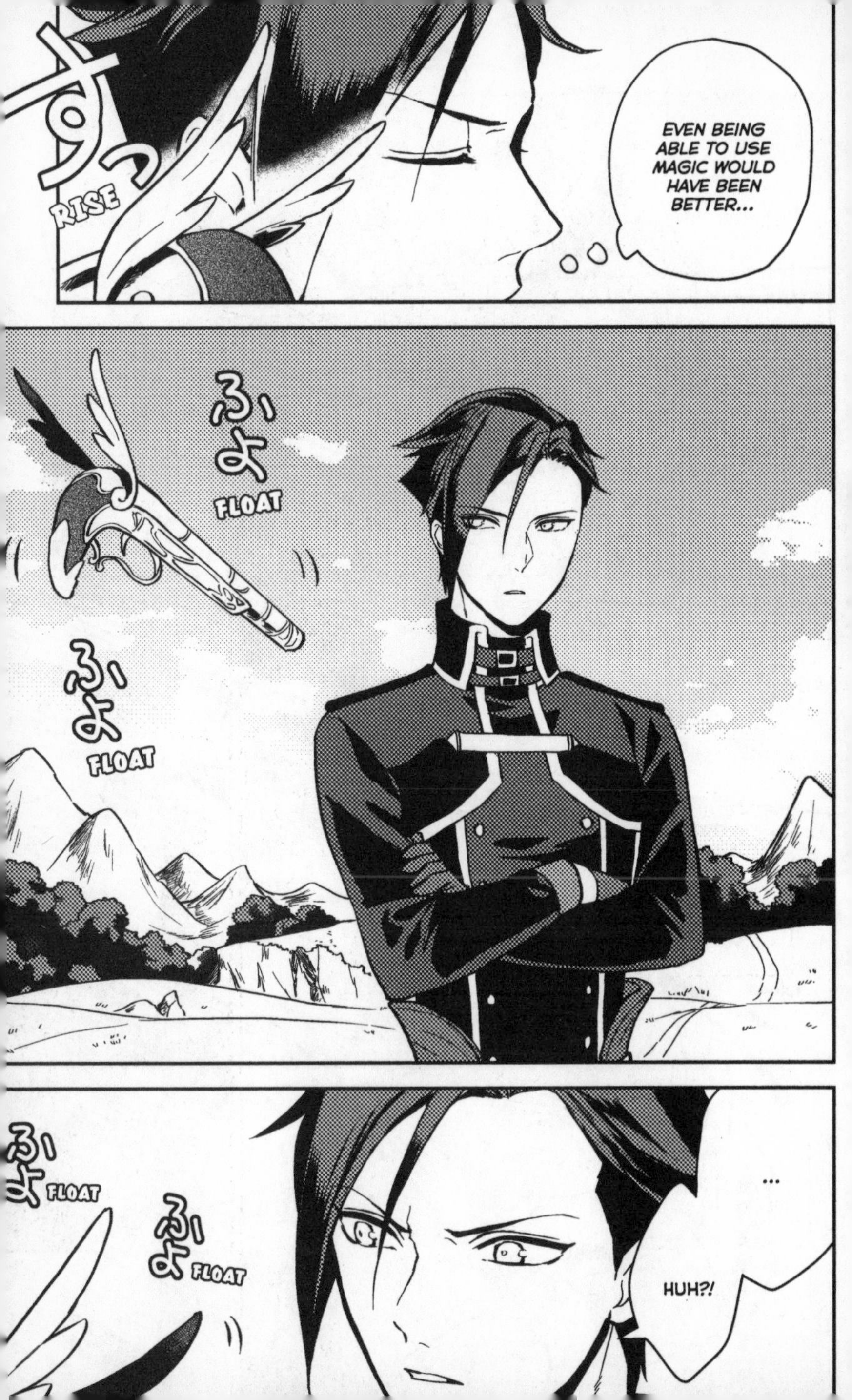
EVEN BEING ABLE TO USE MAGIC WOULD HAVE BEEN BETTER...
すっ
RISE
ふよ
FLOAT
ふよ
FLOAT
...
HUH?!
ふよ
FLOAT
ふよ
FLOAT

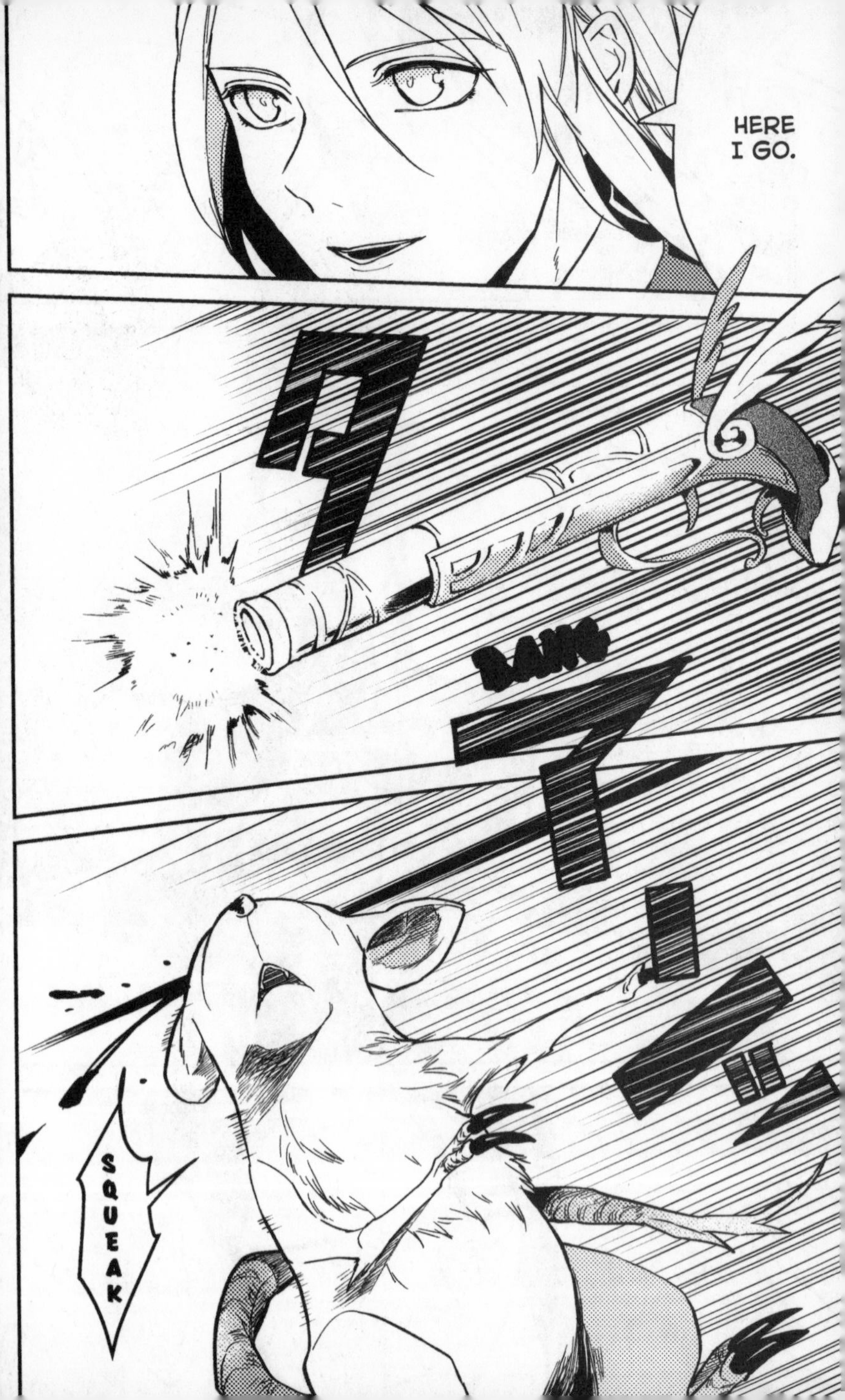
HERE I GO.
SQUEAK

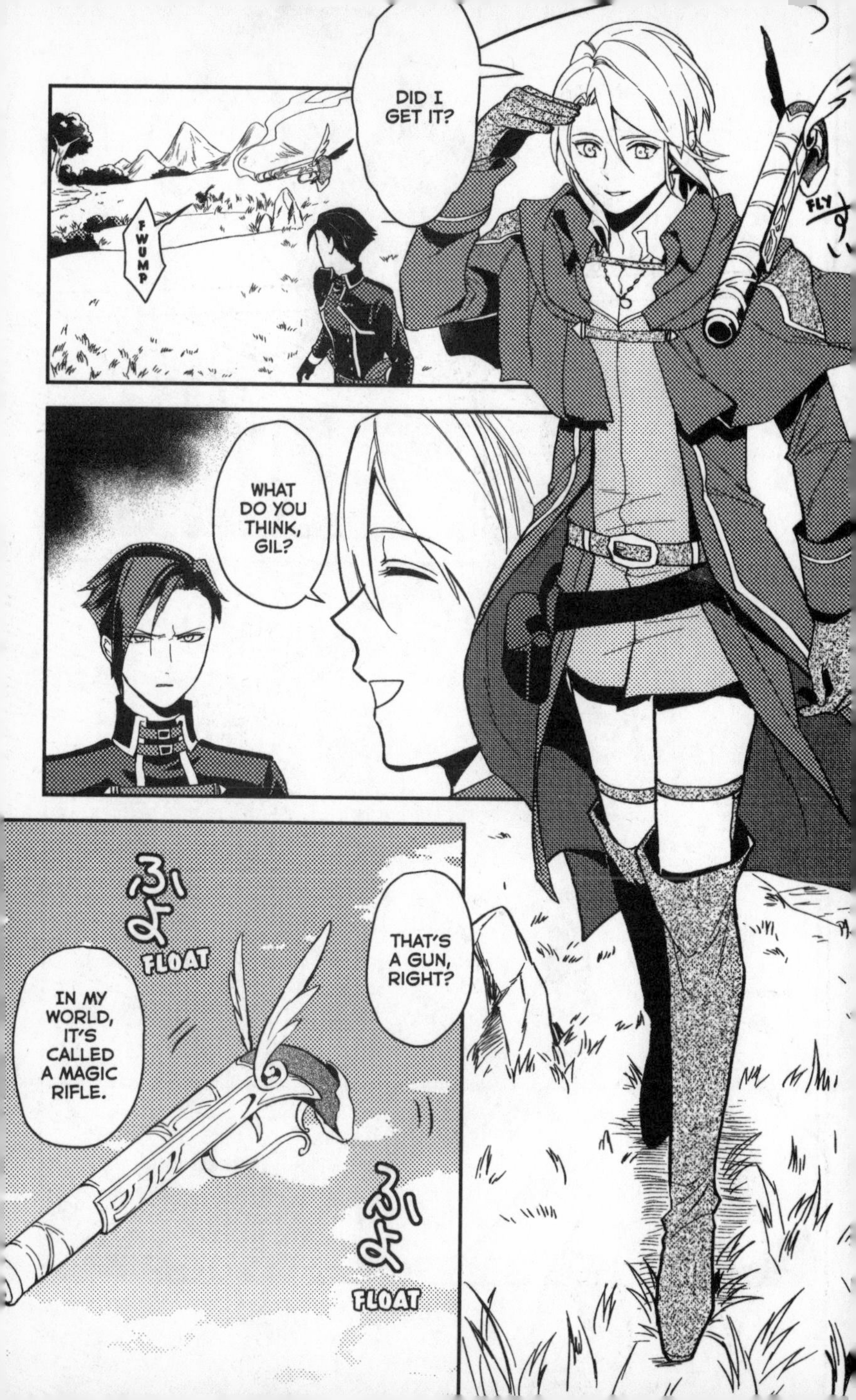
DID I GET IT?
FLY
FWUMP
WHAT DO YOU THINK, GIL?
THAT'S A GUN, RIGHT?
ふよ
FLOAT
IN MY WORLD, IT'S CALLED A MAGIC RIFLE.
ふよ
FLOAT

A RIFLE, HUH?

HOW DO YOU CONTROL IT?

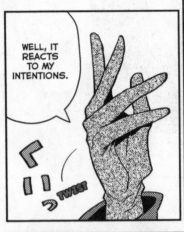

WELL, IT REACTS TO MY INTENTIONS.

TWIST

FLY

FLY

THERE'S ALMOST NO TIME LAG.

IT CAN SHOOT MULTIPLE ROUNDS WITHOUT BEING RELOADED.

SINCE IT'S SO SPECIALIZED, YOU CAN PROBABLY USE IT IN BOTH CLOSE AND LONG-RANGE ATTACKS.

YES, I DON'T BELIEVE THAT'D BE A PROBLEM.

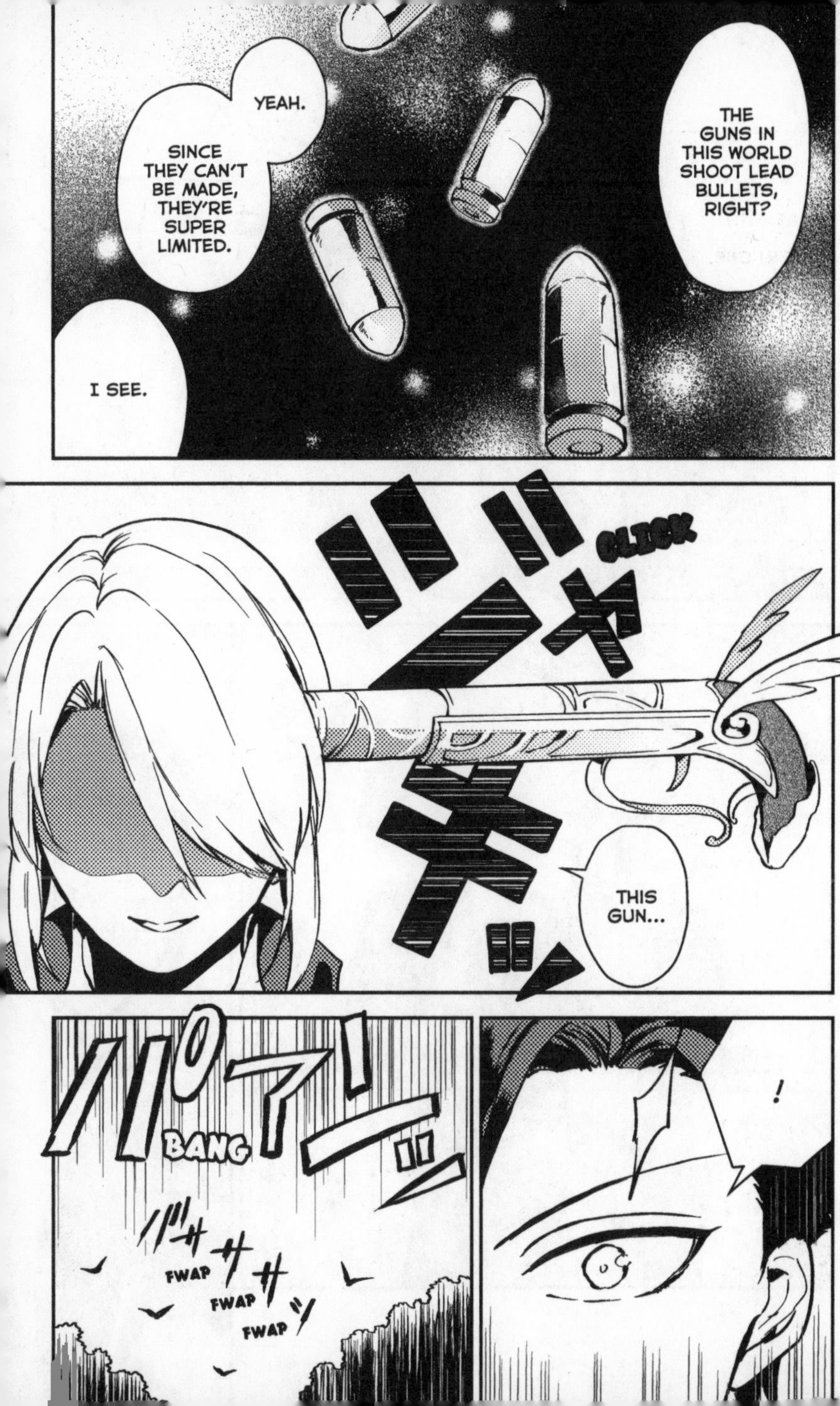
THE GUNS IN THIS WORLD SHOOT LEAD BULLETS, RIGHT?
YEAH.
SINCE THEY CAN'T BE MADE, THEY'RE SUPER LIMITED.
I SEE.
CLICK
THIS GUN...
!
BANG
FWAP
FWAP
FWAP

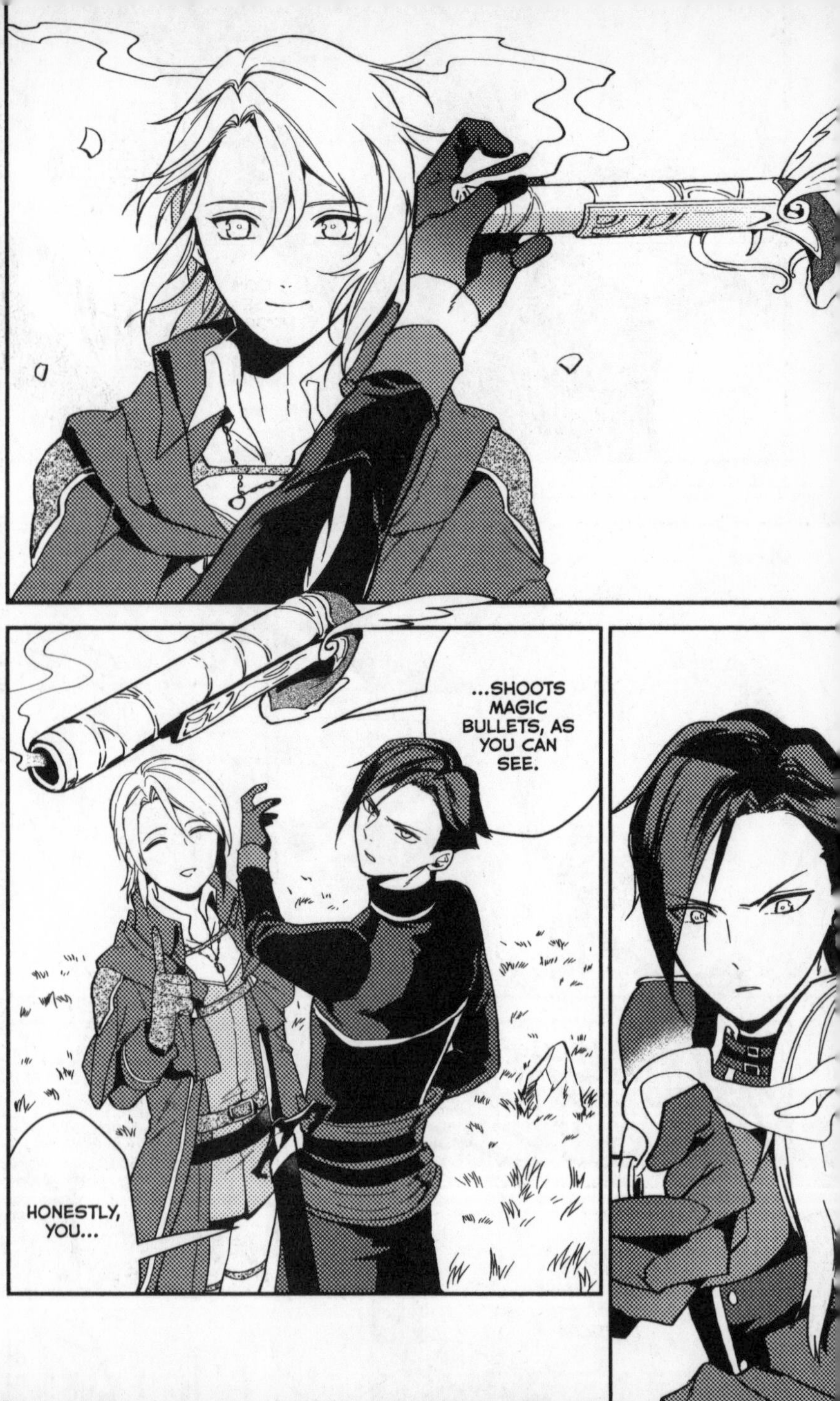
...SHOOTS MAGIC BULLETS, AS YOU CAN SEE.
HONESTLY, YOU...

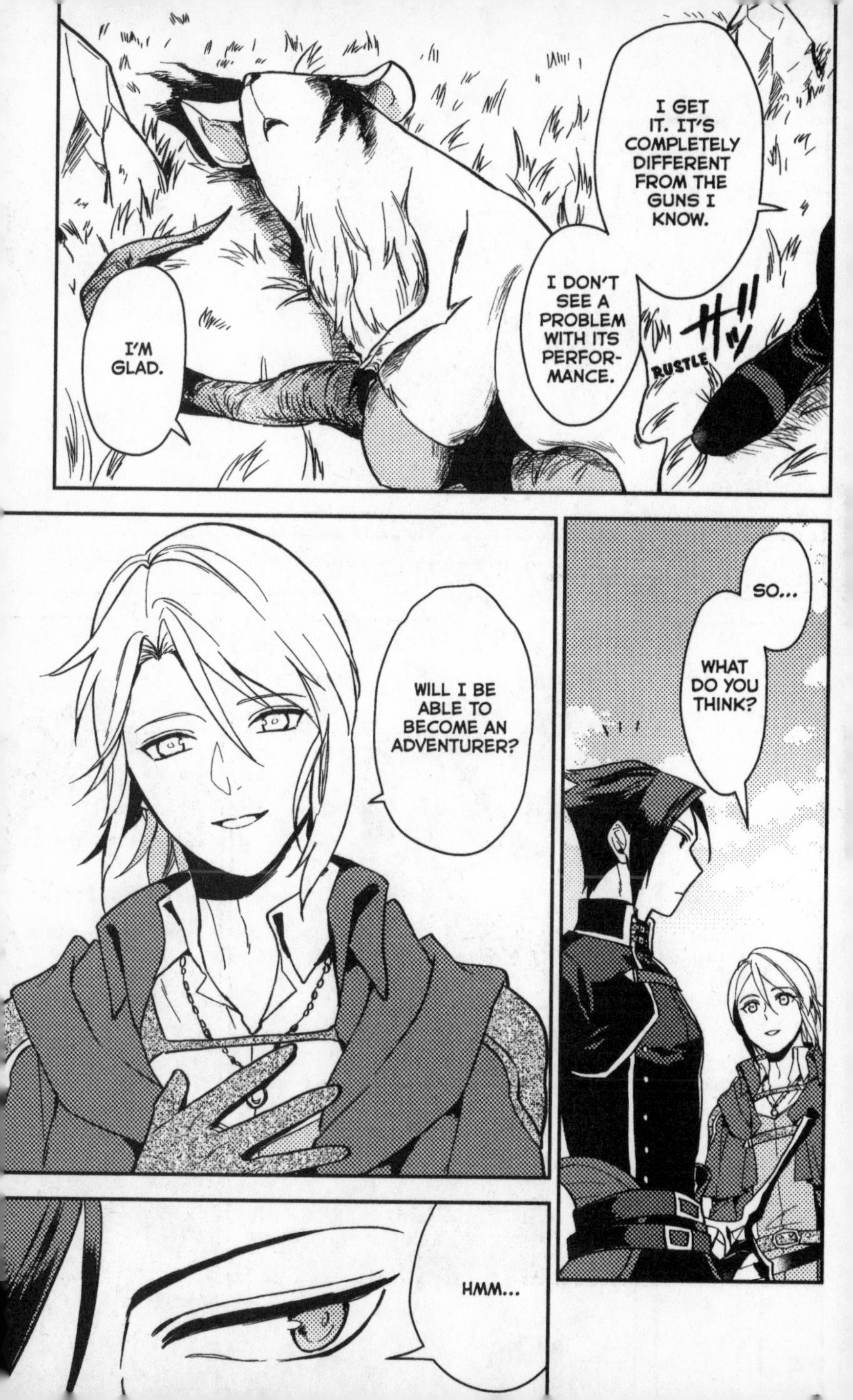
I GET IT. IT'S COMPLETELY DIFFERENT FROM THE GUNS I KNOW.
I DON'T SEE A PROBLEM WITH ITS PERFORMANCE.
RUSTLE
I'M GLAD.
SO...
WHAT DO YOU THINK?
WILL I BE ABLE TO BECOME AN ADVENTURER?
HMM...

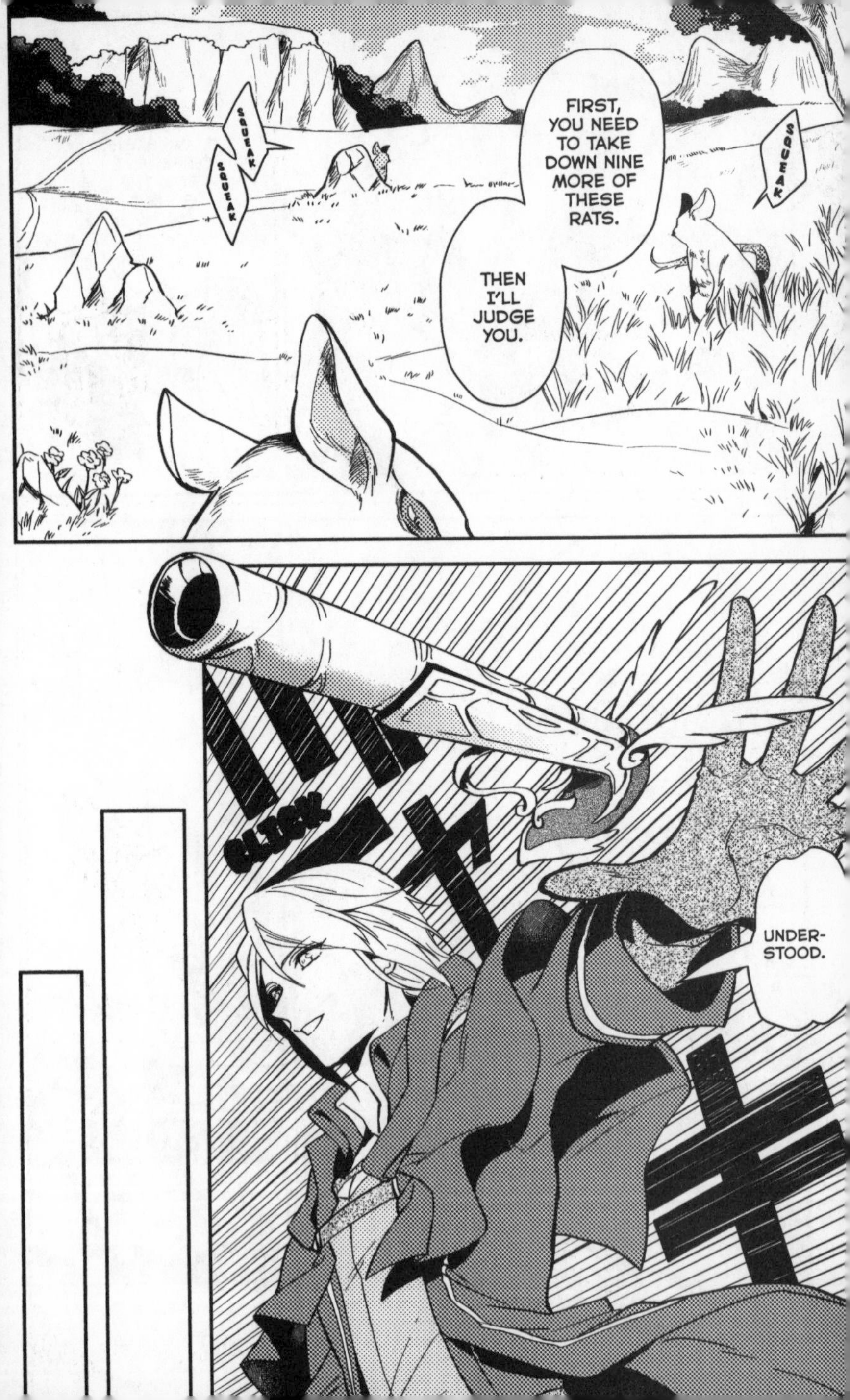
SQUEAK
FIRST, YOU NEED TO TAKE DOWN NINE MORE OF THESE RATS.
THEN I'LL JUDGE YOU.
SQUEAK
SQUEAK
UNDER-STOOD.
CLICK

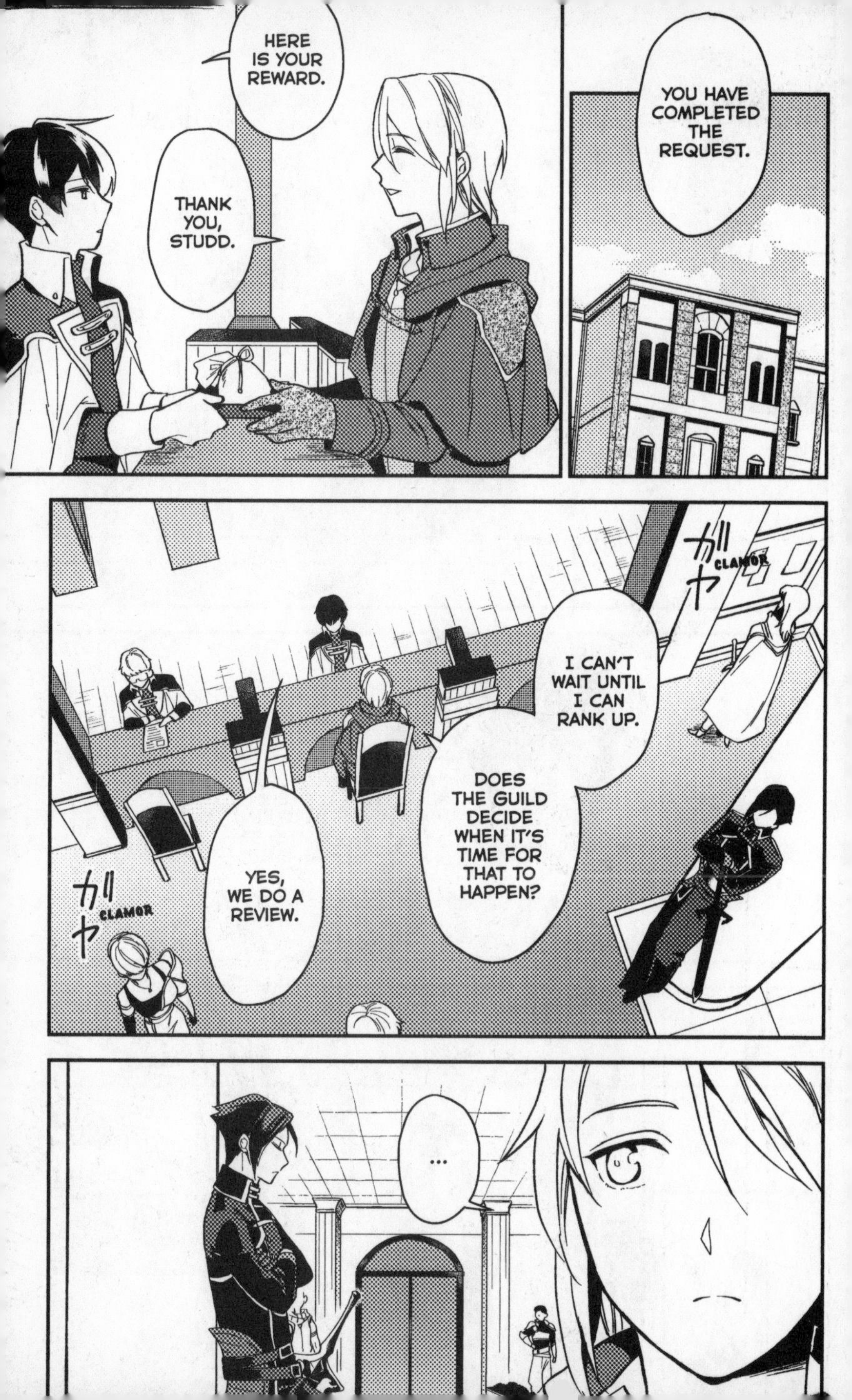
YOU HAVE COMPLETED THE REQUEST.
HERE IS YOUR REWARD.
THANK YOU, STUDD.
ガヤ
CLAMOR
I CAN'T WAIT UNTIL I CAN RANK UP.
DOES THE GUILD DECIDE WHEN IT'S TIME FOR THAT TO HAPPEN?
YES, WE DO A REVIEW.
ガヤ
CLAMOR
...

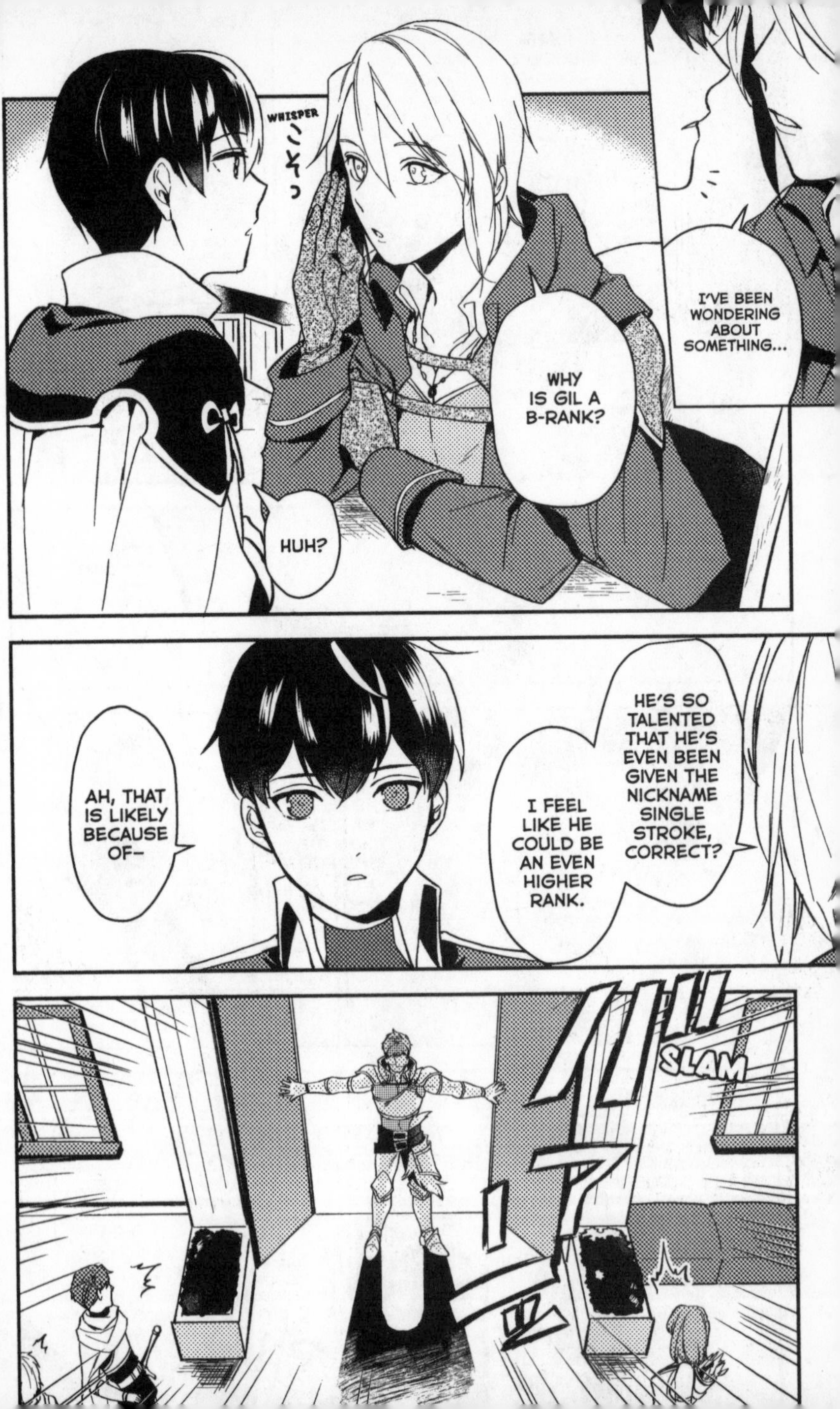
I'VE BEEN WONDERING ABOUT SOMETHING...
WHISPER
WHY IS GIL A B-RANK?
HUH?
HE'S SO TALENTED THAT HE'S EVEN BEEN GIVEN THE NICKNAME SINGLE STROKE, CORRECT?
I FEEL LIKE HE COULD BE AN EVEN HIGHER RANK.
AH, THAT IS LIKELY BECAUSE OF–
SLAM

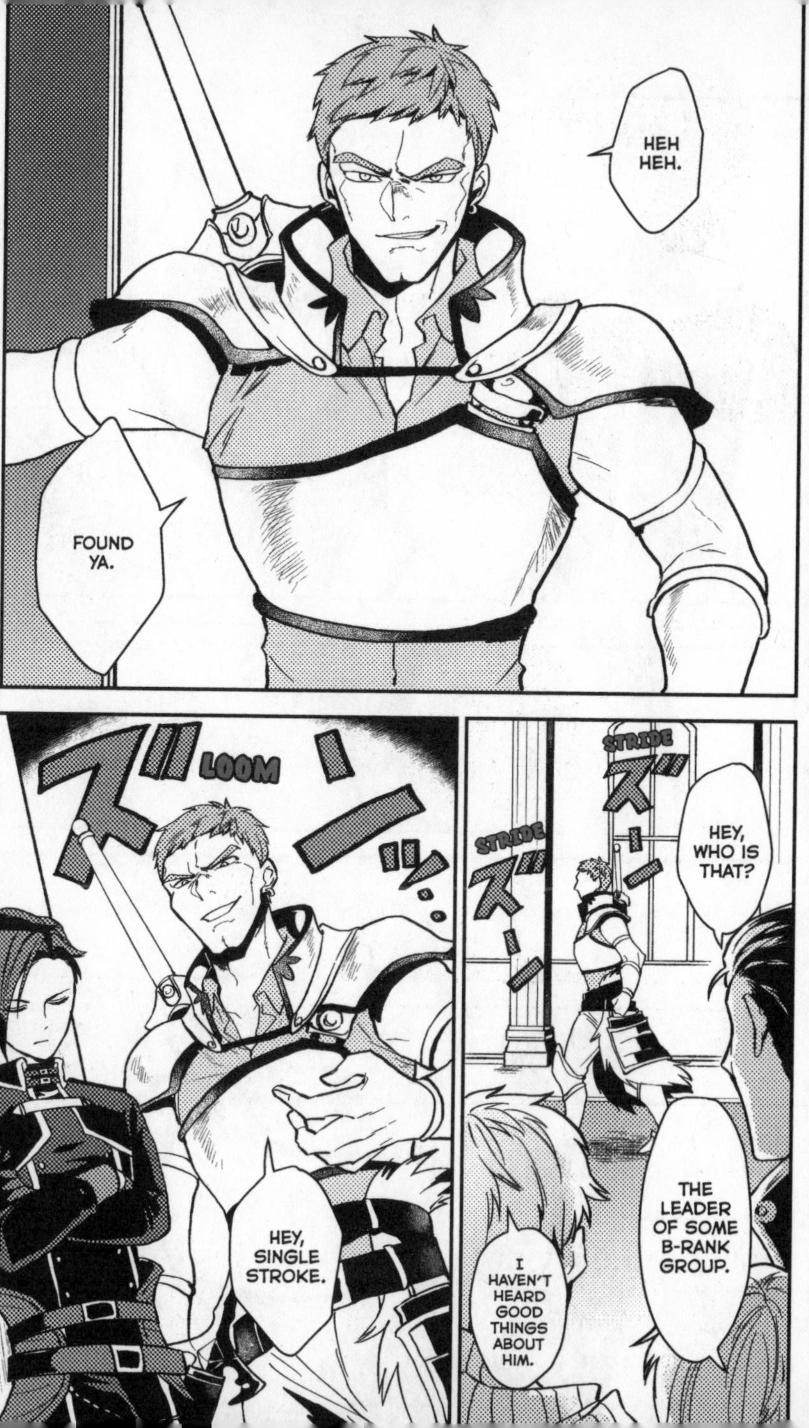
HEH HEH.
FOUND YA.
STRIDE
STRIDE
HEY, WHO IS THAT?
THE LEADER OF SOME B-RANK GROUP.
I HAVEN'T HEARD GOOD THINGS ABOUT HIM.
LOOM
HEY, SINGLE STROKE.

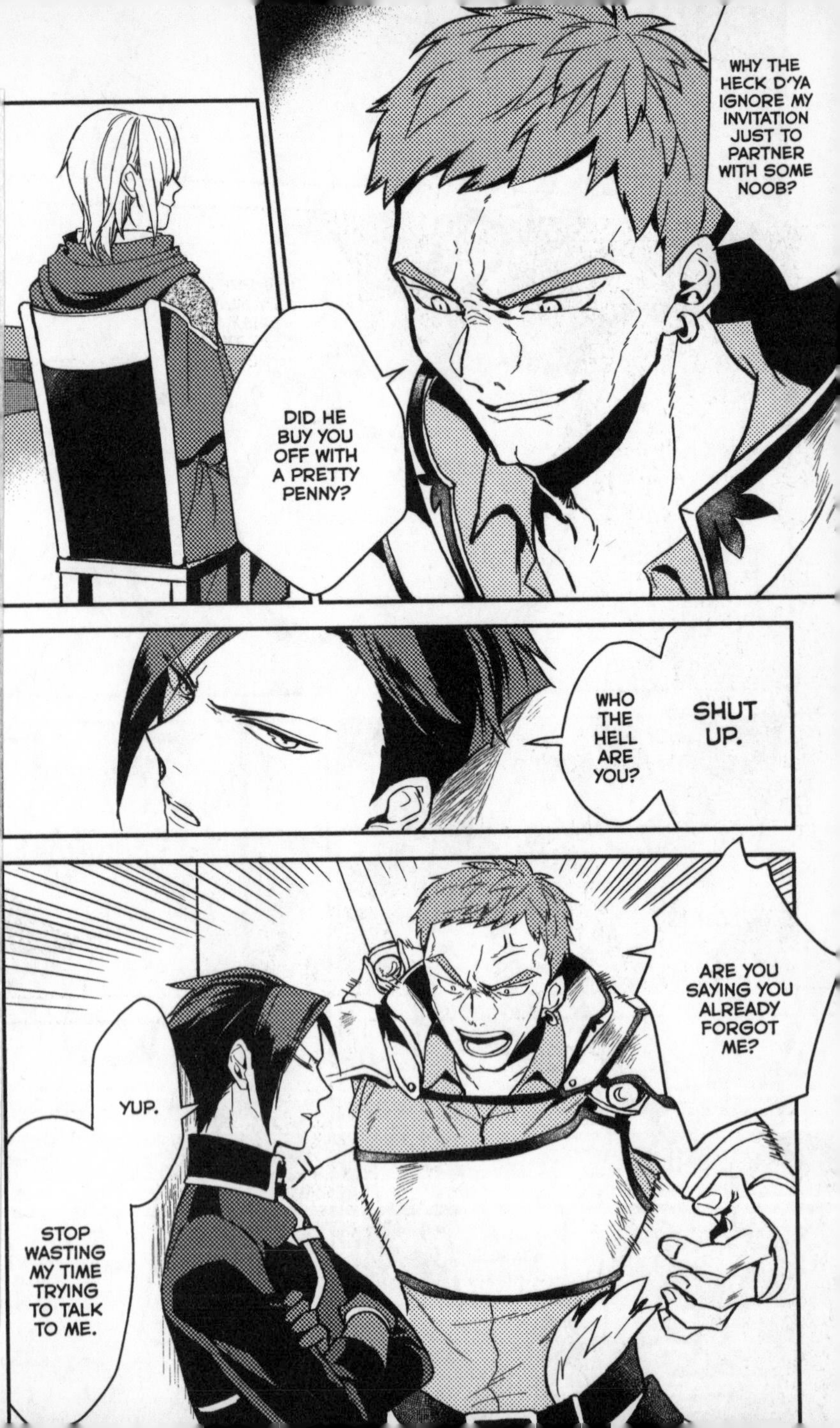
WHY THE HECK D'YA IGNORE MY INVITATION JUST TO PARTNER WITH SOME NOOB?
DID HE BUY YOU OFF WITH A PRETTY PENNY?
SHUT UP.
WHO THE HELL ARE YOU?
ARE YOU SAYING YOU ALREADY FORGOT ME?
YUP.
STOP WASTING MY TIME TRYING TO TALK TO ME.

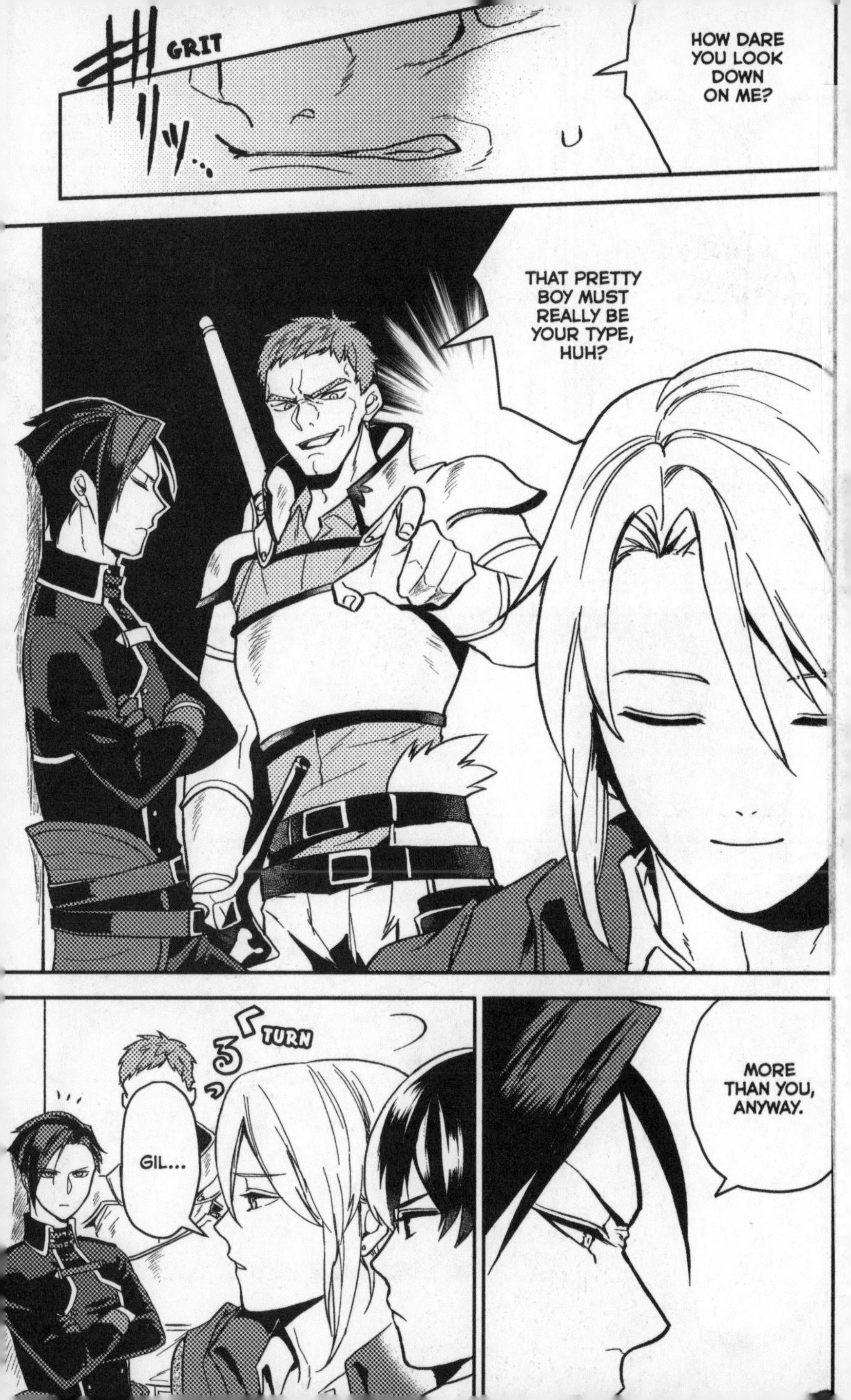
HOW DARE YOU LOOK DOWN ON ME?
GRIT
THAT PRETTY BOY MUST REALLY BE YOUR TYPE, HUH?
MORE THAN YOU, ANYWAY.
TURN
GIL...

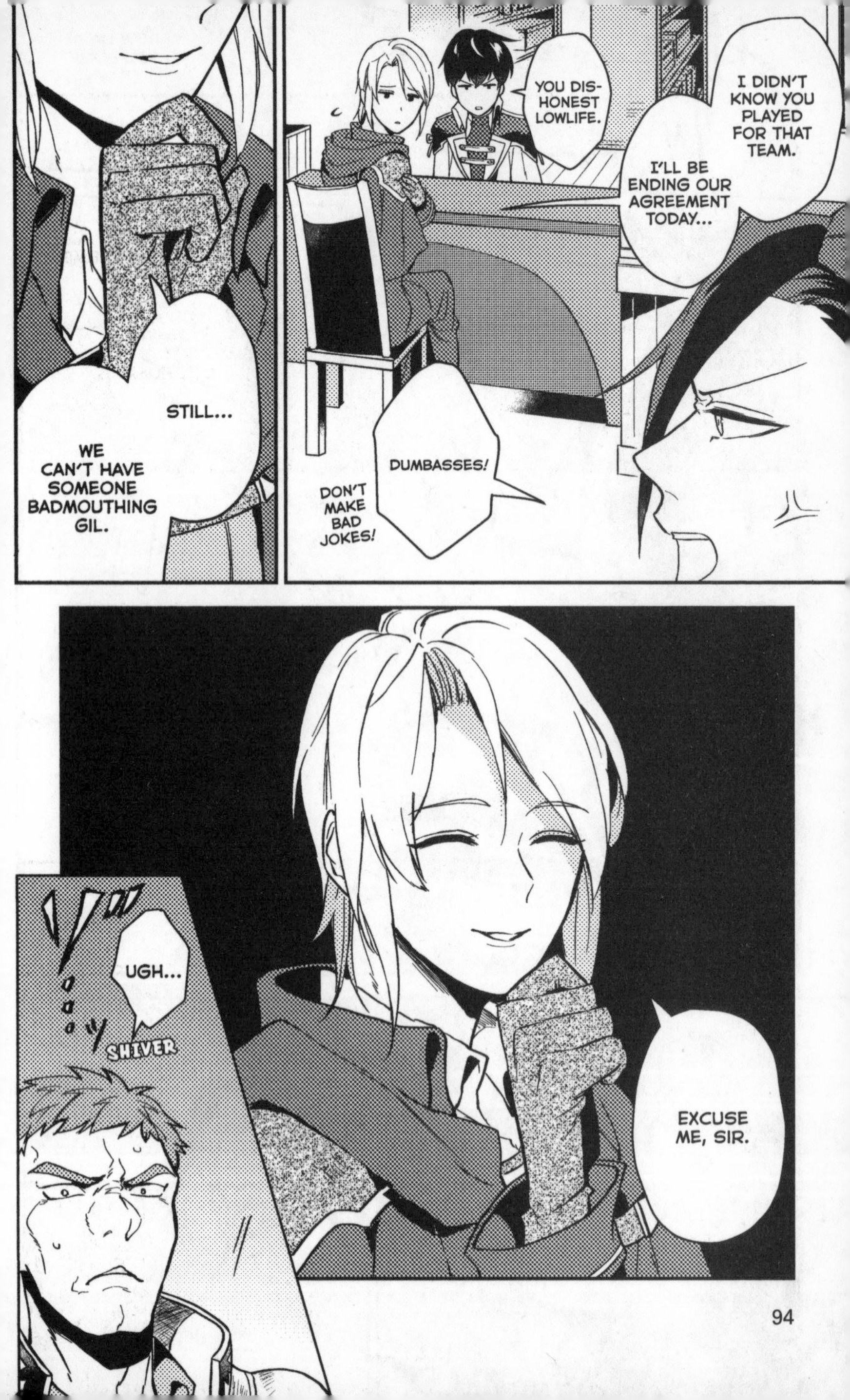
I DIDN'T KNOW YOU PLAYED FOR THAT TEAM.
I'LL BE ENDING OUR AGREEMENT TODAY...
YOU DIS-HONEST LOWLIFE.
DUMBASSES!
DON'T MAKE BAD JOKES!
STILL...
WE CAN'T HAVE SOMEONE BADMOUTHING GIL.
EXCUSE ME, SIR.
UGH...
SHIVER

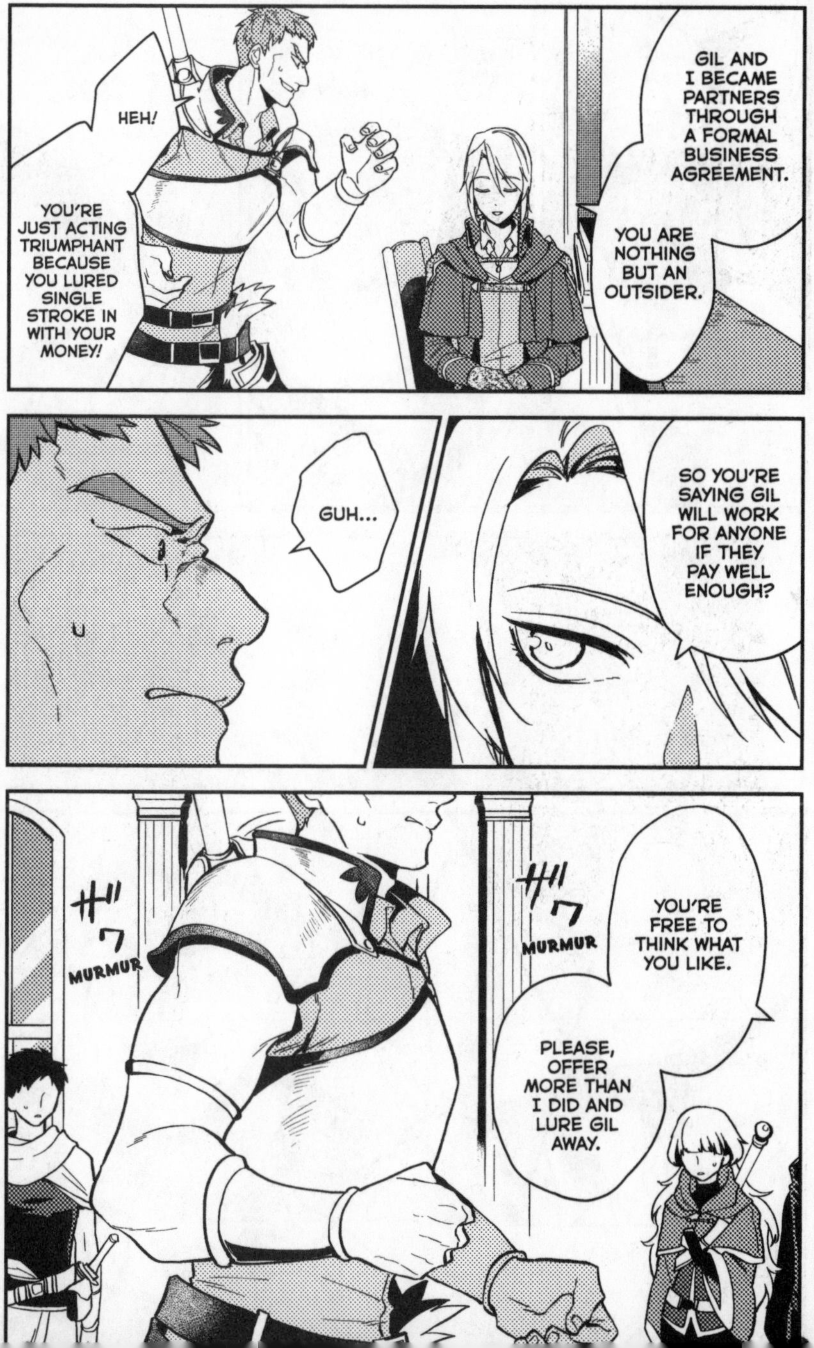
GIL AND I BECAME PARTNERS THROUGH A FORMAL BUSINESS AGREEMENT.
YOU ARE NOTHING BUT AN OUTSIDER.
HEH!
YOU'RE JUST ACTING TRIUMPHANT BECAUSE YOU LURED SINGLE STROKE IN WITH YOUR MONEY!
SO YOU'RE SAYING GIL WILL WORK FOR ANYONE IF THEY PAY WELL ENOUGH?
GUH...
YOU'RE FREE TO THINK WHAT YOU LIKE.
PLEASE, OFFER MORE THAN I DID AND LURE GIL AWAY.
ザワ
MURMUR
ザワ
MURMUR

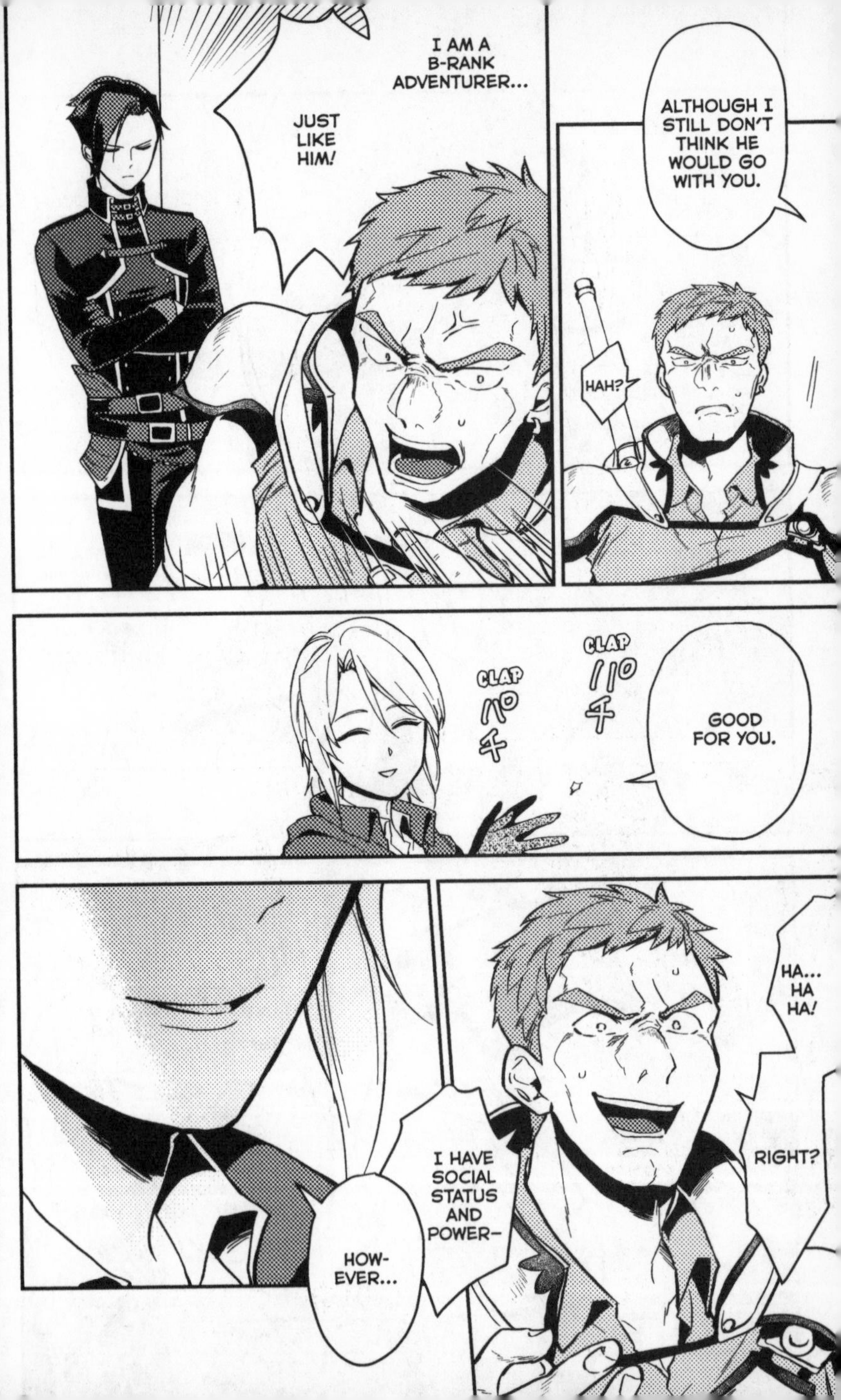
ALTHOUGH I STILL DON'T THINK HE WOULD GO WITH YOU.
HAH?
I AM A B-RANK ADVENTURER...
JUST LIKE HIM!
GOOD FOR YOU.
CLAP
パチ
CLAP
パチ
HA... HA HA!
RIGHT?
I HAVE SOCIAL STATUS AND POWER–
HOW-EVER...

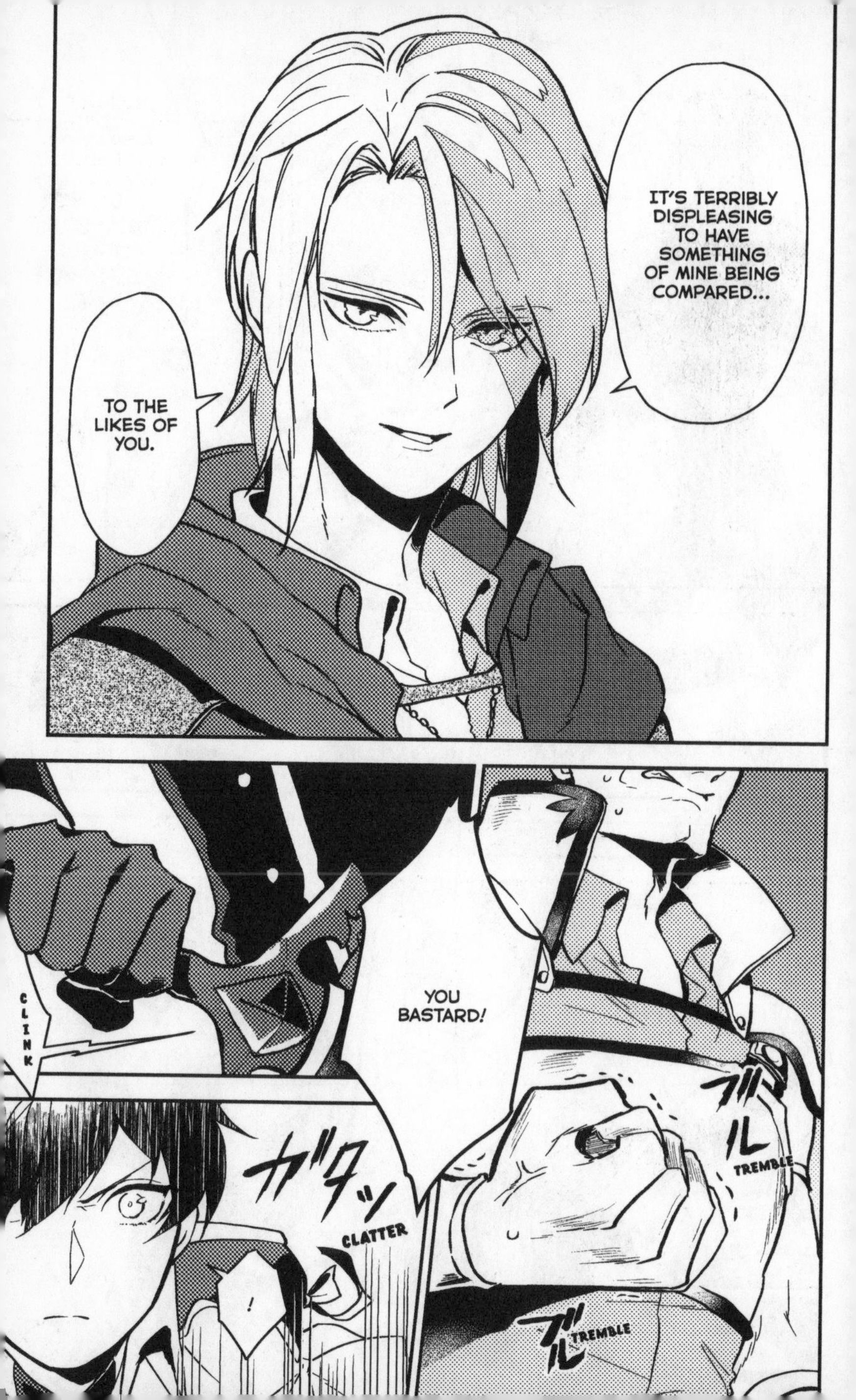
IT'S TERRIBLY DISPLEASING TO HAVE SOMETHING OF MINE BEING COMPARED...
TO THE LIKES OF YOU.
YOU BASTARD!
ブル
TREMBLE
ブル
TREMBLE
CLINK
ガタッ
CLATTER
!

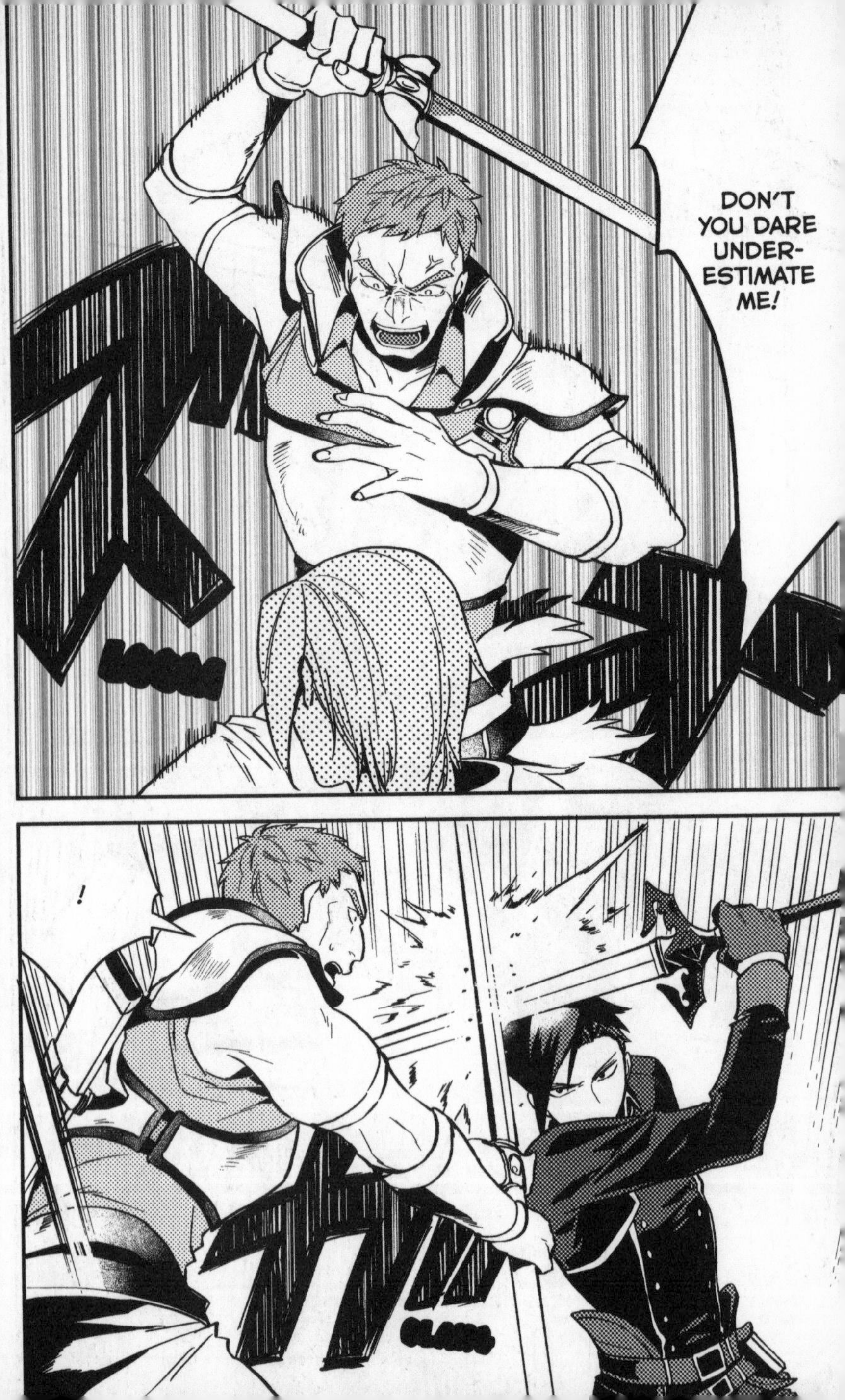
DON'T YOU DARE UNDER-ESTIMATE ME!
!

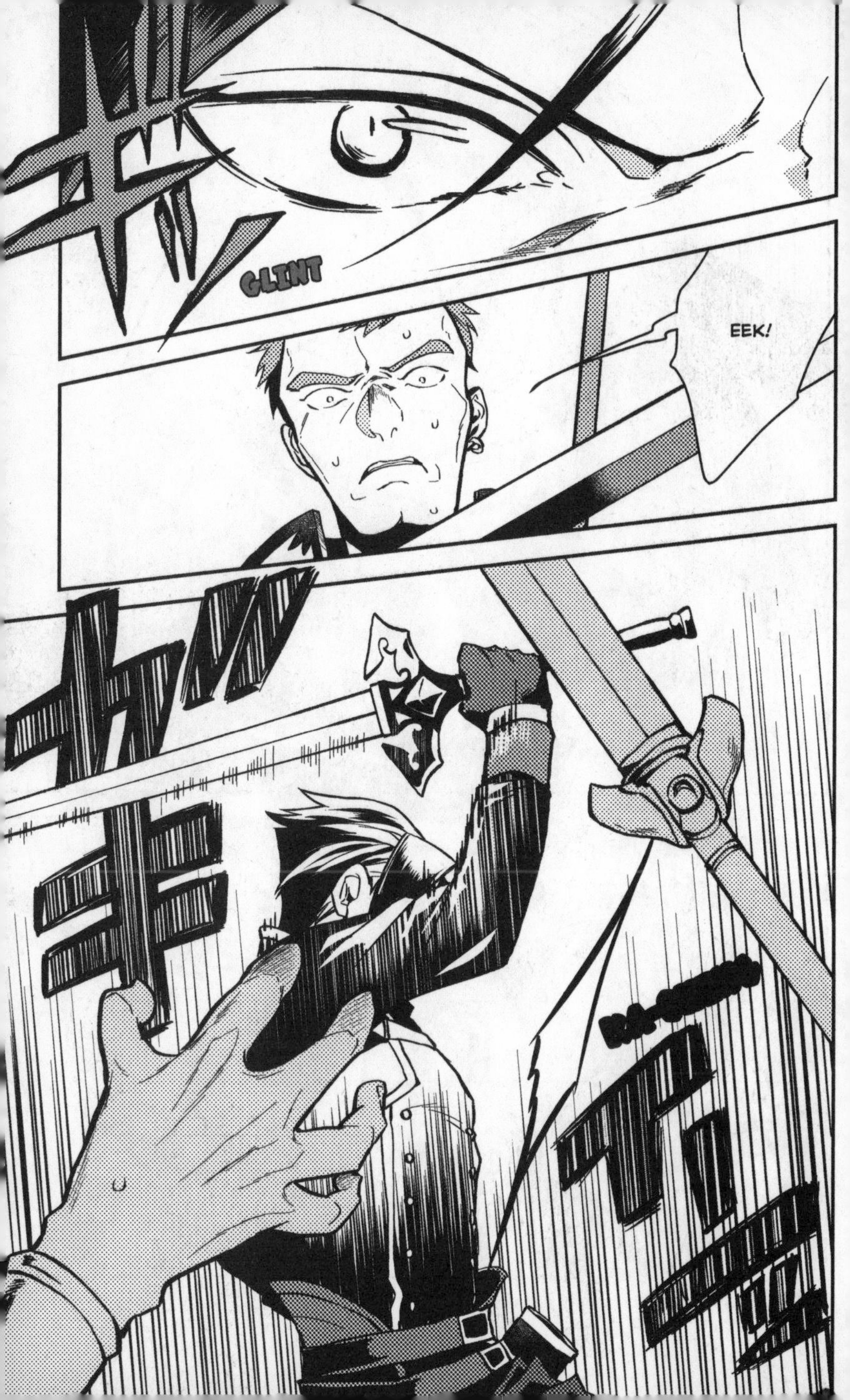
GLINT
EEK!

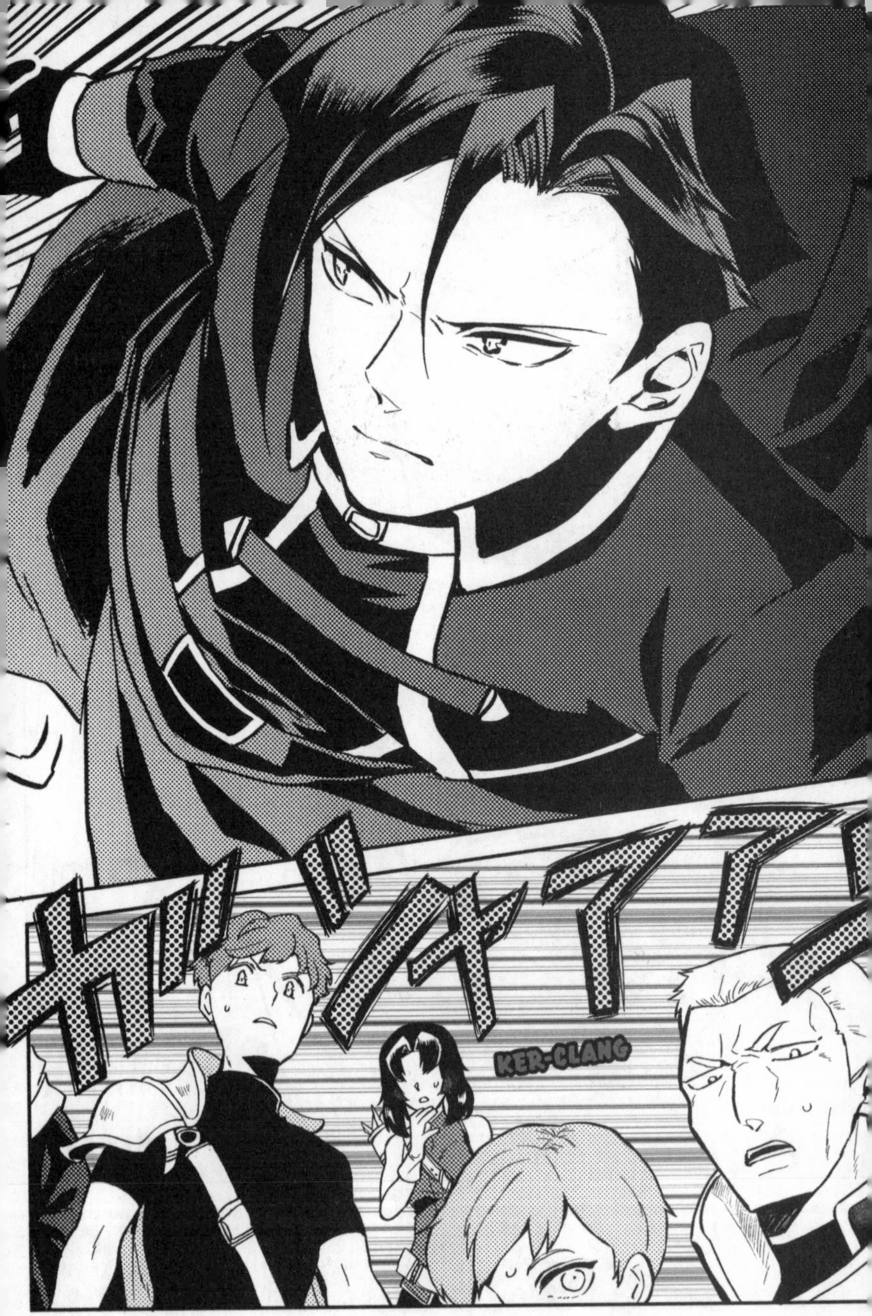
ガッシャアアン
KER-CLANG

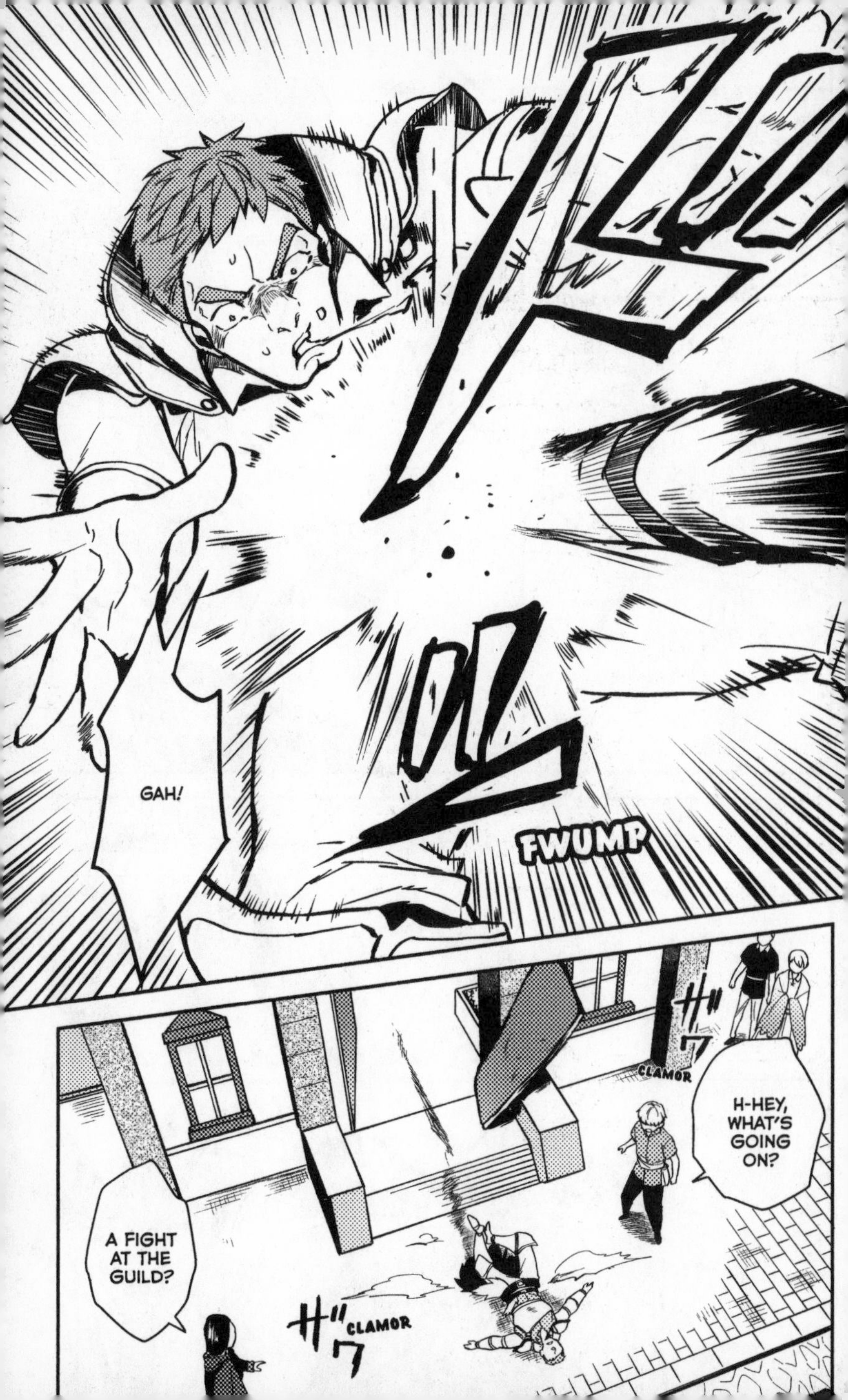
GAH!
FWUMP
CLAMOR
H-HEY, WHAT'S GOING ON?
A FIGHT AT THE GUILD?
CLAMOR

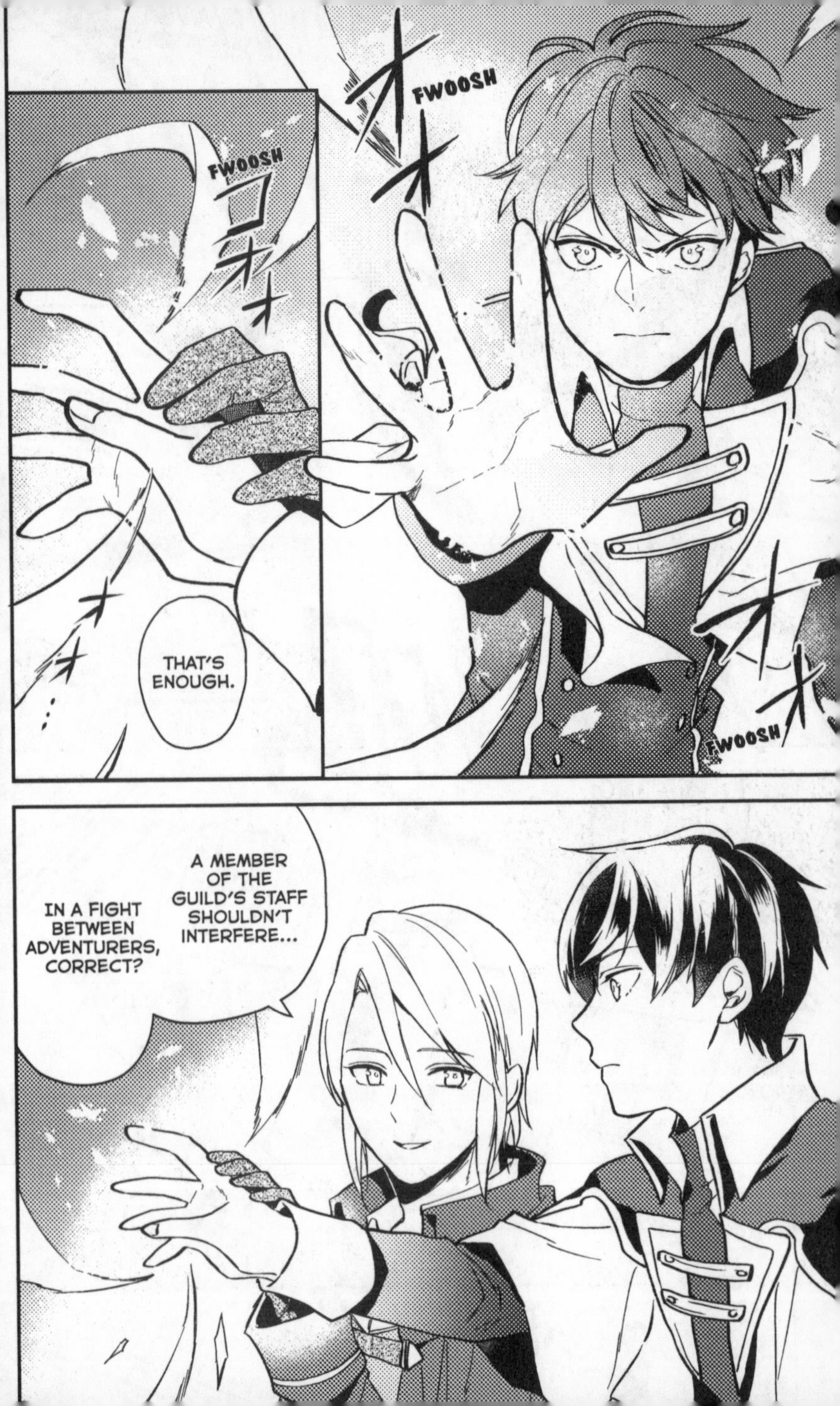
FWOOSH
FWOOSH
FWOOSH
THAT'S ENOUGH.
A MEMBER OF THE GUILD'S STAFF SHOULDN'T INTERFERE...
IN A FIGHT BETWEEN ADVENTURERS, CORRECT?

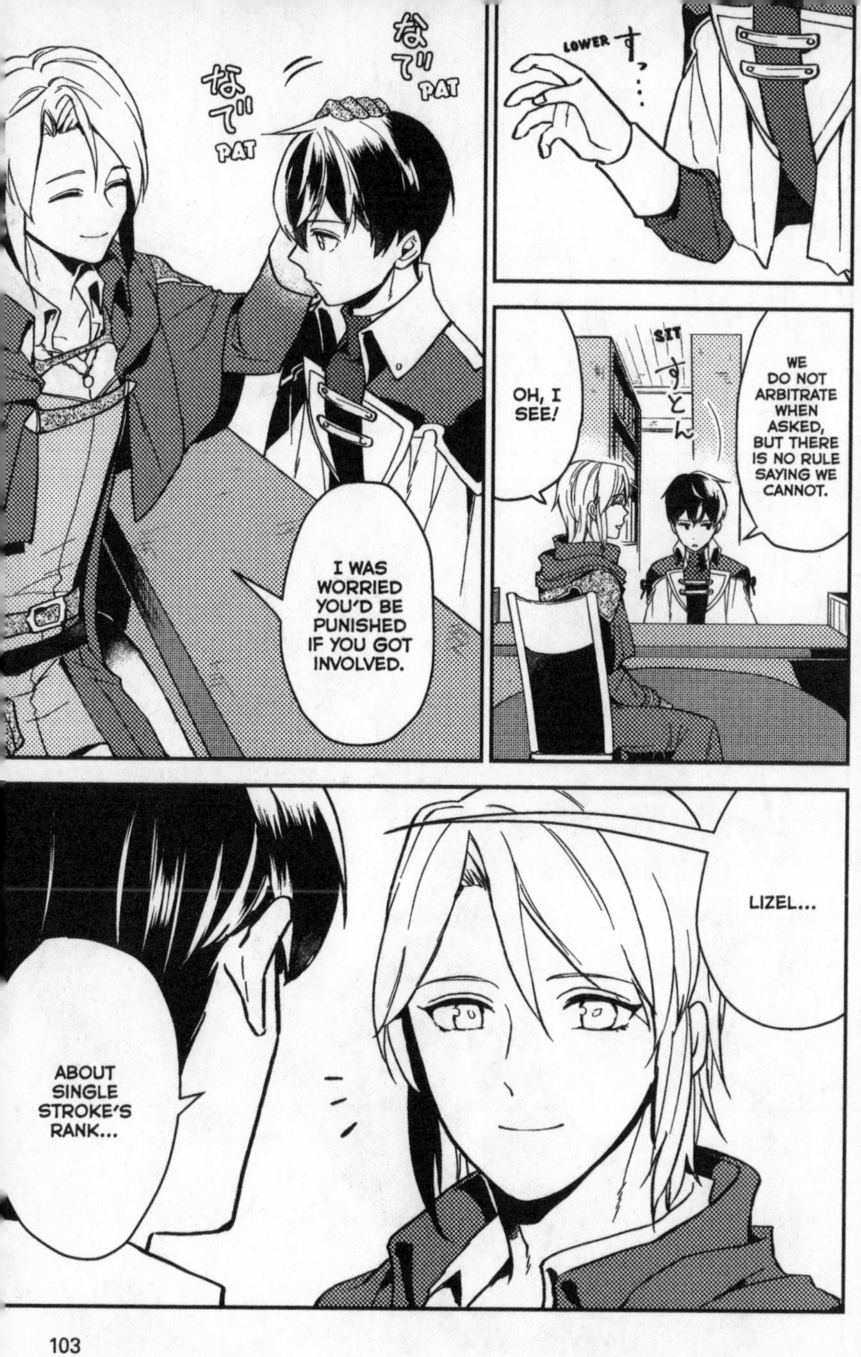

LOWER すっ…
WE DO NOT ARBITRATE WHEN ASKED, BUT THERE IS NO RULE SAYING WE CANNOT.
すとん SIT
OH, I SEE!
なでなで PAT PAT
I WAS WORRIED YOU'D BE PUNISHED IF YOU GOT INVOLVED.
LIZEL...
ABOUT SINGLE STROKE'S RANK...

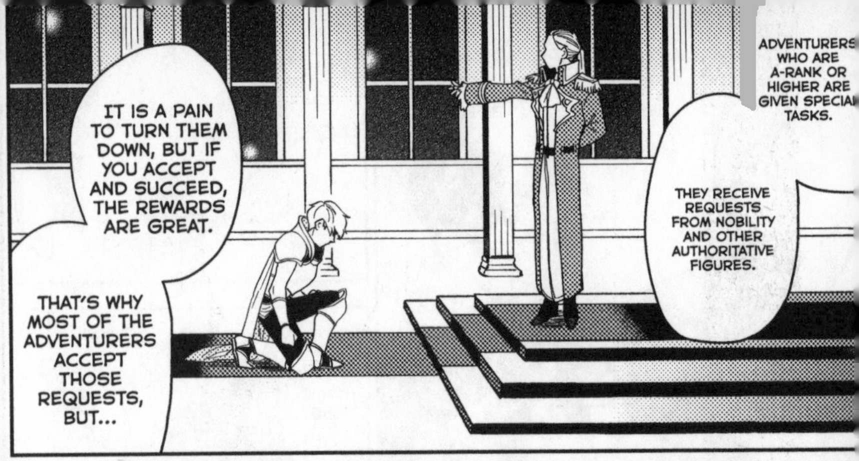
ADVENTURERS WHO ARE A-RANK OR HIGHER ARE GIVEN SPECIAL TASKS.
THEY RECEIVE REQUESTS FROM NOBILITY AND OTHER AUTHORITATIVE FIGURES.
IT IS A PAIN TO TURN THEM DOWN, BUT IF YOU ACCEPT AND SUCCEED, THE REWARDS ARE GREAT.
THAT'S WHY MOST OF THE ADVENTURERS ACCEPT THOSE REQUESTS, BUT...
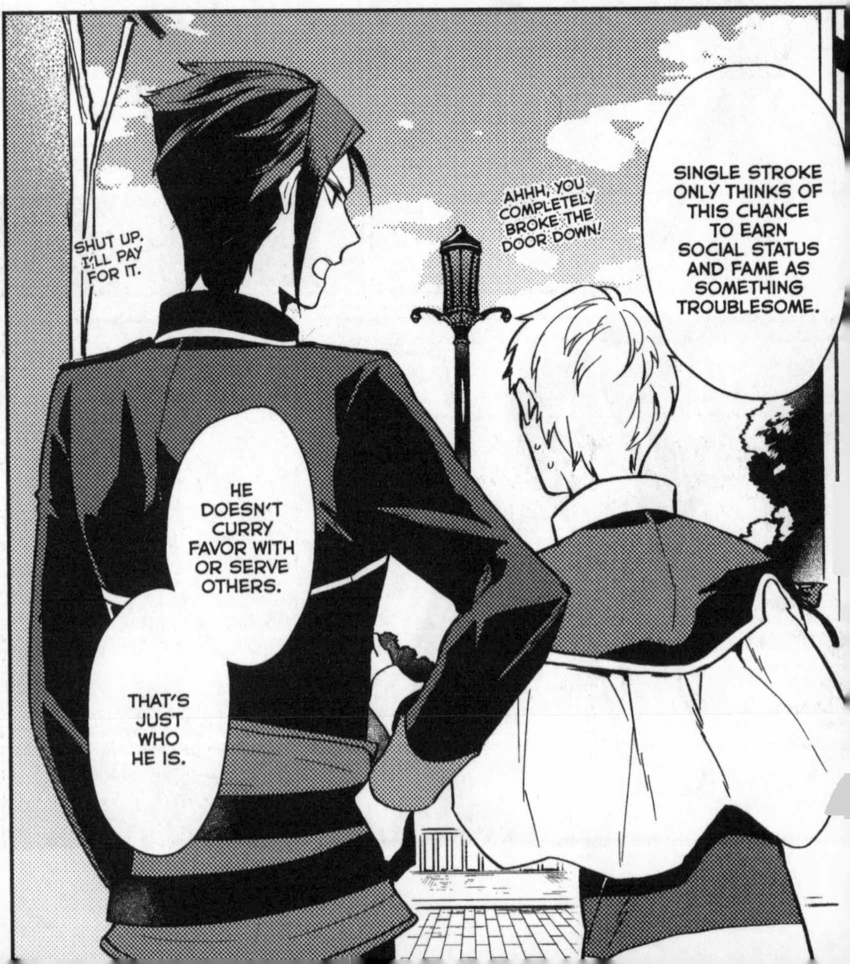
SINGLE STROKE ONLY THINKS OF THIS CHANCE TO EARN SOCIAL STATUS AND FAME AS SOMETHING TROUBLESOME.
AHHH, YOU COMPLETELY BROKE THE DOOR DOWN!
SHUT UP. I'LL PAY FOR IT.
HE DOESN'T CURRY FAVOR WITH OR SERVE OTHERS.
THAT'S JUST WHO HE IS.

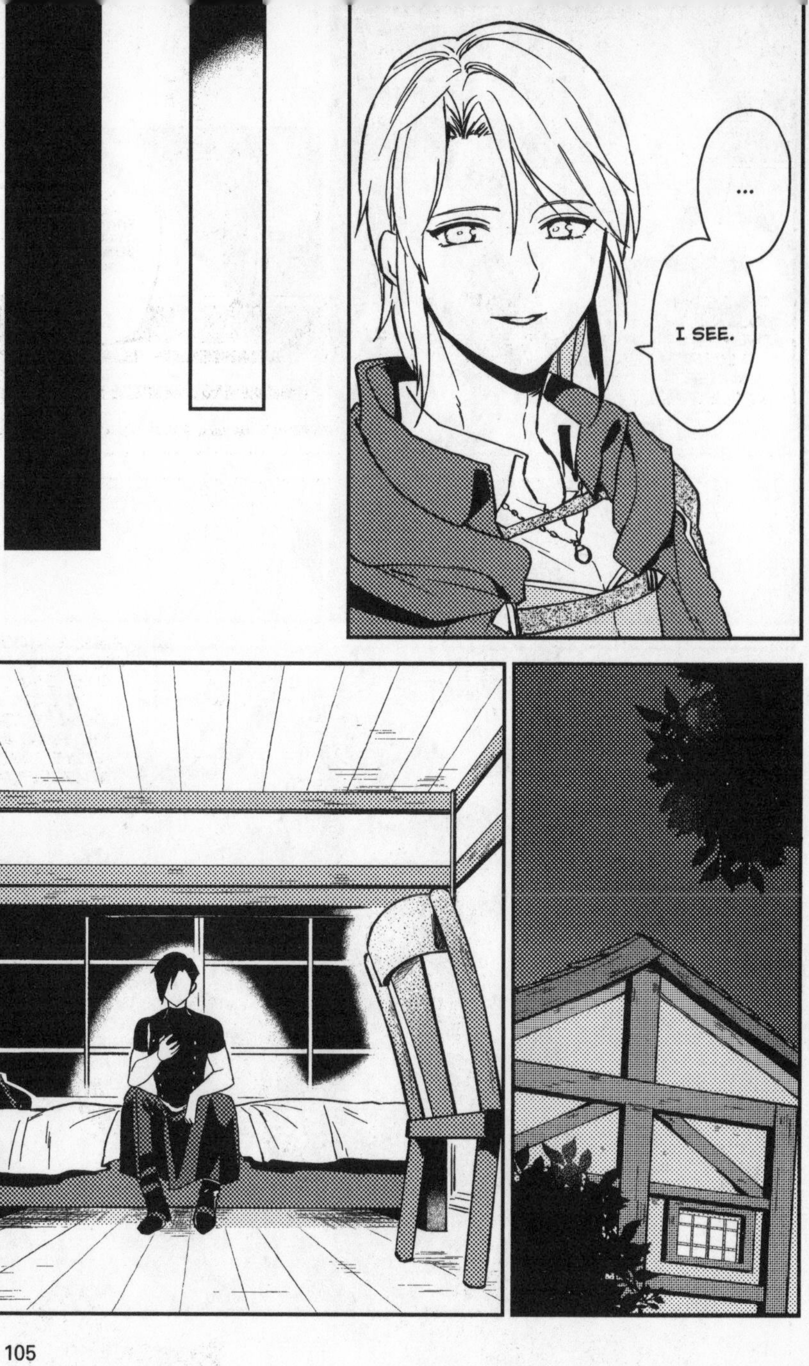
...
I SEE.

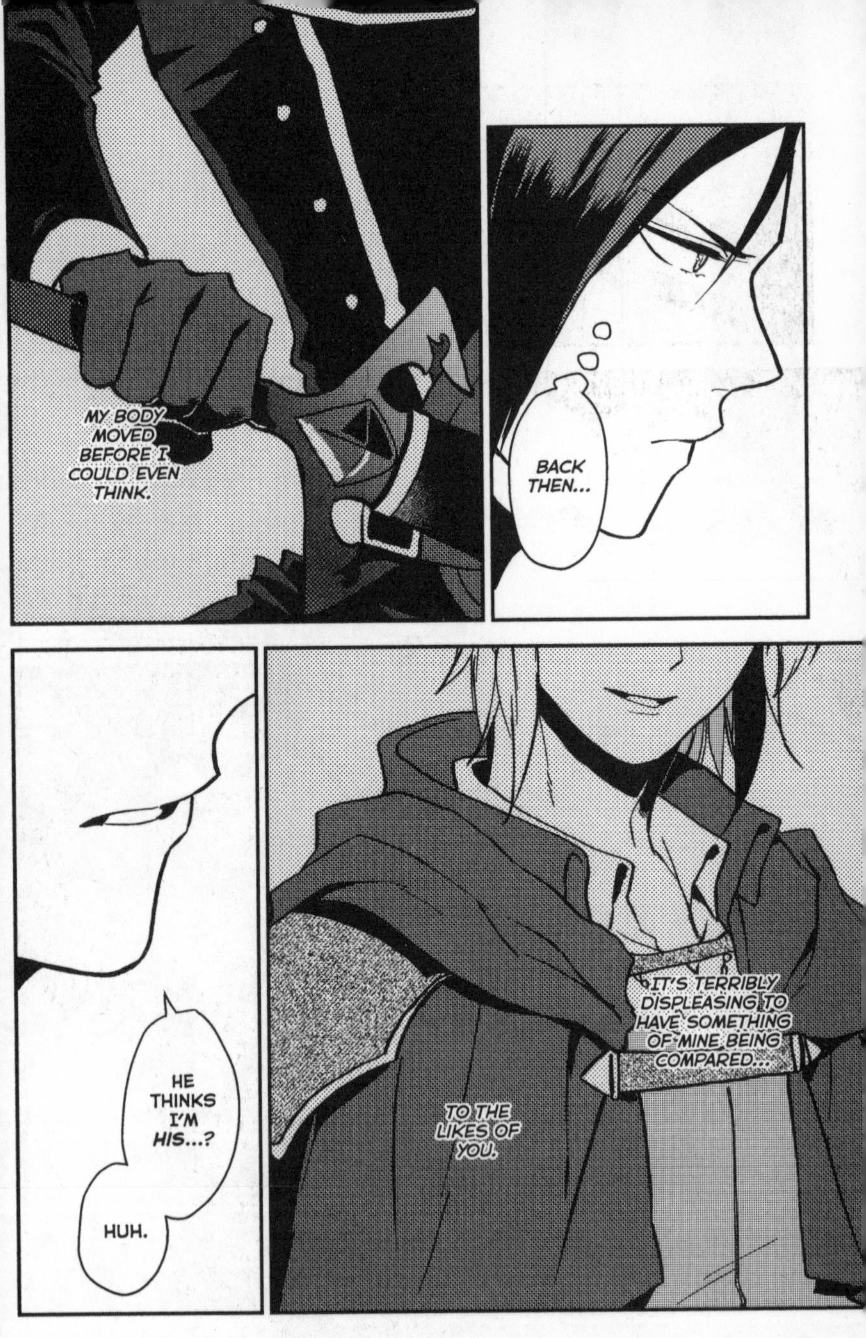
BACK THEN...
MY BODY MOVED BEFORE I COULD EVEN THINK.
IT'S TERRIBLY DISPLEASING TO HAVE SOMETHING OF MINE BEING COMPARED...
TO THE LIKES OF YOU.
HE THINKS I'M *HIS*...?
HUH.

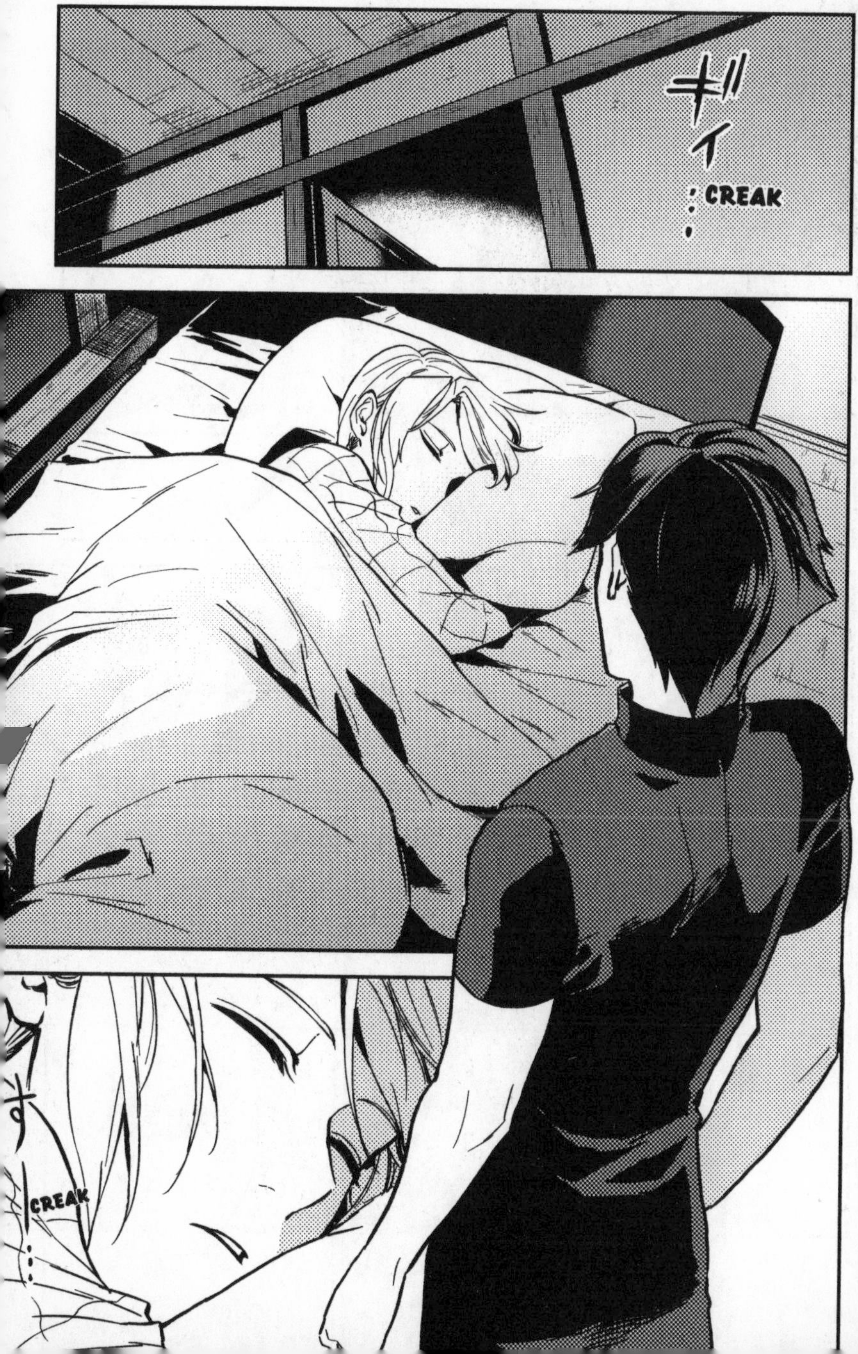
ギィ…
CREAK
CREAK

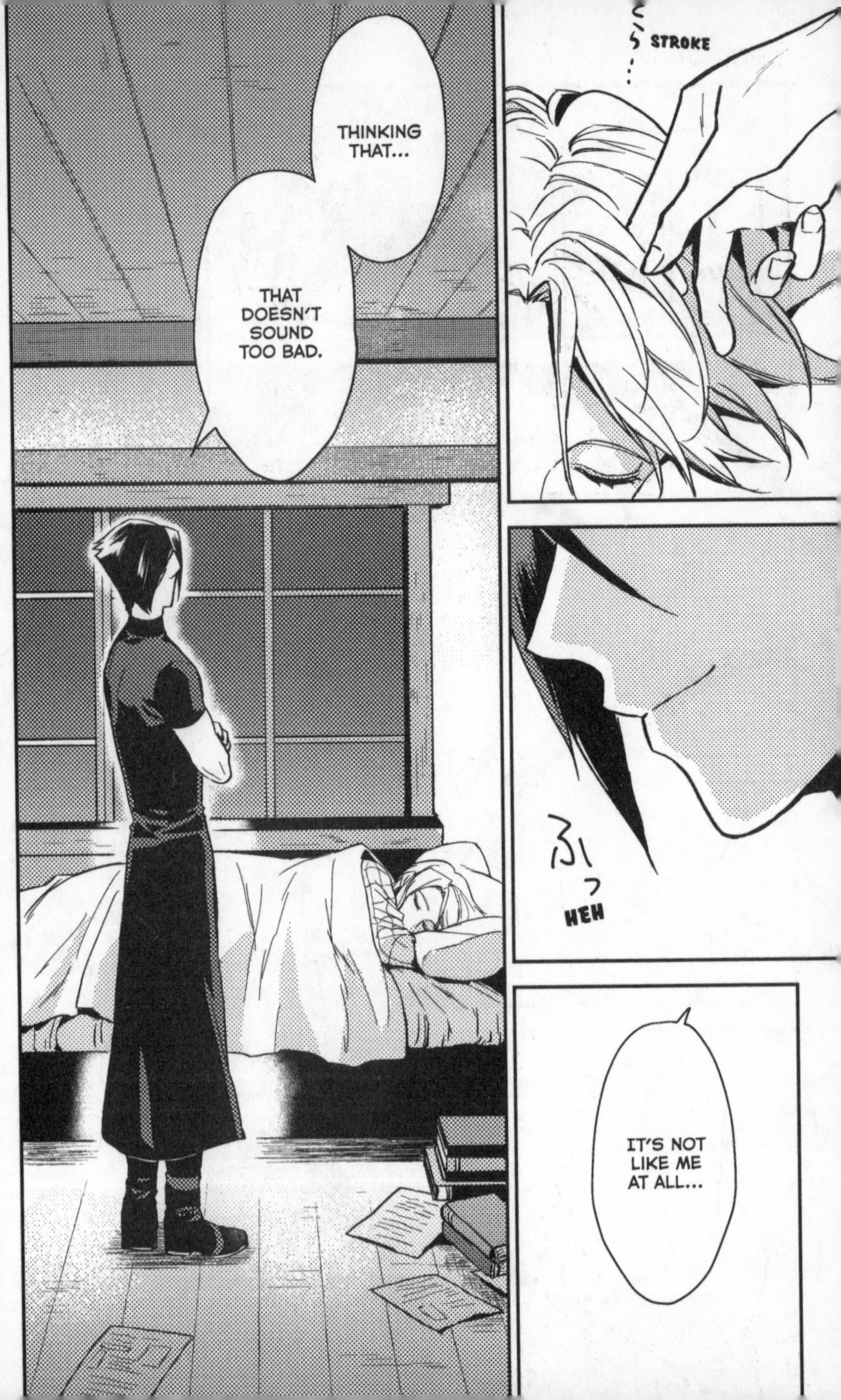
STROKE
ふっ
HEH
IT'S NOT LIKE ME AT ALL...
THINKING THAT...
THAT DOESN'T SOUND TOO BAD.

Chapter 4

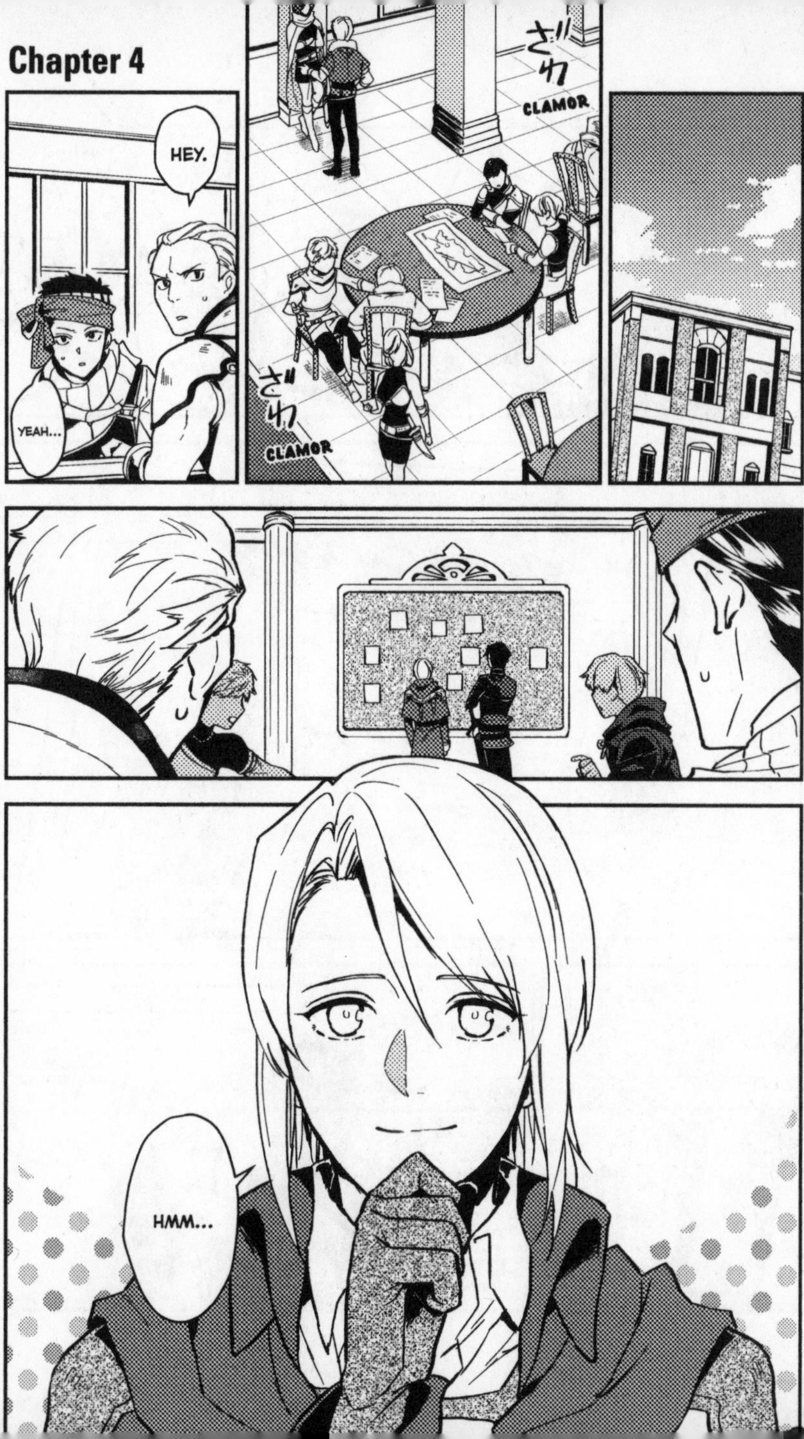
ざわ
CLAMOR
ざわ
CLAMOR
HEY.
YEAH...
HMM...

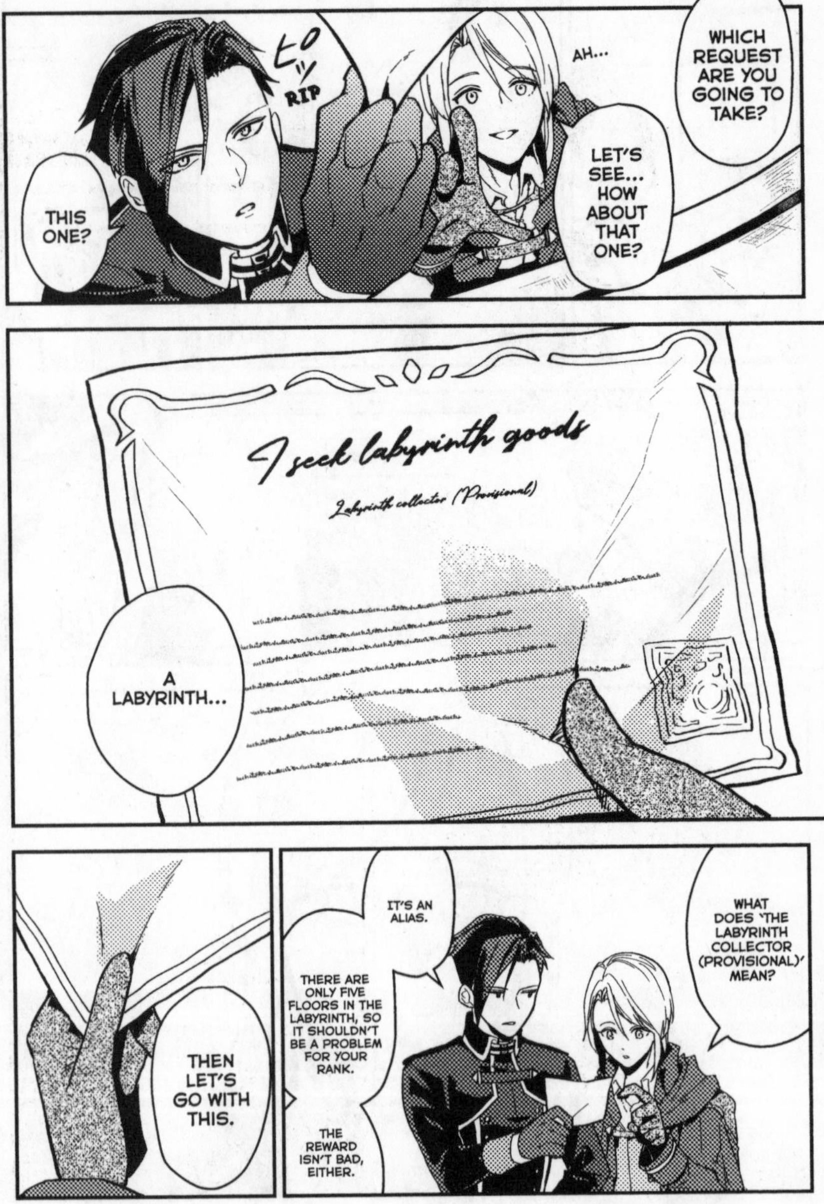
WHICH REQUEST ARE YOU GOING TO TAKE?
AH...
LET'S SEE... HOW ABOUT THAT ONE?
RIP
THIS ONE?
I seek labyrinth goods
Labyrinth collector (Provisional)
A LABYRINTH...
WHAT DOES 'THE LABYRINTH COLLECTOR (PROVISIONAL)' MEAN?
IT'S AN ALIAS.
THERE ARE ONLY FIVE FLOORS IN THE LABYRINTH, SO IT SHOULDN'T BE A PROBLEM FOR YOUR RANK.
THE REWARD ISN'T BAD, EITHER.
THEN LET'S GO WITH THIS.

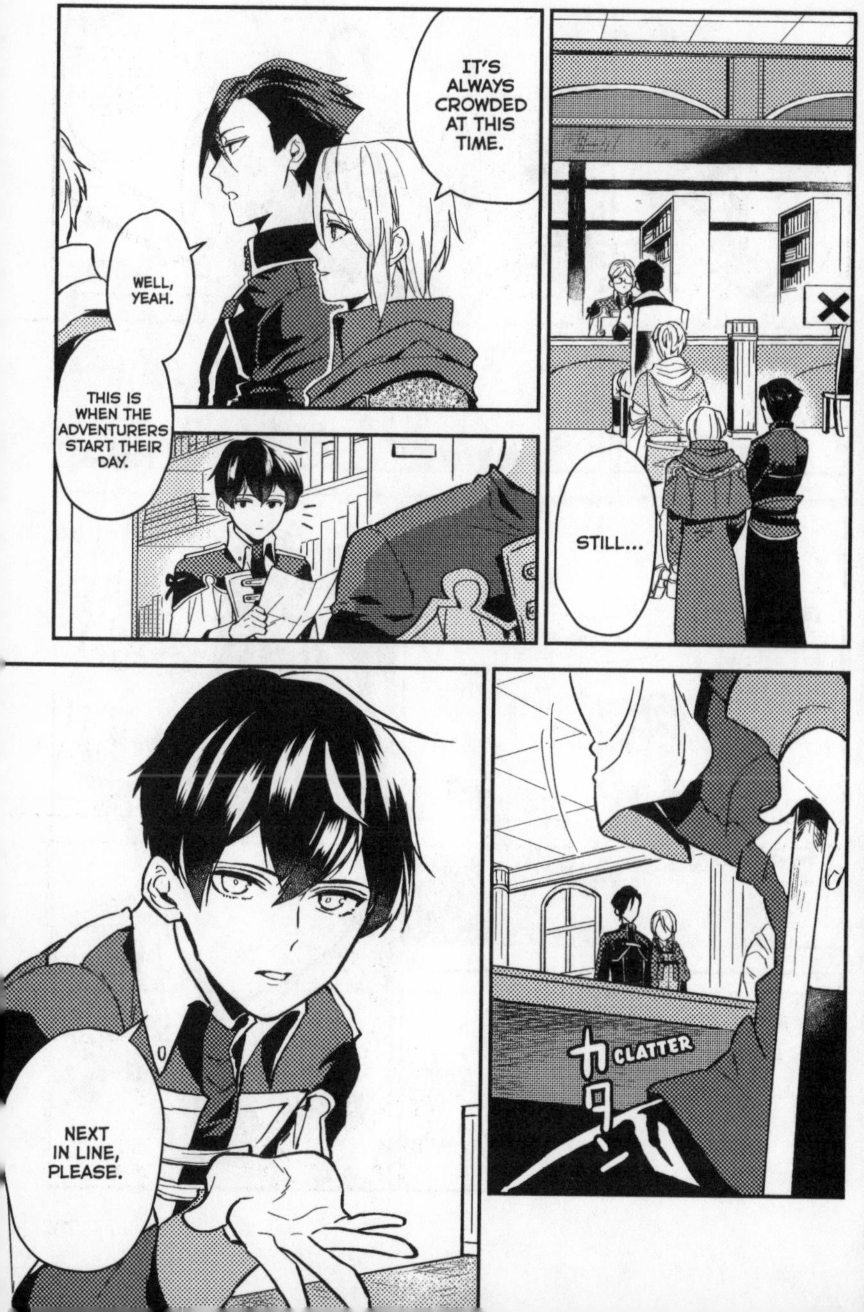
STILL...
IT'S ALWAYS CROWDED AT THIS TIME.
WELL, YEAH.
THIS IS WHEN THE ADVENTURERS START THEIR DAY.
カタン
CLATTER
NEXT IN LINE, PLEASE.

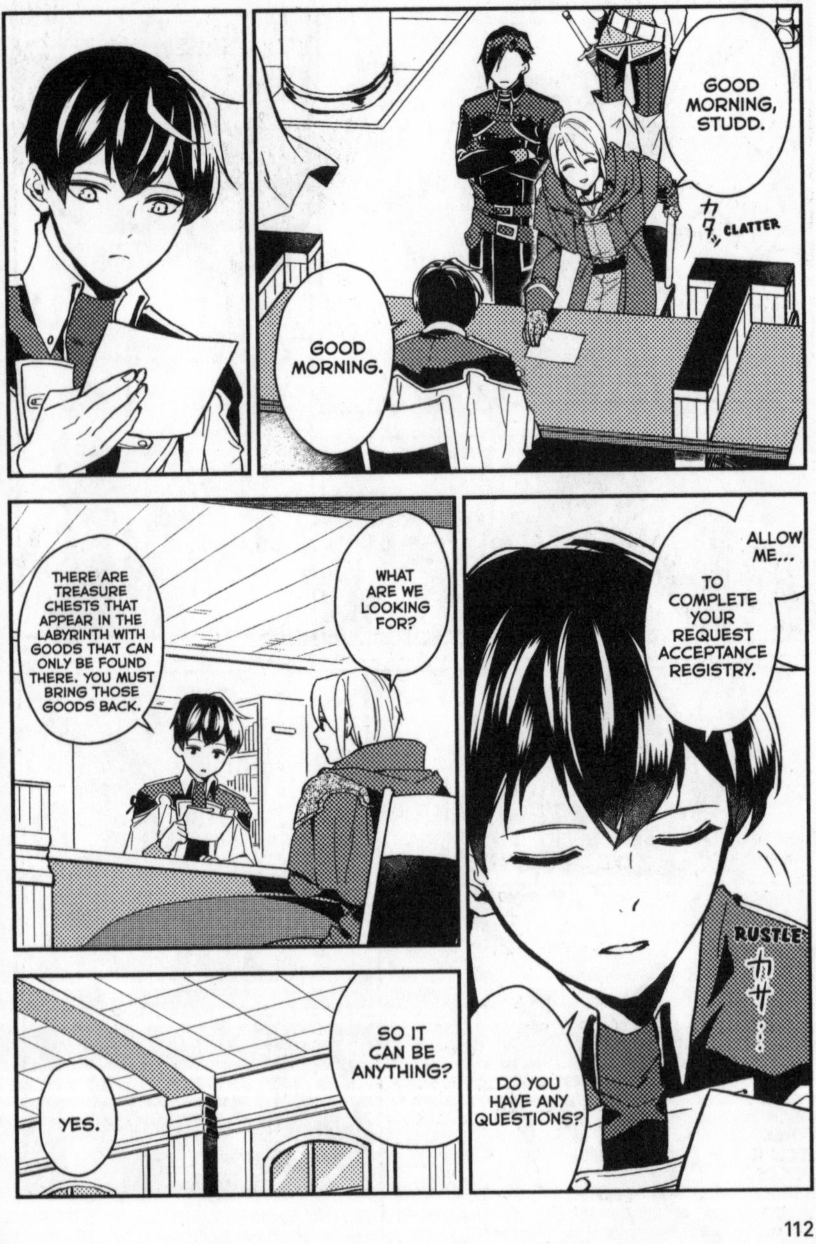
GOOD MORNING, STUDD.
カタッ
CLATTER
GOOD MORNING.
ALLOW ME...
TO COMPLETE YOUR REQUEST ACCEPTANCE REGISTRY.
RUSTLE
カサ…
DO YOU HAVE ANY QUESTIONS?
WHAT ARE WE LOOKING FOR?
THERE ARE TREASURE CHESTS THAT APPEAR IN THE LABYRINTH WITH GOODS THAT CAN ONLY BE FOUND THERE. YOU MUST BRING THOSE GOODS BACK.
SO IT CAN BE ANYTHING?
YES.

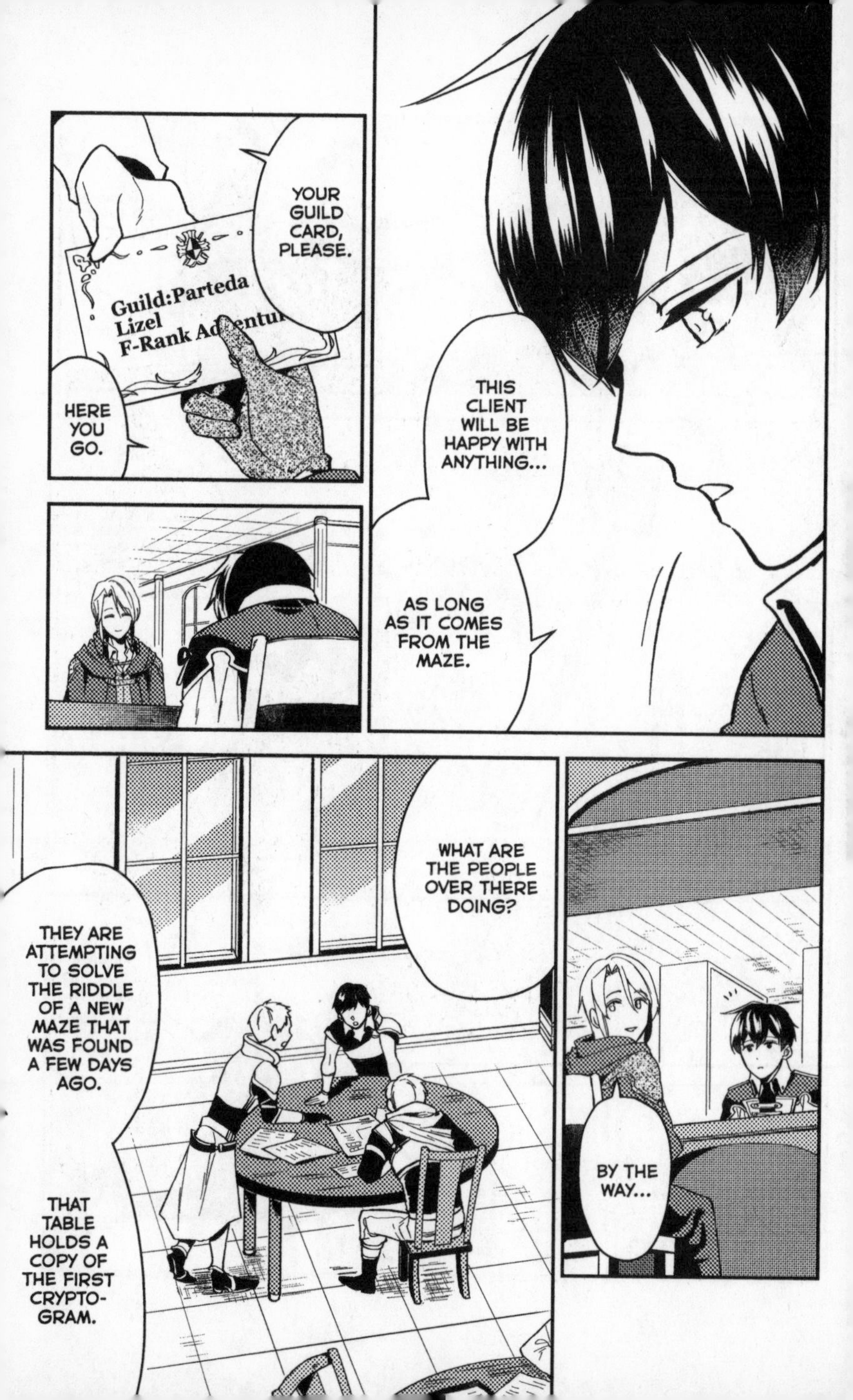
THIS CLIENT WILL BE HAPPY WITH ANYTHING...
AS LONG AS IT COMES FROM THE MAZE.
YOUR GUILD CARD, PLEASE.
Guild:Parteda
Lizel
F-Rank
HERE YOU GO.
BY THE WAY...
WHAT ARE THE PEOPLE OVER THERE DOING?
THEY ARE ATTEMPTING TO SOLVE THE RIDDLE OF A NEW MAZE THAT WAS FOUND A FEW DAYS AGO.
THAT TABLE HOLDS A COPY OF THE FIRST CRYPTO-GRAM.

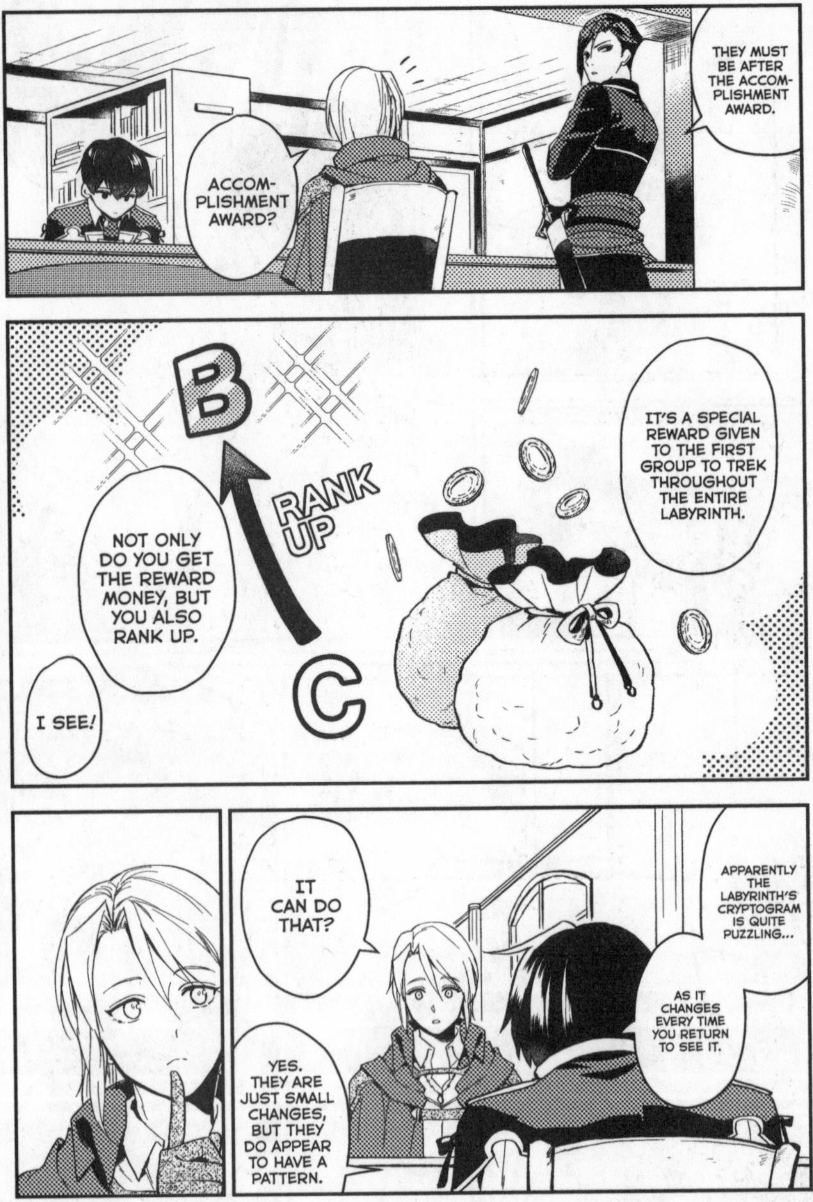
THEY MUST BE AFTER THE ACCOMPLISHMENT AWARD.
ACCOMPLISHMENT AWARD?
IT'S A SPECIAL REWARD GIVEN TO THE FIRST GROUP TO TREK THROUGHOUT THE ENTIRE LABYRINTH.
B
RANK UP
C
NOT ONLY DO YOU GET THE REWARD MONEY, BUT YOU ALSO RANK UP.
I SEE!
APPARENTLY THE LABYRINTH'S CRYPTOGRAM IS QUITE PUZZLING...
AS IT CHANGES EVERY TIME YOU RETURN TO SEE IT.
IT CAN DO THAT?
YES. THEY ARE JUST SMALL CHANGES, BUT THEY DO APPEAR TO HAVE A PATTERN.

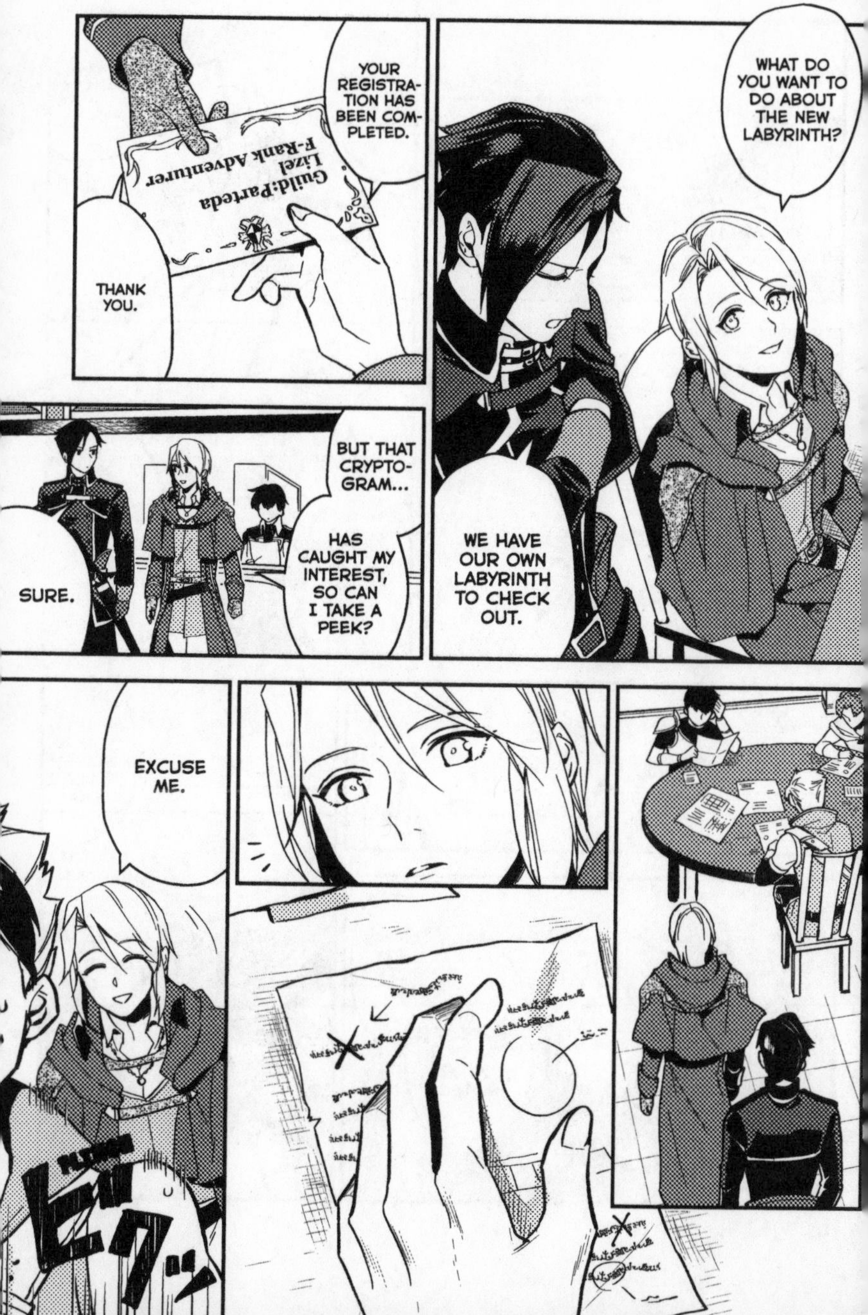
WHAT DO YOU WANT TO DO ABOUT THE NEW LABYRINTH?
WE HAVE OUR OWN LABYRINTH TO CHECK OUT.
YOUR REGISTRATION HAS BEEN COMPLETED.
Guild:Parteda
Lizel
F-Rank Adventurer
THANK YOU.
BUT THAT CRYPTOGRAM...
HAS CAUGHT MY INTEREST, SO CAN I TAKE A PEEK?
SURE.
EXCUSE ME.

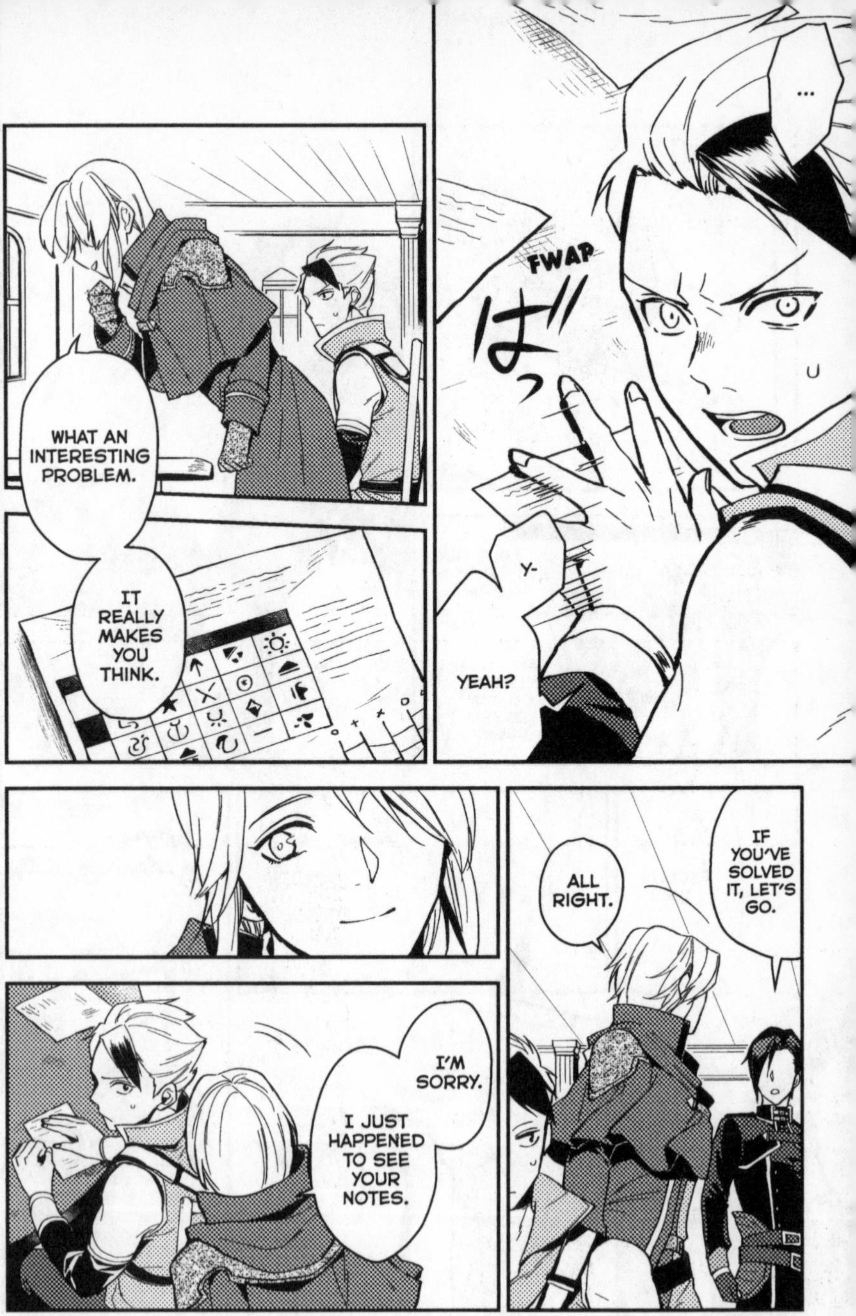
...
FWAP
ばっ
Y-
YEAH?
WHAT AN INTERESTING PROBLEM.
IT REALLY MAKES YOU THINK.
IF YOU'VE SOLVED IT, LET'S GO.
ALL RIGHT.
I'M SORRY.
I JUST HAPPENED TO SEE YOUR NOTES.

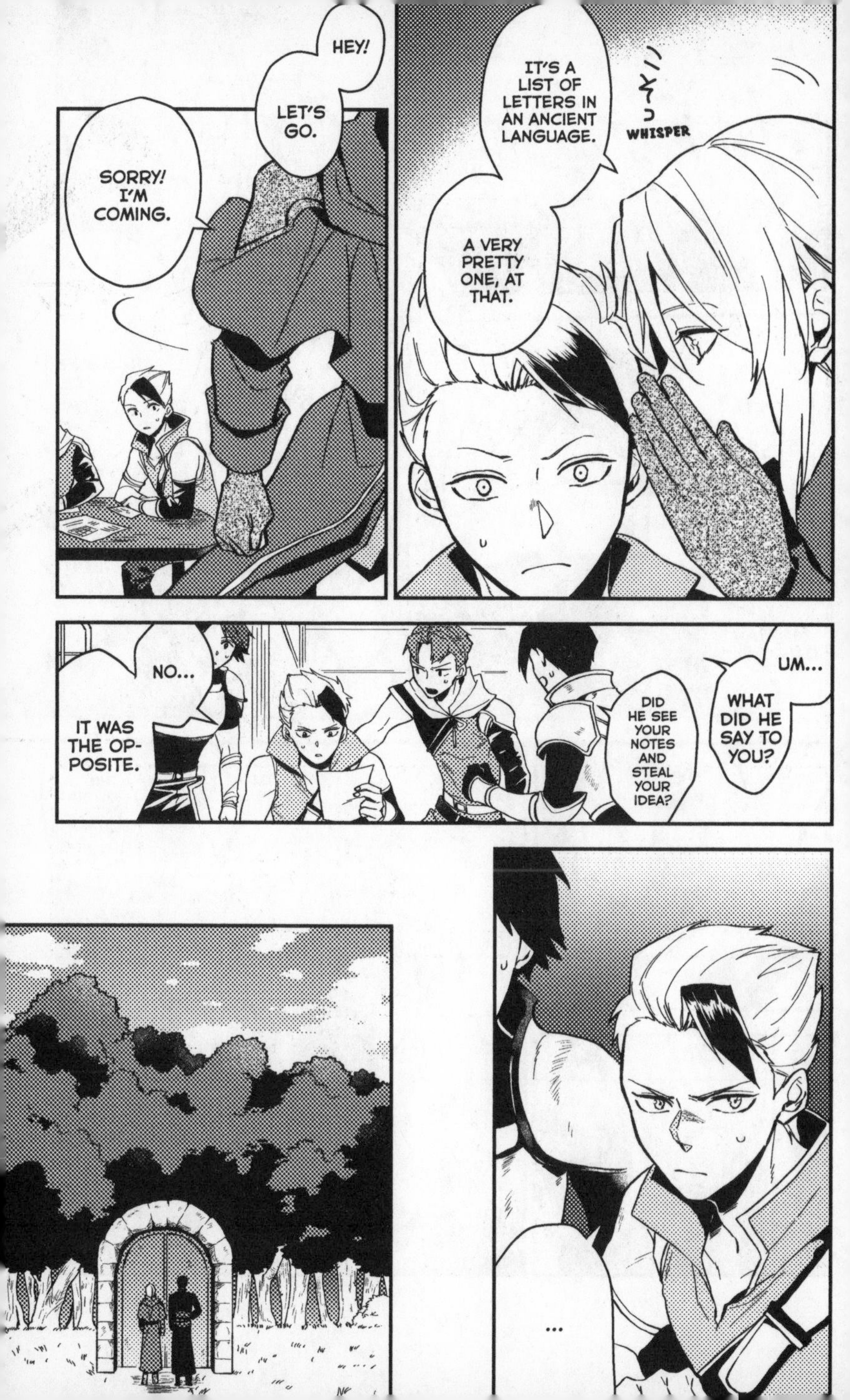
IT'S A LIST OF LETTERS IN AN ANCIENT LANGUAGE.
こそっ
WHISPER
A VERY PRETTY ONE, AT THAT.
HEY!
LET'S GO.
SORRY! I'M COMING.
UM...
WHAT DID HE SAY TO YOU?
DID HE SEE YOUR NOTES AND STEAL YOUR IDEA?
NO...
IT WAS THE OP-POSITE.
...

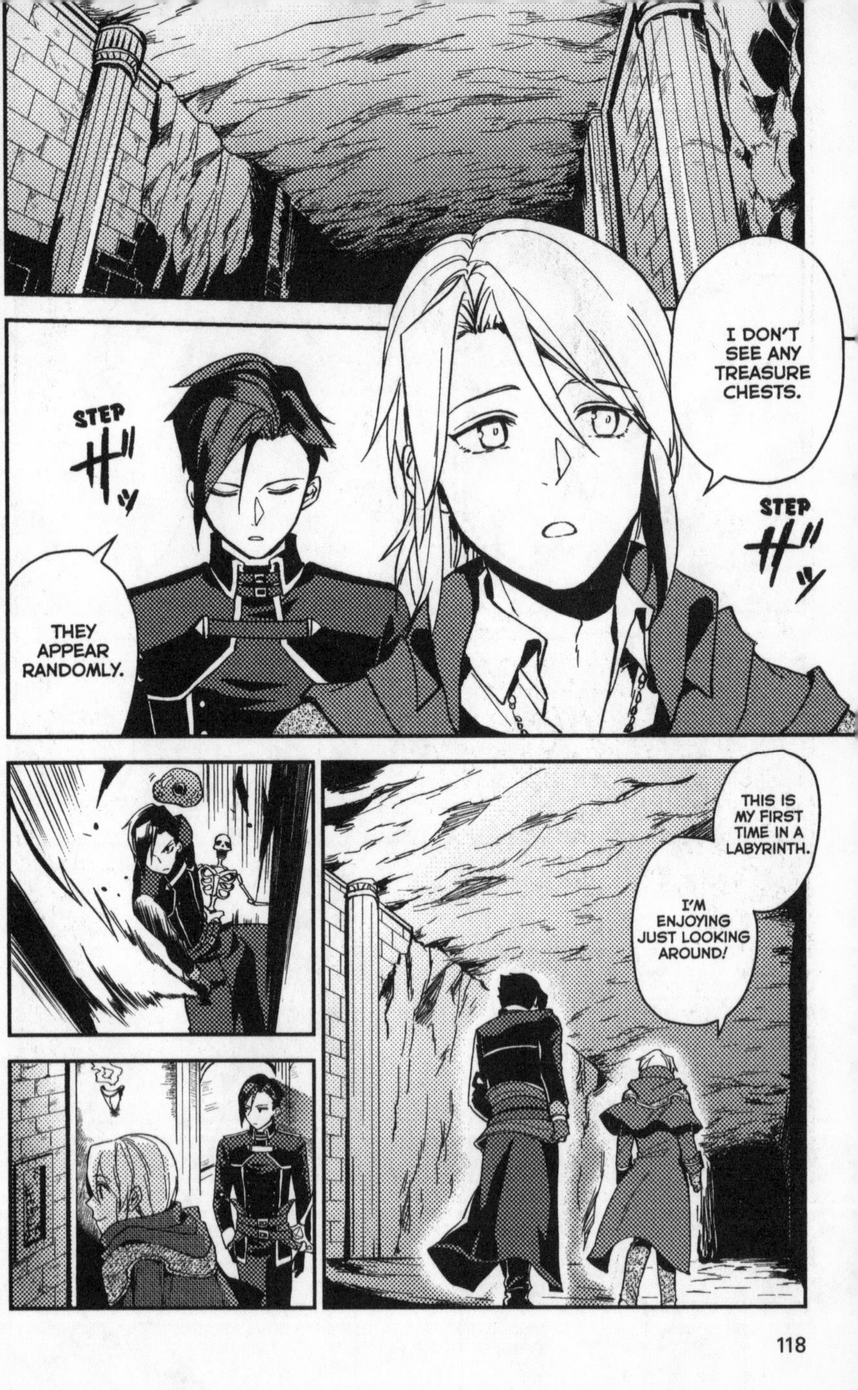
I DON'T SEE ANY TREASURE CHESTS.
STEP
STEP
THEY APPEAR RANDOMLY.
THIS IS MY FIRST TIME IN A LABYRINTH.
I'M ENJOYING JUST LOOKING AROUND!

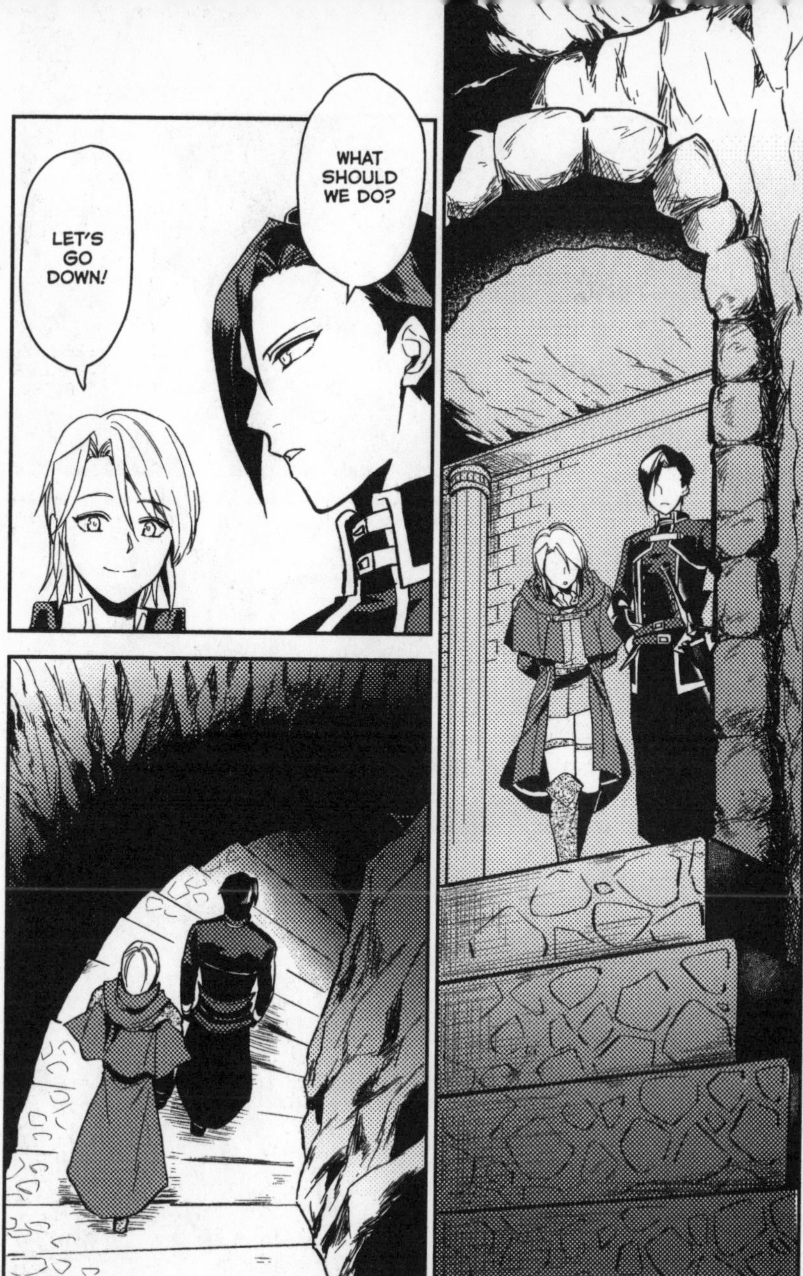
WHAT SHOULD WE DO?
LET'S GO DOWN!

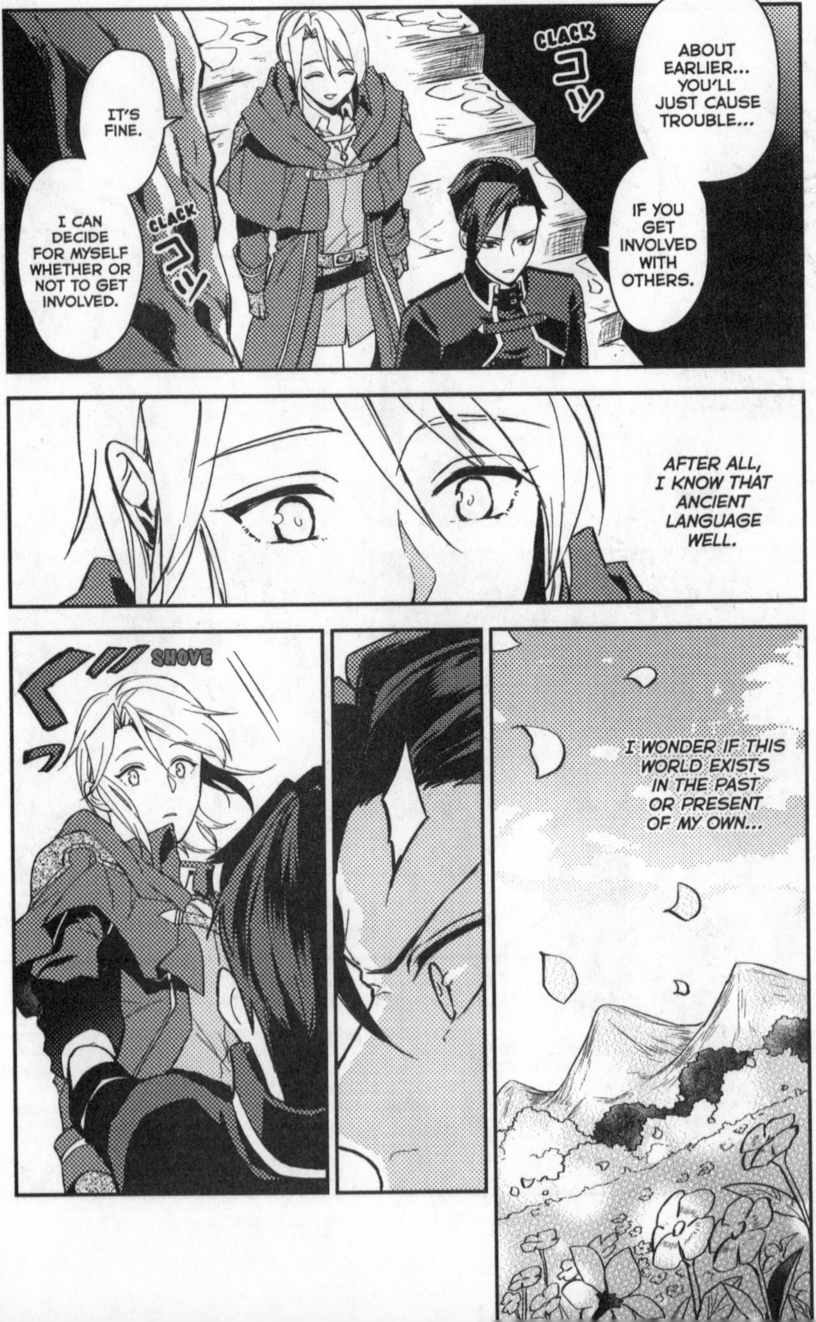
CLACK
コツ
ABOUT EARLIER... YOU'LL JUST CAUSE TROUBLE...
IF YOU GET INVOLVED WITH OTHERS.
IT'S FINE.
CLACK
コツ
I CAN DECIDE FOR MYSELF WHETHER OR NOT TO GET INVOLVED.
AFTER ALL, I KNOW THAT ANCIENT LANGUAGE WELL.
I WONDER IF THIS WORLD EXISTS IN THE PAST OR PRESENT OF MY OWN...
SHOVE

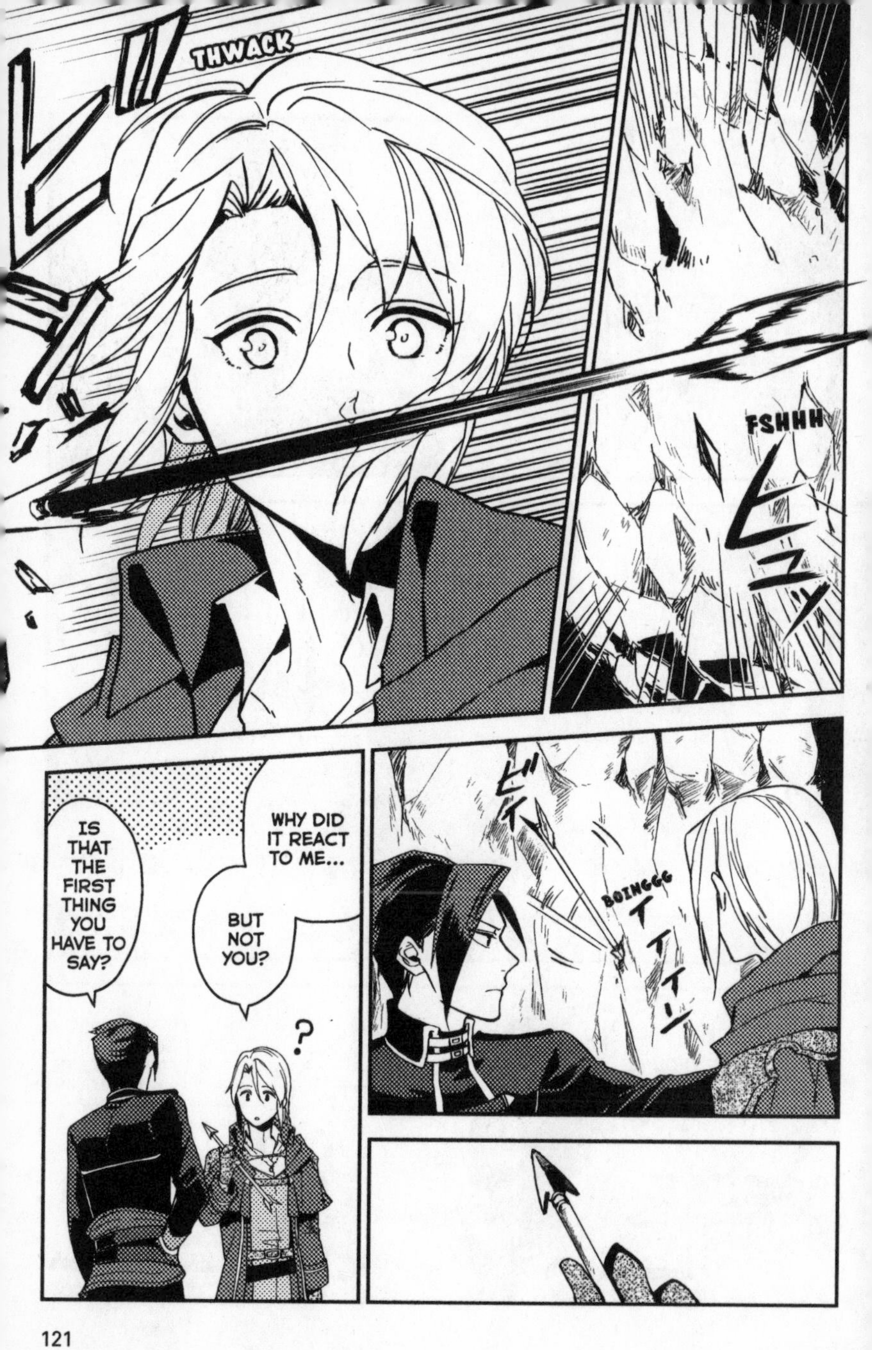

FSHHH
THWACK
BOINGGG
WHY DID IT REACT TO ME...
BUT NOT YOU?
IS THAT THE FIRST THING YOU HAVE TO SAY?
?

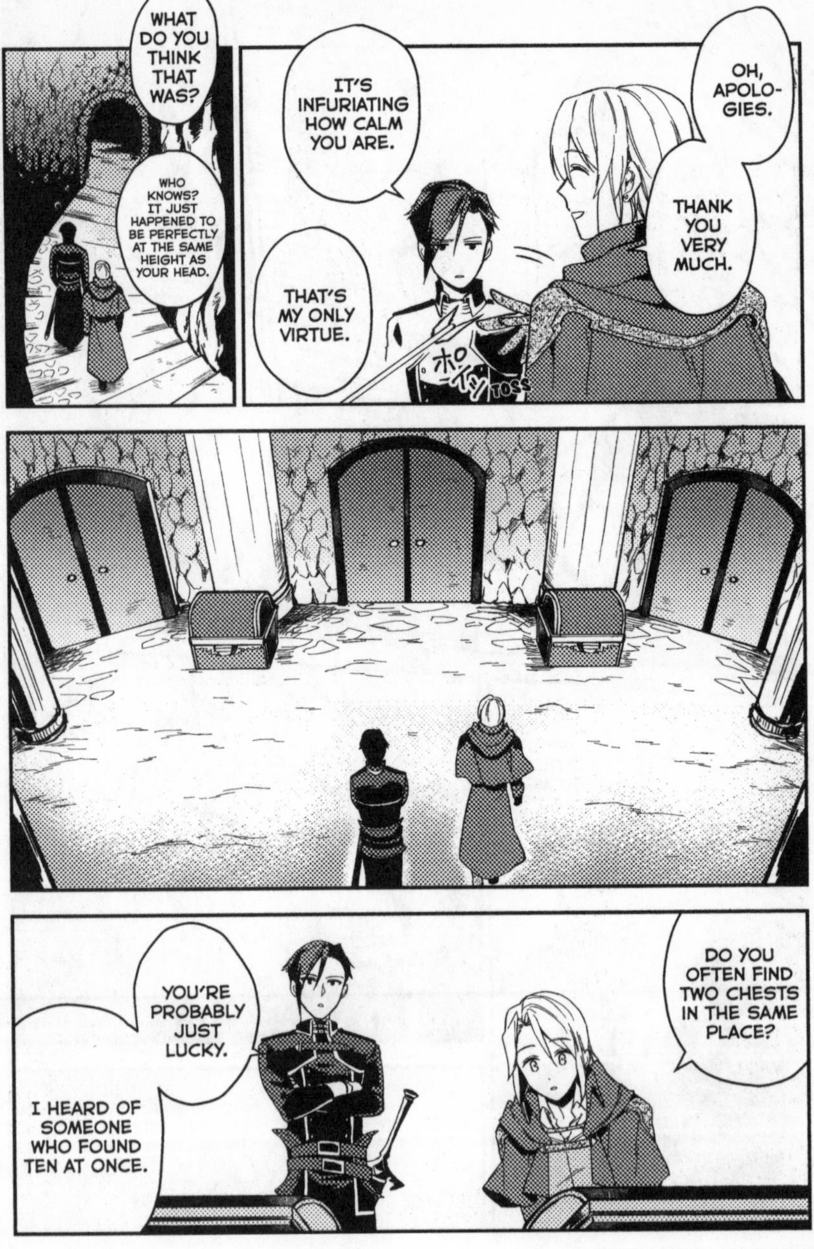
OH, APOLOGIES.
IT'S INFURIATING HOW CALM YOU ARE.
THANK YOU VERY MUCH.
THAT'S MY ONLY VIRTUE.
ホイッ TOSS
WHAT DO YOU THINK THAT WAS?
WHO KNOWS? IT JUST HAPPENED TO BE PERFECTLY AT THE SAME HEIGHT AS YOUR HEAD.
DO YOU OFTEN FIND TWO CHESTS IN THE SAME PLACE?
YOU'RE PROBABLY JUST LUCKY.
I HEARD OF SOMEONE WHO FOUND TEN AT ONCE.

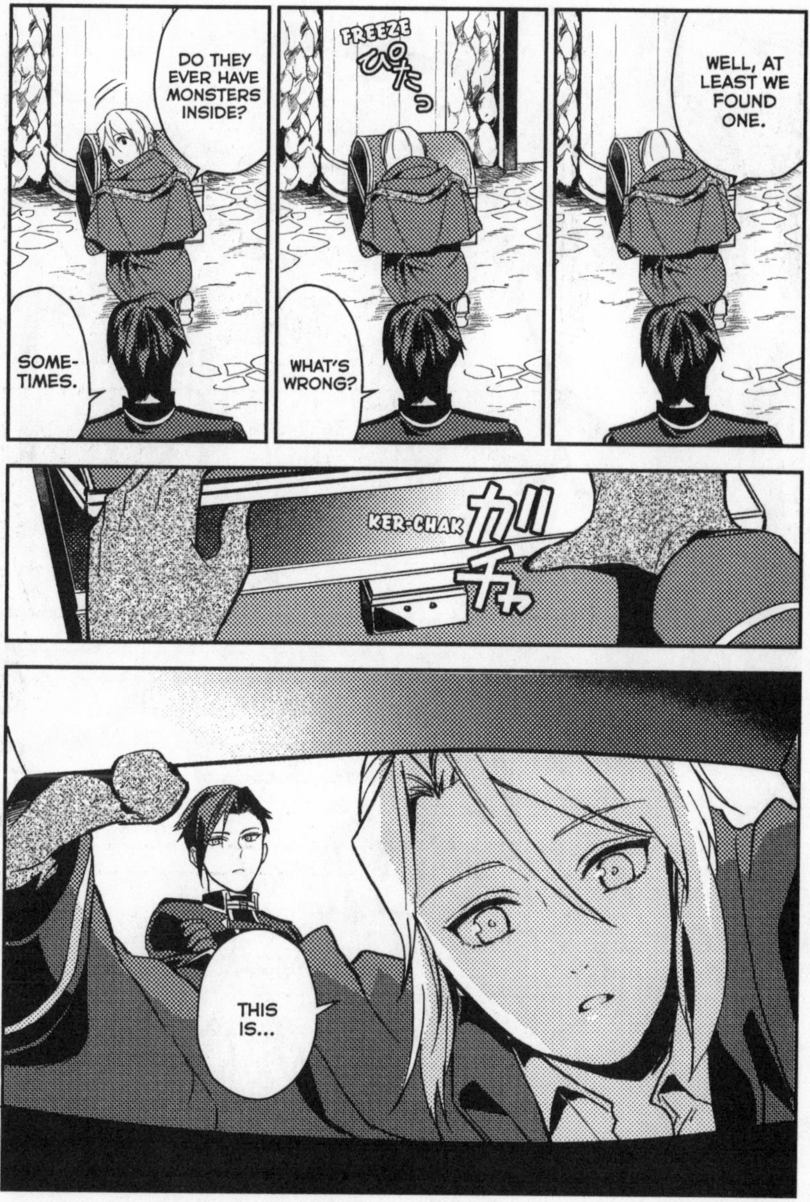
WELL, AT LEAST WE FOUND ONE.
FREEZE
ぴたっ
WHAT'S WRONG?
DO THEY EVER HAVE MONSTERS INSIDE?
SOME-TIMES.
KER-CHAK
THIS IS...

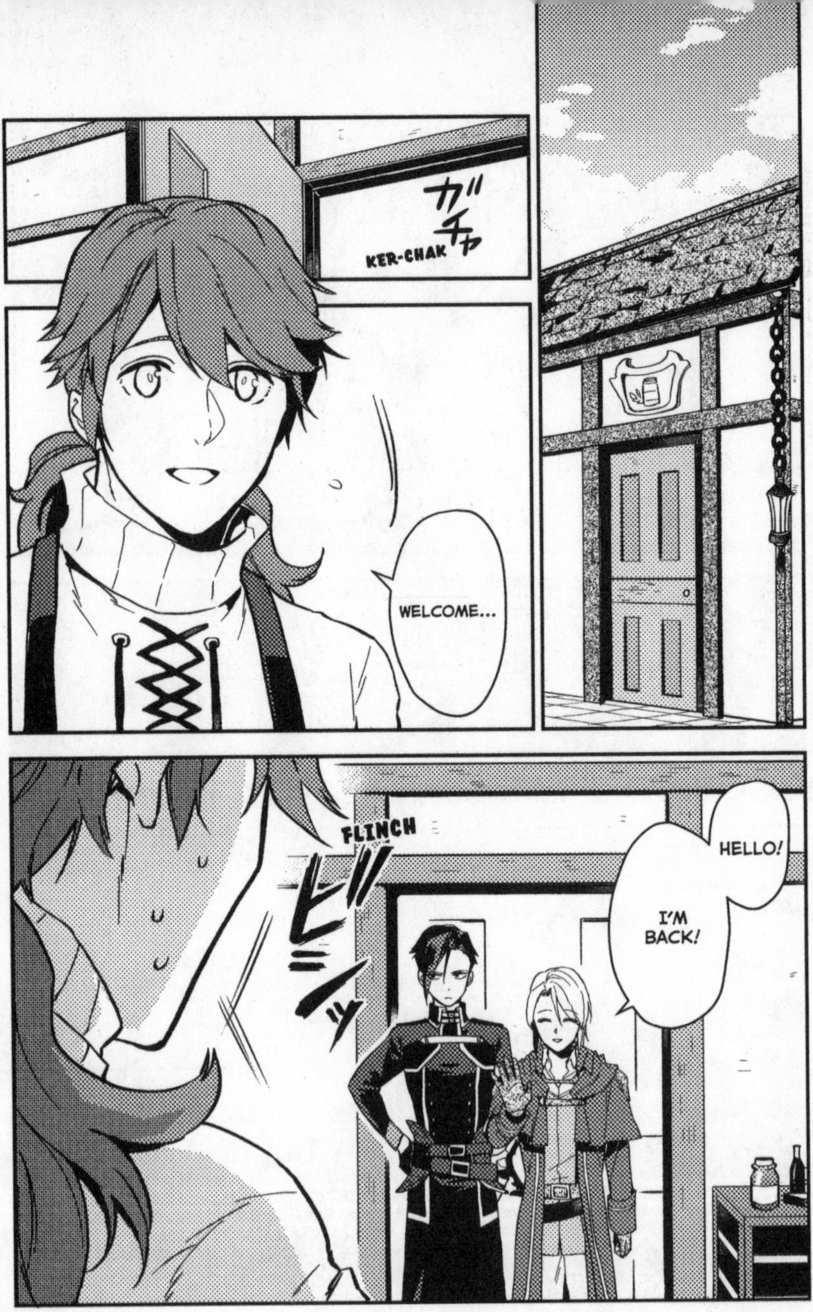
ガチャ
KER-CHAK
WELCOME...
HELLO!
I'M BACK!
FLINCH

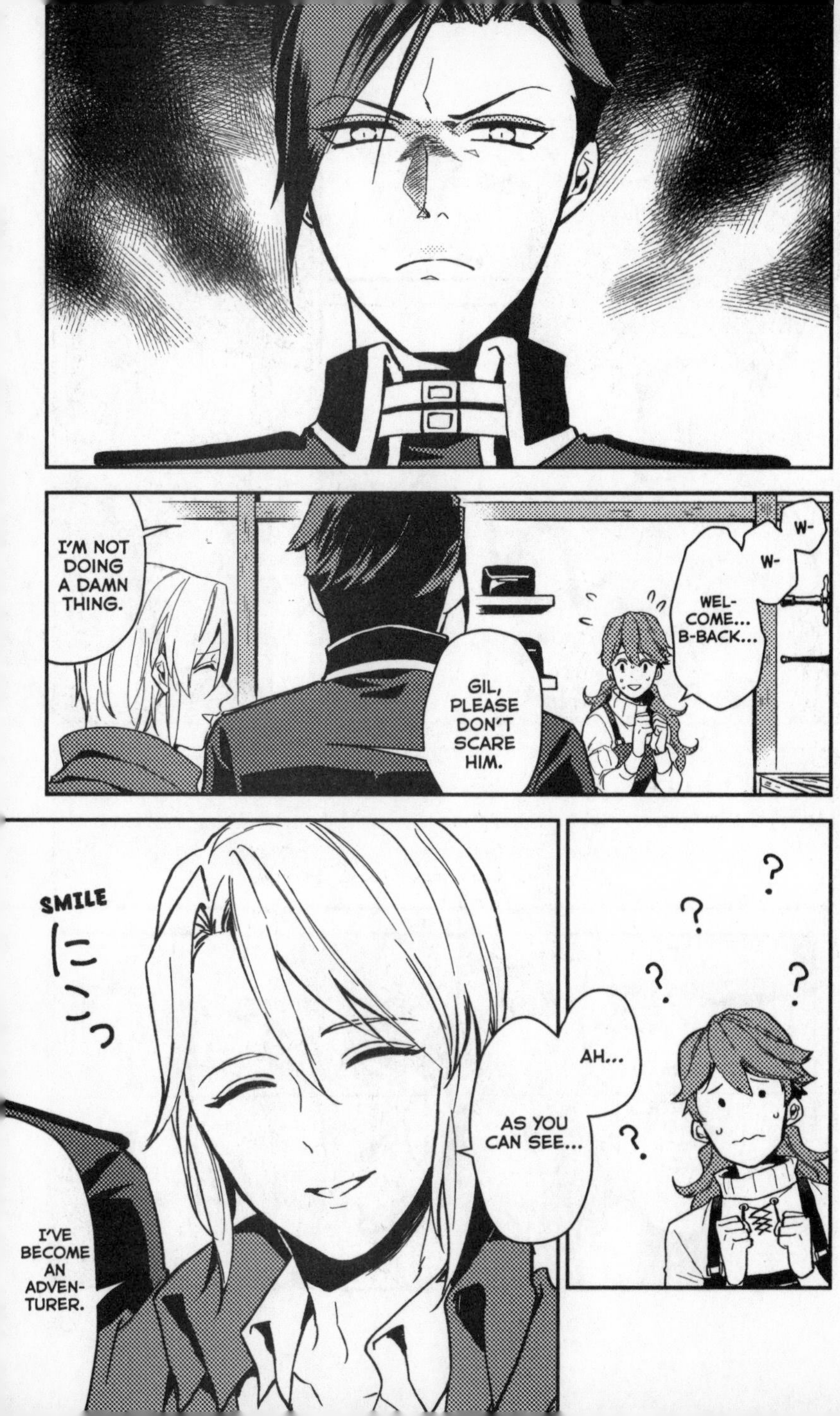
W- W- WELCOME... B-BACK...
GIL, PLEASE DON'T SCARE HIM.
I'M NOT DOING A DAMN THING.
? ? ? ? ?
AH... AS YOU CAN SEE...
SMILE
にこっ
I'VE BECOME AN ADVENTURER.

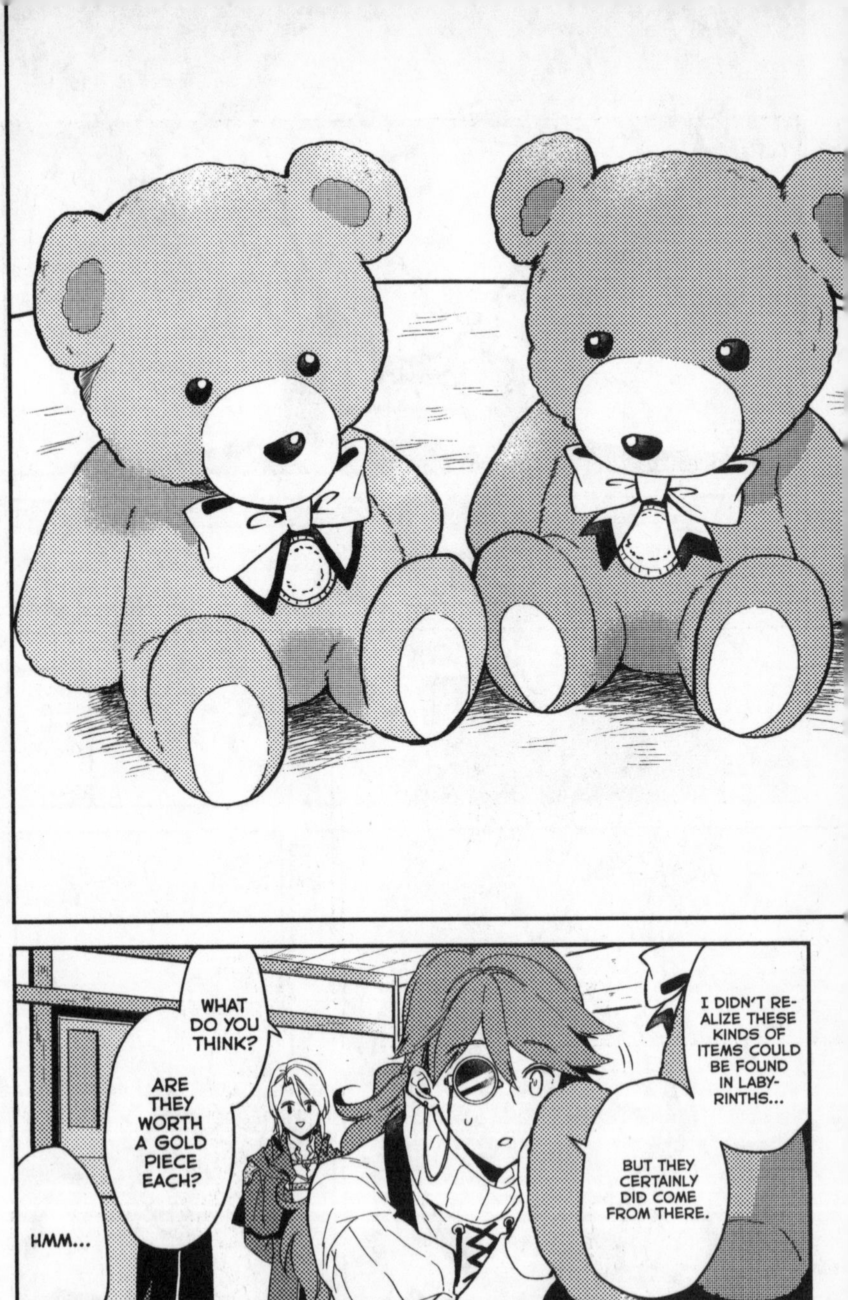
I DIDN'T RE-ALIZE THESE KINDS OF ITEMS COULD BE FOUND IN LABY-RINTHS...
BUT THEY CERTAINLY DID COME FROM THERE.
WHAT DO YOU THINK?
ARE THEY WORTH A GOLD PIECE EACH?
HMM...

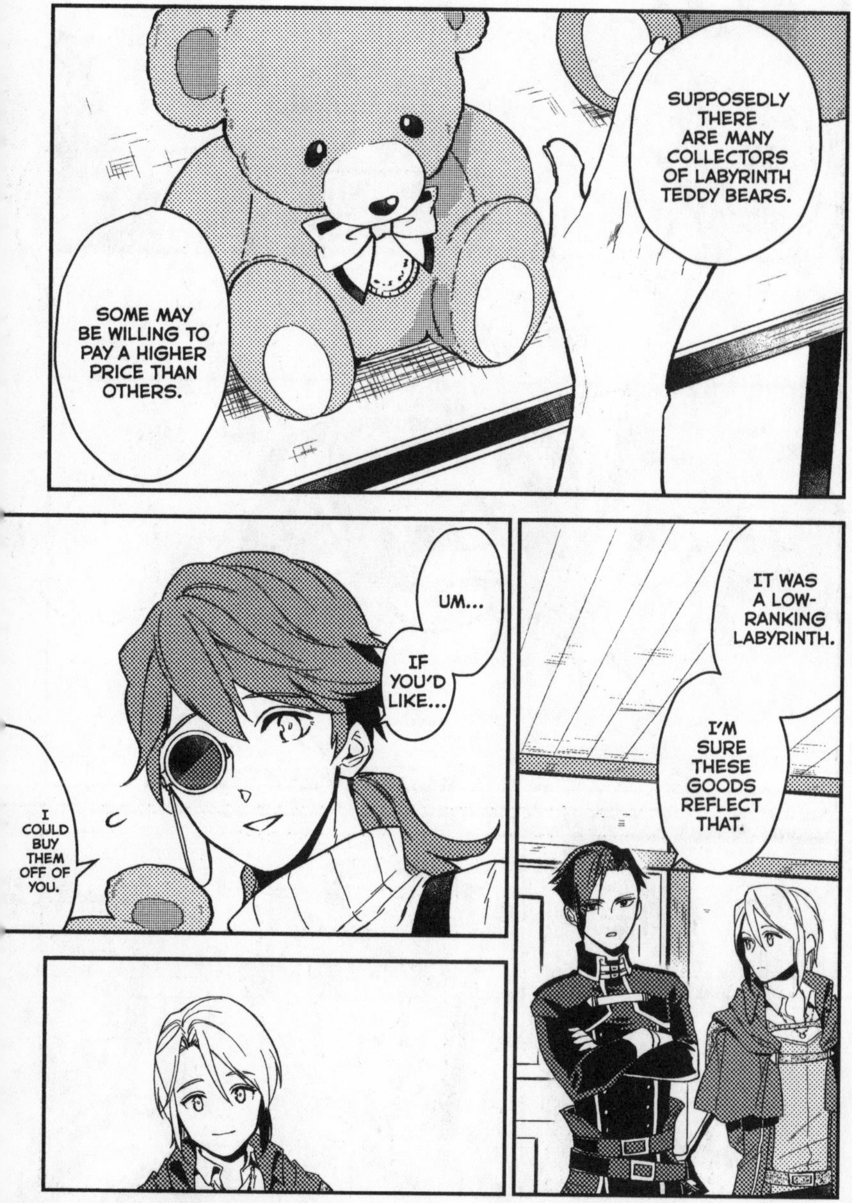
SUPPOSEDLY THERE ARE MANY COLLECTORS OF LABYRINTH TEDDY BEARS.
SOME MAY BE WILLING TO PAY A HIGHER PRICE THAN OTHERS.
IT WAS A LOW-RANKING LABYRINTH.
I'M SURE THESE GOODS REFLECT THAT.
UM...
IF YOU'D LIKE...
I COULD BUY THEM OFF OF YOU.

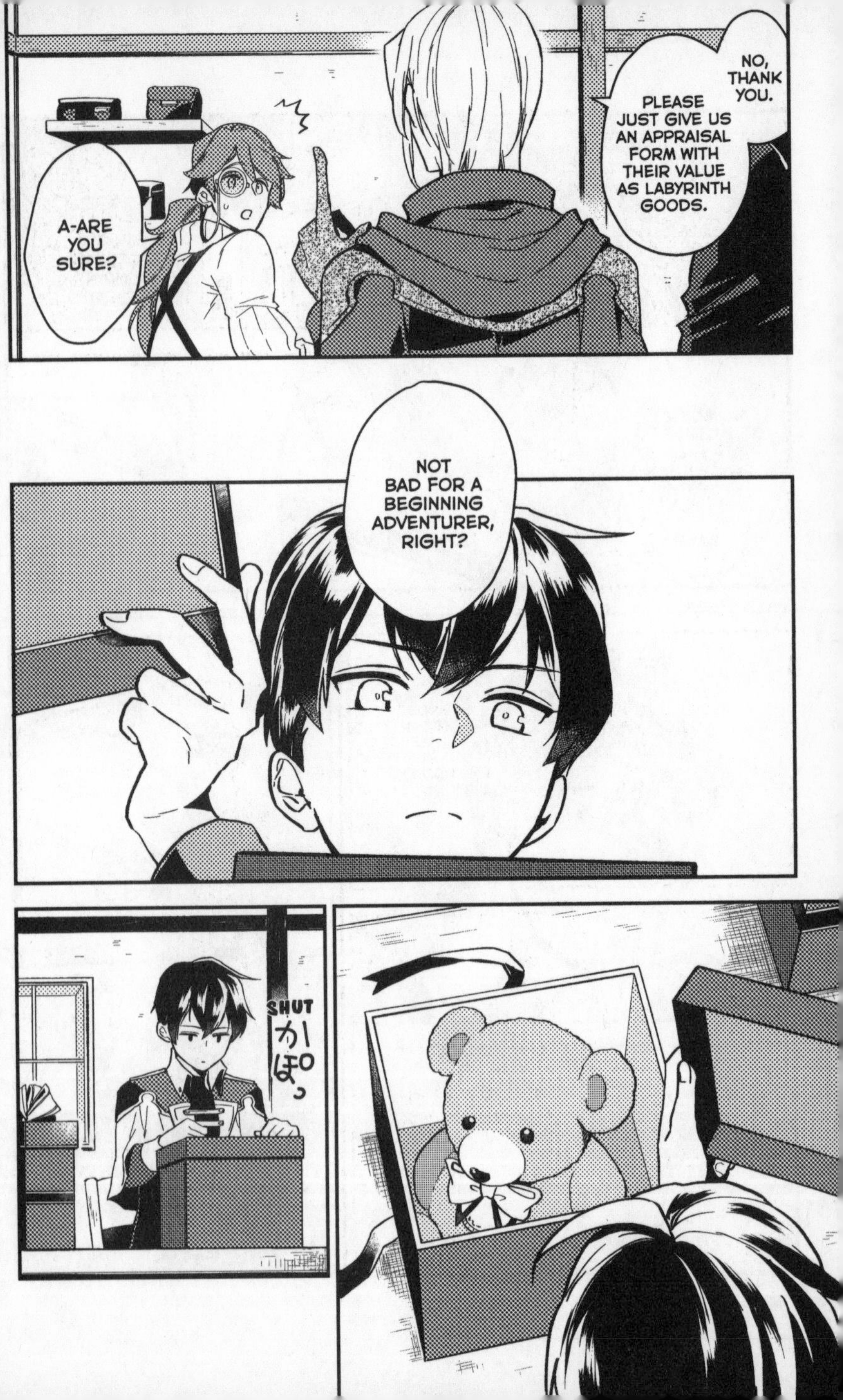
NO, THANK YOU.
PLEASE JUST GIVE US AN APPRAISAL FORM WITH THEIR VALUE AS LABYRINTH GOODS.
A-ARE YOU SURE?
NOT BAD FOR A BEGINNING ADVENTURER, RIGHT?
SHUT
かぽっ

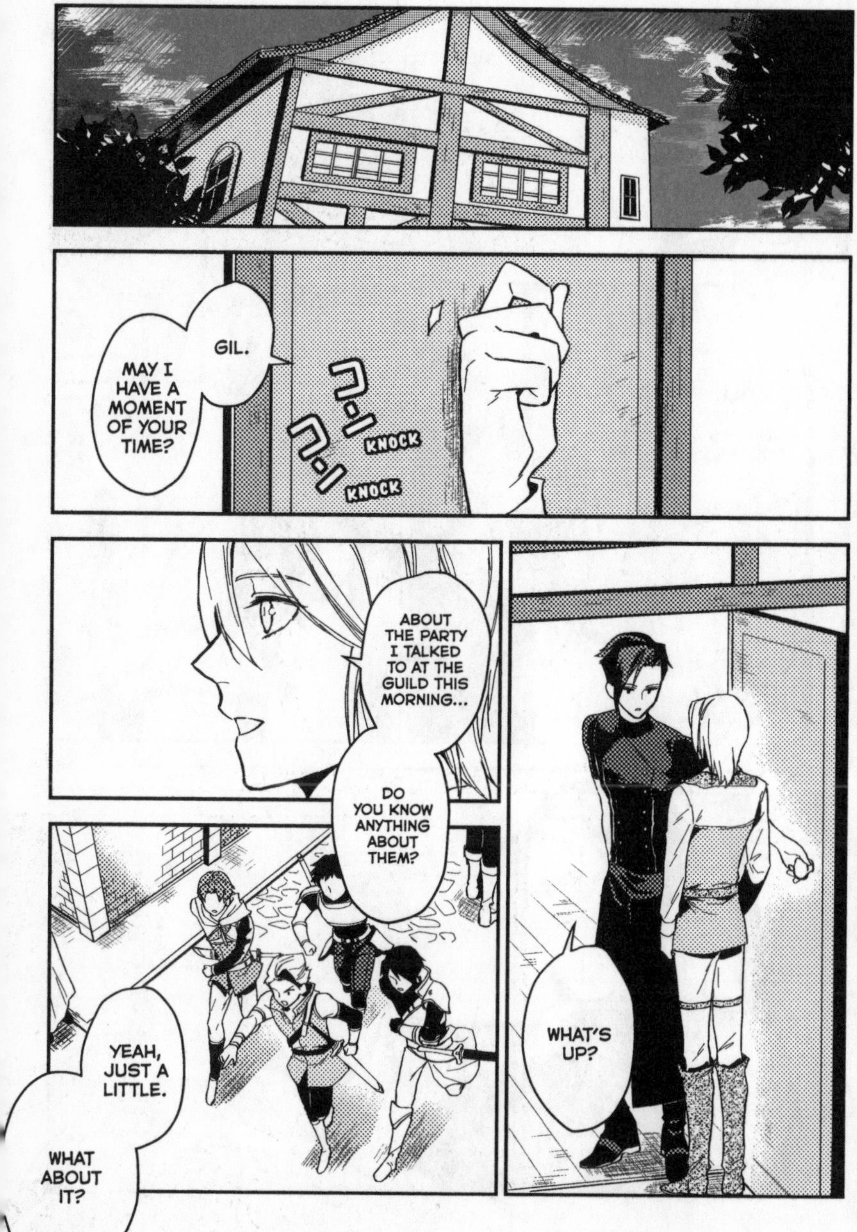
KNOCK
KNOCK
GIL.
MAY I HAVE A MOMENT OF YOUR TIME?
WHAT'S UP?
ABOUT THE PARTY I TALKED TO AT THE GUILD THIS MORNING...
DO YOU KNOW ANYTHING ABOUT THEM?
YEAH, JUST A LITTLE.
WHAT ABOUT IT?

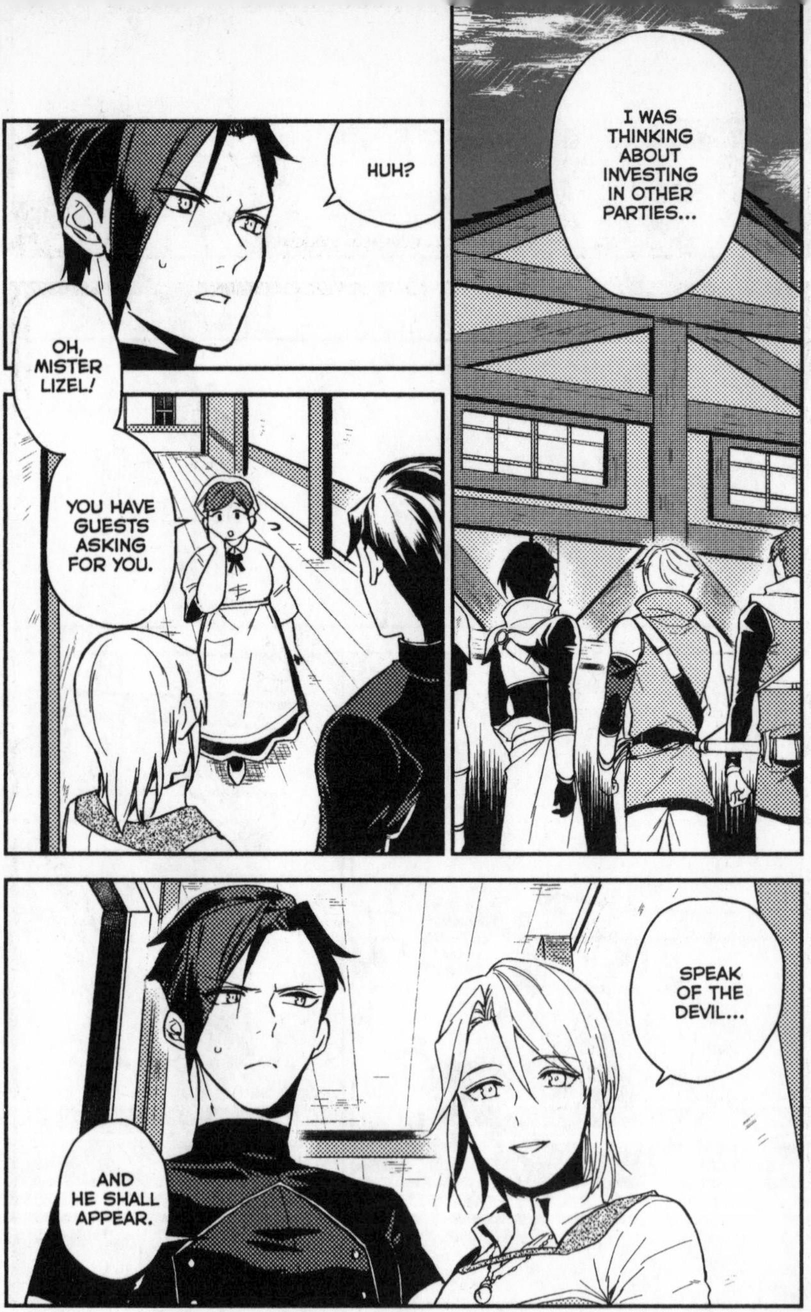
I WAS THINKING ABOUT INVESTING IN OTHER PARTIES...
HUH?
OH, MISTER LIZEL!
YOU HAVE GUESTS ASKING FOR YOU.
SPEAK OF THE DEVIL...
AND HE SHALL APPEAR.

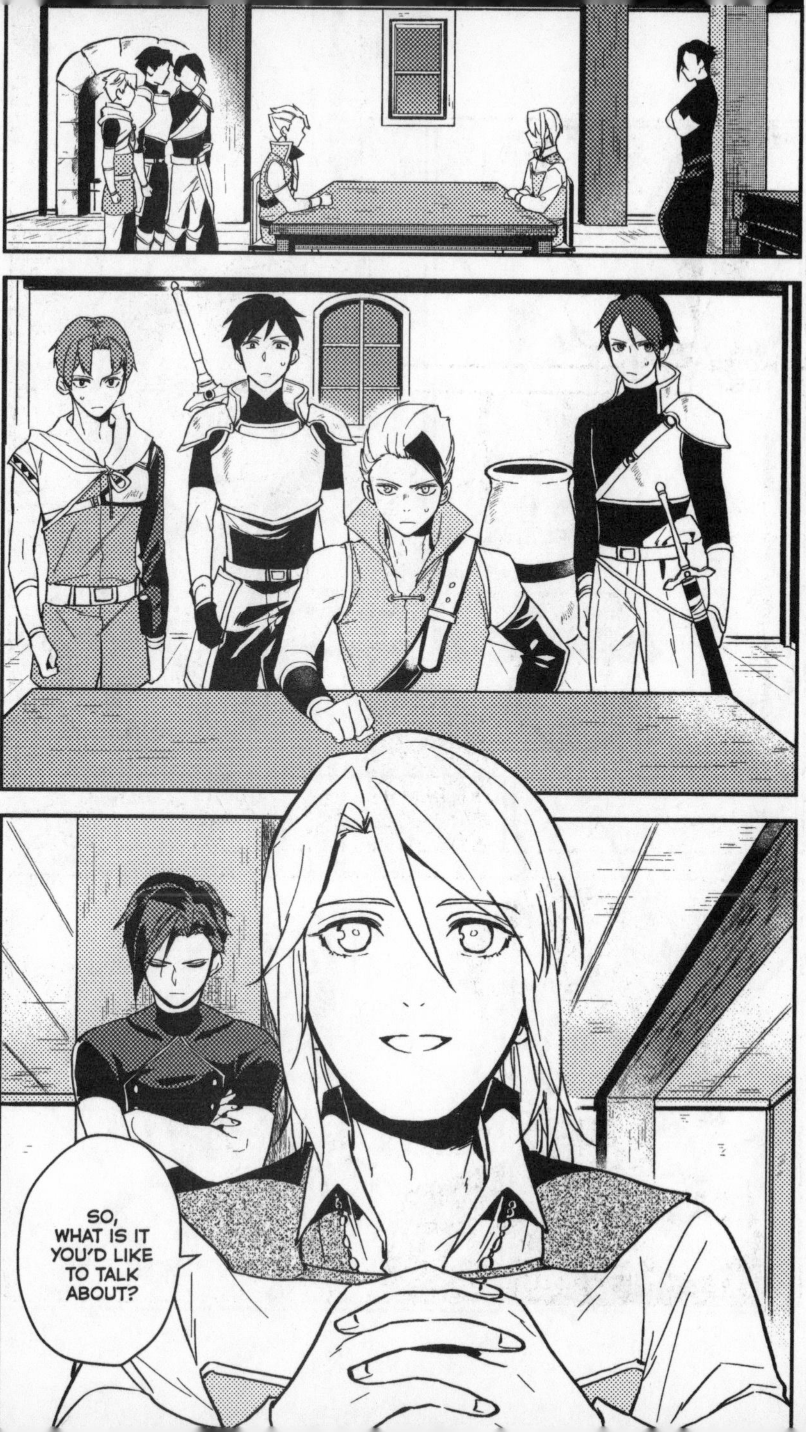
SO, WHAT IS IT YOU'D LIKE TO TALK ABOUT?

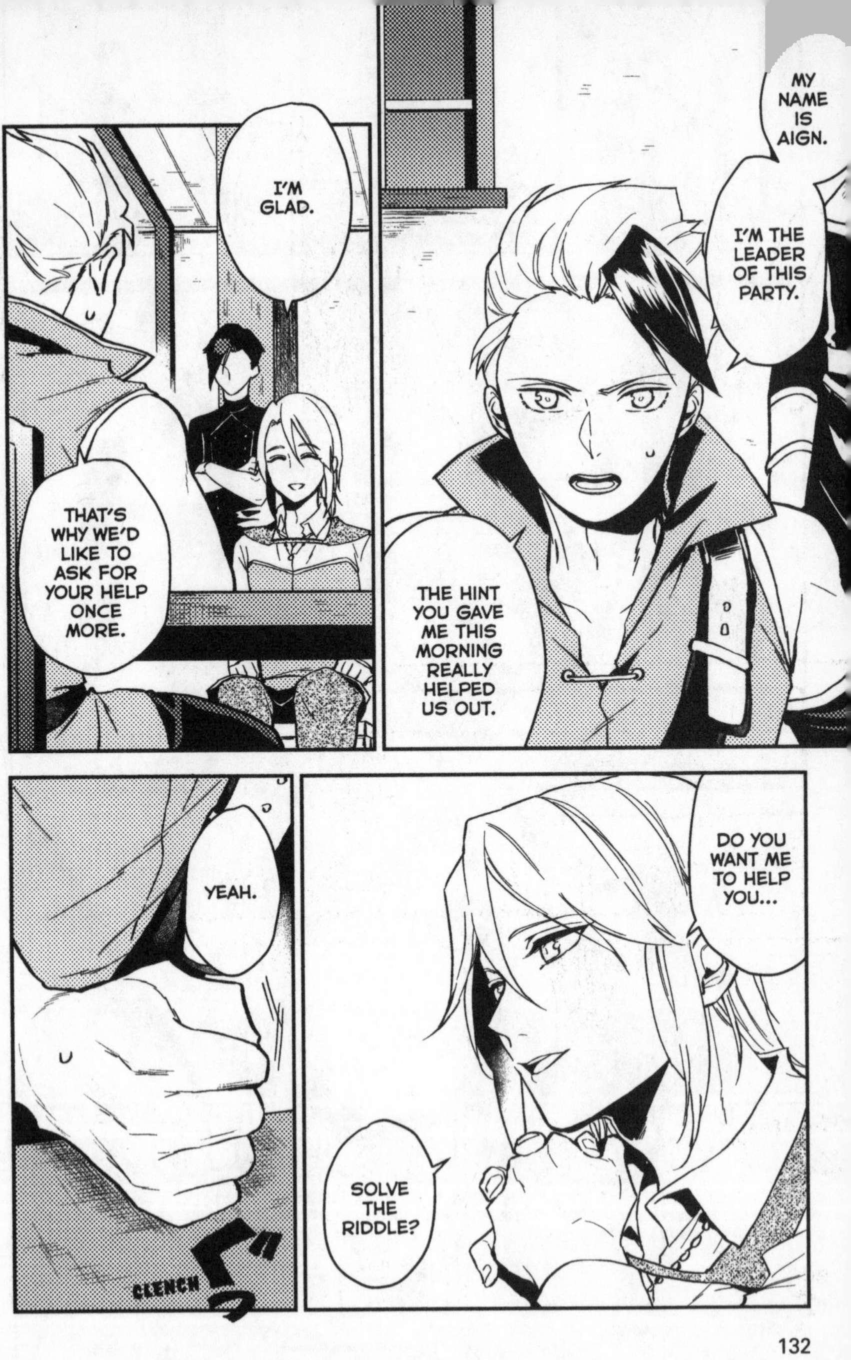
MY NAME IS AIGN.
I'M THE LEADER OF THIS PARTY.
THE HINT YOU GAVE ME THIS MORNING REALLY HELPED US OUT.
I'M GLAD.
THAT'S WHY WE'D LIKE TO ASK FOR YOUR HELP ONCE MORE.
DO YOU WANT ME TO HELP YOU...
SOLVE THE RIDDLE?
YEAH.
CLENCH

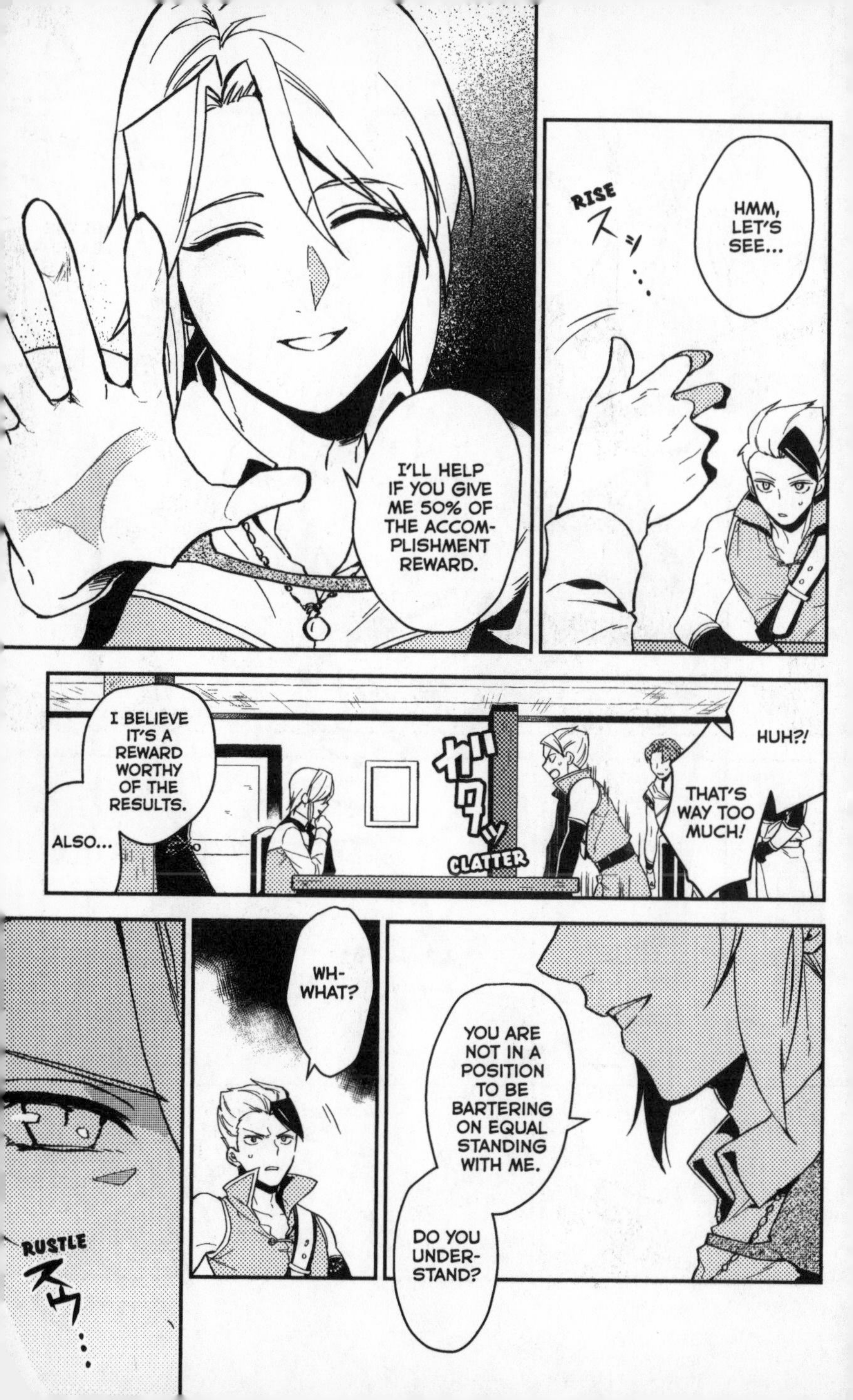

HMM, LET'S SEE...
RISE
I'LL HELP IF YOU GIVE ME 50% OF THE ACCOMPLISHMENT REWARD.
HUH?!
THAT'S WAY TOO MUCH!
CLATTER
I BELIEVE IT'S A REWARD WORTHY OF THE RESULTS.
ALSO...
YOU ARE NOT IN A POSITION TO BE BARTERING ON EQUAL STANDING WITH ME.
DO YOU UNDERSTAND?
WH-WHAT?
RUSTLE

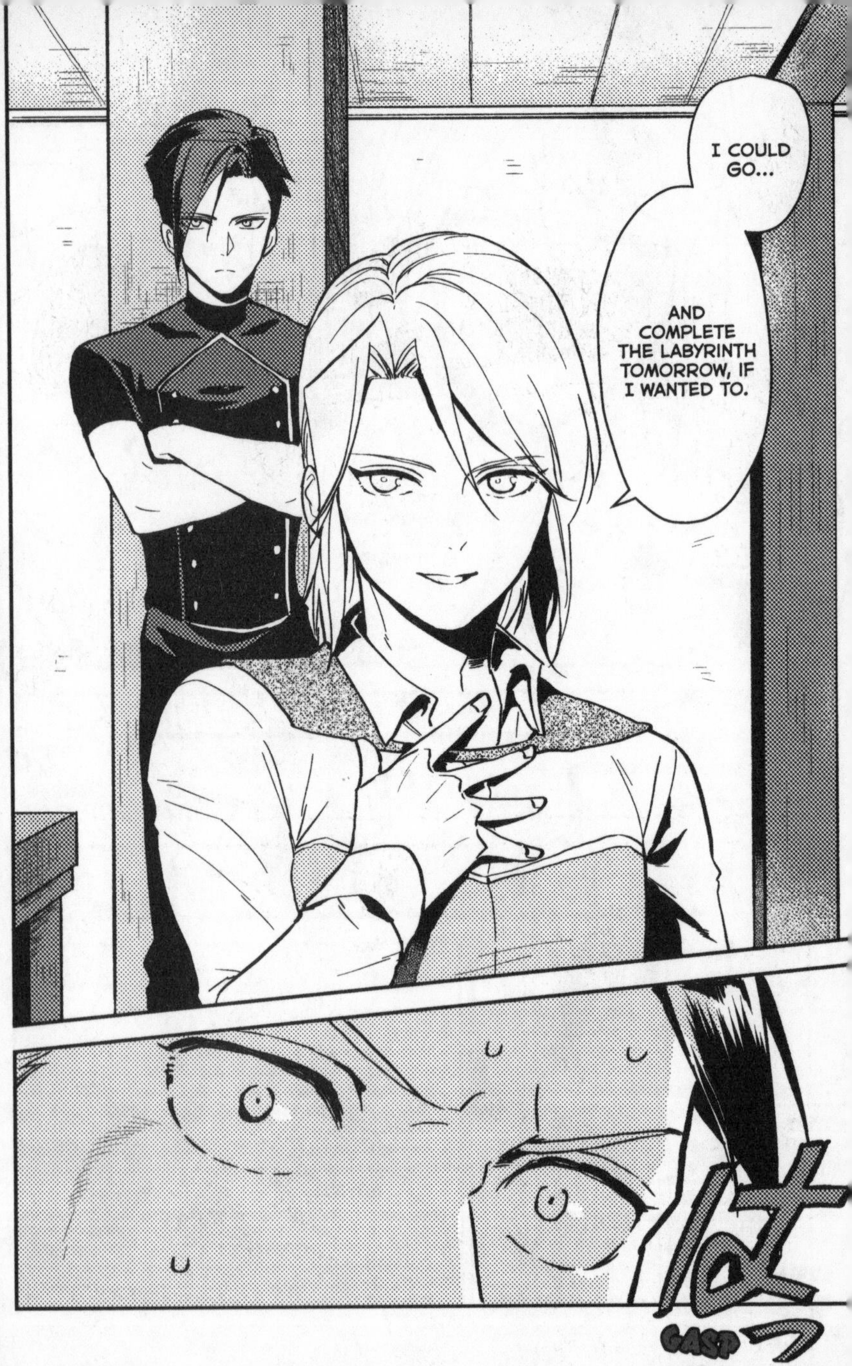
I COULD GO...
AND COMPLETE THE LABYRINTH TOMORROW, IF I WANTED TO.
GASP

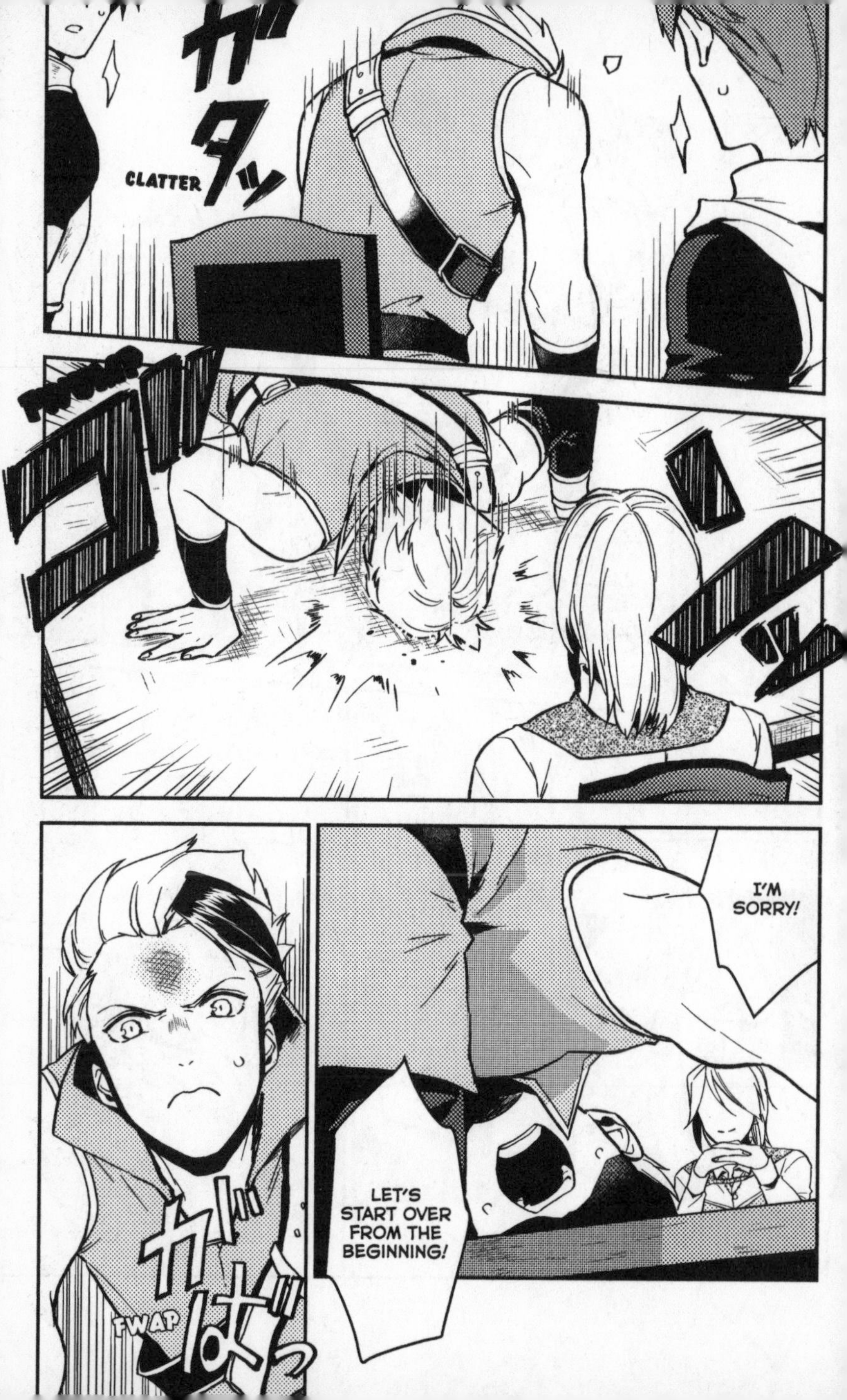
CLATTER
I'M SORRY!
LET'S START OVER FROM THE BEGINNING!
FWAP

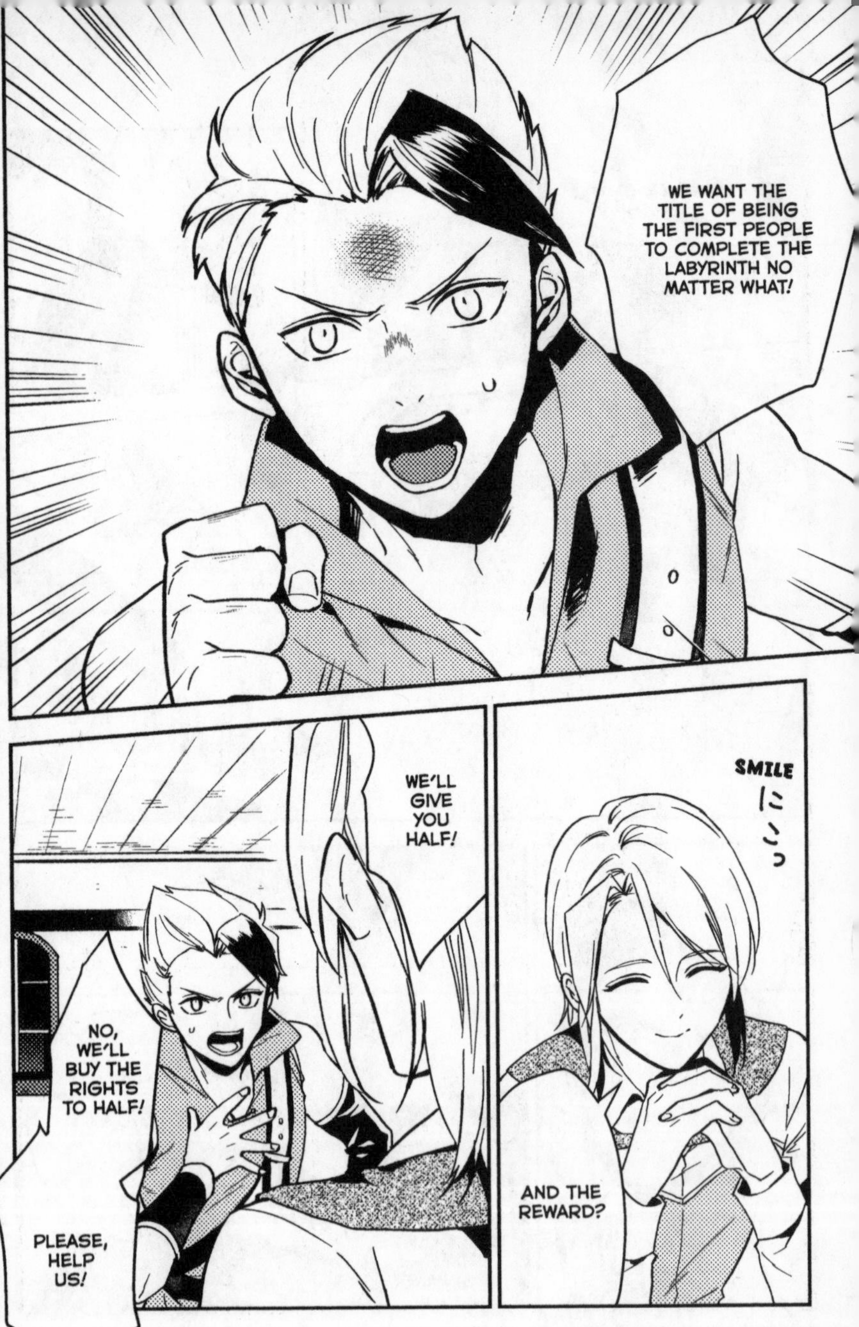
WE WANT THE TITLE OF BEING THE FIRST PEOPLE TO COMPLETE THE LABYRINTH NO MATTER WHAT!
SMILE
にこっ
AND THE REWARD?
WE'LL GIVE YOU HALF!
NO, WE'LL BUY THE RIGHTS TO HALF!
PLEASE, HELP US!

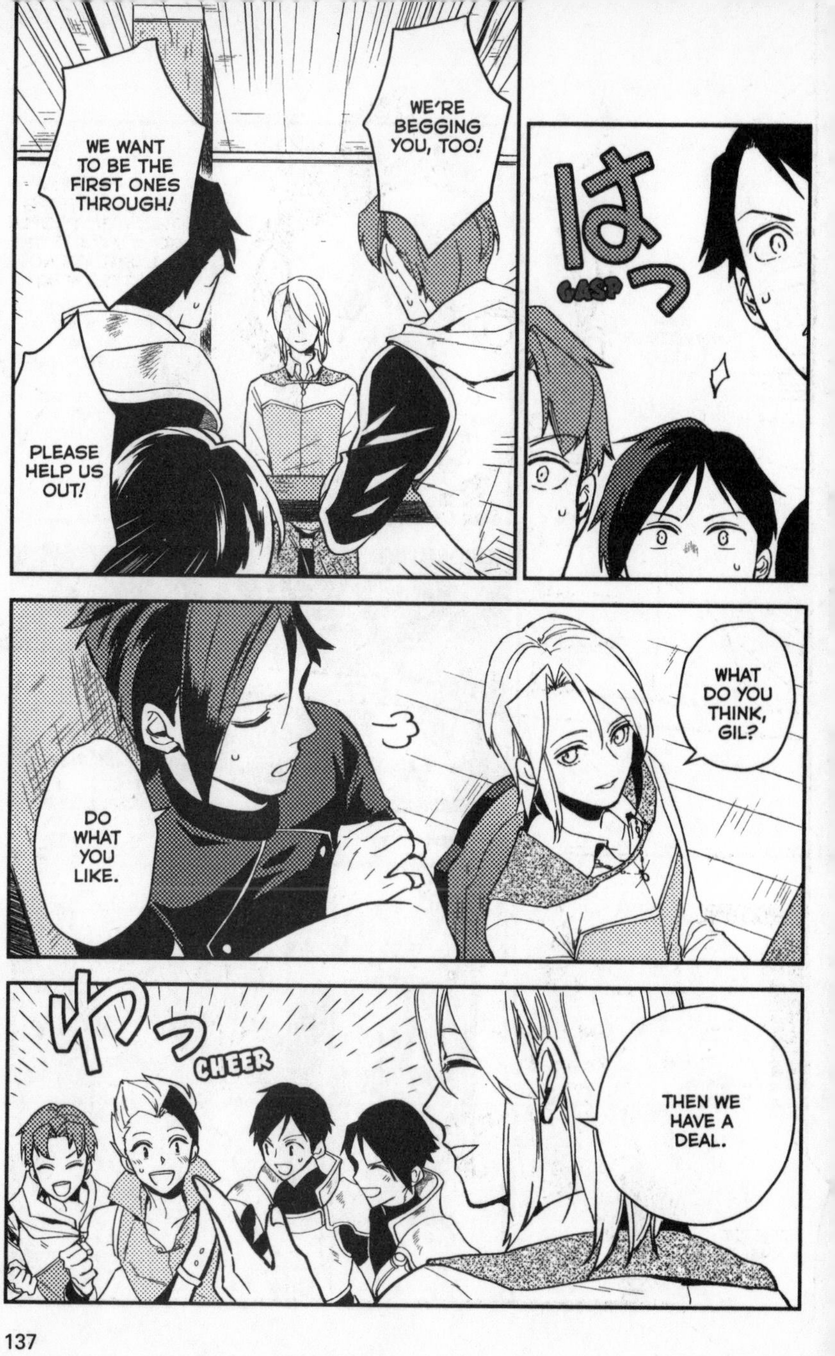
はっ
GASP
WE'RE BEGGING YOU, TOO!
WE WANT TO BE THE FIRST ONES THROUGH!
PLEASE HELP US OUT!
WHAT DO YOU THINK, GIL?
DO WHAT YOU LIKE.
THEN WE HAVE A DEAL.
わっ
CHEER

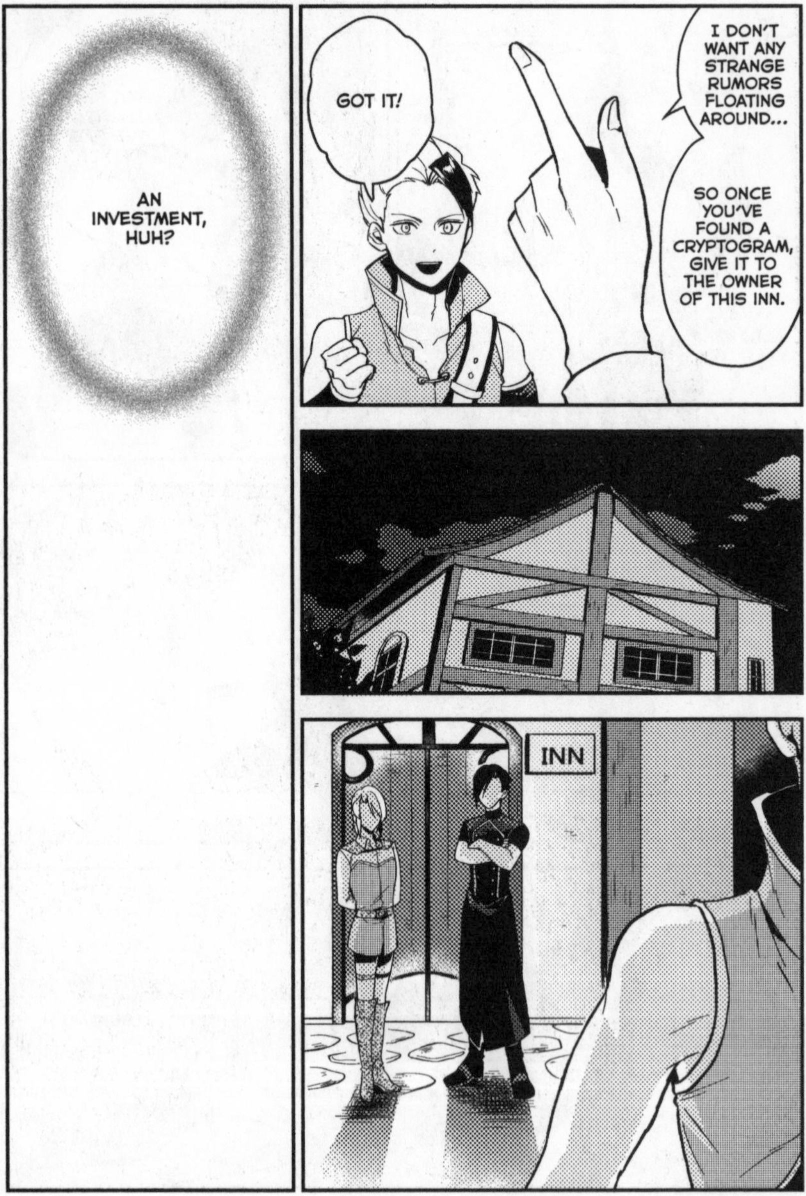
I DON'T WANT ANY STRANGE RUMORS FLOATING AROUND...
SO ONCE YOU'VE FOUND A CRYPTOGRAM, GIVE IT TO THE OWNER OF THIS INN.
GOT IT!
INN
AN INVESTMENT, HUH?

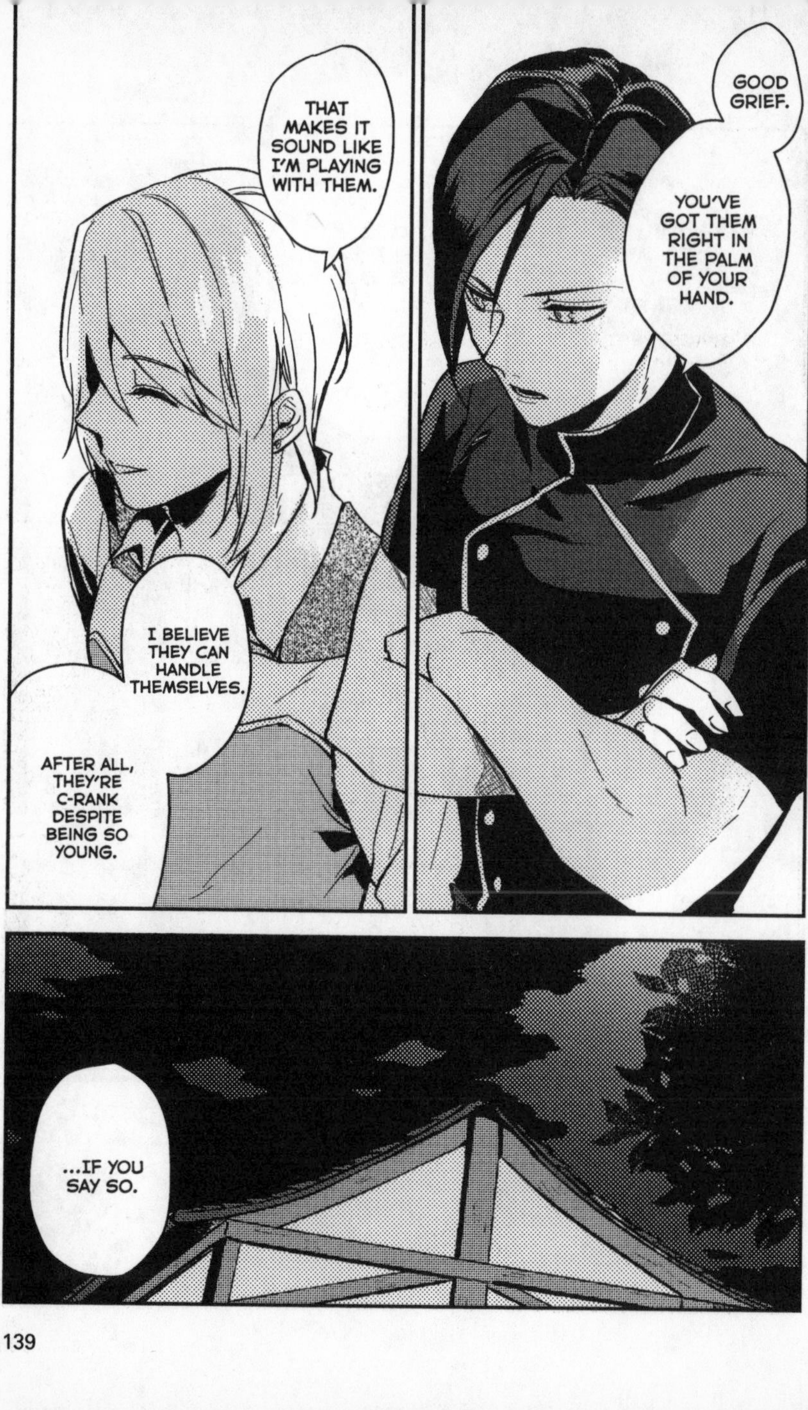
GOOD GRIEF.
YOU'VE GOT THEM RIGHT IN THE PALM OF YOUR HAND.
THAT MAKES IT SOUND LIKE I'M PLAYING WITH THEM.
I BELIEVE THEY CAN HANDLE THEMSELVES.
AFTER ALL, THEY'RE C-RANK DESPITE BEING SO YOUNG.
...IF YOU SAY SO.

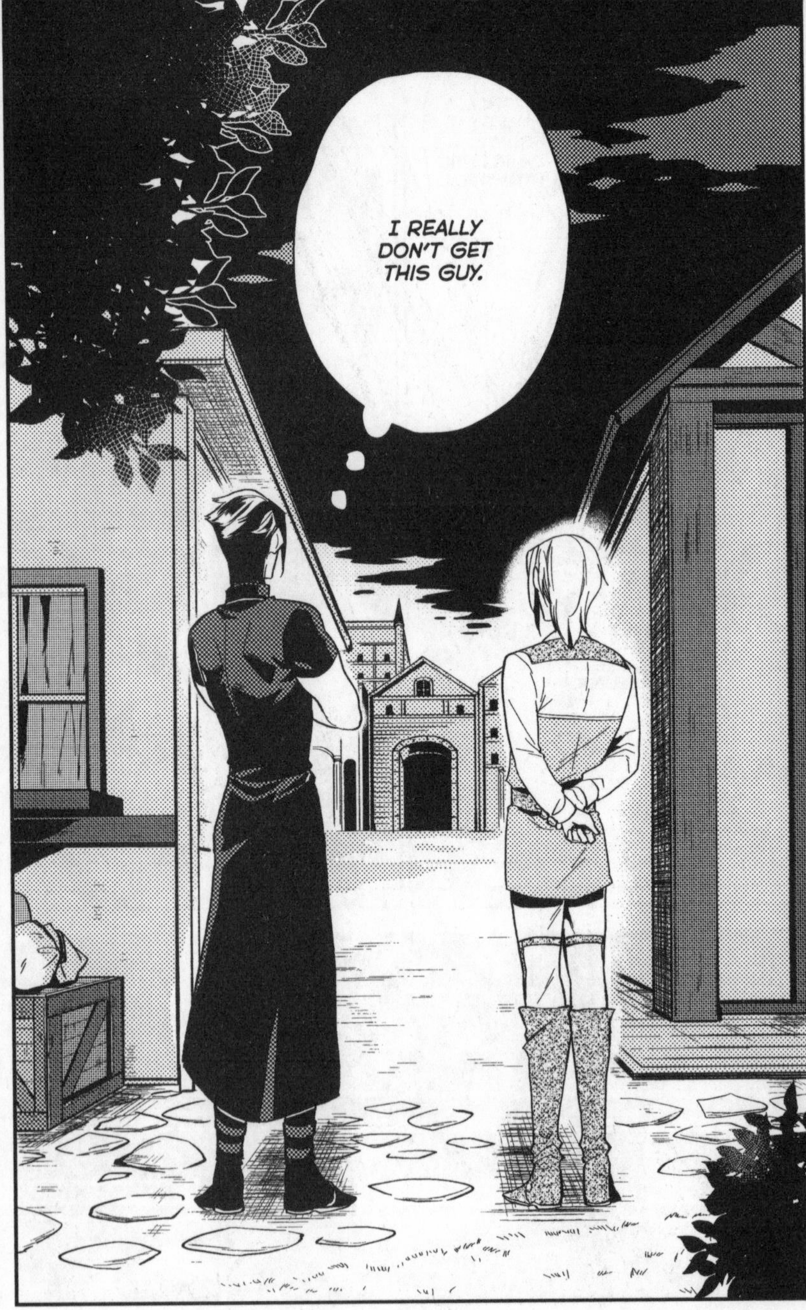
I REALLY DON'T GET THIS GUY.

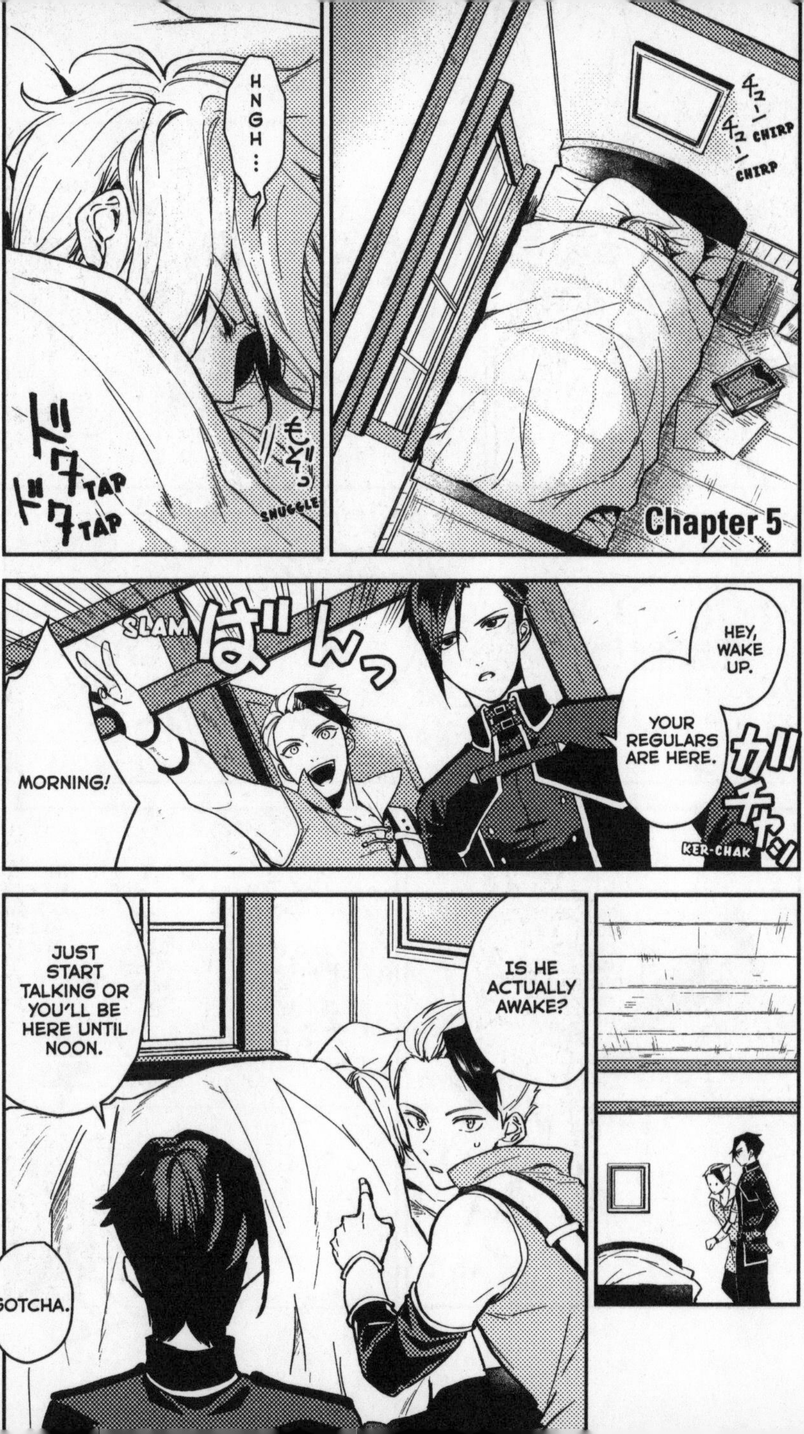
チュンチュン
CHIRP CHIRP
Chapter 5
HNGH...
もぞっ
SNUGGLE
ドクドク
TAP TAP
HEY, WAKE UP.
YOUR REGULARS ARE HERE.
ガチャ!!
KER-CHAK
ばんっ
SLAM
MORNING!
IS HE ACTUALLY AWAKE?
JUST START TALKING OR YOU'LL BE HERE UNTIL NOON.
GOTCHA.

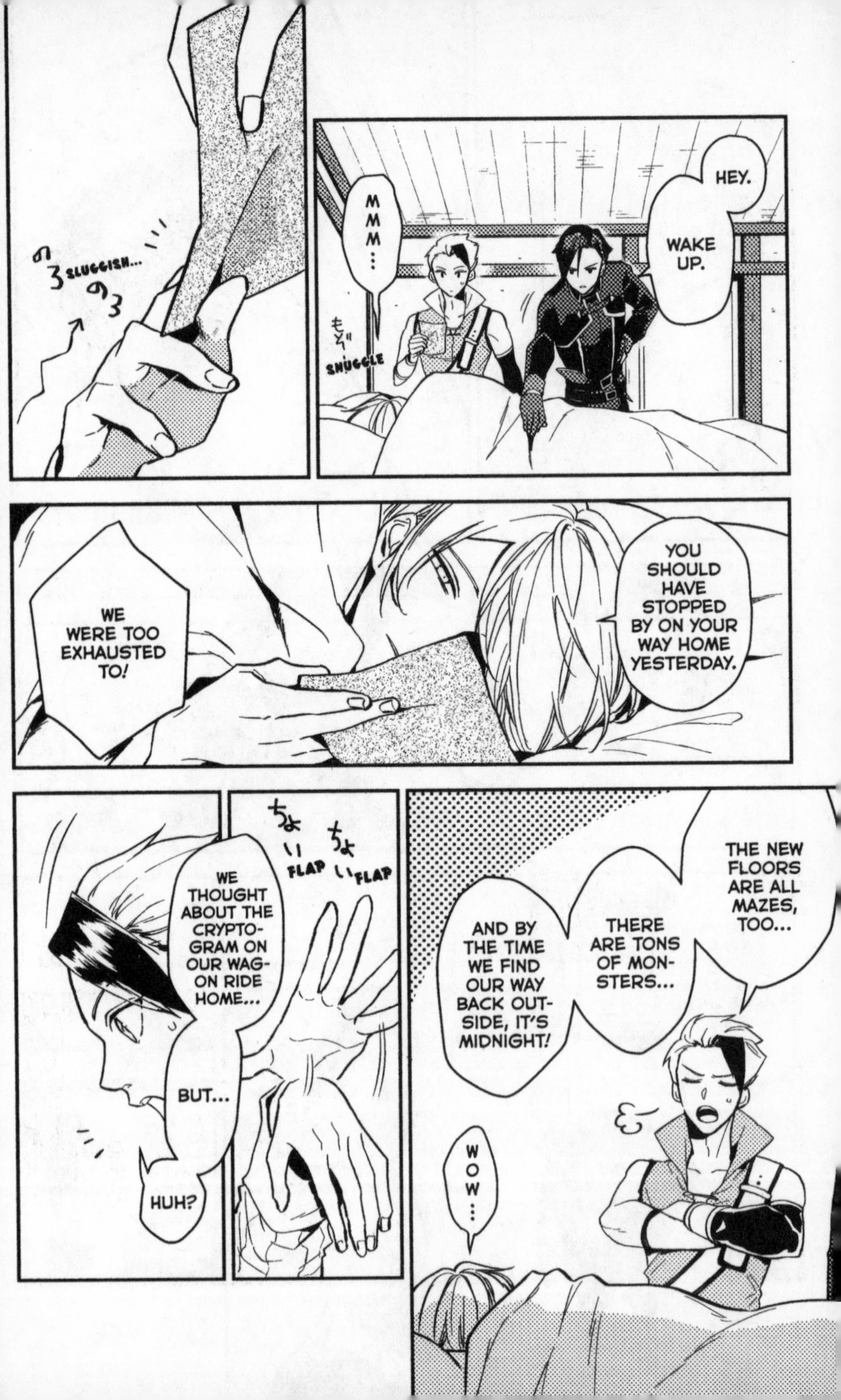
HEY.
WAKE UP.
MMM...
もぞ
SNUGGLE
のろ SLUGGISH... のろ
YOU SHOULD HAVE STOPPED BY ON YOUR WAY HOME YESTERDAY.
WE WERE TOO EXHAUSTED TO!
THE NEW FLOORS ARE ALL MAZES, TOO...
THERE ARE TONS OF MON-STERS...
AND BY THE TIME WE FIND OUR WAY BACK OUT-SIDE, IT'S MIDNIGHT!
WOW...
ちょい FLAP ちょい FLAP
WE THOUGHT ABOUT THE CRYPTO-GRAM ON OUR WAG-ON RIDE HOME...
BUT...
HUH?

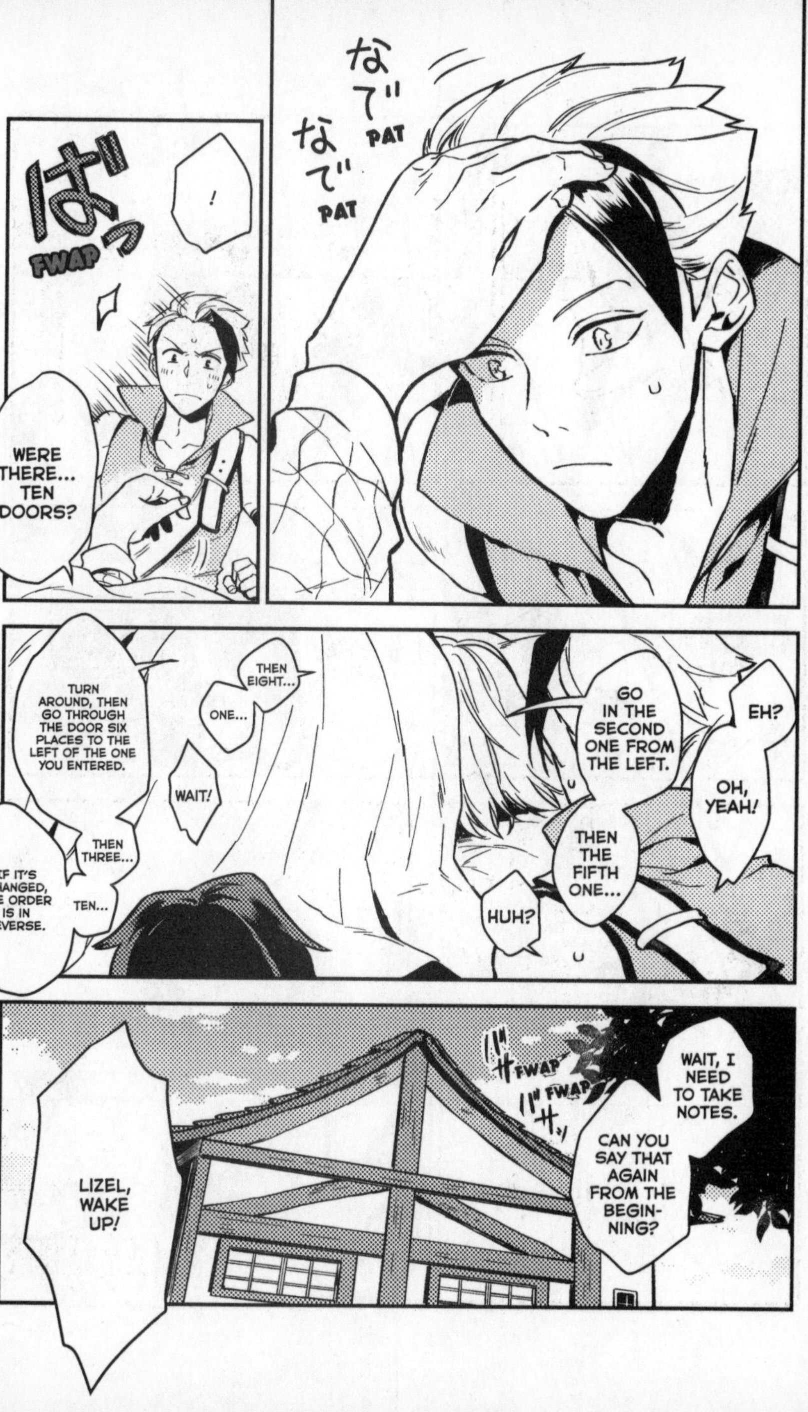

なで
PAT
なで
PAT
ばっ
FWAP
!
WERE THERE... TEN DOORS?
EH?
GO IN THE SECOND ONE FROM THE LEFT.
OH, YEAH!
THEN THE FIFTH ONE...
HUH?
THEN EIGHT...
ONE...
WAIT!
TURN AROUND, THEN GO THROUGH THE DOOR SIX PLACES TO THE LEFT OF THE ONE YOU ENTERED.
THEN THREE...
TEN...
IF IT'S CHANGED, THE ORDER IS IN REVERSE.
WAIT, I NEED TO TAKE NOTES.
CAN YOU SAY THAT AGAIN FROM THE BEGINNING?
FWAP
FWAP
LIZEL, WAKE UP!

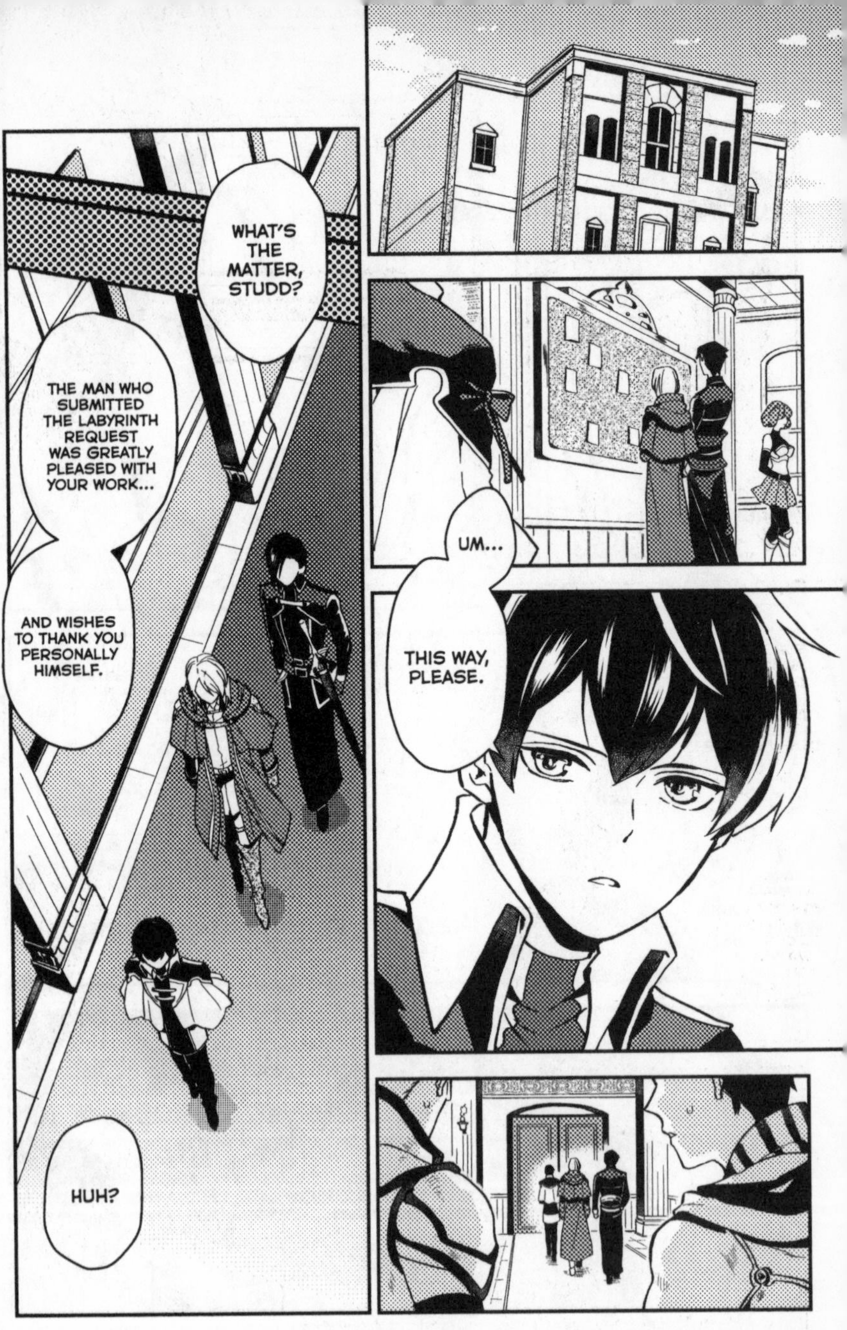
UM...
THIS WAY, PLEASE.
WHAT'S THE MATTER, STUDD?
THE MAN WHO SUBMITTED THE LABYRINTH REQUEST WAS GREATLY PLEASED WITH YOUR WORK...
AND WISHES TO THANK YOU PERSONALLY HIMSELF.
HUH?

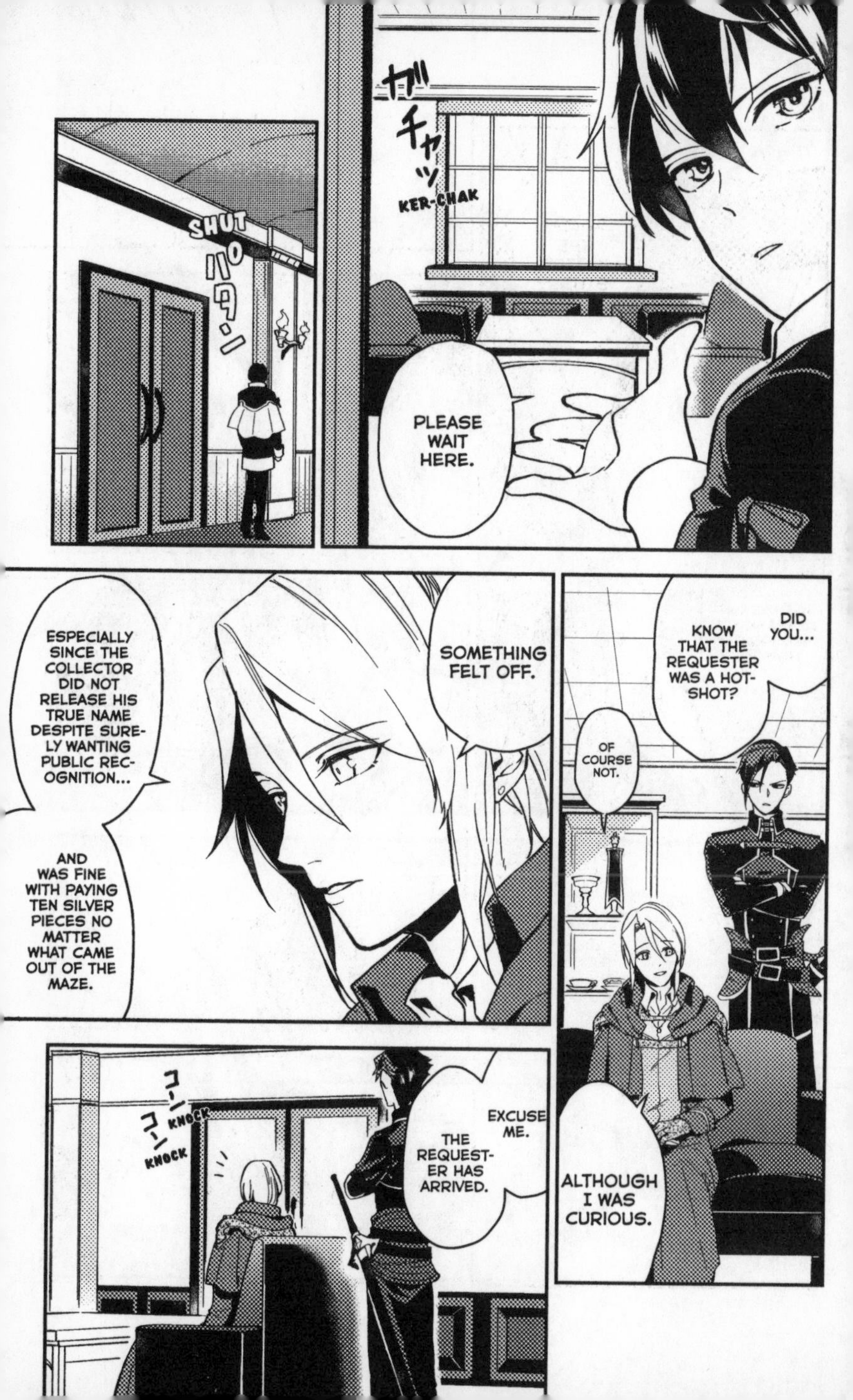
ガチャッ
KER-CHAK
PLEASE WAIT HERE.
SHUT
バタン
DID YOU...
KNOW THAT THE REQUESTER WAS A HOT-SHOT?
OF COURSE NOT.
ALTHOUGH I WAS CURIOUS.
SOMETHING FELT OFF.
ESPECIALLY SINCE THE COLLECTOR DID NOT RELEASE HIS TRUE NAME DESPITE SURELY WANTING PUBLIC RECOGNITION...
AND WAS FINE WITH PAYING TEN SILVER PIECES NO MATTER WHAT CAME OUT OF THE MAZE.
コン
KNOCK
コン
KNOCK
EXCUSE ME.
THE REQUESTER HAS ARRIVED.

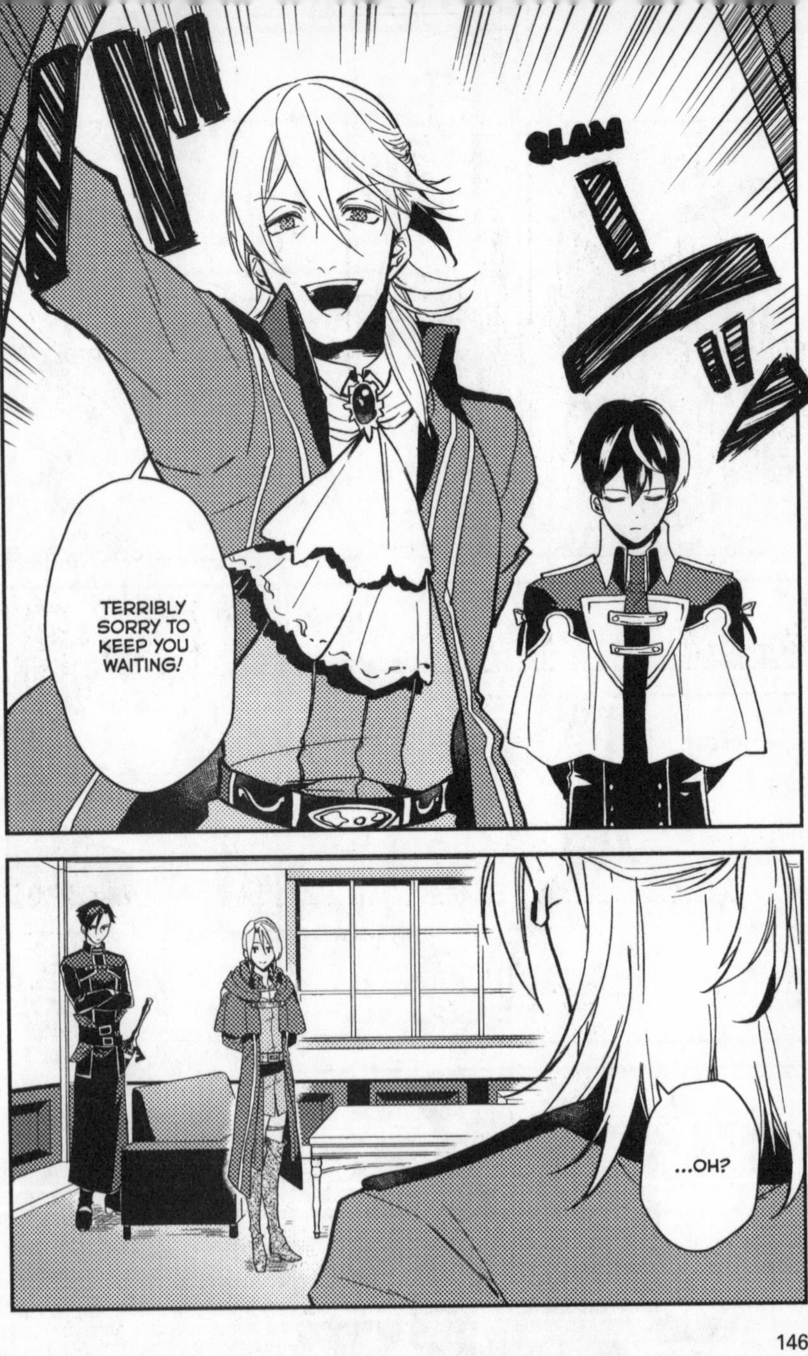
SLAM
TERRIBLY SORRY TO KEEP YOU WAITING!
...OH?

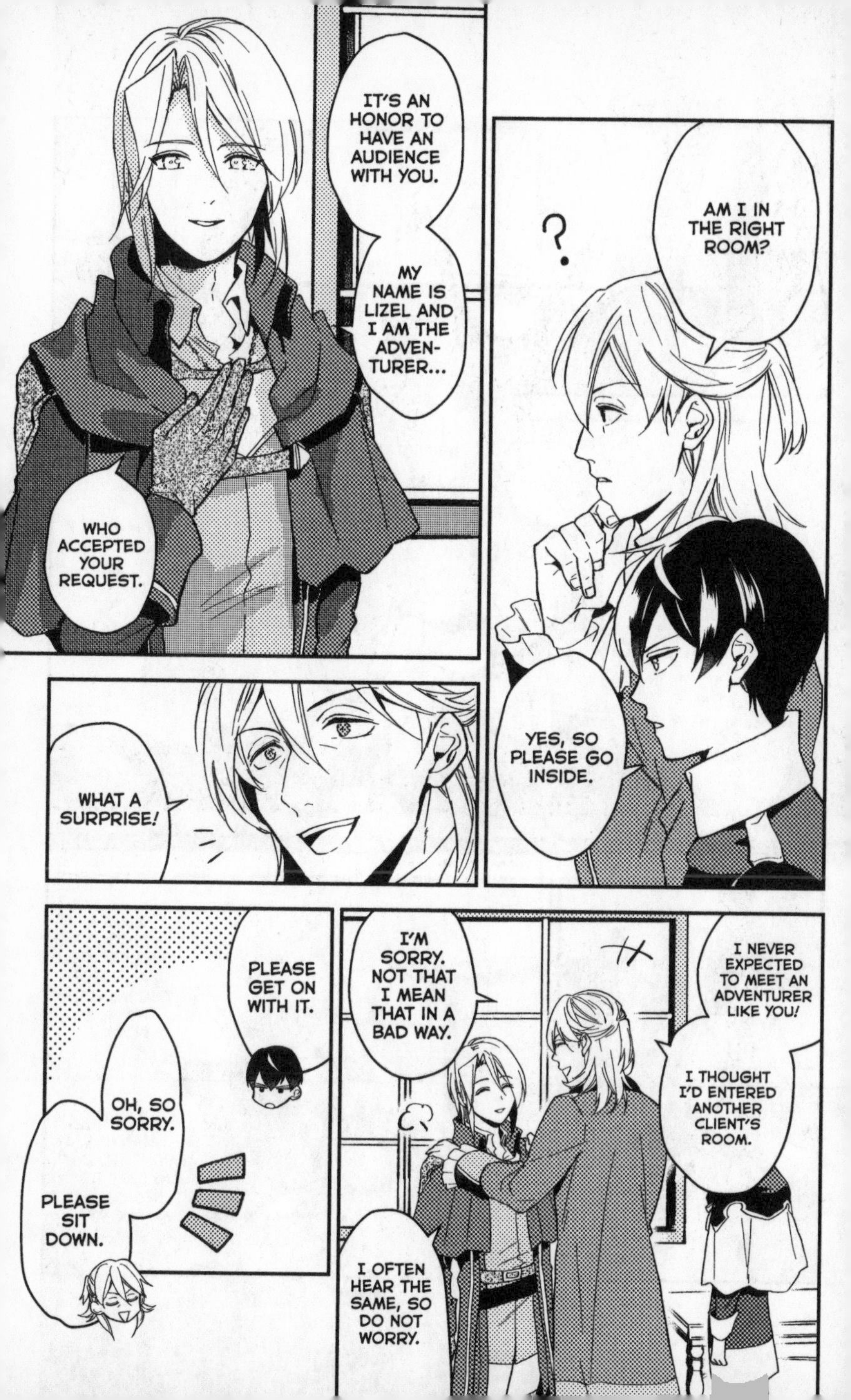
?
AM I IN THE RIGHT ROOM?
YES, SO PLEASE GO INSIDE.
IT'S AN HONOR TO HAVE AN AUDIENCE WITH YOU.
MY NAME IS LIZEL AND I AM THE ADVEN-TURER...
WHO ACCEPTED YOUR REQUEST.
WHAT A SURPRISE!
I NEVER EXPECTED TO MEET AN ADVENTURER LIKE YOU!
I THOUGHT I'D ENTERED ANOTHER CLIENT'S ROOM.
I'M SORRY. NOT THAT I MEAN THAT IN A BAD WAY.
I OFTEN HEAR THE SAME, SO DO NOT WORRY.
PLEASE GET ON WITH IT.
OH, SO SORRY.
PLEASE SIT DOWN.

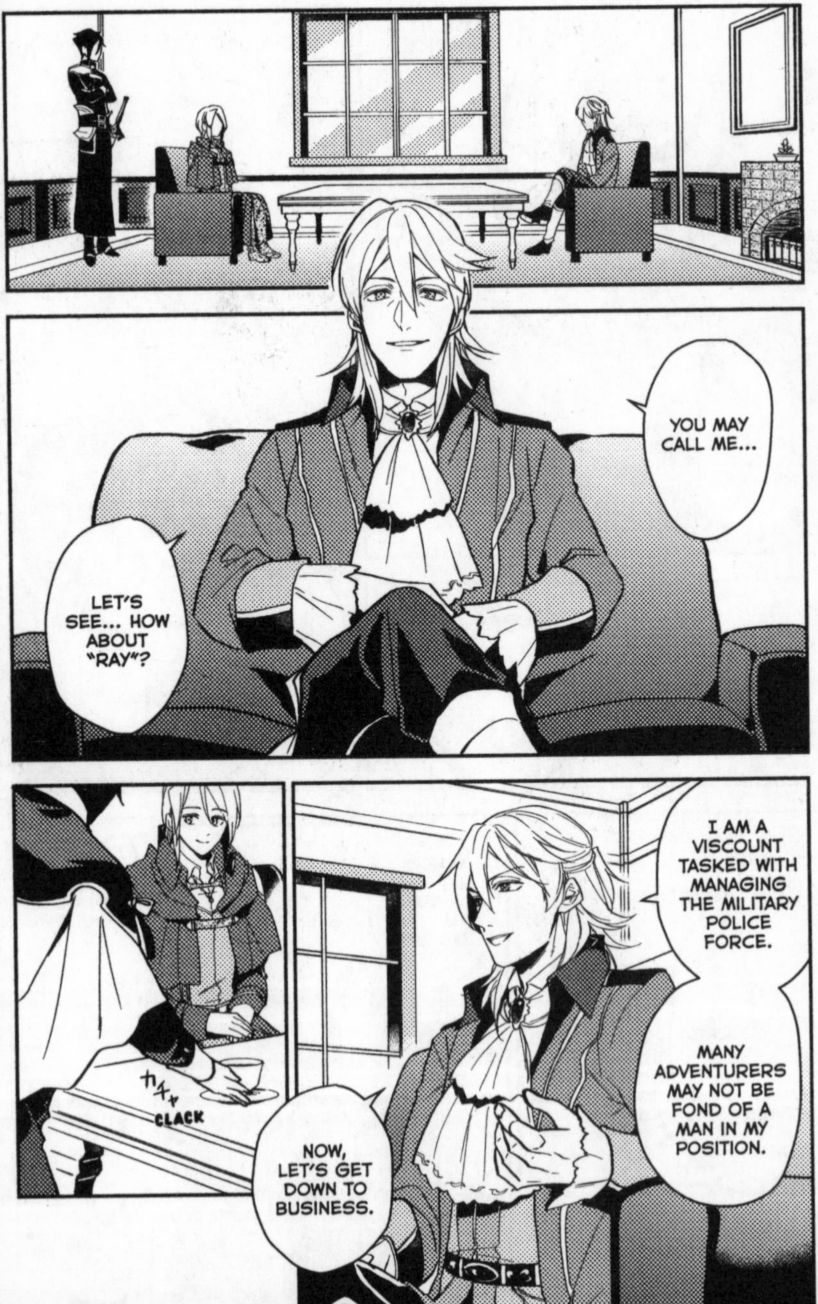
YOU MAY CALL ME...
LET'S SEE... HOW ABOUT "RAY"?
I AM A VISCOUNT TASKED WITH MANAGING THE MILITARY POLICE FORCE.
MANY ADVENTURERS MAY NOT BE FOND OF A MAN IN MY POSITION.
NOW, LET'S GET DOWN TO BUSINESS.
カチャ
CLACK

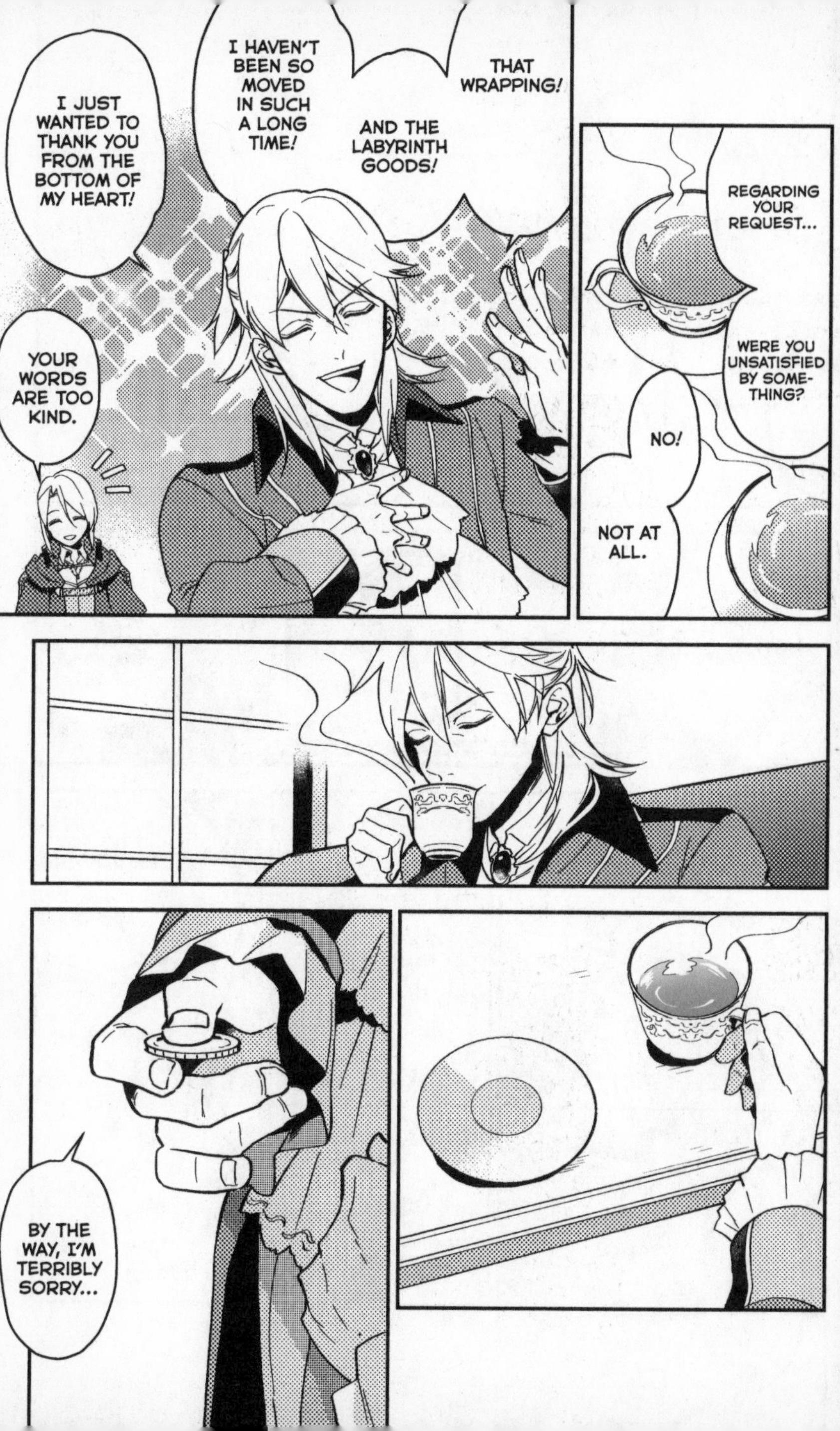
REGARDING YOUR REQUEST...
WERE YOU UNSATISFIED BY SOME-THING?
NO!
NOT AT ALL.
THAT WRAPPING!
AND THE LABYRINTH GOODS!
I HAVEN'T BEEN SO MOVED IN SUCH A LONG TIME!
I JUST WANTED TO THANK YOU FROM THE BOTTOM OF MY HEART!
YOUR WORDS ARE TOO KIND.
BY THE WAY, I'M TERRIBLY SORRY...

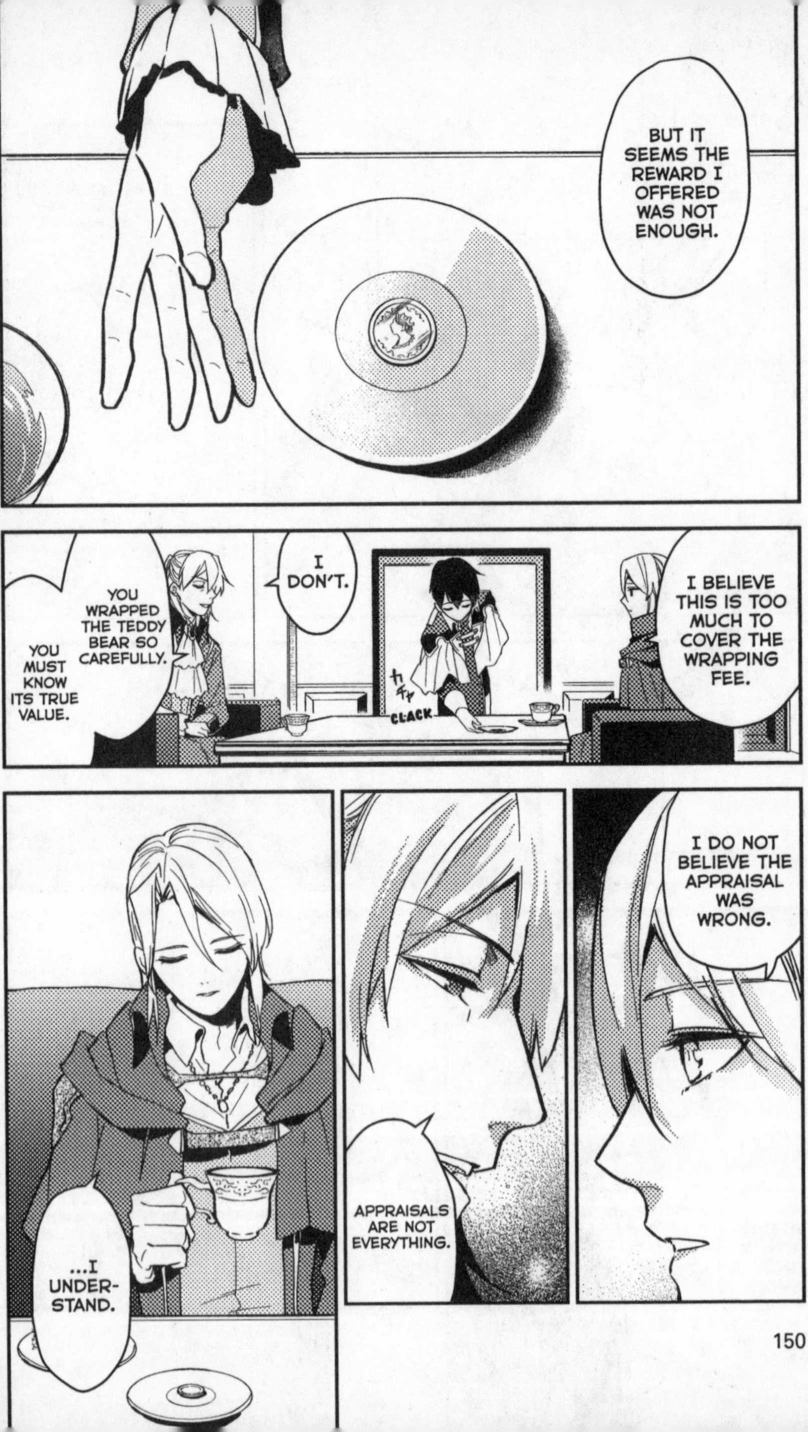
BUT IT SEEMS THE REWARD I OFFERED WAS NOT ENOUGH.
I BELIEVE THIS IS TOO MUCH TO COVER THE WRAPPING FEE.
カチャ
CLACK
I DON'T.
YOU WRAPPED THE TEDDY BEAR SO CAREFULLY.
YOU MUST KNOW ITS TRUE VALUE.
I DO NOT BELIEVE THE APPRAISAL WAS WRONG.
APPRAISALS ARE NOT EVERYTHING.
...I UNDER-STAND.

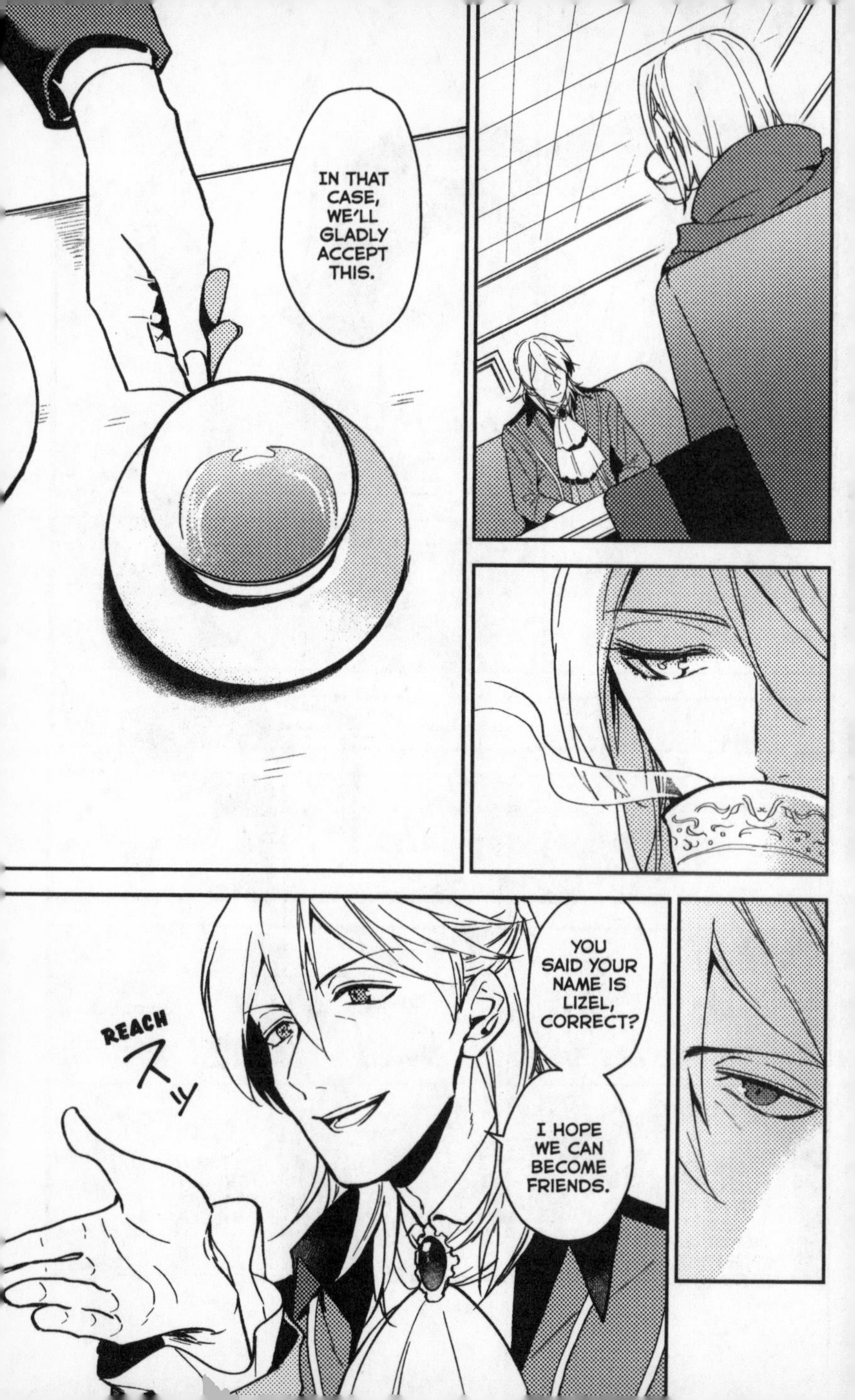
IN THAT CASE, WE'LL GLADLY ACCEPT THIS.
YOU SAID YOUR NAME IS LIZEL, CORRECT?
I HOPE WE CAN BECOME FRIENDS.
REACH
スッ

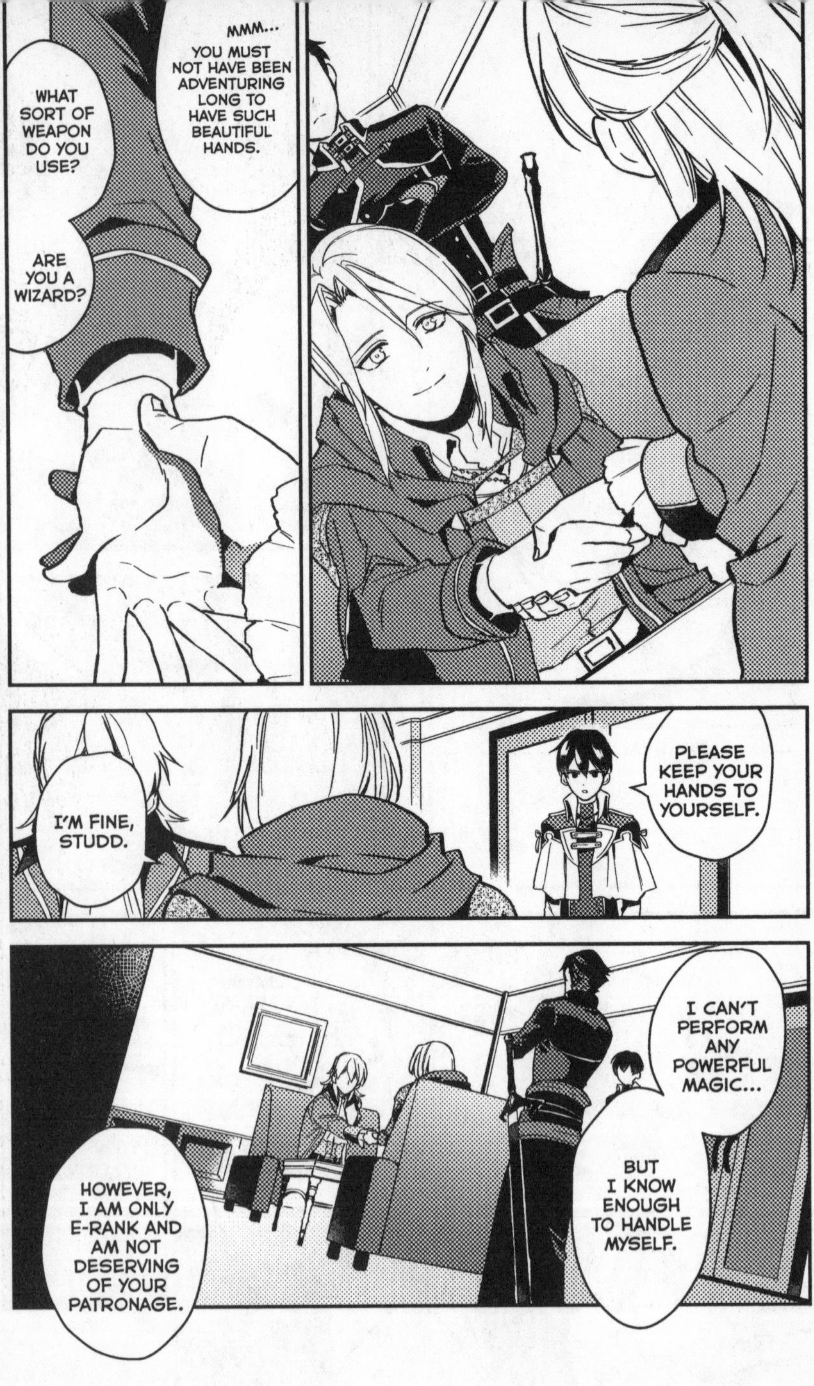
MMM... YOU MUST NOT HAVE BEEN ADVENTURING LONG TO HAVE SUCH BEAUTIFUL HANDS.
WHAT SORT OF WEAPON DO YOU USE?
ARE YOU A WIZARD?
PLEASE KEEP YOUR HANDS TO YOURSELF.
I'M FINE, STUDD.
I CAN'T PERFORM ANY POWERFUL MAGIC...
BUT I KNOW ENOUGH TO HANDLE MYSELF.
HOWEVER, I AM ONLY E-RANK AND AM NOT DESERVING OF YOUR PATRONAGE.

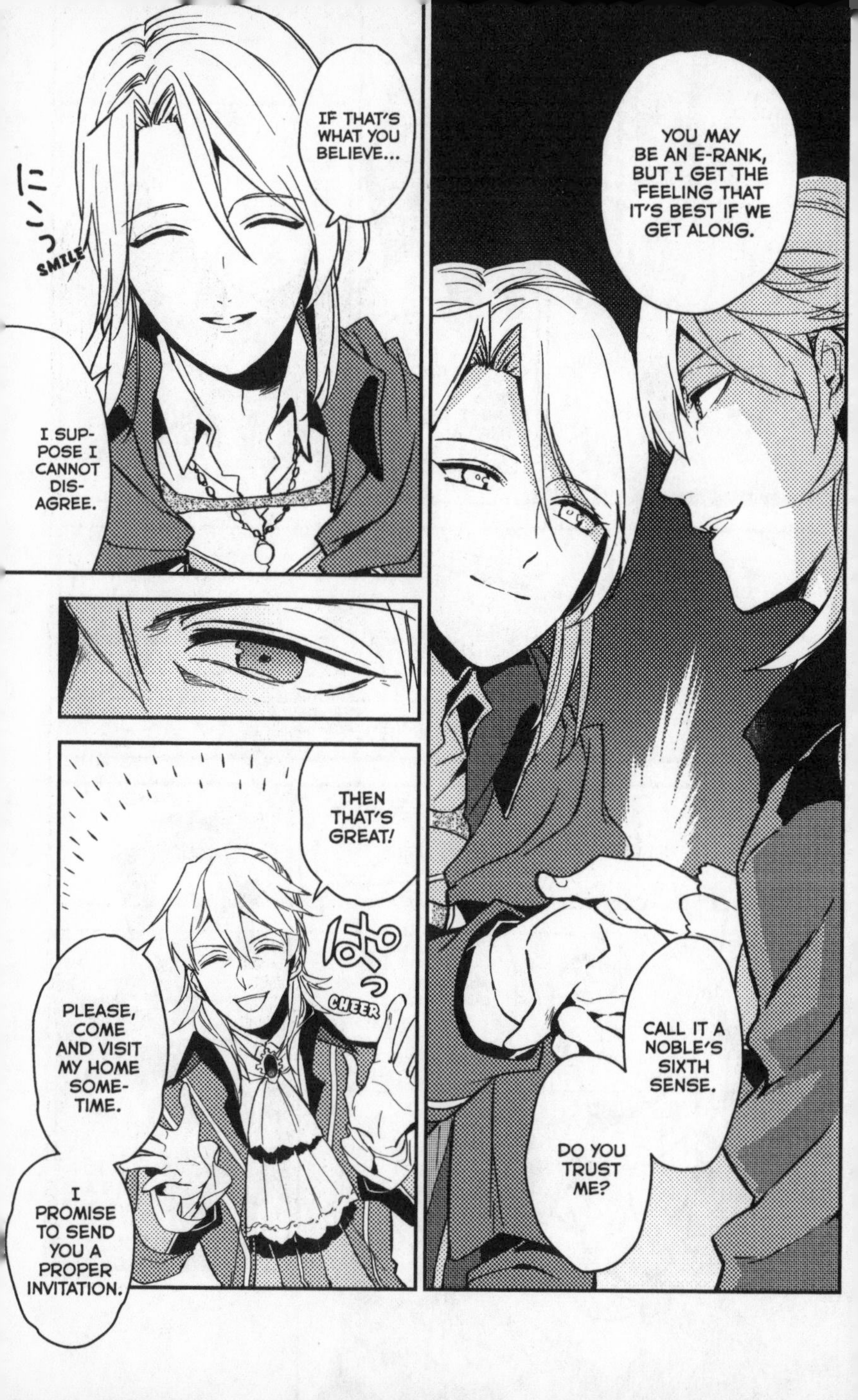
YOU MAY BE AN E-RANK, BUT I GET THE FEELING THAT IT'S BEST IF WE GET ALONG.
CALL IT A NOBLE'S SIXTH SENSE.
DO YOU TRUST ME?
IF THAT'S WHAT YOU BELIEVE...
にこっ
SMILE
I SUP-POSE I CANNOT DIS-AGREE.
THEN THAT'S GREAT!
ぱっ
CHEER
PLEASE, COME AND VISIT MY HOME SOME-TIME.
I PROMISE TO SEND YOU A PROPER INVITATION.

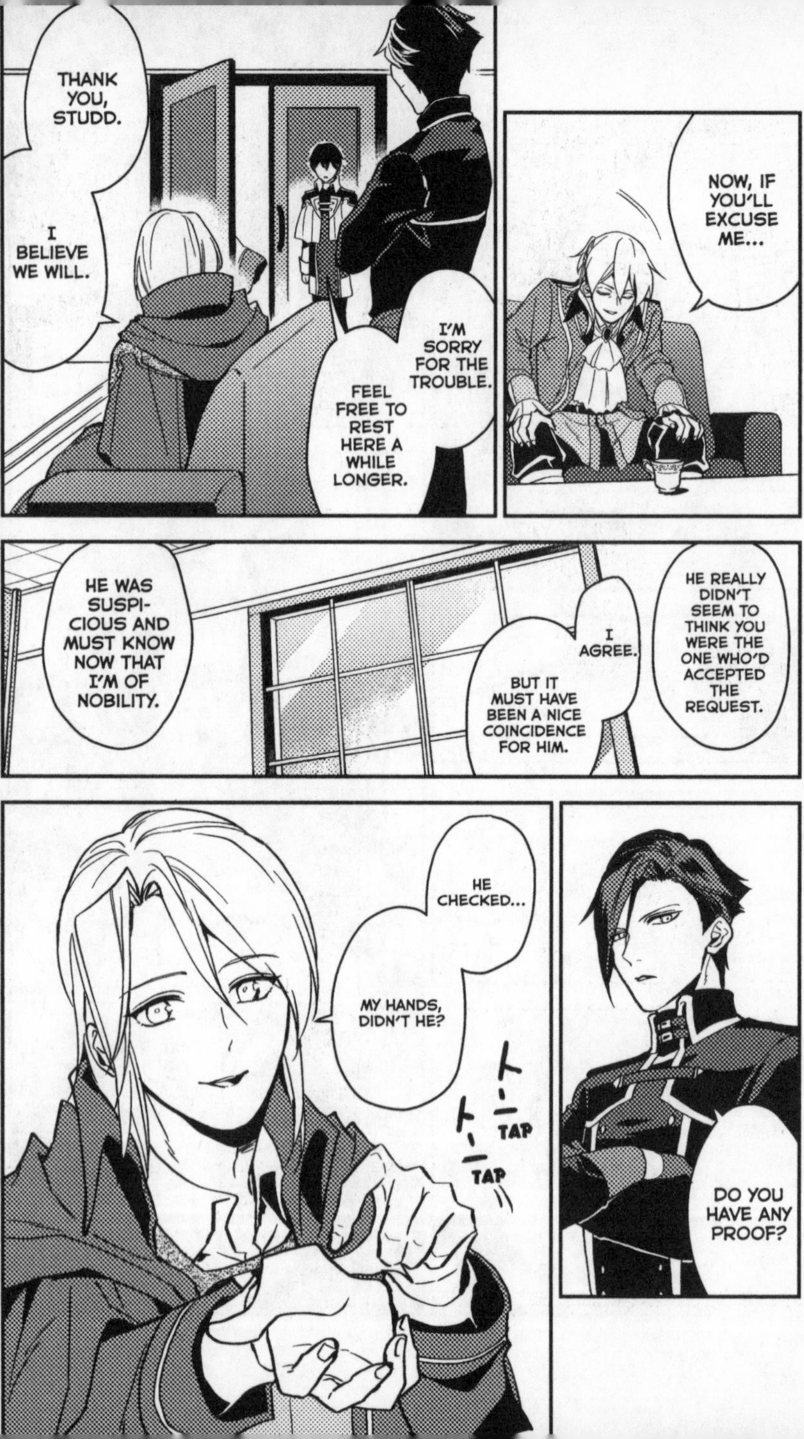
NOW, IF YOU'LL EXCUSE ME...
I'M SORRY FOR THE TROUBLE.
FEEL FREE TO REST HERE A WHILE LONGER.
THANK YOU, STUDD.
I BELIEVE WE WILL.
HE REALLY DIDN'T SEEM TO THINK YOU WERE THE ONE WHO'D ACCEPTED THE REQUEST.
I AGREE.
BUT IT MUST HAVE BEEN A NICE COINCIDENCE FOR HIM.
HE WAS SUSPICIOUS AND MUST KNOW NOW THAT I'M OF NOBILITY.
DO YOU HAVE ANY PROOF?
HE CHECKED...
MY HANDS, DIDN'T HE?
TAP
TAP

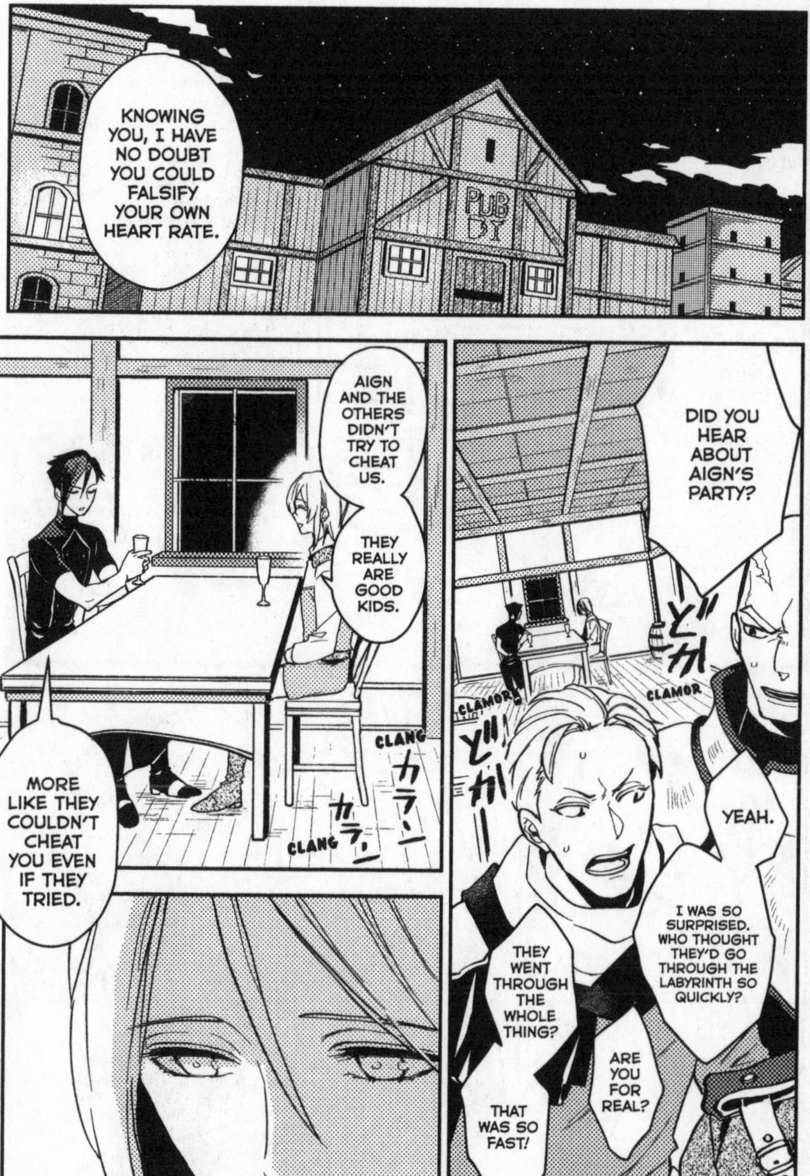
KNOWING YOU, I HAVE NO DOUBT YOU COULD FALSIFY YOUR OWN HEART RATE.
DID YOU HEAR ABOUT AIGN'S PARTY?
CLAMOR
CLAMOR
YEAH.
I WAS SO SURPRISED. WHO THOUGHT THEY'D GO THROUGH THE LABYRINTH SO QUICKLY?
THEY WENT THROUGH THE WHOLE THING?
ARE YOU FOR REAL?
THAT WAS SO FAST!
AIGN AND THE OTHERS DIDN'T TRY TO CHEAT US.
THEY REALLY ARE GOOD KIDS.
CLANG
CLANG
MORE LIKE THEY COULDN'T CHEAT YOU EVEN IF THEY TRIED.

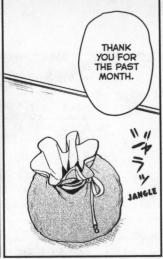

THANK YOU FOR THE PAST MONTH.

JANGLE

BUT YOU WEREN'T ABLE TO TAKE ALL MY MONEY.

THAT'S BECAUSE YOU MADE A TON AT THE LAST MINUTE.

THAT SEEMS LIKE A LOT.

IT'S TO SHOW MY APPRECIATION...

AND TO SAVE A FUTURE RESERVATION.

TWITCH

A RESERVATION?

156

IF I NEED YOUR HELP IN THE FUTURE...

WILL YOU BE AVAILABLE TO ASSIST ME?

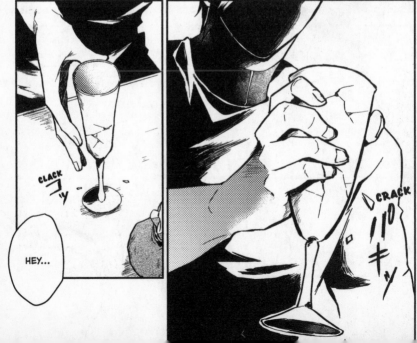

CLACK

HEY...

CRACK

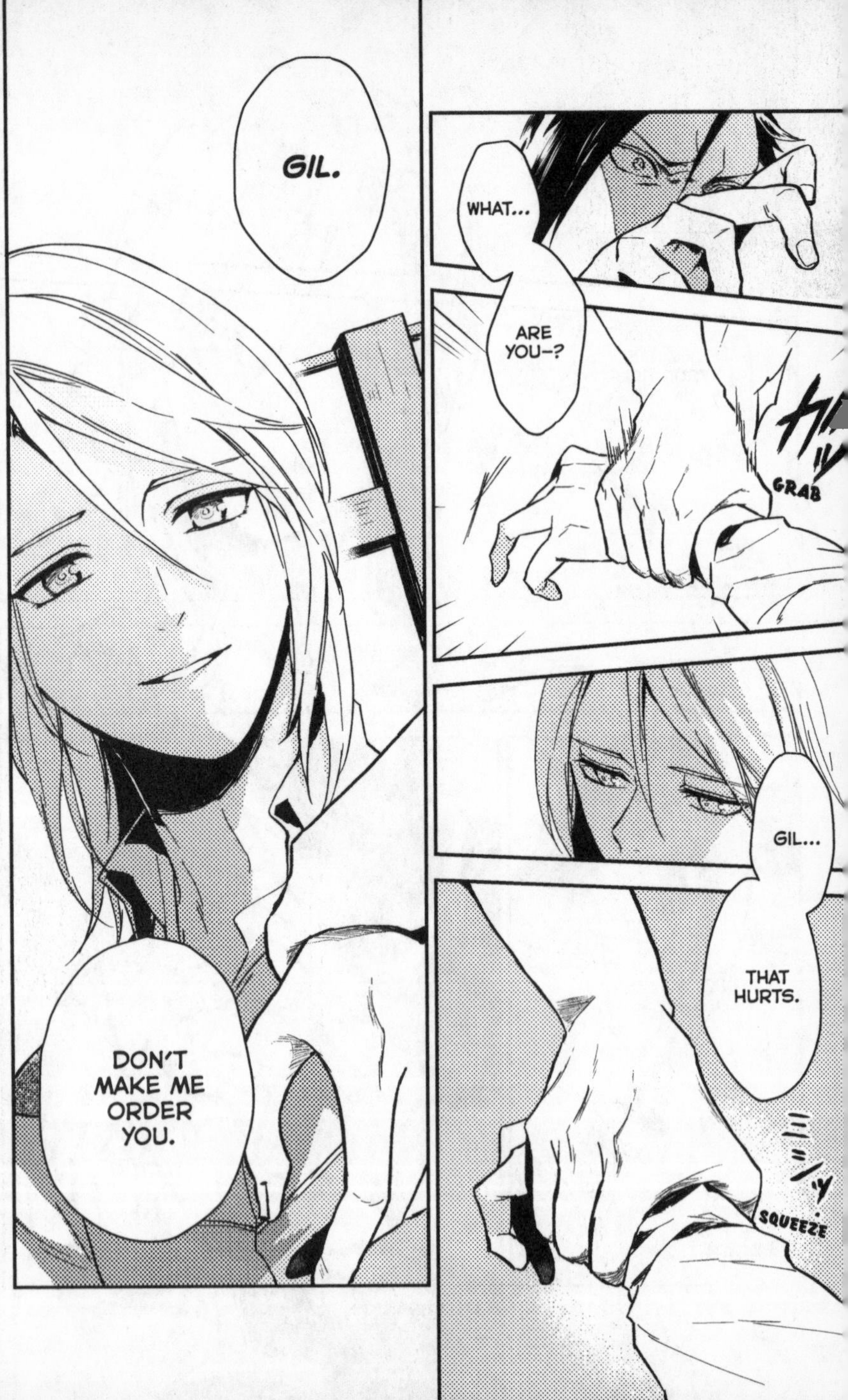
WHAT...
ARE YOU–?
GRAB
GIL...
THAT HURTS.
SQUEEZE
GIL.
DON'T MAKE ME ORDER YOU.

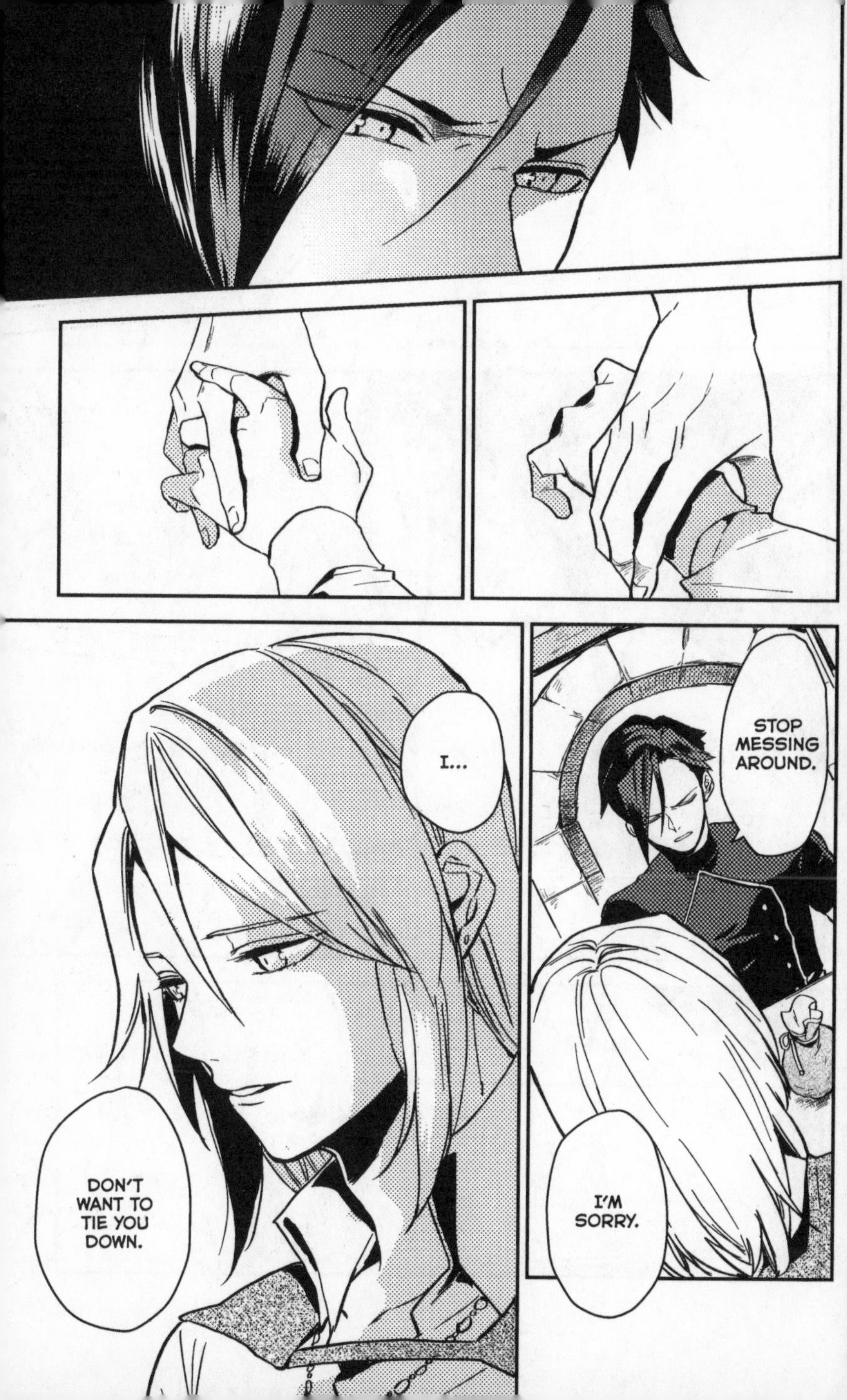
STOP MESSING AROUND.
I'M SORRY.
I...
DON'T WANT TO TIE YOU DOWN.

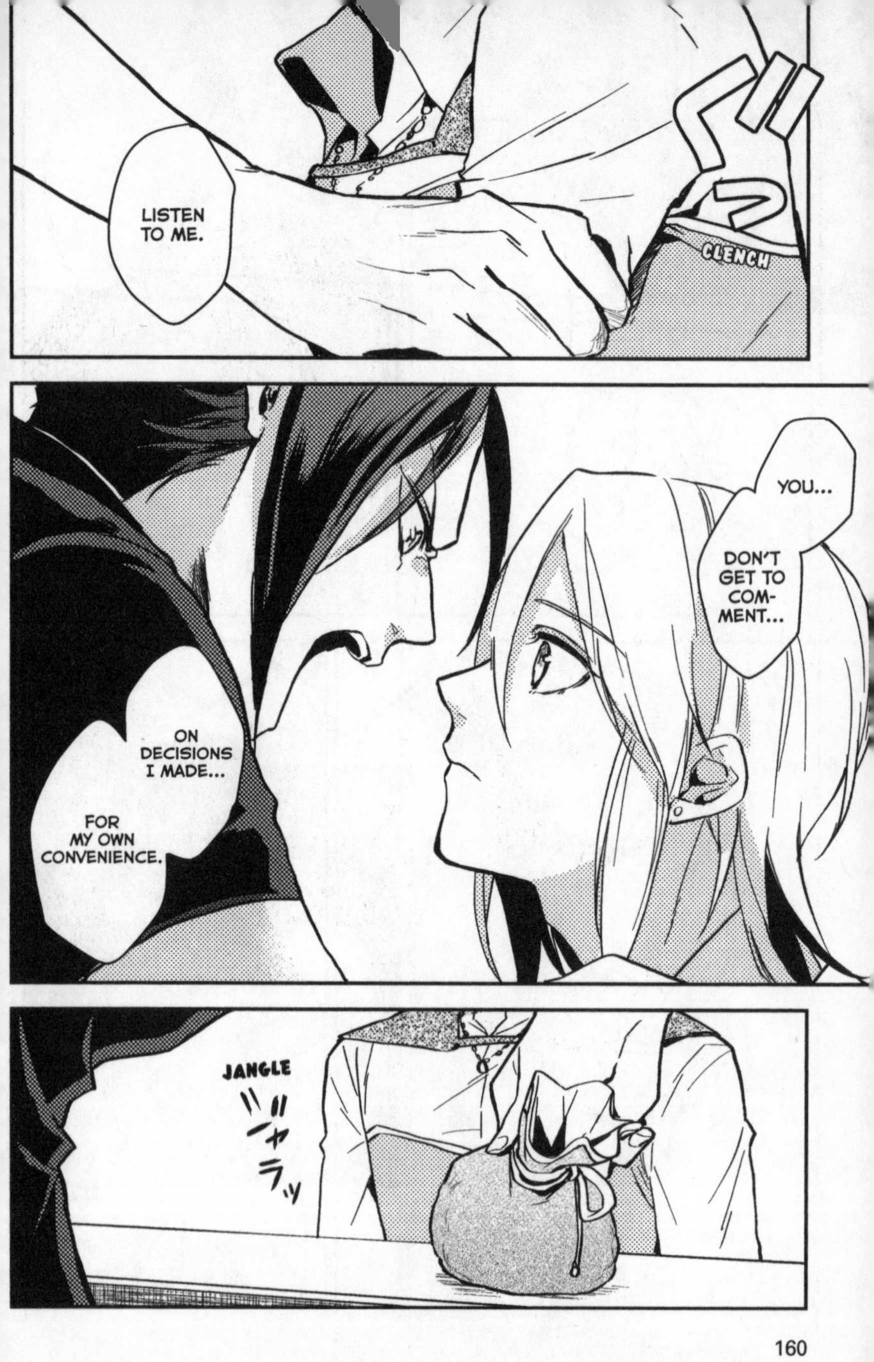
LISTEN TO ME.
CLENCH
YOU...
DON'T GET TO COM-MENT...
ON DECISIONS I MADE...
FOR MY OWN CONVENIENCE.
JANGLE
ジャラッ

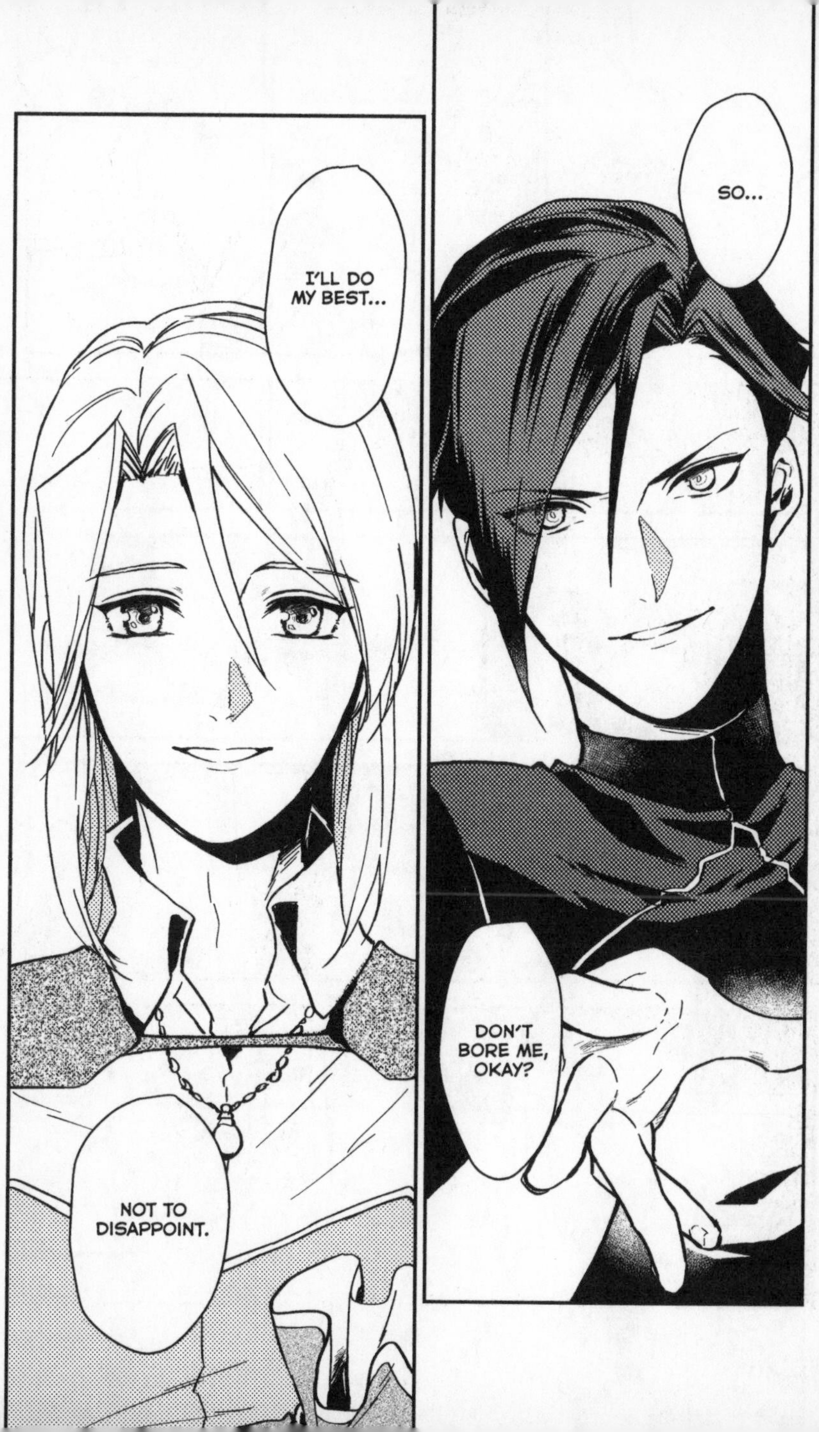
SO...
DON'T BORE ME, OKAY?
I'LL DO MY BEST...
NOT TO DISAPPOINT.

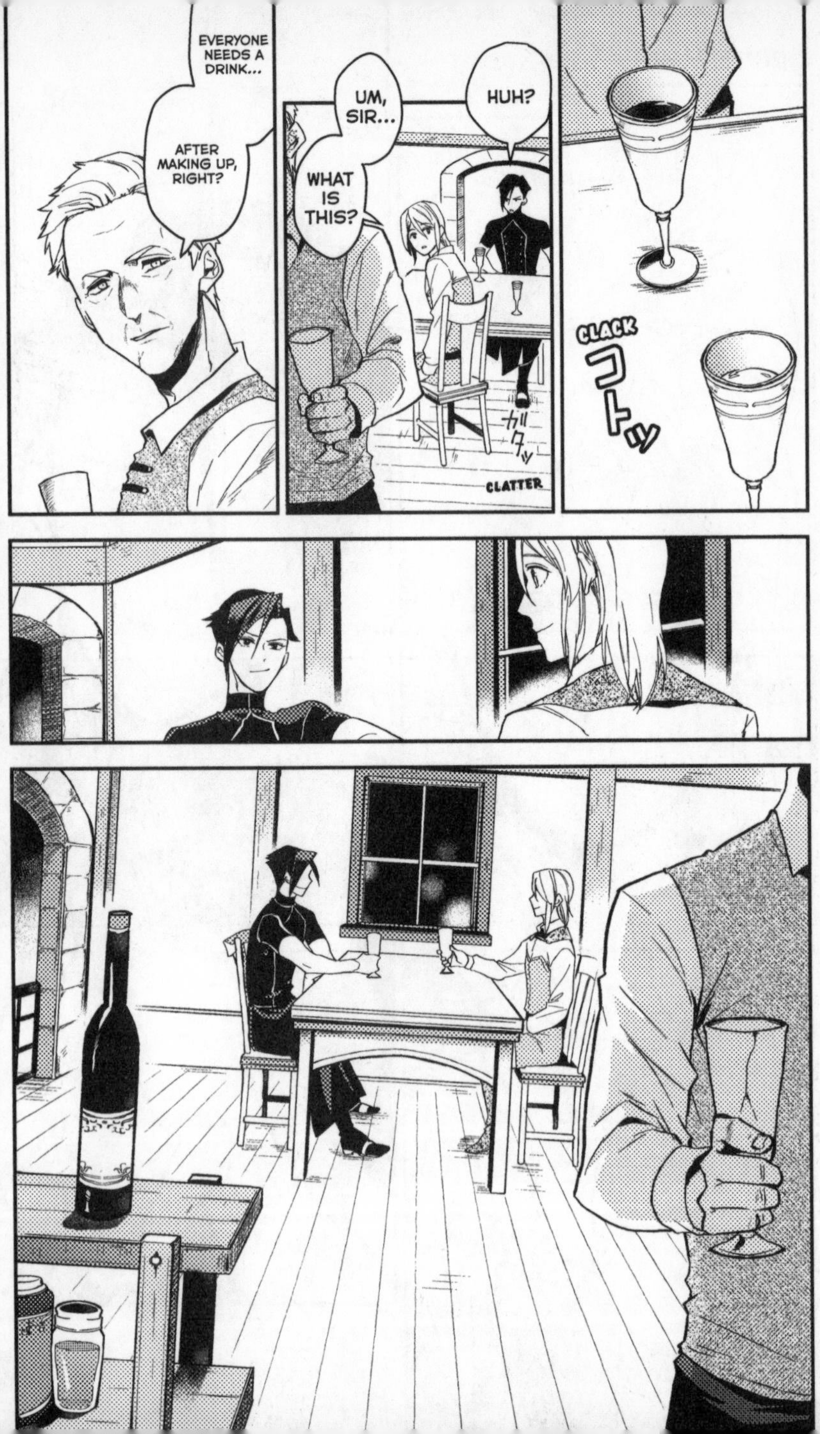
CLACK
コトッ
HUH?
UM, SIR...
WHAT IS THIS?
ガタッ
CLATTER
EVERYONE NEEDS A DRINK...
AFTER MAKING UP, RIGHT?

Bonus Manga Chapter

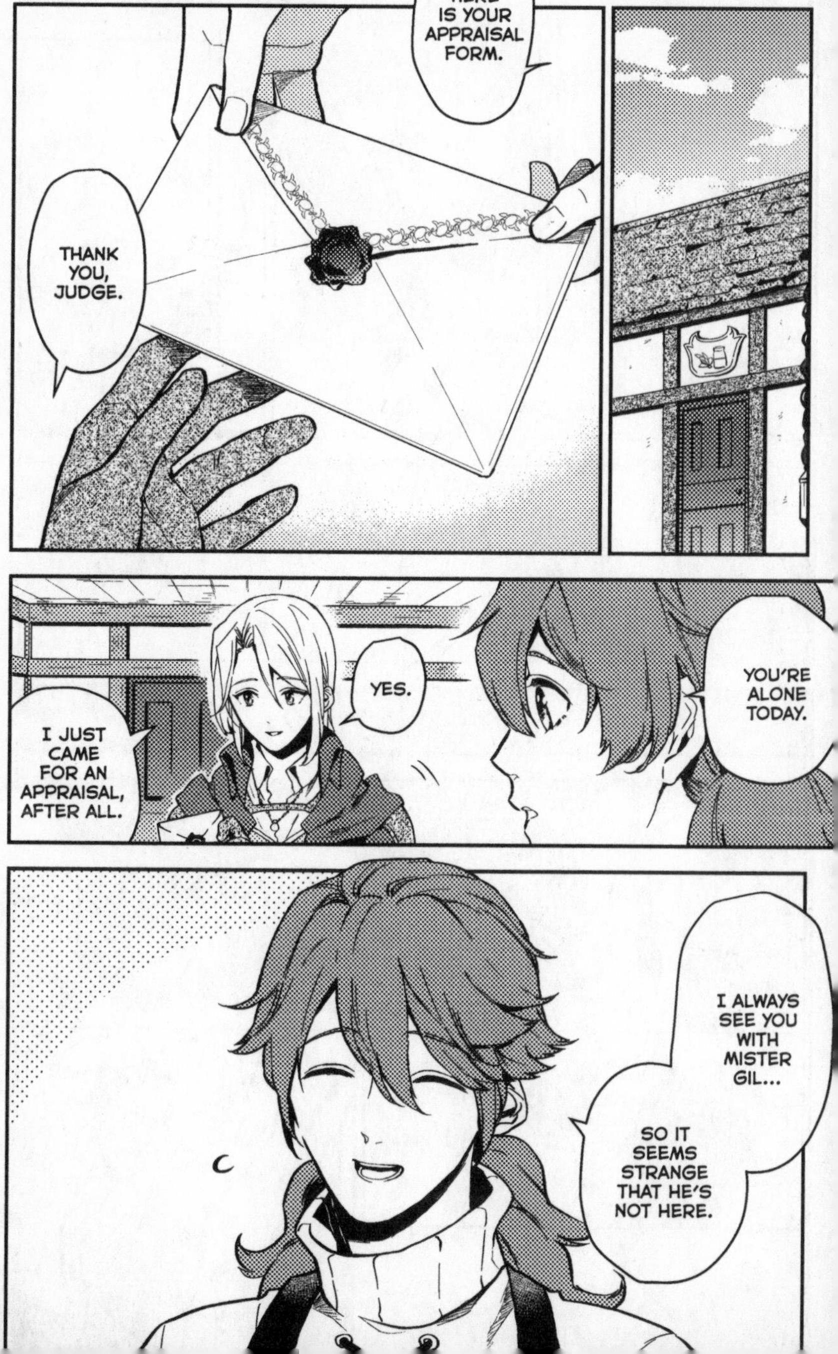
HERE IS YOUR APPRAISAL FORM.
THANK YOU, JUDGE.
YOU'RE ALONE TODAY.
YES.
I JUST CAME FOR AN APPRAISAL, AFTER ALL.
I ALWAYS SEE YOU WITH MISTER GIL...
SO IT SEEMS STRANGE THAT HE'S NOT HERE.

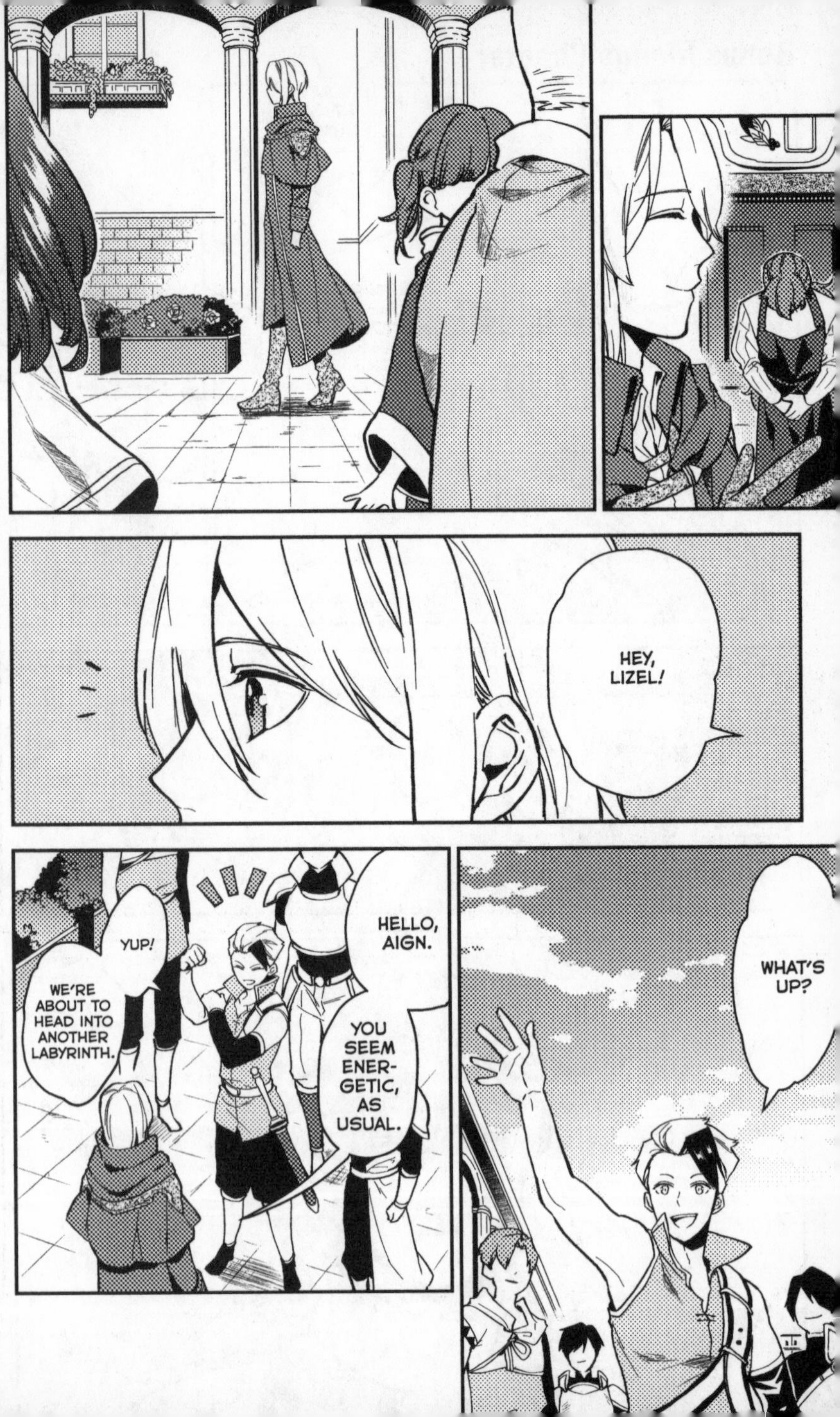
HEY, LIZEL!
WHAT'S UP?
HELLO, AIGN.
YOU SEEM ENER-GETIC, AS USUAL.
YUP!
WE'RE ABOUT TO HEAD INTO ANOTHER LABYRINTH.

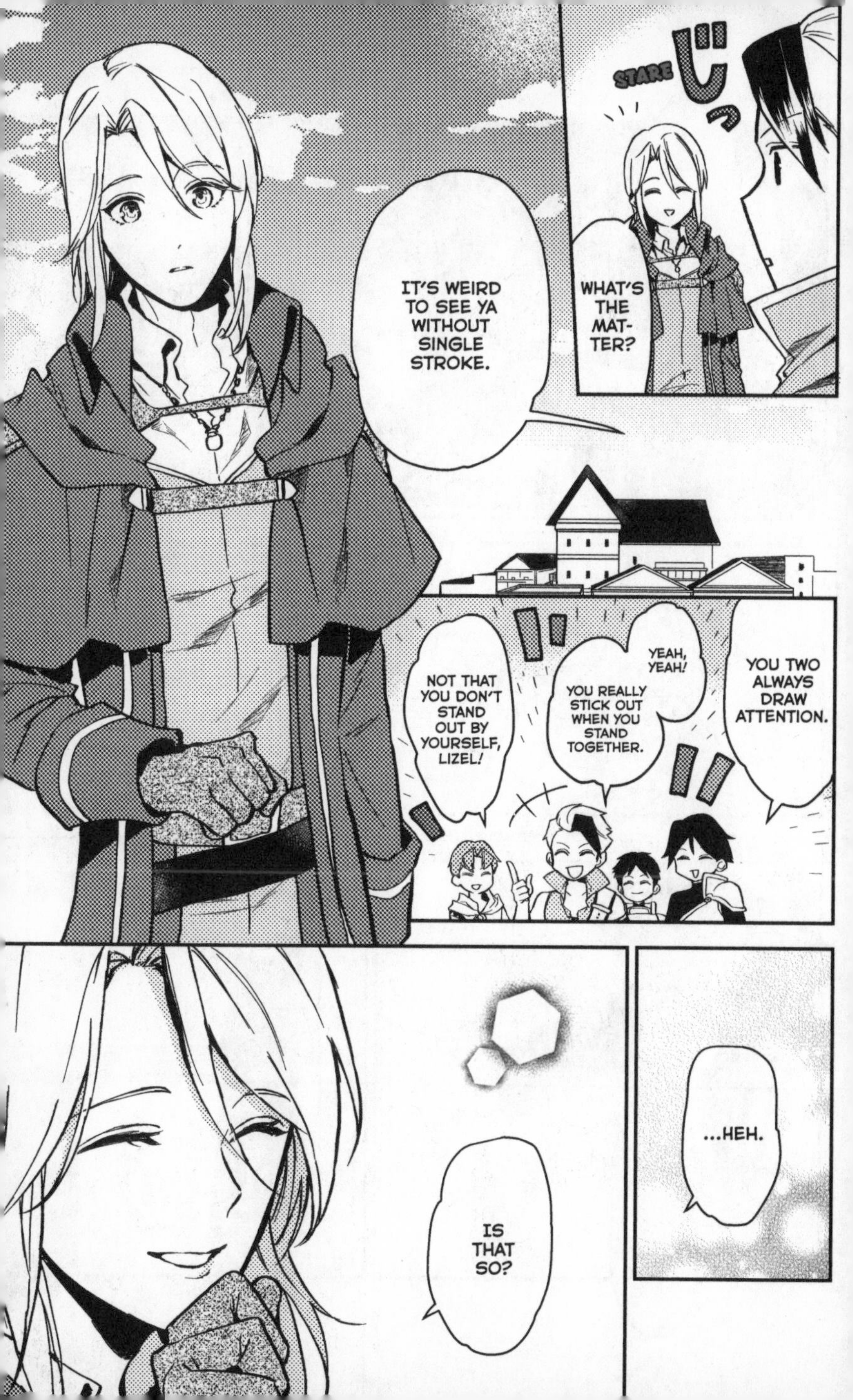
STARE
WHAT'S THE MATTER?
IT'S WEIRD TO SEE YA WITHOUT SINGLE STROKE.
YOU TWO ALWAYS DRAW ATTENTION.
YEAH, YEAH!
YOU REALLY STICK OUT WHEN YOU STAND TOGETHER.
NOT THAT YOU DON'T STAND OUT BY YOURSELF, LIZEL!
...HEH.
IS THAT SO?

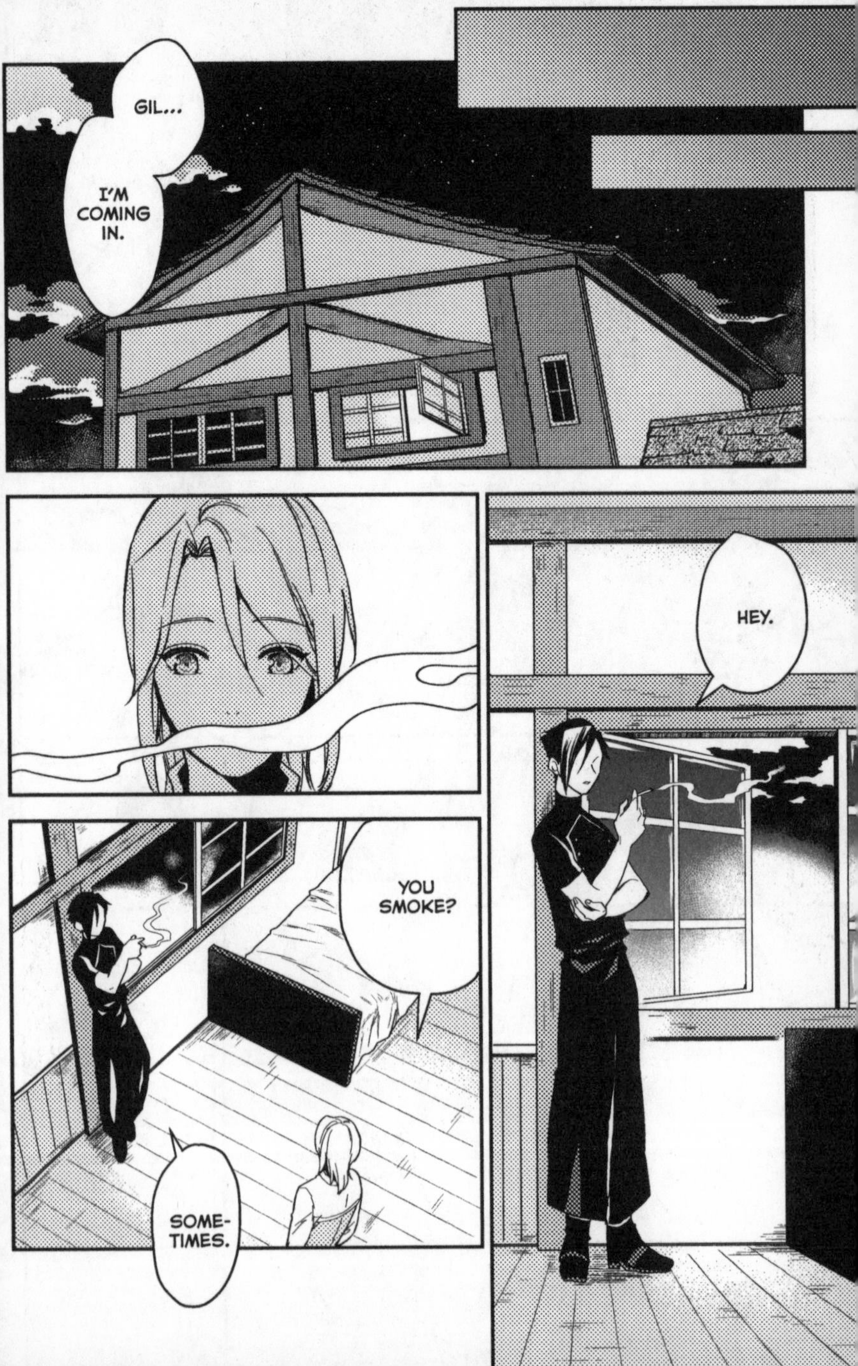
GIL...
I'M COMING IN.
HEY.
YOU SMOKE?
SOME-TIMES.

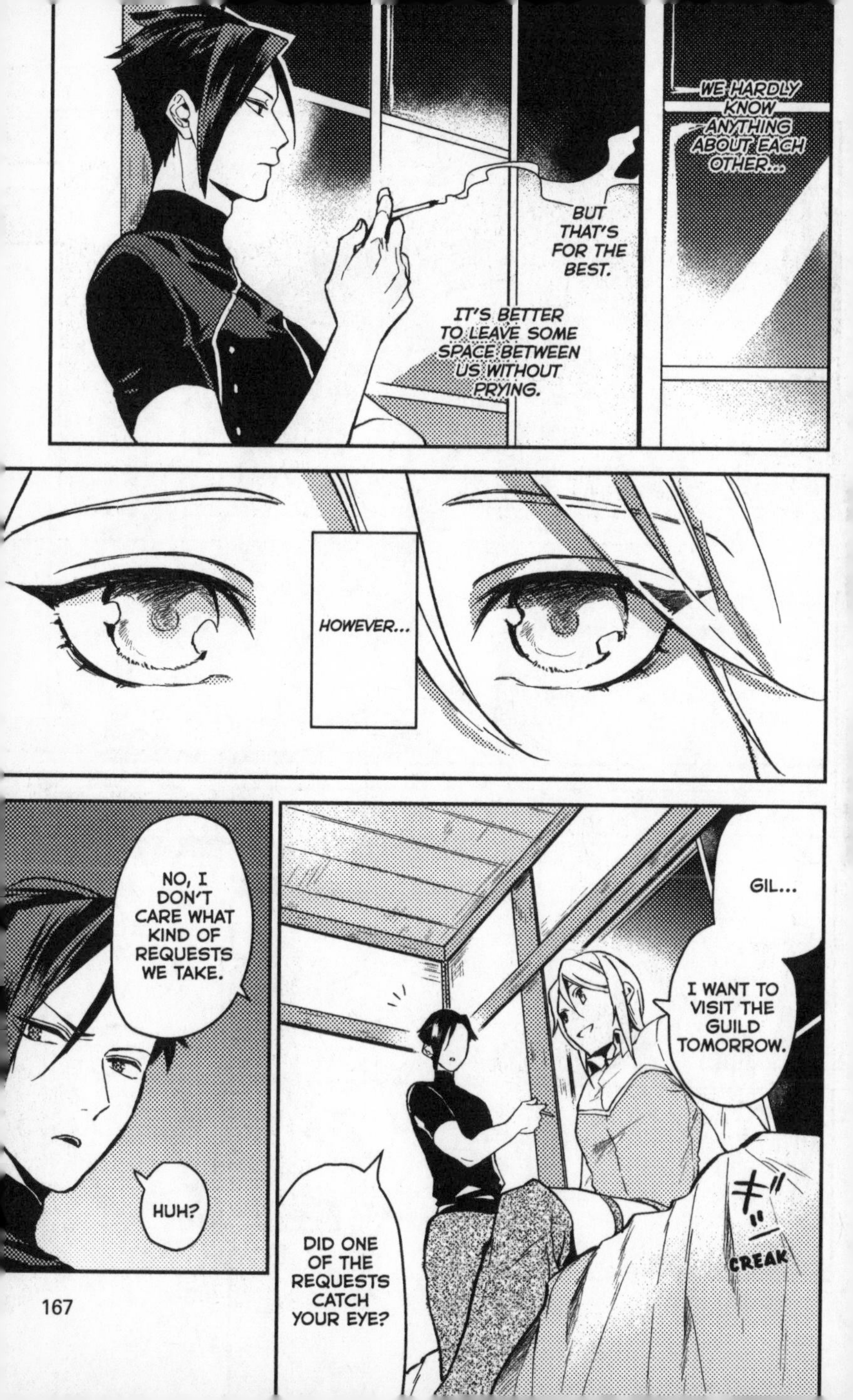
WE HARDLY KNOW ANYTHING ABOUT EACH OTHER...
BUT THAT'S FOR THE BEST.
IT'S BETTER TO LEAVE SOME SPACE BETWEEN US WITHOUT PRYING.
HOWEVER...
GIL...
I WANT TO VISIT THE GUILD TOMORROW.
ギ"
CREAK
DID ONE OF THE REQUESTS CATCH YOUR EYE?
NO, I DON'T CARE WHAT KIND OF REQUESTS WE TAKE.
HUH?

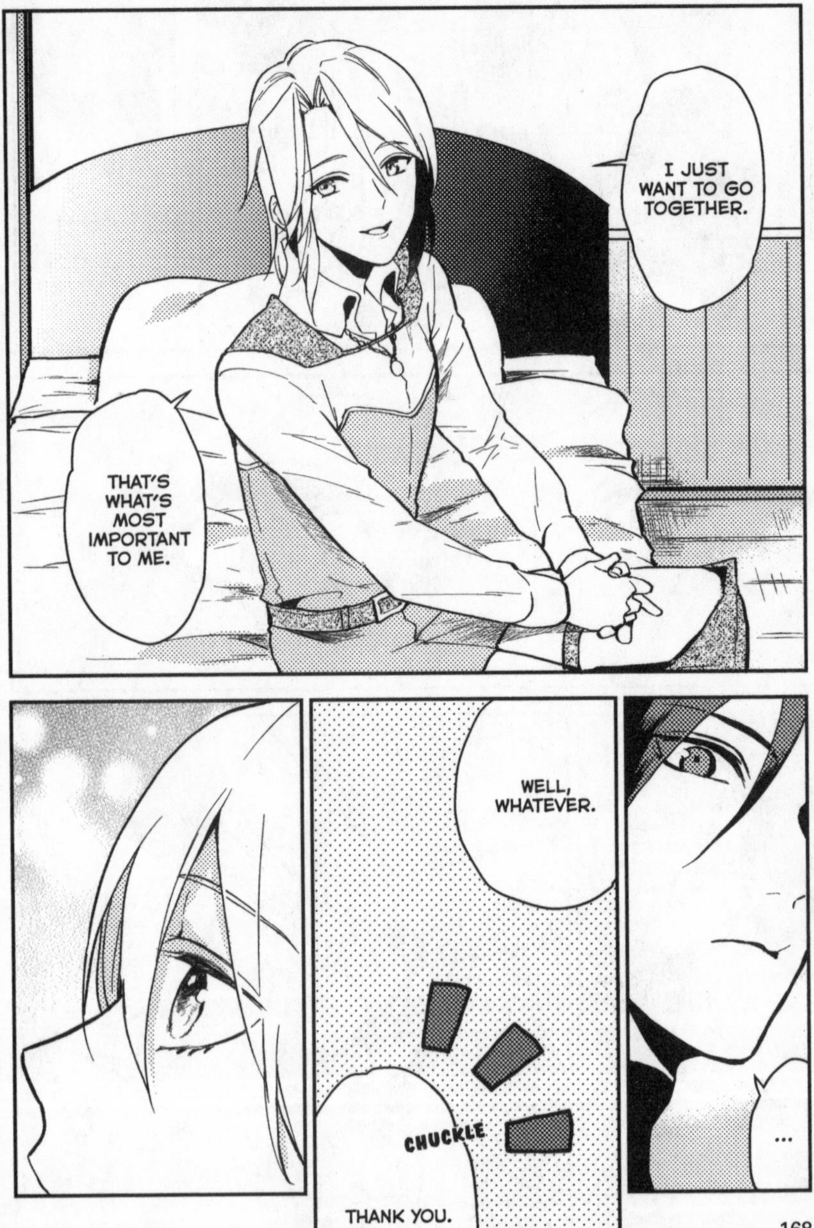
I JUST WANT TO GO TOGETHER.
THAT'S WHAT'S MOST IMPORTANT TO ME.
...
WELL, WHATEVER.
CHUCKLE
THANK YOU.

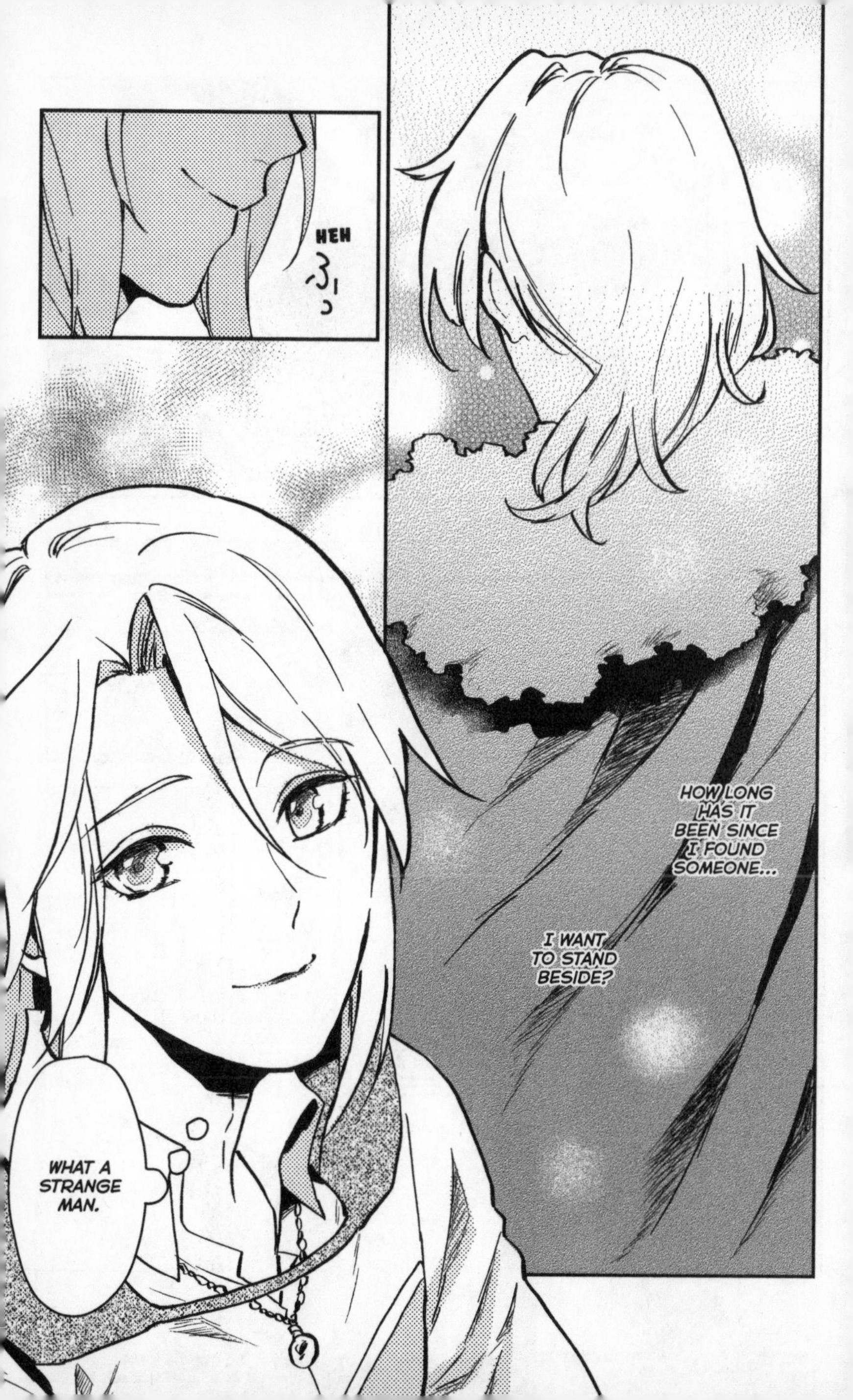
HOW LONG HAS IT BEEN SINCE I FOUND SOMEONE...
I WANT TO STAND BESIDE?
HEH
ふっ
WHAT A STRANGE MAN.

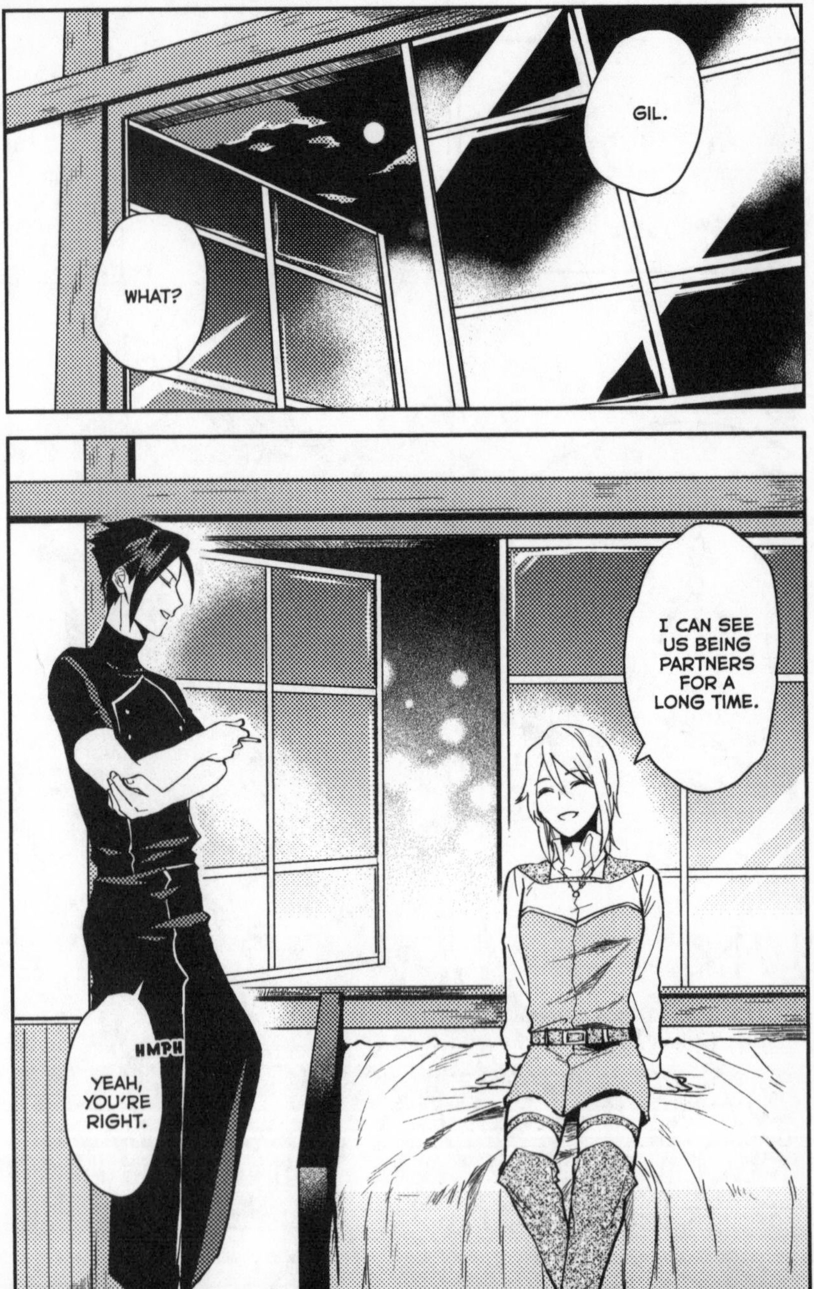
GIL.
WHAT?
I CAN SEE US BEING PARTNERS FOR A LONG TIME.
HMPH
YEAH, YOU'RE RIGHT.

A Gentle Noble's
VACATION
RECOMMENDATION
End of Volume 1

It's nice to meet you! I'm Momochi.
This is my first time publishing a comic, so after I was given the opportunity I had to fight an unusual amount of anxiety. Now that it's been published without any major problems, I feel like I can take a breath of relief.

In the next volume, more charming characters will continue to be introduced alongside Lizel and Gil. I hope fans of the original light novel series as well as fans who learned about the series through the manga can enjoy it!

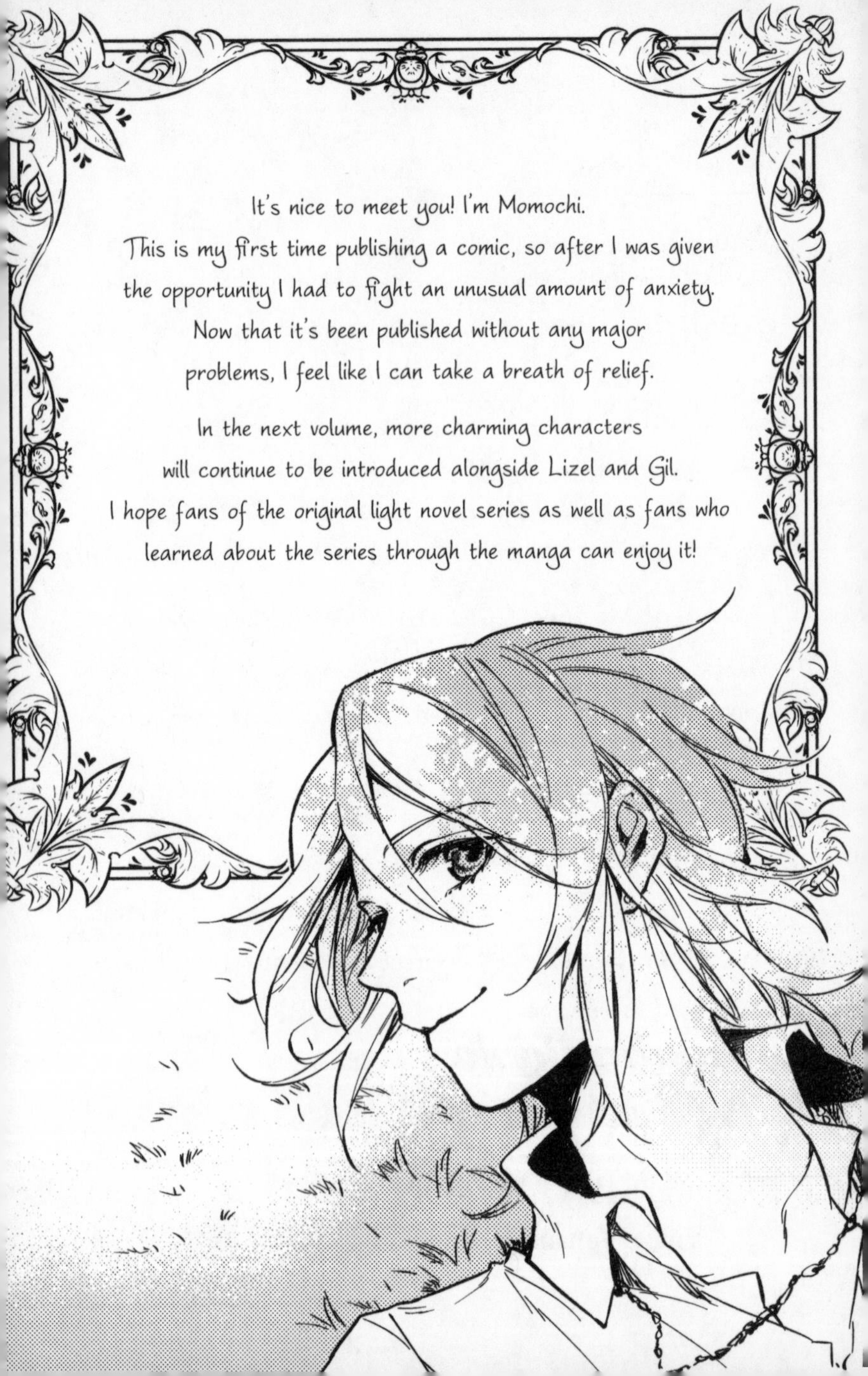

POST SCRIPT

Thanks to the love and devotion of the series' fans, Lizel's vacation has finally been adapted into a manga! I've received many comments from devoted fans, such as "I collected all the books!" and "I wish they hadn't cut out this scene!" and "Gil was unexpectedly expressive." Every comment makes me as happy as can be. You've all been so kind. For those new to the series, hello! I'm Misaki.

In any case, Momochi-sensei's Lizel is absolutely marvelous! In contrast to the angelic Lizel drawn by Sando-sensei, who was in charge of character design and illustrations for the novels, Momochi-sensei shows us a Lizel who is a little devilish but adorable when he's just woken up. Isn't his sleepy face the cutest?! In the original novels, Lizel is wishy-washy and peculiarly reserved, which almost makes him a poor protagonist. To think he could become this lively! At the same time as I cry tears of gratitude, I also live in fear of readers' opinions.

Momochi-sensei has brought Lizel and the other characters to life so that they can continue to enjoy their vacations. Please continue to relax alongside them in future volumes!

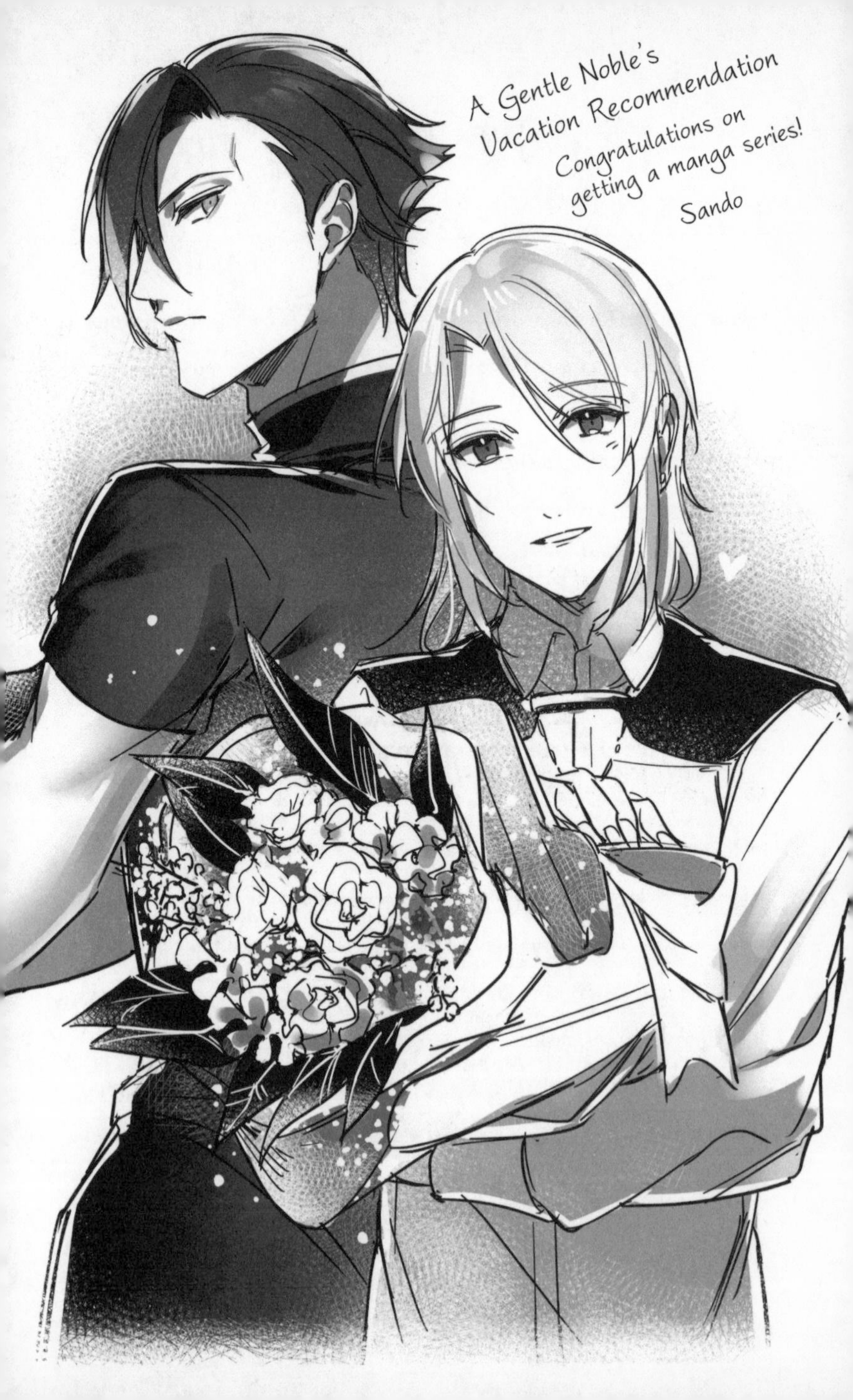
A Gentle Noble's
Vacation Recommendation
Congratulations on
getting a manga series!
Sando

A Gentle Noble's
VACATION
RECOMMENDATION

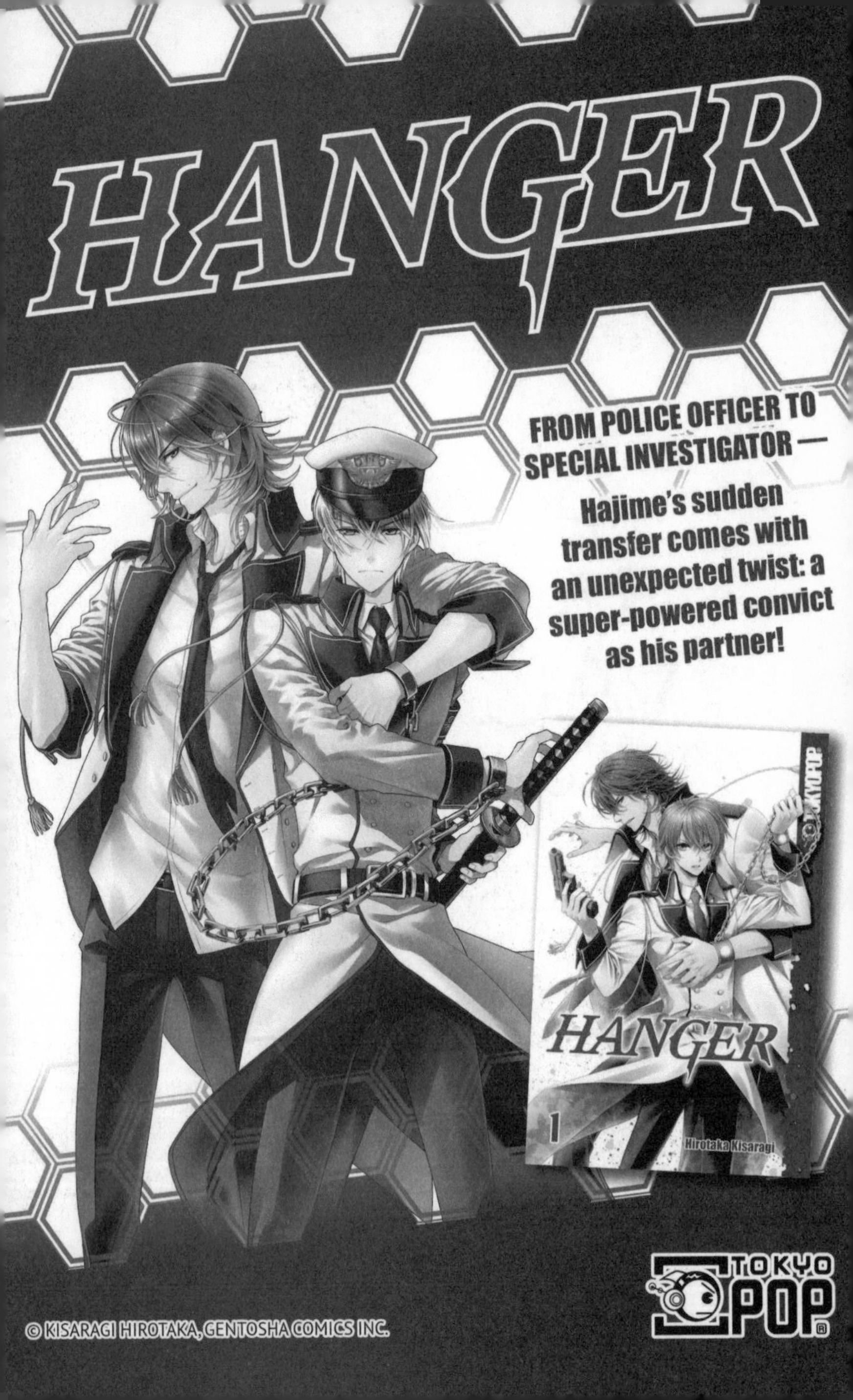
HANGER
FROM POLICE OFFICER TO SPECIAL INVESTIGATOR —
Hajime's sudden transfer comes with an unexpected twist: a super-powered convict as his partner!
TOKYOPOP
HANGER
1
Hirotaka Kisaragi
TOKYO POP
© KISARAGI HIROTAKA, GENTOSHA COMICS INC.

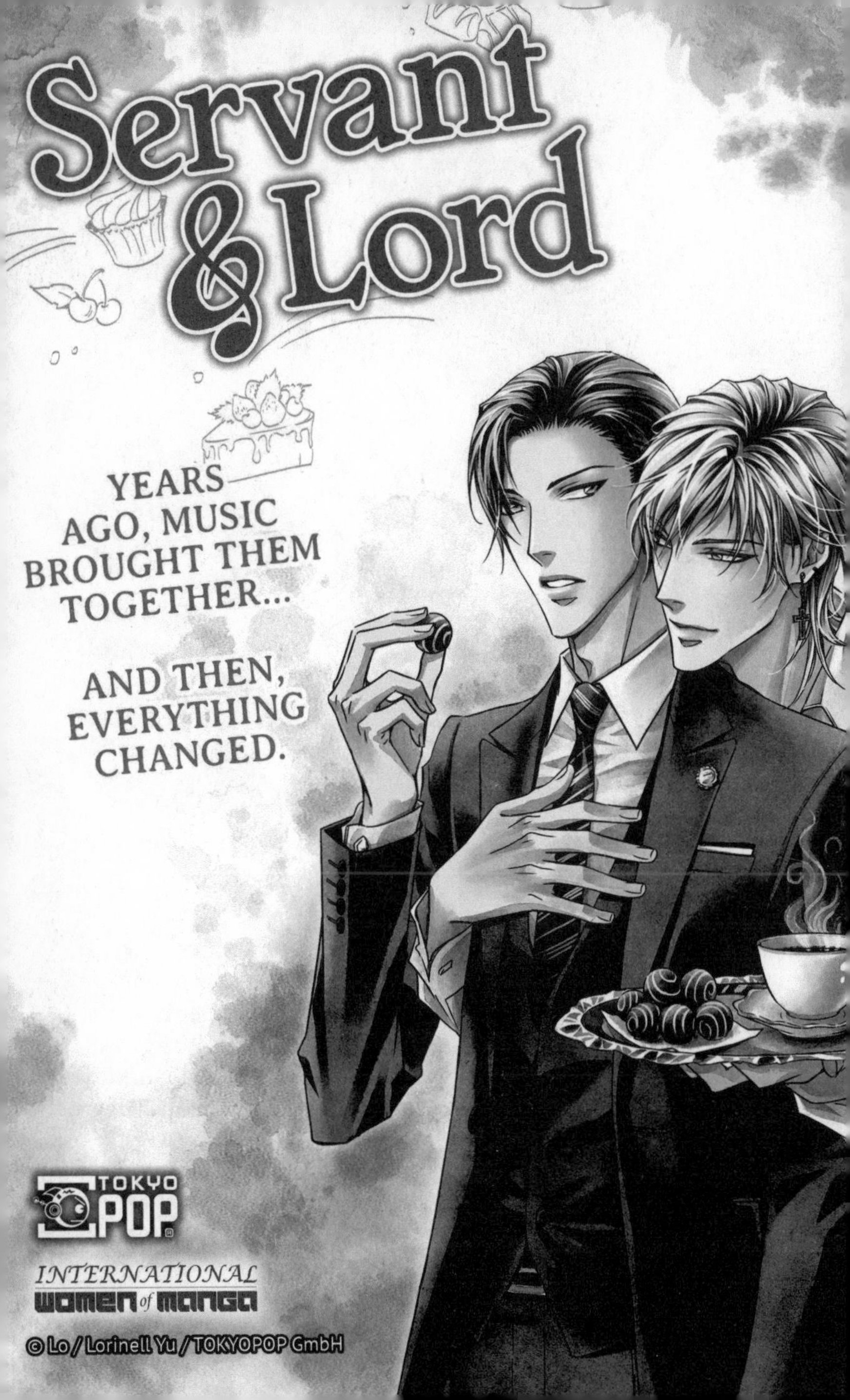
Servant & Lord
YEARS AGO, MUSIC BROUGHT THEM TOGETHER...
AND THEN, EVERYTHING CHANGED.
TOKYOPOP
INTERNATIONAL WOMEN of MANGA
© Lo / Lorinell Yu / TOKYOPOP GmbH

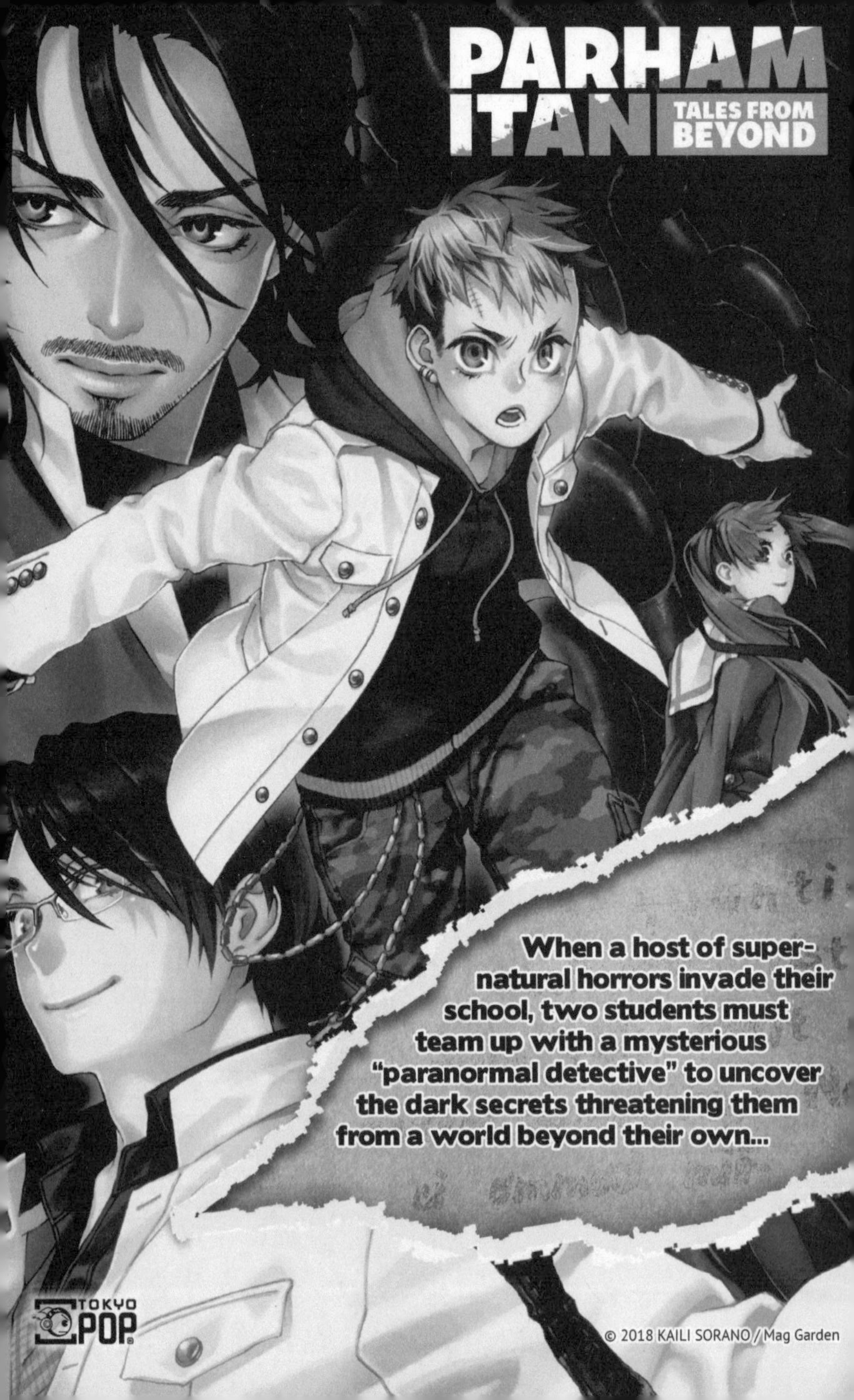

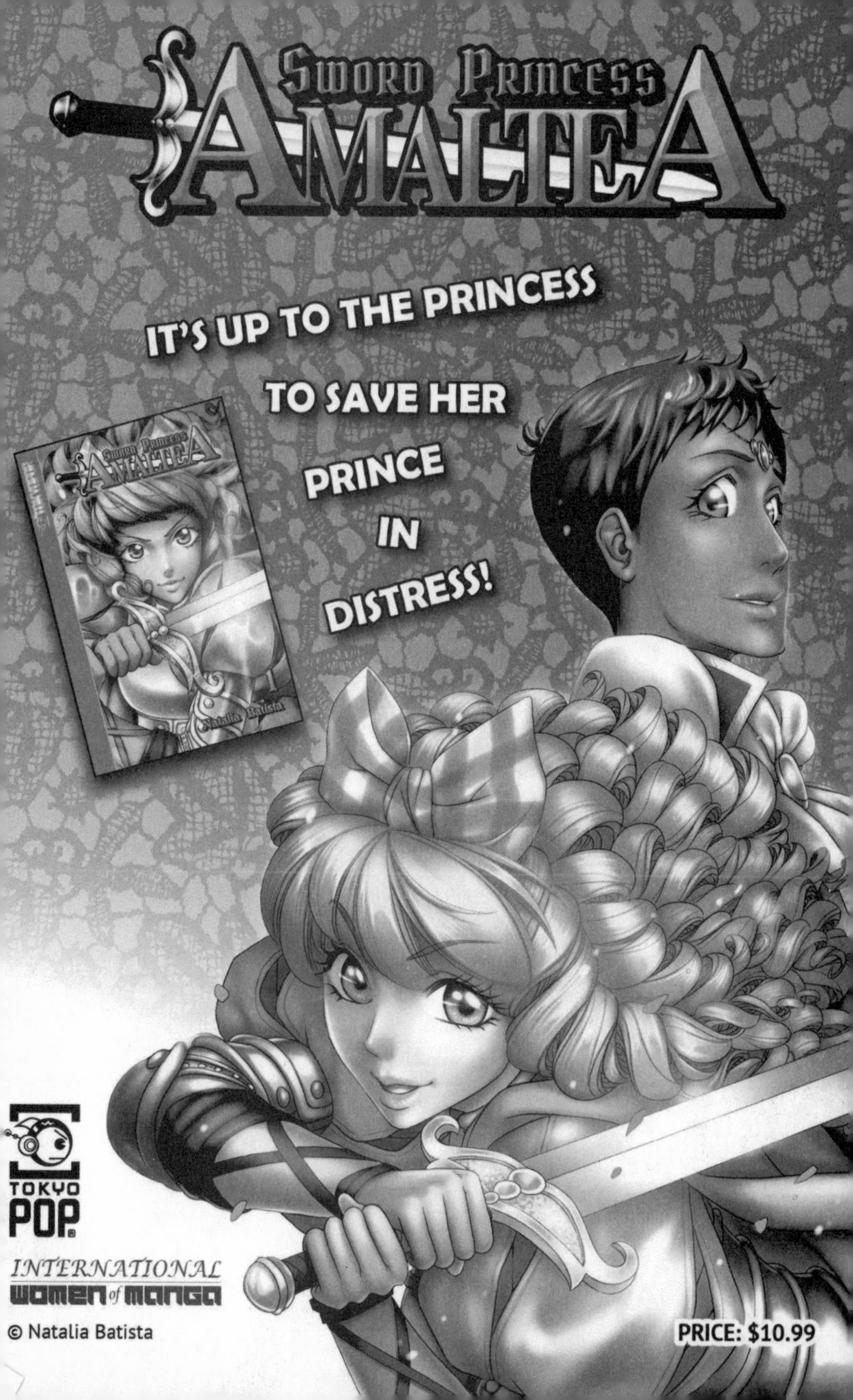

Sword Princess
AMALTEA
IT'S UP TO THE PRINCESS
TO SAVE HER
PRINCE
IN
DISTRESS!
Sword Princess
AMALTEA
Natalia Batista
TOKYO
POP
INTERNATIONAL
women of manga
© Natalia Batista
PRICE: $10.99

Long ago, an ancient hero sealed
away the underworld. Now, with
that sacred barrier broken, it's up
to Rin and the mysterious demon
Aghyr to restore balance to the
Kingdom of Nohmur!

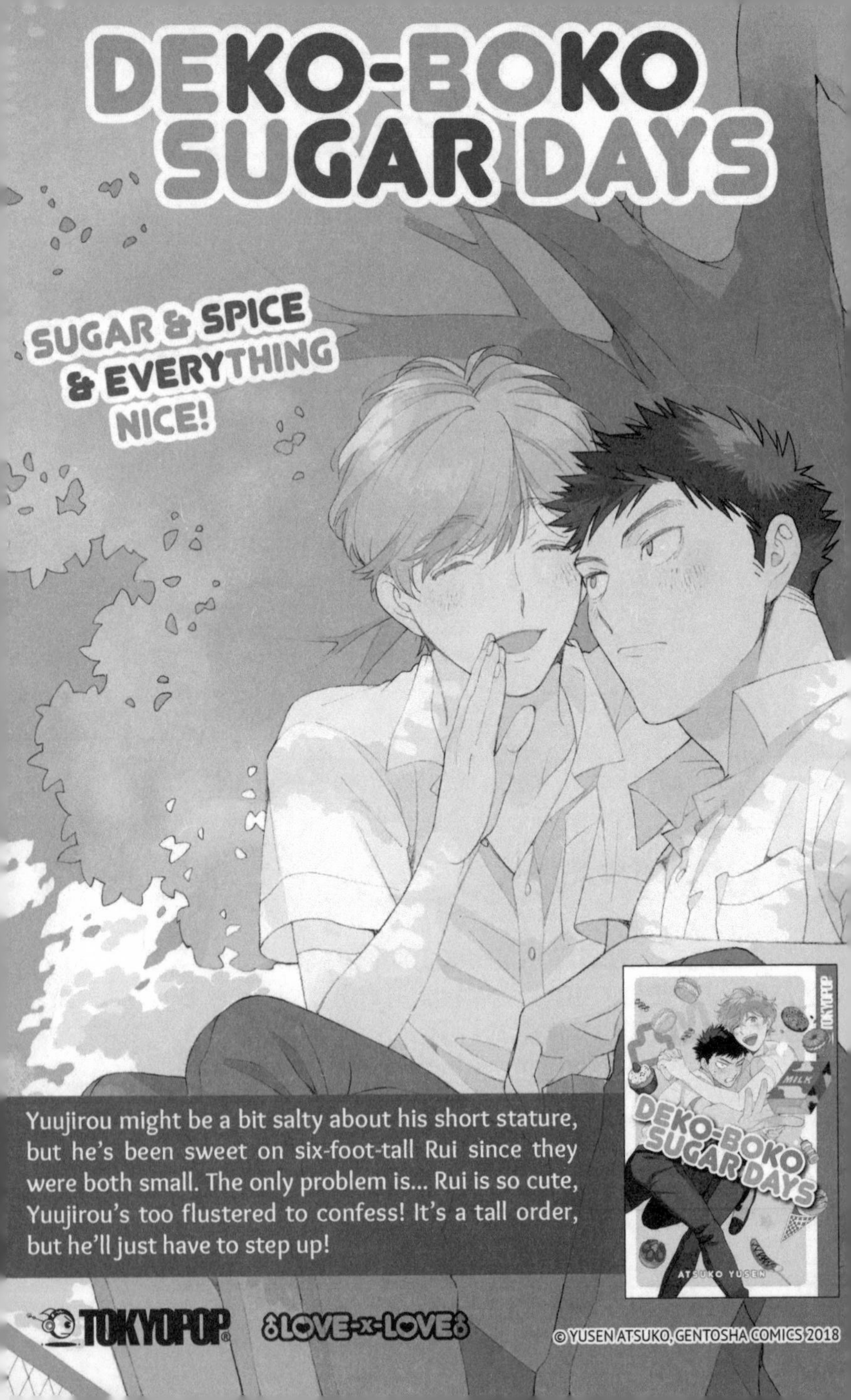
DEKO-BOKO SUGAR DAYS
SUGAR & SPICE & EVERYTHING NICE!
Yuujirou might be a bit salty about his short stature, but he's been sweet on six-foot-tall Rui since they were both small. The only problem is... Rui is so cute, Yuujirou's too flustered to confess! It's a tall order, but he'll just have to step up!
TOKYOPOP
MILK
DEKO-BOKO SUGAR DAYS
ATSUKO YUSEN
TOKYOPOP
LOVE x LOVE
© YUSEN ATSUKO, GENTOSHA COMICS 2018

REPLAY

There's nothing Yuta loves more than baseball...

Except **Ritsu**.

A heartwarming love story about growing up and facing the future together.

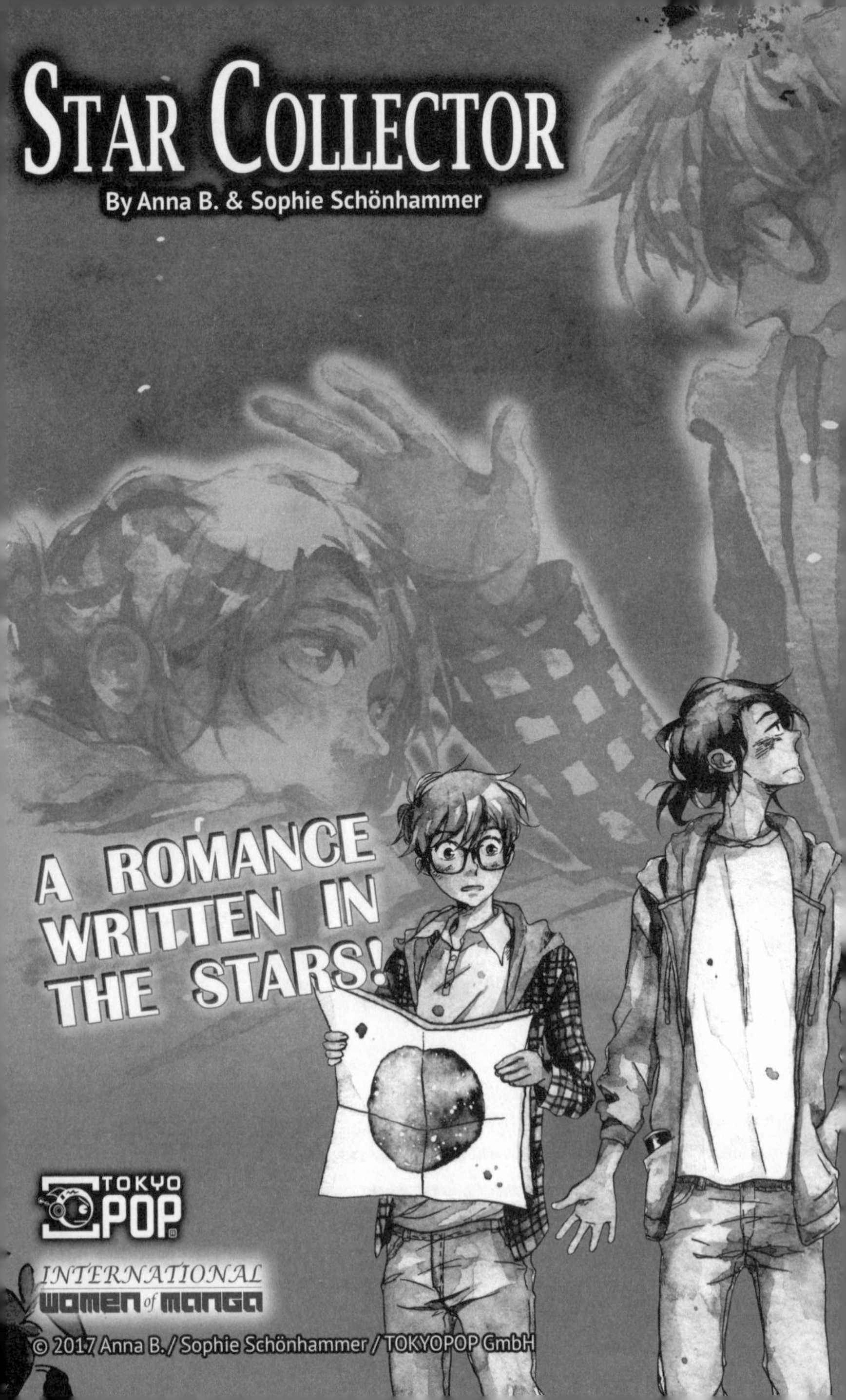
STAR COLLECTOR
By Anna B. & Sophie Schönhammer
A ROMANCE WRITTEN IN THE STARS!
TOKYO POP
INTERNATIONAL WOMEN of MANGA
© 2017 Anna B. / Sophie Schönhammer / TOKYOPOP GmbH

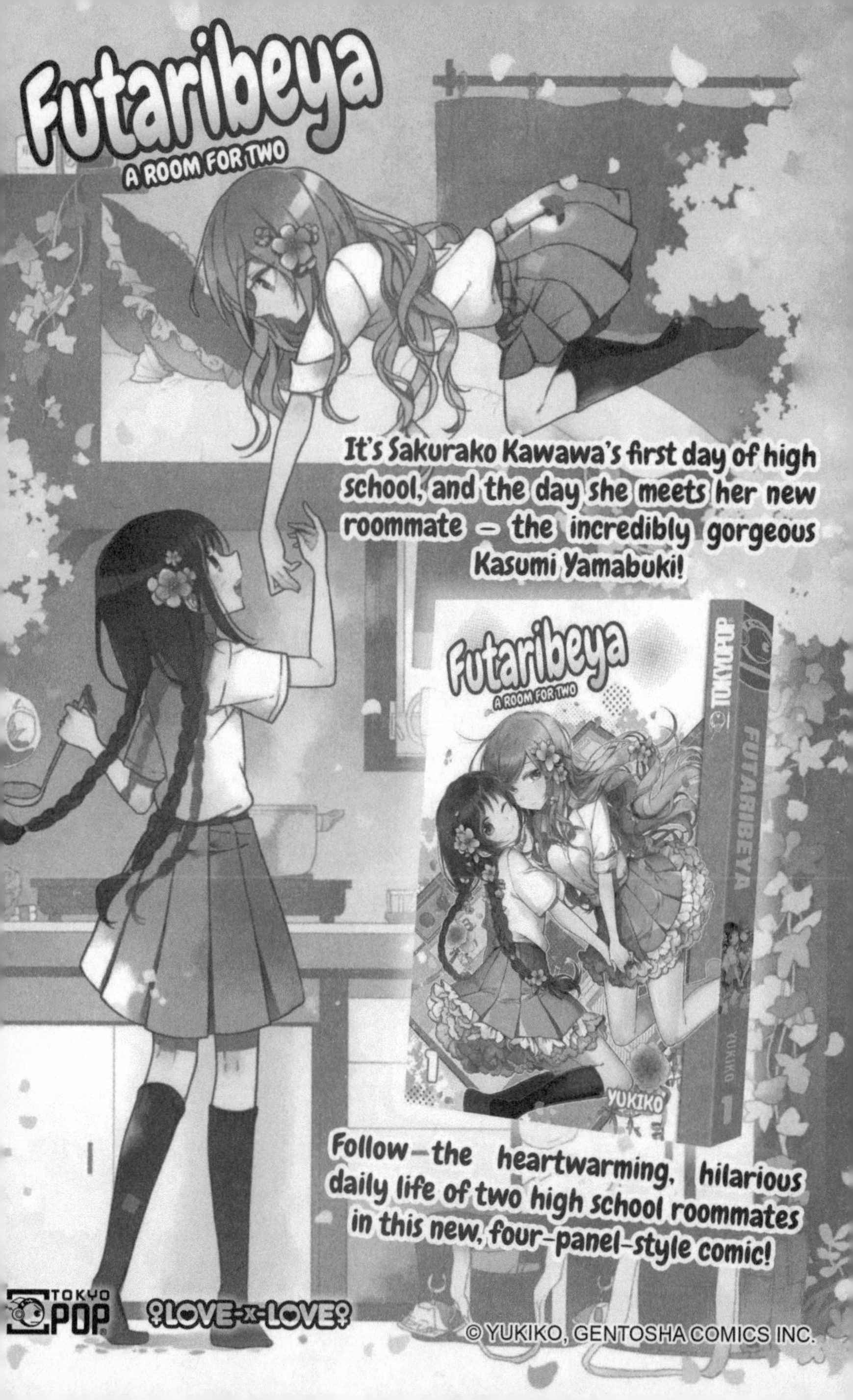
Futaribeya
A ROOM FOR TWO
It's Sakurako Kawawa's first day of high school, and the day she meets her new roommate – the incredibly gorgeous Kasumi Yamabuki!
Futaribeya
A ROOM FOR TWO
TOKYOPOP
FUTARIBEYA
YUKIKO
1
YUKIKO
1
Follow the heartwarming, hilarious daily life of two high school roommates in this new, four-panel-style comic!
TOKYOPOP
LOVE x LOVE
© YUKIKO, GENTOSHA COMICS INC.

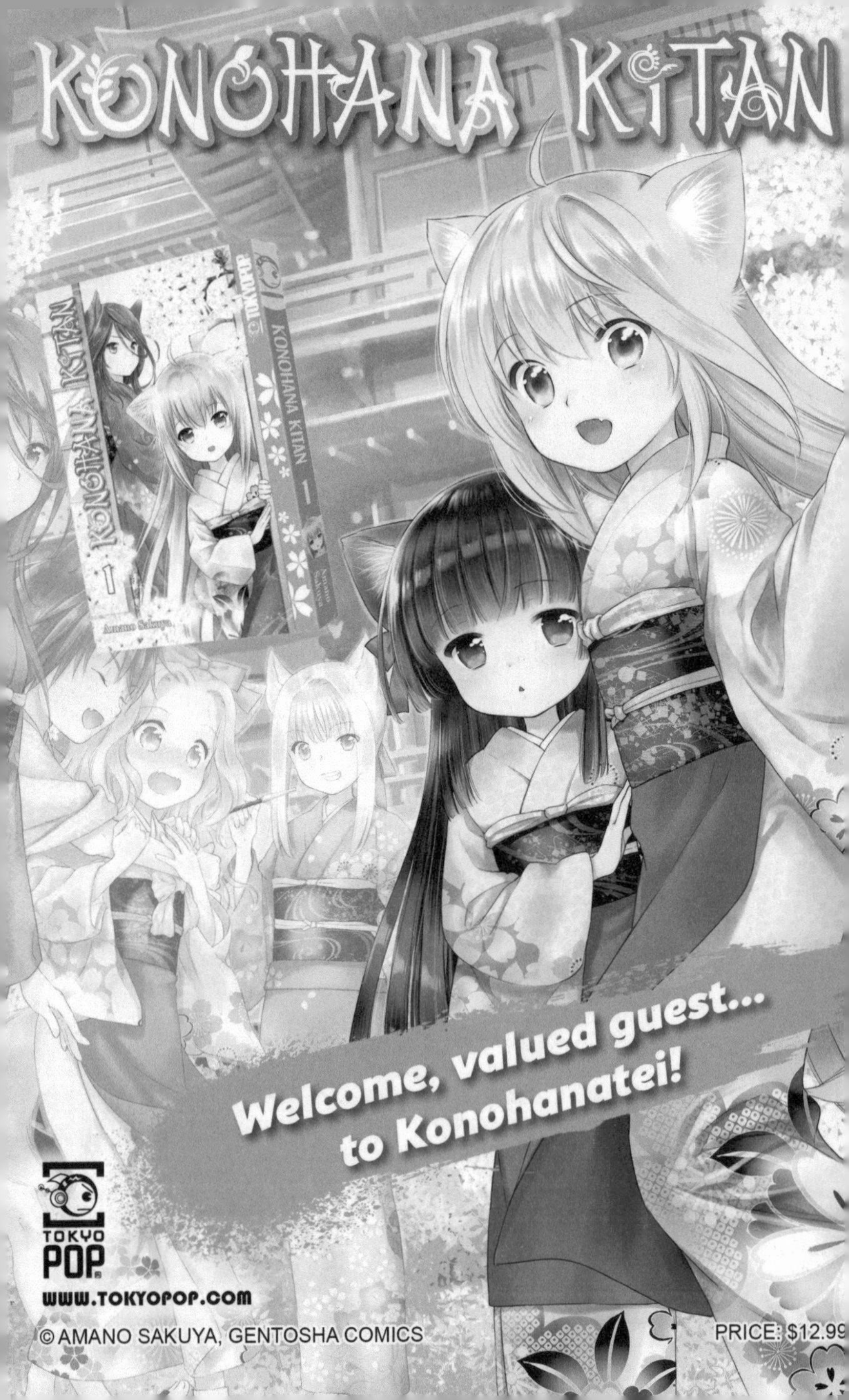
KONOHANA KITAN
KONOHANA KITAN 1
Amano Sakuya
TOKYOPOP
Welcome, valued guest...
to Konohanatei!
TOKYO POP
WWW.TOKYOPOP.COM
© AMANO SAKUYA, GENTOSHA COMICS
PRICE: $12.99

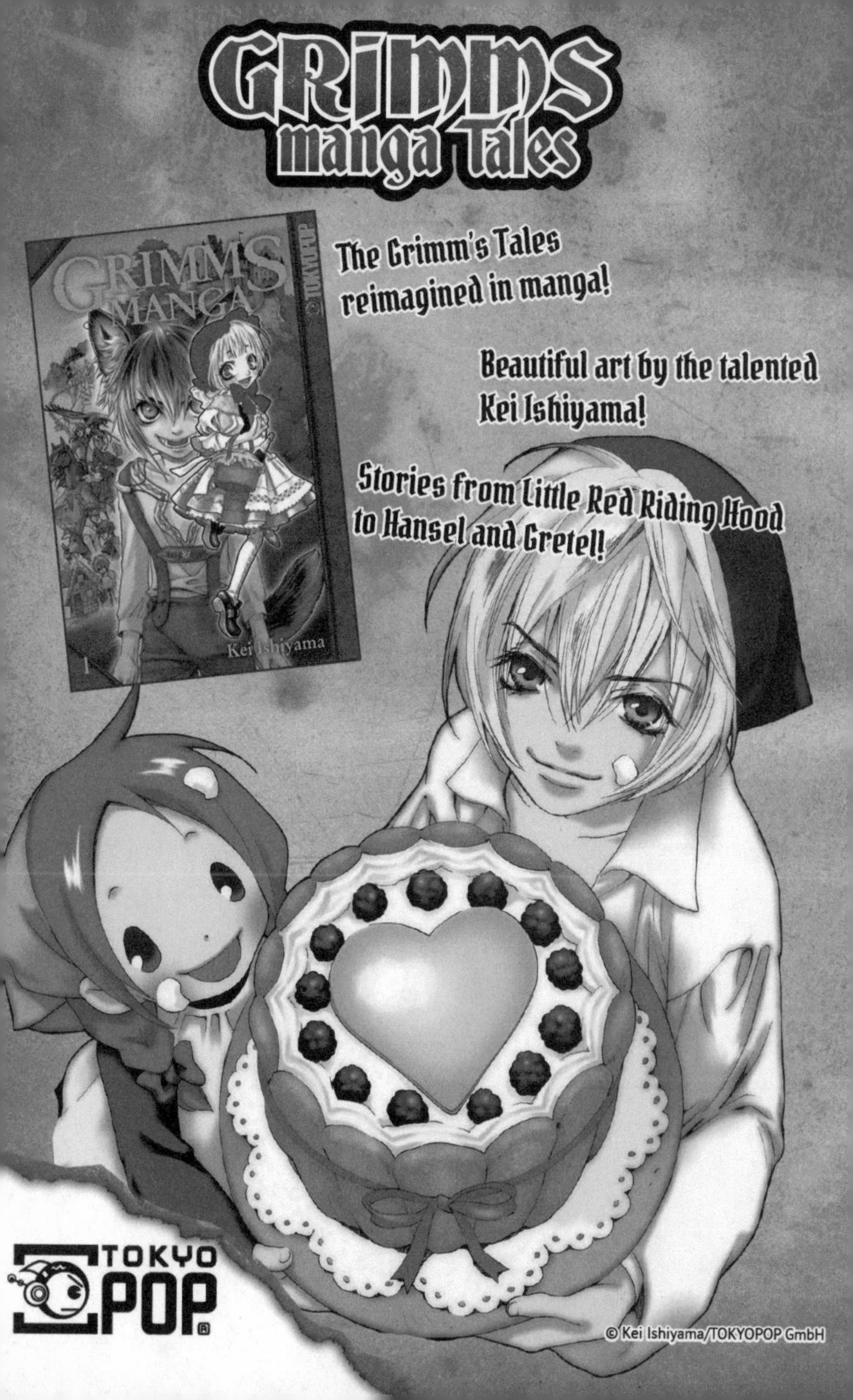
GRIMMS
manga Tales
The Grimm's Tales
reimagined in manga!
Beautiful art by the talented
Kei Ishiyama!
Stories from Little Red Riding Hood
to Hansel and Gretel!
TOKYOPOP
© Kei Ishiyama/TOKYOPOP GmbH

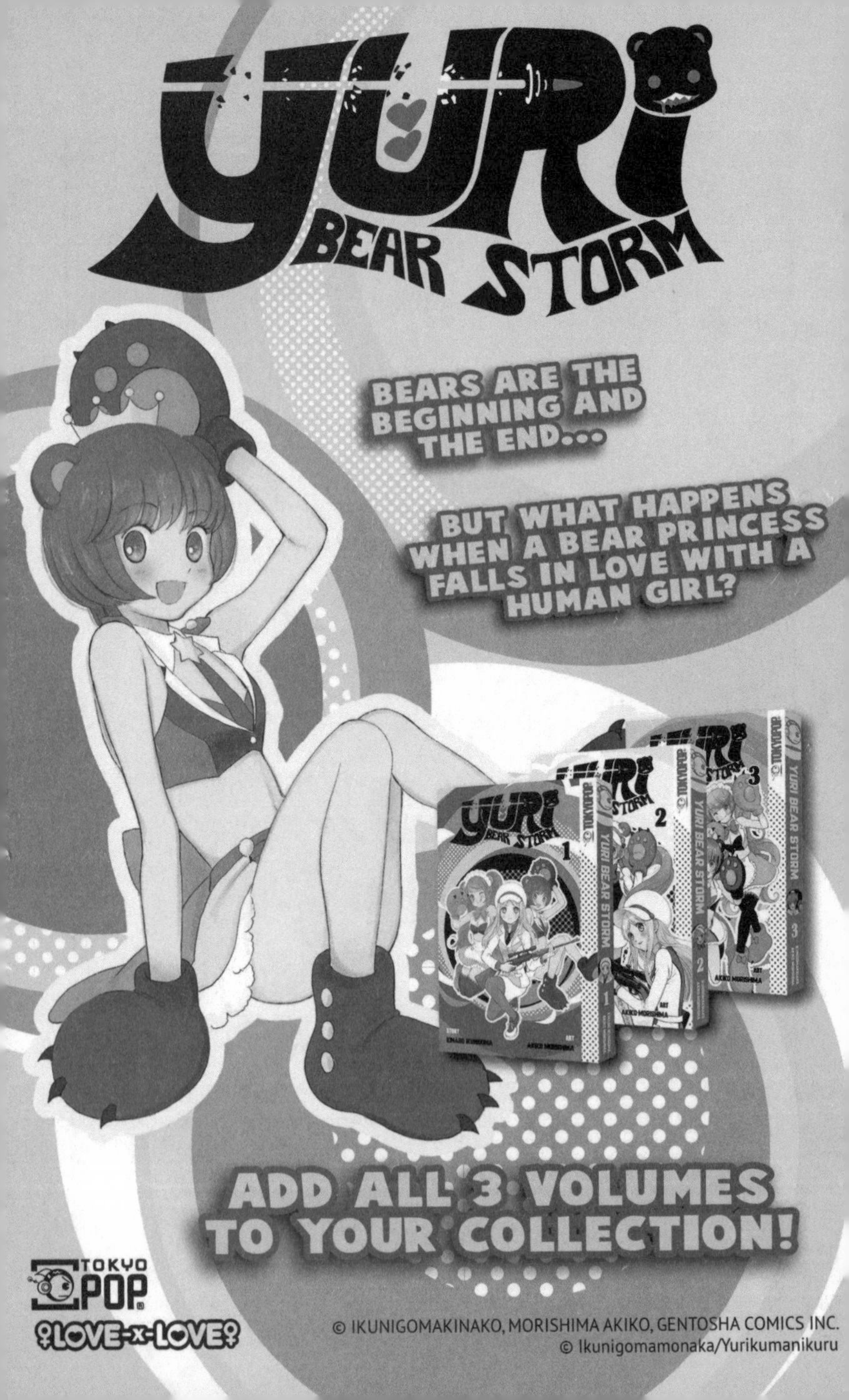

YURI BEAR STORM
BEARS ARE THE BEGINNING AND THE END...
BUT WHAT HAPPENS WHEN A BEAR PRINCESS FALLS IN LOVE WITH A HUMAN GIRL?
ADD ALL 3 VOLUMES TO YOUR COLLECTION!
TOKYO POP
LOVE x LOVE
© IKUNIGOMAKINAKO, MORISHIMA AKIKO, GENTOSHA COMICS INC.
© Ikunigomamonaka/Yurikumanikuru

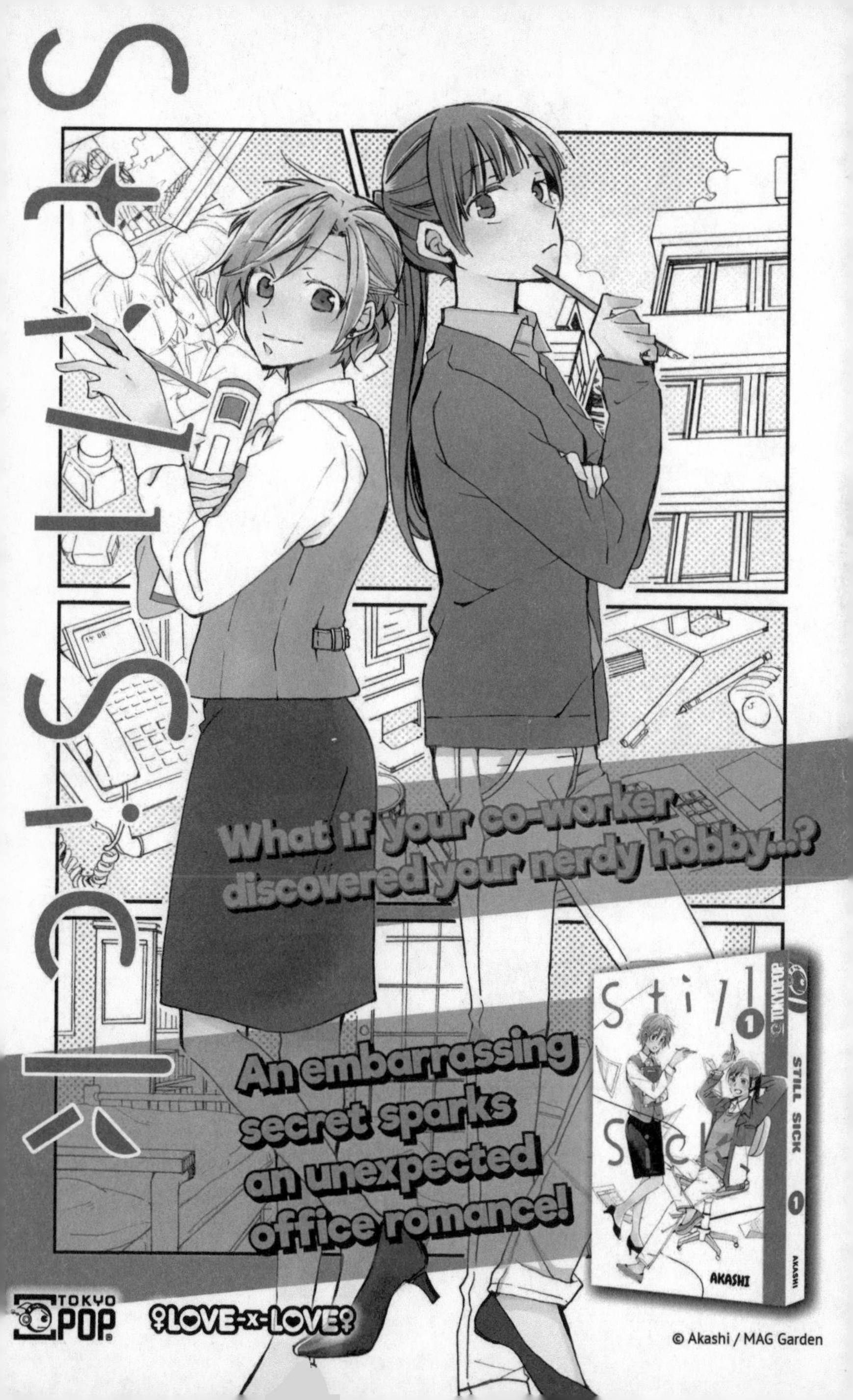

Still Sick
What if your co-worker discovered your nerdy hobby...?
An embarrassing secret sparks an unexpected office romance!
Still 1 Sick
STILL SICK 1
AKASHI
TOKYOPOP
LOVE x LOVE
© Akashi / MAG Garden

GOLDFISCH

Join Morrey and his swimmingly cute pet Otta on his adventure to reverse his Midas-like powers and save his frozen brother. Mega-hit shonen manga from hot new European creator Nana Yaa!

The Little Fox & Tanuki

KORISENMAN

A modern-day fable for all ages inspired by Japanese folklore!

Senzou the black fox was punished by having his powers taken away. Now to get them back, he must play babysitter to an adorable baby tanuki!

©2019 Mi Tagawa / MAG Garden

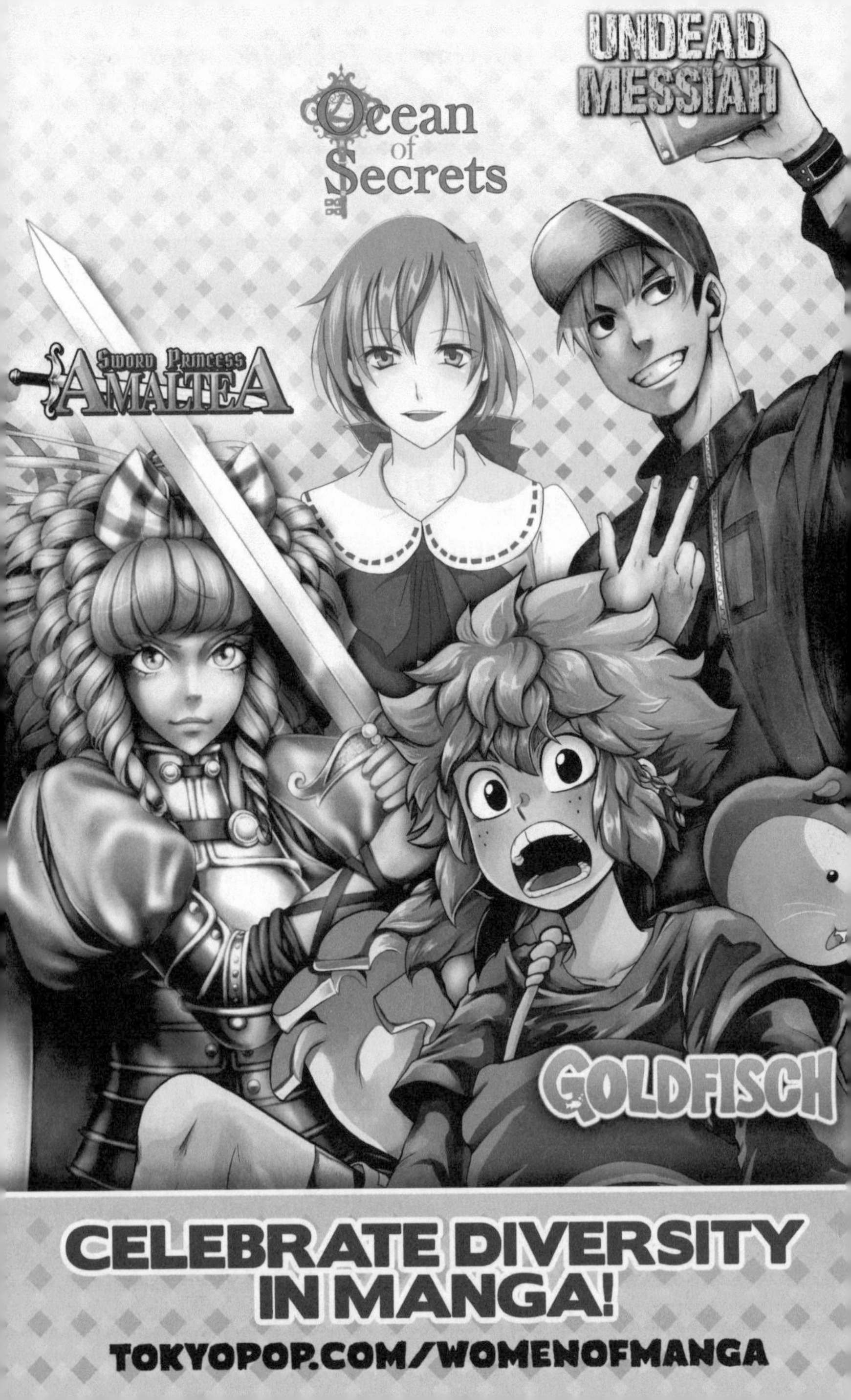
UNDEAD MESSIAH
Ocean of Secrets
Sword Princess AMALTEA
GOLDFISCH
CELEBRATE DIVERSITY IN MANGA!
TOKYOPOP.COM/WOMENOFMANGA

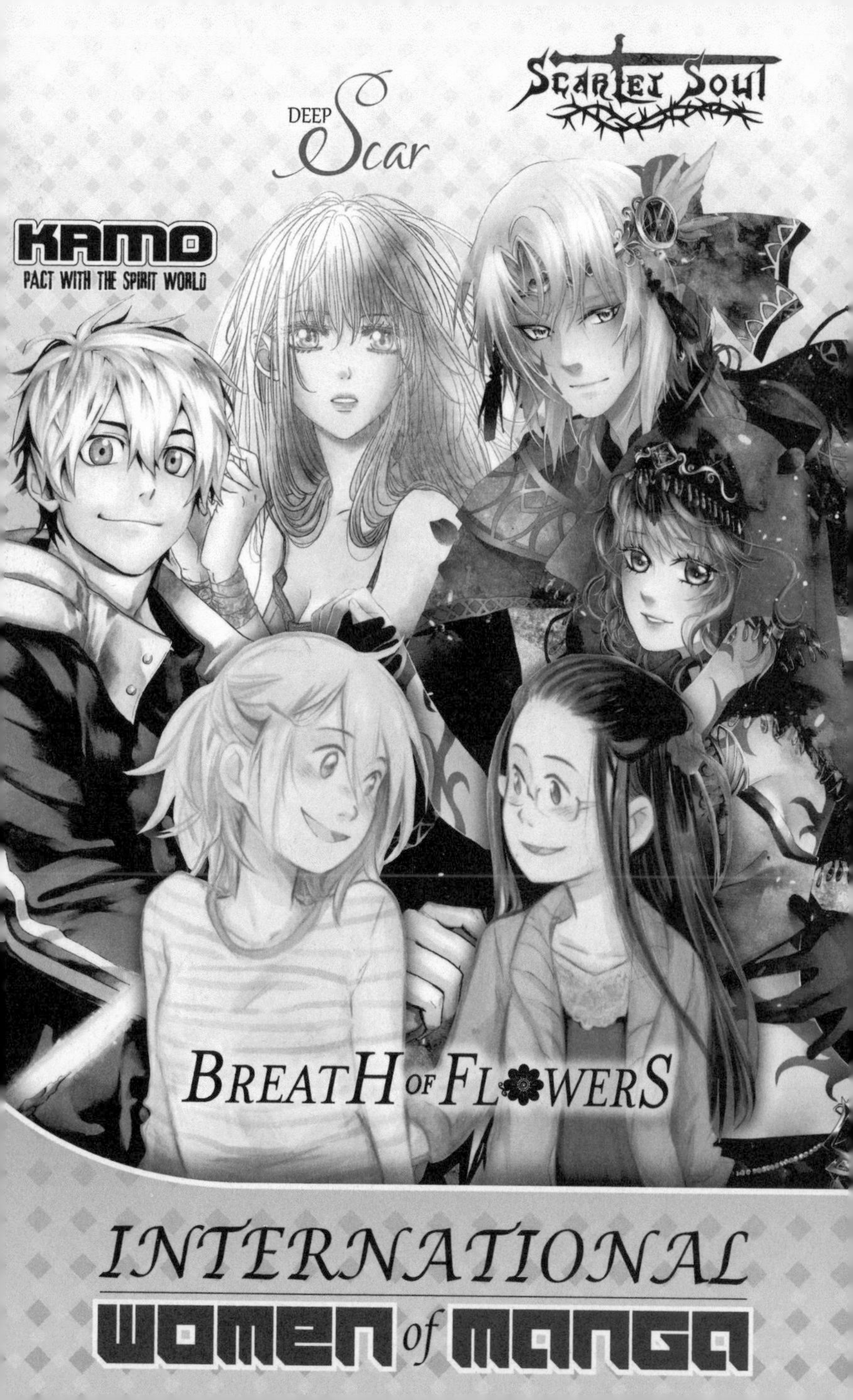
Scarlet Soul
DEEP Scar
KAMO
PACT WITH THE SPIRIT WORLD
BREATH OF FLOWERS
INTERNATIONAL
WOMEN of MANGA

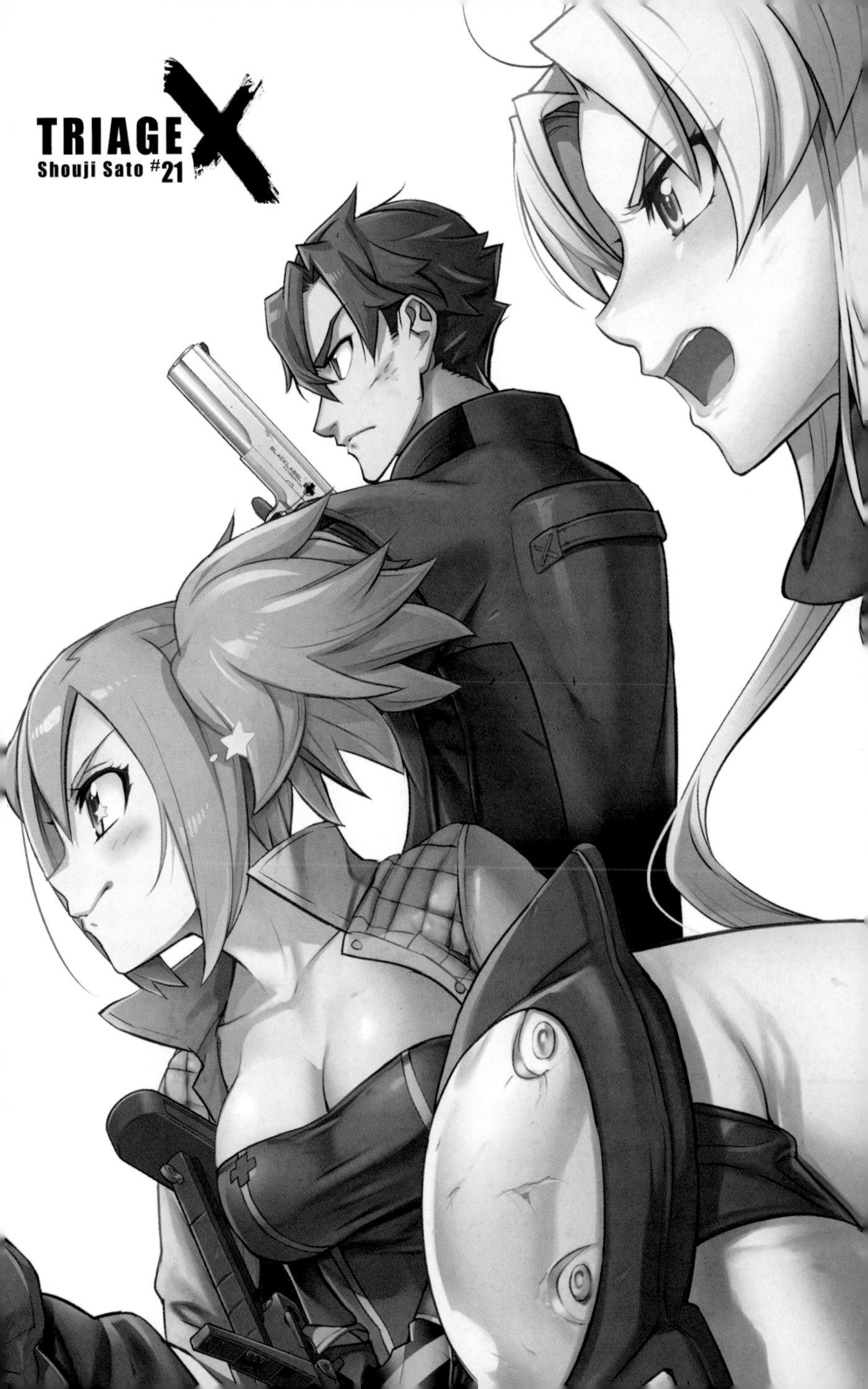
TRIAGE X
Shouji Sato #21

CONTENTS

TRIAGE
X